BRITISH NAVAL TRAWLERS AND DRIFTERS
IN TWO WORLD WARS

By Steve R Dunn

The Power and the Glory: Royal Navy Fleet Reviews from Earliest Times to 2005.

Battle in the Baltic: The Royal Navy and the Fight to Save Estonia and Latvia, 1918–1920.

Southern Thunder: The Royal Navy and the Scandinavian Trade in World War One.

Bayly's War: The Battle for the Western Approaches in the First World War.

Securing the Narrow Sea: The Dover Patrol, 1914–1918.

Blockade: Cruiser warfare and the starvation of Germany in World War One.

Formidable: A true story of disaster and courage.

The Coward? The rise and fall of the Silver King.

The Scapegoat: The life and tragedy of a fighting admiral and Churchill's role in his death.

BRITISH NAVAL TRAWLERS AND DRIFTERS

IN TWO WORLD WARS

FROM THE JOHN LAMBERT COLLECTION

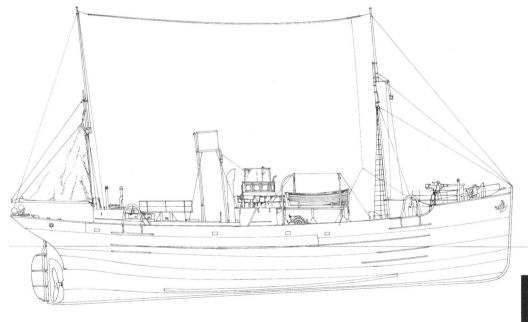

Edited and introduced by

STEVE R DUNN

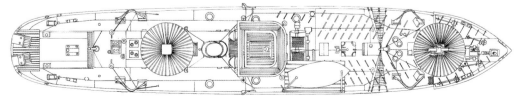

Seaforth

PUBLISHING

Title page illustration: HM *Castle*-class Admiralty standard trawler, general arrangement, 1917.

First published in Great Britain in 2021 by
Seaforth Publishing,
A division of Pen & Sword Books Ltd,
47 Church Street,
Barnsley S70 2AS

www.seaforthpublishing.com

British Library Cataloguing in Publication Data
A catalogue record for this book is available from the British Library

ISBN 978 1 5267 9486 4 (HARDBACK)
ISBN 978 1 5267 9487 1 (EPUB)
ISBN 978 1 5267 9488 8 (KINDLE)

All uncredited photographs are from the John Lambert collection

Pen & Sword Books Limited incorporates the imprints of Atlas, Archaeology, Aviation, Discovery, Family History, Fiction, History, Maritime, Military, Military Classics, Politics, Select, Transport, True Crime, Air World, Frontline Publishing, Leo Cooper, Remember When, Seaforth Publishing, The Praetorian Press, Wharncliffe Local History, Wharncliffe Transport, Wharncliffe True Crime and White Owl

Typeset and designed by Ian Hughes, Mousemat Design Ltd
Printed and bound in India by Replika Press Pvt Ltd

Contents

Second World War

Appendices

Three fishers went sailing out into the West,
Out into the West as the sun went down;
Each thought on the woman who lov'd him the best
And the children stood watching them out of the town …

CHARLES KINGSLEY, 'THREE FISHERS' (1851)

Dusk off the Foreland – the last light going
And the traffic crowding through,
And five damned trawlers with their sirens blowing
Heading the whole review!
'Sweep completed in the fairway.
No more mines remain.
Send back *Unity, Claribel, Assyrian, Stormcock,* and *Golden Gain*'.

RUDYARD KIPLING, 'MINESWEEPERS' (*SONGS FROM BOOKS,*1914)

She'd a gun at her bow that was Newcastle's best,
And a gun at her stern that was fresh from the Clyde,
And a secret her skipper had never confessed,
Not even at dawn, to his newly wed bride;
And a wireless that whispered above like a gnome,
The laughter of London, the boasts of Berlin.
O, it may have been mermaids that lured her from home,
But nobody knew where *Kilmeny* had been.

It was dark when *Kilmeny* came home from her quest,
With her bridge dabbled red where her skipper had died;
But she moved like a bride with a rose at her breast;
And 'Well done, *Kilmeny*!' the admiral cried.
Now at sixty-four fathom a conger may come,
And nose at the bones of a drowned submarine;
But late in the evening *Kilmeny* came home,
And nobody knew where *Kilmeny* had been.

ALFRED NOYES, 'KILMENY – A SONG OF THE TRAWLERS' (1917)

Syringa was a 'Tree'-class Admiralty trawler purchased in 1935, previously named *Cape Kanin* and sold back into trade in 1947 as *Davaar Island*.

Preface

How would the ordinary person in the street respond if they were to be asked 'what was the most numerous war vessel type used by the Royal Navy in each of the First and Second World Wars?' He or she might reply 'destroyers'; 'sloops'; or 'motor launches'; it is unlikely that they would say 'fishing boats'.

Yet that would be the true answer, and by some distance. Trawlers and drifters served in their thousands; and, in their tens of thousands, so did their fishermen crews.

The age-old fishing ports of Grimsby and Hull, Lowestoft and Great Yarmouth, Aberdeen, Fleetwood, and their like, sent men and ships to war in two global conflicts where the humble fishing vessel, unchanged in concept (if not propulsion) for centuries, fought against the latest hi-tech warfare innovations of those times.

However, this service, and sacrifice, goes relatively unsung and unnoticed by commentators and historians, more focused on the ironclad delights of battleships or aircraft carriers, cruisers or submarines, Jutland or Norway, and their part in the two great conflicts of 1914–18 and 1939–45.

This book tells the story of how fishing vessels came to be the answer to the strategic or tactical conundrums posed by new technology, previously ignored or overlooked by the Admiralty. It relates how trawlermen and skippers became part of the Royal Navy, the roles they played, the conditions they served under and the bravery that they showed. Importantly it also examines the ships themselves;

their design, construction, arming, usage and development. In this, both author and reader are well served by the detailed drawings and plans depicted herein and taken from the John Lambert Collection, an archive which also provided many of the photographs used in the volume. It is the bringing to life of these depictions that is the main purpose of the book and they will no doubt be of considerable interest to modellers and students of historical naval architecture.

The book is divided into two sections. The first part tells how the fishing fleet developed into an integral part of the Royal Navy's pre-1914 plans and details some of the activities and actions of trawlers and drifters at war in 1914–18. The second investigates the armed fishing fleet in the struggle of 1939–45.

In the end, it would not be overstating the case to suggest that without the use of trawlers, whalers, drifters – and their crews – in the sea fight for survival during two world wars, Britain would have lost command of the sea, the 'Sovereignty of the Seas' held dear by British monarchs from Edward III onwards. And hence the country would have lost its freedom and nationhood. Their quotidian but valuable service is often overlooked. Hopefully, this volume goes some way to redress that failing.

The book does not follow a strict chronology; rather each subject is explored before moving on. The twenty-four-hour clock is used throughout. Where an original text used ante or post meridian, the times have been converted.

Cape Portland was built in 1936 and taken up on the outbreak of the
Second World War. She served as an auxiliary boarding vessel until being
transferred to the Portuguese navy in 1943 (where shew was named P-5)
and returned to the RN in 1945

Hugh John Lambert

(22 August 1937 – 11 January 2016)

Hugh John Lambert – Hugh to his family, but John to the world at large – was one of a generation of naval writers who were, in the strictest sense, amateurs, but who brought a new level of technical interest, deep personal enthusiasm, and, in John's case, hands-on experience, that radically changed the way warships were described and understood.

John was trained as a technical draughtsman but showed an early interest in the sea, joining the Royal Naval Volunteer Reserve in order to ensure that his National Service would be in the Royal Navy. Called up in 1956, his engineering background made him a natural candidate for Stoker branch, and he enjoyed naval life so much he signed up for nine years' service, during which time he became familiar with most of the machinery to be found in the warships of that era. Much of his time was spent in aircraft carriers – *Theseus*, *Ocean*, *Albion* and *Bulwark* – which took him around the world and into action at Suez and in the Far East.

He left the Navy as a Petty Officer in 1965 and joined the Metropolitan Police, but in his spare time slowly began a career as a writer on warship topics. Initially, these were short magazine pieces, usually accompanied by one of his own plans, but he soon acquired a following among ship modellers looking for detailed and reliable reference material. As evidence of this demand built up, he began to sell copies of his plans separately and from about 1976 started producing more elaborate drawings specifically for his plans service. By now his police career was of secondary importance to him, and he regularly turned down promotion in order to have enough freedom to pursue his real interests. Nevertheless, he remained in the force for nearly twenty-five years before taking early retirement.

In the meantime, he continued to write regularly for magazines and periodicals like *Model Boats*, *Airfix Magazine*, *Scale Models*, *Warship*, *Model Shipwright* and *Marine Modelling International*, his output eventually totalling at least 350 articles. His particular obsession was always the smaller types, from destroyers downwards, and especially Coastal Forces, on which he became uniquely expert. Because of his interest in these largely ignored craft, he was forced to become an immensely diligent researcher, seeking out copies of plans, technical manuals, photos and data from obscure archives and any of the wartime builders and suppliers who remained in business at the time. He also tracked down individuals with first-hand knowledge, quizzing them about any and every elusive detail of the ship or weapons system he was working on. A combination of this painstaking research and highly professional draughtsmanship made his plans uniquely valuable.

It was inevitable that his expertise would attract publishing interest, and in 1984 he was commissioned to provide the line illustrations for John Campbell's *Naval Weapons of World War Two*. This began a fruitful partnership with Conway Maritime Press that led to John's first book, *The Fairmile D Motor Torpedo Boat* in the publishers' 'Anatomy of the Ship' series. This was released in 1985, followed in 1986 by another in the same series on *The Submarine Alliance* which he co-wrote with David Hill. He then launched into a broader and more ambitious multi-volume work, *Allied Coastal Forces of World War II*, with the US Navy material being supplied by Al Ross, a long-time American collaborator with shared interests. Volume I: *Fairmile Designs and US Submarine Chasers*, was published in 1990, with Volume II: *Vosper Designs and US ELCOs* following in 1993, but a planned third volume never materialised. The two existing volumes have been reprinted by Seaforth in 2018–19 and the feasibility of completing the third volume from surviving material is under consideration.

In the new century, John reverted to smaller scale works, publishing *Flower Class Corvettes in World War II* (in the Warship Perspective series) with Alan Raven in 2000, and two 'Specials' in the ShipCraft series (both with Les Brown): *Flower Class Corvettes* in 2008 and *Allied Torpedo Boats* in 2010.

Part of the reason for his apparently low output at this time was that he was working on a large project he clearly expected to become his magnum opus – a complete encyclopaedia of British naval weapons used between 1939 and 1945 on destroyer-size and smaller vessels, the rationale being that they were open mountings that would present difficulties to any modeller seeking to portray them in detail. He completed the vast majority of the drawings required, but as his health deteriorated he was not able to write up any of the accompanying text, so the project was a long way from completion when he died in 2016.

Seaforth Publishing acquired all of John's existing drawings, photographs and research materials with a view to fulfilling his ambition, and this book is one of a series reproducing all his significant weapons drawings in logical, thematic collections. This third and final volume follows the earlier ones devoted to destroyer weapons, and those of escorts and minesweepers.

Now completed, this project is therefore a posthumous but fitting conclusion to a career of immense significance to all those interested in warships.

Cherwell was originally the *Mersey*-class Admiralty trawler *James Jones*, built by Cochrane's in 1918. She was sold (and renamed) in 1920, only to be taken up again in 1939. From 1942, Cherwell was used as a boom defence vessel.

Publishers' Note

John Lambert's fascination with small craft inevitably drew him to the trawlers and drifters that played such an important role in both world wars, and the drawings he made of a number of these form the core of this book. The plans of the vessels were drawn on large sheets, usually 32 by 24 inches but a few of 32 by 17 inches. Rather than adopt a specific scale, his style was to make the maximum use of space, so the drawings often present a very crowded appearance, with details, annotation and the scale bar filling blank areas between the main profiles and deck plans.

This presents a bit of a challenge in converting them to book form if material is not to disappear into the gutter between pages. The simplest solution would be to print them in their entirety on a single page, but that would make the drawings disappointingly small scale. The solution we have adopted is – in effect – to print each drawing across a double-page spread, but digitally separating the two halves into individual views, so that no details of significance are lost in the binding. This is particularly the solution where the size of whole vessels in some drawings has forced some profiles and deck plans to run across two pages.

The main portfolio of plans is organised chronologically and is divided between the two world wars. It should be noted that in John Lambert's collection were discovered some original builders' plans and these have been spliced into the run of drawings presented here.

As John Lambert never finished any description to accompany the plans, we are grateful to Steve Dunn for agreeing to sort the material into a coherent collection and for providing an introduction that goes well beyond a commentary on the drawings and the vessels they depict, but also describes the fascinating contribution that these vessels and their crews made to the Allied victory in two world wars.

Part One

The First World War

1: A Change of Strategy

By 1897, Queen Victoria had ruled Britain for fifty years. As queen of the United Kingdom of Great Britain and Ireland and Empress of India (from 1876) she was ruler of the globe's largest ever maritime empire. And disposed at her service was the world's biggest navy. At the naval celebration of her Diamond Jubilee on 26 June, 165 British warships were drawn up in the Solent in magnificent array, decked with ensigns and bunting, all in sumptuous flag-waving glory.

The composition of the fleet was a function of the needs of empire. Firstly, cruisers of medium size and exceptional endurance to patrol the colonial outposts of Britain's territories and keep the sea lanes free for trade. The Victorians divided these vessels into three classes, plus armoured cruisers – in reality small battleships which could be employed as an admiral's flagship and fight anything that they could not out-sail. Cruisers were not meant to be used in the line of battle. They were intended to exercise control, sovereignty of the sea, rather than the gaining of it. In peacetime they signified presence, a visible symbol of the fleet and by extension the power of the British nation.

Secondly, gun vessels, heavy guns on shallow keels for coastal bombardment or defence and policing the imperial waterways. And thirdly, the battlefleet to fight the foreign foe, the chief candidate for which was still at this time France.

Britain was a thalassocracy. The need to protect the trade and boundaries of empire created the need for an overwhelmingly powerful (and expensive) navy. Commerce was also the fountainhead of a large merchant shipping fleet. By 1914, Britain – with over 20 million tons – owned more steam and motor ship tonnage than Germany (by a factor of four), the USA (by a factor of ten) or France (also by ten). Indeed, British cargo tonnage was greater than the aggregate of Germany, America, France, Norway, Sweden and Denmark in total.[1]

Britain predominated in commercial fishing too. The nation lived by and from the sea. From the earliest times, the sea had provided a rich source of food for the inhabitants of the British Isles. Oyster shells are found in Stone Age middens. They were a commonplace food in taverns and markets throughout the eighteenth and nineteenth centuries, so much so that apprentices complained about the quantity of oysters they were forced to eat. Salmon was a food for the masses from medieval until modern times, as were cod and herring, often preserved by salting. Days on which only fish could be eaten were prescribed not just by canon law but also by royal decree; for keeping a healthy fishing fleet in work and profit was good not just for landing fees and taxes but also to ensure that a pool of experienced seafaring men was available for naval duties, as required.

For fishing was a major source of employment as well as of food. During the fifteenth century, Bristol was the second biggest port in the kingdom. Bristol's fishermen caught cod in Newfoundland, and from the city John Cabot sailed in 1479 and made landfall in North America. Ports such as Aberdeen, Lowestoft and Great Yarmouth depended on the herring trade, as to a lesser extent did Grimsby and Hull, and waxed fat on it. Of Yarmouth, Daniel Defoe wrote as early as 1724 that 'the ships ride here so close, and as it were, keeping up one another, with their head-fasts on shore, that for half a mile together, they go cross the stream with their bowsprits over the land, their bowes, or heads, touching the very wharf; so that one may walk from ship to ship as on a floating bridge, all along by the shore-side'.[2]

Such sights continued untrammelled into the twentieth century. Initially, trawlers were wooden-hulled vessels, often owed by the skipper and powered by sail. The first steam fishing vessel emerged in Leith in 1875 when David Allan and Co converted a drifter to steam power. Two years later Allan designed and built the first screw-propelled steam trawler in the world. This was *Pioneer*, fishery number LH 854, with a two-cylinder compound engine by another Leith company, Oliver and Turnbull. Just to be sure, *Pioneer* also had two masts and carried a full set of sails. She ran aground and was wrecked in 1880.

By the beginning of the twentieth century, the wood-built craft had largely been displaced by steel-hulled vessels fitted with triple-expansion steam engines, and usually owned by companies rather than skippers. Only Lowestoft and Brixham retained substantial fleets of sailing trawlers.

The pre-eminent fishing ports in Britain during the early 1900s were Grimsby and Hull. From the latter, some 2,900 men in four trawler fleets (Gamecock,* Red Cross, Great Northern and Hellyers) set forth. They would stay out to sea, often voyaging for 1,000 miles or more, under the supervision of an 'admiral', off-loading their catch into a fast 'cutter' (a sort of super-trawler) which took it to London where the best prices could be obtained. From Grimsby, some 2,750 men worked around Dogger Bank, Heligoland and out to Icelandic waters or the White Sea. These skippers generally took their catch back to port after every trip, for sale in the local fish market. Aberdeen had the largest Scottish fleet, and Fleetwood and

---

* The largest.

Milford Haven were important west coast fishing ports.

And then there was herring. Herring was a delicacy on the Continent and was caught relatively easily round the coast of Scotland; off the east coast during winter and spring, off the north of Scotland and Shetland during the summer months and, in the autumn, off East Anglia (see plate 1).

Because herring is a fatty fish, it has to be cured as quickly as possible to prevent it from rotting. By 1907, 2.5 million barrels of fish (perhaps 250,000 tons) were cured and exported, the main markets being Germany, Eastern Europe and Russia; pre-1914 the 'Russian market purchased seventy-five per cent of the Scottish cured herring production'.[3]

Scottish fishermen, and their accompanying wives and 'herring girls',* followed the shoals around the coast of Britain: from Stornoway to Lerwick, then to Peterhead and down the east coast to Great Yarmouth. Here, in the autumn, there were large camps of Scottish fisher-lasses set up on the quayside, gutting and packing the 'silver darlings'.

By the eve of the First World War, there were 45,382 British fishermen across the country catching 800,000 tons of fish a year in 7,271 fishing craft (excluding the smallest craft). Of these, the steam trawling fleet numbered 1,657 boats across England, Wales and Scotland and steam drifters another 1,555 vessels.[4] Those directly

involved in employment in the fishing industry numbered some 100,000 in 1913.[5]

All of Britain's maritime trade and fishing pre-eminence depended on maintaining control and command of the seas, the Sovereignty of the Seas demanded by King Edward III and most of the monarchs who followed him. And this dominion was exercised by the Royal Navy, the Senior Service, 'Our Wonderful Navy … the sure shield in peace and war'.[6]

But beneath the surface, something threatening was stirring; and a Kraken was about to wake. Three trends, two technical, one political, began a convergence that would threaten the Royal Navy battlefleet's supremacy.

First, came the rapid and innovative industrial growth of Germany and her desire for both an empire and naval fleet to meet her ruler's self-perceived personal and national status. Germany's ambition frightened France, which sought protection through an alliance of mutual support and defence with Russia. Such was French fear of Germany that in 1904 she also signed an Entente Cordiale with Britain, her hereditary enemy, which harmonised relations between the two countries.

Running in parallel to these developments came the dawning realisation in the navy, and especially in the fertile brain of First Sea Lord (from 1904 to 1910) Admiral Sir John (Jacky) Fisher, that Germany

---

* In 1913, 12,000 women herring gutters followed the fleet; 5,000 of them arrived at Great Yarmouth.

1. Scottish herring drifters at Fraserburgh in the 1880s.
(author's collection)

not France would be Britain's most likely foe and that the battle ground would be the North Sea. As historian Andrew Lambert has written, 'by early 1906 the centre of naval effort was shifting from the Mediterranean to the North Sea; Germany was not only the most likely but also the only realistic enemy. Russia was no longer a naval power and the French navy had collapsed.'[7] And the North Sea is a small, often shallow, confined space in which to manoeuvre a battlefleet.

The other two technological innovations which would disturb the Royal Navy's hundred-year long *Pax Britannica*, were the development of undersea weapons; mines and the torpedo-carrying submarine.

Mines

Mines were not a new weapon. At its simplest, a sea mine is an explosive device laid in the waterway with the intention of sinking or damaging surface or undersea vessels. Barrels of 'Greek fire' (a mixture of sulphur, naphtha, nitre and maybe phosphorous) were used extensively by, for instance, the Byzantine empire in its struggles against Muslim invaders from around 672 CE. The ignited weapon was floated on the tidal stream towards enemy ships. In January 1778, during the American War of Independence, the Connecticut-born inventor David Bushnell floated a large number of explosive-filled kegs towards the British fleet at night; in what was perhaps the first mine-countermeasure operation, the British sent small boats to intercept the barrels. And during the War of 1812, the Americans laid a defensive minefield in order to keep British ships out of New York harbour, possibly the first use of such a stratagem. By the end of the war the Americans were using mines so extensively that British ships had to remain offshore.

The first British warship to be mined was probably the two-gun paddle packet vessel HMS *Merlin*, in June 1855 during the Crimean War. She struck a Russian device in the Baltic but suffered only minor damage.

In the American Civil War, the Confederates made use of mines in harbours, bays and rivers. When on 5 August 1863 Admiral Davy Farragut was attacking Mobile, Alabama, the Confederacy's last major open port on the Gulf of Mexico, he found the bay heavily mined with tethered naval mines, then known as 'torpedoes'. The monitor USS *Tecumseh* hit one and sank, causing his ships to pull back. From his place of observation high in the rigging, Farragut gave the order which has gone down in history as 'full speed ahead and damn the torpedoes'.*

Germany and Russia both gained useful knowledge as to the potential of the mine. During the Schleswig-Holstein conflict (1848–51) the Prussians used electrically controlled mines to protect Kiel harbour from the Danish fleet. And in the Crimean War (1854–56) the Russians laid minefields to defend the Baltic harbours of Sveaborg, Kronstadt and Bomarsund and the Black Sea port of Sevastapol. Some of these used controlled mines detonated via cables from the shore but the vast majority were moored contact mines.

However, in Britain, there was a strong body of opinion at the Admiralty that the widespread deployment of mines was poor strategy. 'Mines were regarded as sneaky weapons, resented because they seemed to favour weaker powers by denying Britain the fruits of her overwhelming maritime superiority.'[8]

Such denigration was also because the Admiralty saw mines as a defensive weapon and the navy prided itself on being an offensive force, seeking the next Trafalgar which would destroy the German High Seas Fleet in a climacteric sea battle. Mining near enemy coasts would deter the foe from coming out into open seas for that much wished for culmination.

As a result, although much technical innovation had taken place at HMS *Vernon*, the navy's torpedo and mine school, the navy had not especially focused on the development of the mine as a serious weapon of war. As naval historian Nick Lambert noted, 'since 1894 Admiralty policy had been to supress the system and suspend further experimentation … in the hope that rival powers perhaps would not realise its full potential'[9] and adopt them too.

But the Russo-Japanese War of 1904–5 re-awakened some Admiralty interest. Each side in the war had made extensive use of mines as both a defensive and offensive tactic. As one example, on 15 May 1904 two Japanese battleships, *Yashima* and *Hatsuse*, were lured into a newly laid Russian minefield off Port Arthur; each ship struck at least two mines. The *Hatsuse* sank within minutes, taking 450 sailors to their deaths, while the *Yashima* sank under tow to Korea for repair. Overall, losses to mines by both sides amounted to three battleships, five cruisers and three destroyers, together with thousands of sailors, including the charismatic Russian fleet commander Vice Admiral Stepan Makarov.

As a result of this intelligence, the Royal Navy developed the 'Navy Spherical Mine' in 1906. This was a so-called 'mechanical mine'. German-developed contact mines used what would prove to be the more effective Hertz horn system (see appendix 1). Even so, at the Hague conference of 1907, Britain proposed restrictions on the localities where mines could be sown. This motion was voted down by thirty-seven of the forty-four states attending; those voting against such constraints included the USA and Germany.

By 1914, the navy's main mine weapon was the Navy Spherical Mine Mark I and II (a moored mine using an automatic anchor, an arm-operated firing mechanism and a charge of about 250lb of gun cotton). Only 4,000 were available for the start of the war against Germany, again highlighting the continued lack of emphasis placed on the weapon. In the words of one historian, 'after 1911 mining effectively fell off the back of the truck'.[10] Indeed, mine stocks were so sparse at the start of the First World War that in November 1914 Britain was forced to acquire 1,000 Russian mines left at Port Arthur at the end of the Russo-Japanese War. These latter were Hertz horn devices.

Worse still, in practice British mines proved to be woefully inadequate, with problems concerning mooring wires, sinkers and

---

* But which was probably 'Damn the torpedoes, four bells, Captain Drayton, go ahead. Jouett, full speed' (Spears, *David G. Farragut*, p 407).

firing pistols. All of which lent weight to those voices in the Admiralty who opposed mining on principle. Eventually, better types were developed by the simple expedient of copying German mines; these were contact mines using Hertz horns which were seen to work all too well. Information about the German mines had, in fact, been obtained by the Intelligence Service pre-1914, yet 'in spite of this information we ourselves clung to an obsolete and ineffectual type of mine for nearly two years after the outbreak of war'.[11] This again perhaps reflects the lack of high-level interest in mining as a strategy.

The German navy had taken a different view of the mine, as perhaps befitted the weaker force; maybe this led to their development of a far superior product. The naval writer Peter Smith has noted that 'Germany was fully committed to the offensive use of these weapons [mines] and had few scruples how and where they could be used'.[12] When war came, Germany had immediately laid mines in defence of its harbours and in minefields across major trade routes. She had also dropped drifting mines, unmoored, to roam the seas on tide and wind, seeking an unlucky victim. In both of these latter two activities Germany was in defiance of international law as then defined, and as adumbrated at, inter alia, the 1907 Hague Convention and the 1909 Declaration of London.

Minesweeping

The problem of the sea mine called for the remedy of minesweeping. Perhaps not surprisingly, given that the Royal Navy had not embraced the use of mines, it had not thought very much about the use of minesweepers either.

Some experiments had been carried out. Trials with explosive sweeps to detonate mines had been undertaken in 1905 and the previous year there had been experiments using ships' cutters and picket boats to sweep mines. But standard doctrine was countermining. In the Mediterranean Fleet there had also been tests involving picket boat 'creeping' and tugs, together with destroyers preceding fleet heavy units.

After the Russo-Japanese War, a Mining Committee had been established at the Admiralty and in November 1908 it reported some far-reaching conclusions. The abolition of both countermining and explosives sweeps* was recommended, and accepted. Instead the committee plumped for the fixed-wire sweep; converted torpedo gunboats were to be used as fleet minesweepers and specifications for replacement vessels specifically designed for minesweeping were drawn up. Nothing more was done to further this latter recommendation. The Mining Committee also considered the use of trawlers, of which more in the following chapter.

Thus Britain entered the First World War with a small fleet of minesweepers which were actually old torpedo boats, dating from the nineteenth century, and which had been converted to fit the

minesweeping needs as then perceived. They were only ten in number and were fitted out as mine sweepers at the end of 1908 and during 1909. But surely, ten mine clearance vessels would hardly be enough in time of war?

Submarines

The first recognisable submarine might be said to be *Nautilus*, built in 1797 by the American engineer and inventor Robert Fulton during the war between Revolutionary France and Britain. It was a submersible with an explosive charge on a spar attached to the bow. Fulton offered it to the French, the Dutch and the French again before approaching the British. But the Royal Navy had limited interest; why would they encourage a cheap technology which would allow lesser players into their game?

The invention of the locomotive torpedo by the English engineer Robert Whitehead in 1866 was the next game changer with regard to cheaply eroding the superiority of an expensive surface fleet. He persuaded the Royal Navy to buy some manufacturing rights in 1871 and the navy started producing the torpedo at the Royal Laboratories at Woolwich, England. These were initially fitted to torpedo boats, small, fast and manoeuvrable, and by the 1880s more of the world's navies began to deploy torpedo vessels. Naval architects also started to envision submarines armed with Whitehead torpedoes.

In 1887, Queen Victoria was able to view an early example of the type at the naval review held in honour of her Golden Jubilee in 1887. This was another *Nautilus*, a Nordenfelt experimental steam-driven submarine, built by the Naval Construction Company at Barrow. She was the third Nordenfelt to be built in British yards, the first two having been purchased by the Turkish navy. The British naval attaché noted that the Ottomans had little faith in the boats and that 'the general opinion of naval officers is much opposed to them'.[13] Captain Lord Beresford had gone aboard her at Tilbury Docks in the January; she had submerged as planned but then refused to rise to the surface. 'The Thames mud held us fast. In this emergency I suggested rolling her by moving the people quickly from side to side.' This expedient eventually succeeded but 'by the time she came to the surface the air was very foul'.[14] The Nordenfelts were not particularly successful. When operating near the surface they were fast and manageable, but when completely submerged they lacked longitudinal stability.†

Nevertheless, the Royal Navy did eventually develop its own submarine, HMS *Holland I*. She was ordered from John Philip Holland, an Irish engineer who had designed submersibles for the US Navy at the end of the nineteenth century, and laid down in 1901 at Barrow-in-Furness. The Royal Navy fitted their new submarine with Whitehead torpedoes; for some naval visionaries, the combination of torpedo and undersea vessel was a *Gestalt*. One

---

* These employed a wire with a sliding charge which could be fired electronically when they encountered a mine. They worked but required skilled operators and were not reliable.

† *Nautilus*'s career was not long. After the review she sailed for Russia, becoming a total loss on the coast of Jutland during the passage. The tsar's government refused Nordenfelt's claims for compensation and denied that it had ever intended to purchase the vessel.

such was Jacky Fisher who, as Third Sea Lord and again as First Sea Lord, pushed for their development. In 1904 he wrote, 'I don't think it is even faintly realised … the immense impending revolution which the submarine will effect as a weapon of war.'[15]

But for many in the navy, submarines remained a toy, 'Fisher's toys' as Beresford (now an admiral) contemptuously called them. Fisher's successor as executive head of the navy, Admiral Sir Arthur Wilson, was resolutely unimpressed by the claims of submarine warfare. He shared the view, held by most senior officers in the navy, that submarines were an undesirable and distrusted class of ship. Many sailors believed them to be a dishonourable and underhand weapon, suitable only for weaker nations and then only for coastal defence. Indeed, Wilson described submarines as 'underhand, unfair and damned un-English' and stated that enemy submarine crews should be hanged as pirates if captured.[16] While in office Wilson did much to retard the development of the weapon for the RN, in part because he did not want to set an example which would be followed by weaker, foreign navies.

Wilson's successor, Admiral Francis Bridgeman, also disliked them; and Rear Admiral the Hon Horace Hood spoke for many when he wrote 'really these submarines are the Devil; it is a great misfortune they were ever invented'.[17]

Nonetheless, successive naval manoeuvres confirmed the potency that submarines could possess. In the 1904 summer trials, the umpires 'considered that the subs fully achieved their various functions'. In 1908, the navy deployed twenty-five undersea boats for defensive work off the Firth of Forth; and in 1909 they were 'used very successfully for coast defence'. In the 1913 anti-invasion manoeuvres, the submarine commanders 'considered … that an enemy's transports could be so damaged so as to render a military landing on any part of our coasts ineffectual'.[18] According to Commander Reginald A R Plunkett,* 'the big ship officer now realises what a serious menace threatens him'.[19]

But as for countering submarines, no one seemed to have a clue. As Admiral Sir Percy Scott put it, 'with regard to attacking submarines … a committee had certainly been at work for some time, but had evolved nothing'.[20]

And Germany did not share the British dislike of the submarine. In 1903 the Friedrich Krupp Germaniawerft dockyard in Kiel completed the first fully functional German-built submarine, *Forelle*. By 1912 they were building boats with diesel engines (the *U-19* class of four) and when war finally broke out, Germany had forty-eight submarines in service or under construction.

A Change of Strategy

The concatenation of mines and torpedo-equipped submarines, coming together as they did, caused Jacky Fisher to question the accepted doctrine of the navy – that of close blockade of an enemy's ports and sea bases.

Britain's nineteenth-century navy had largely been configured on the principle that France would be the enemy. The major naval bases were Portsmouth and Plymouth, facing the enemy across the English Channel. There was little in the way of defence facing Germany across the North Sea.

Furthermore, Britain's naval strategy had been to follow the Nelsonian doctrine of 'close blockade'. The fleet would be deployed close up to the enemy's ports preventing exit of its ships, or forcing it to seek battle, and stopping the inflow of war materials. Close blockade had some advantages, the best perhaps being that it was legal under the dictates of the Hague Convention.

But the materiel changes noted above had undermined this strategy completely. Mines, the torpedo and the submarine had redefined the rules. Fisher was one of the few Royal Navy leaders who clearly saw that the advent of new technologies had revolutionised naval warfare.

More than anyone, Fisher recognised that the coming of the torpedo-armed submarine, and the availability of mines, meant that the narrow waters of the North Sea and English Channel became a high-risk environment for large and expensive capital ships. Rather than chance battleships in such a situation, it was better, he argued, to police those waters through 'flotilla defence', using large numbers of torpedo boats (surface vessels carrying on-deck torpedoes), submarines and torpedo boat destroyers (more usually abbreviated to 'destroyers') to render the waters uninhabitable for enemy battleships or potential invasion fleets.

When Winston Churchill became First Lord of the Admiralty in 1911, Fisher, now out of office, kept prodding him to force the Admiralty to examine the potential of the submarine, and more so Fisher's ideas for the North Sea, which had now coalesced around the strategy of so-called 'distant blockade' – the shutting off of the whole of the North Sea at its northern and southern exits. Under this plan the British fleet would be held beyond the northern blockade to enter the disputed seas only when the enemy battlefleet itself ventured out. Otherwise small ships would patrol and keep free the North Sea and English Channel and prevent German trade and ships entering or leaving.

Both ideas appealed to Churchill, especially Fisher's theory of 'flotilla defence' primarily for its economy, given the pressing political need to stabilise the Naval Estimates. But exercises proved that the navy did not have enough cruisers or destroyers to support such a strategy.

Nonetheless, distant blockade became the de facto strategy as fear of the submarine and mine menace in the closed waters of the North Sea grew amongst the naval planners. At the outbreak of war Britain had nowhere near enough small craft to pursue such a policy and instead settled for patrols by ancient cruisers to the north and destroyers in the south, assisted by old pre-dreadnought battleships from Sheerness and Portland; while the Grand Fleet stayed well to the north, with its base in Scapa Flow.

Where were the vessels needed to patrol the North Sea, and keep the seaway free for trade, to come from?

---

* From 1916, known as Reginald Aylmer Ranfurly Plunkett-Ernle-Erle-Drax.

2: Cometh the Hour, Cometh the Men

The sudden uptick in interest in mining as a weapon of war, due to its success in the Russo-Japanese War, led to a concomitant curiosity regarding minesweeping, for which no ready solution had seemed apparent from the experience in the conflict. And the growing realisation that submarines were not just 'toys' but a clear and present danger to the battlefleet (and to trade) kindled the desire for patrol vessels – hardy, versatile enough to sweep for mines and seek out underwater threats, capable of surviving in the stormy conditions of the North Sea and readily available in time of war. The Royal Navy had spent several fortunes on warships; but these were battleships, destroyers to protect them, cruisers to seek out the enemy. No one had thought it fit to invest in patrol vessels to the extent that now seemed necessary, especially at a time of budget scrutiny when early twentieth-century Liberal governments sought to increase expenditure on social causes, such as old age pensions. Some senior officers began to think through the problem, especially with regard to mines.

History has not been kind to Admiral Lord Charles William de la Poer Beresford, First Baron Beresford of Metemmeh and Curraghmore (plate 2), and with some justification. Self-important and vain, he was a member of parliament, vitriolic enemy of Fisher, and the man of whom it was said 'in the navy we knew he was not a sailor, but thought he was a politician; in the House of Commons they knew he was not a politician but thought he was a sailor'.[1]

Nonetheless, it was to Beresford that the navy owed the insight that fishing trawlers might be the answer to the problem of minesweeping (and by extension, general patrol work).

While in command of the Mediterranean Fleet during 1905, Beresford had instigated experiments in minesweeping using his ships' small boats. In

2. Admiral Lord Charles Beresford.
(photo; Library of Congress)

1907, he was appointed to command the Channel Fleet, and proceeded to take it on a grand tour of the British Isles, primarily intended to boost his own popularity and provide more publicity for his war with Fisher. As one lieutenant in the fleet noted, the cruises were 'principally a processional career around the ports of Britain ... I do not recall that any serious problems of war were either attempted or solved [but] Lord Charles received deputations, addressed crowded meetings in his honour, and became freeman of innumerable cities.'[2]

On 27 June 1907, Beresford's peregrinations brought him to Grimsby. In company, the admiral had his flagship, the pre-dreadnought battleship *King Edward VII*; five more battleships, *Britannia, Dominion, Hindustan, Illustrious* and *Swiftsure*; the cruisers *Gladiator, Sentinel* and *Talbot*; and the torpedo boats *Avon, Coquette, Blackwater, Cynthia, Flirt, Gala, Gypsy, Kangaroo, Lee, Leopard, Osprey* and *Waveney*.

Here, the mayor visited the flagship, and festivities and a civic luncheon were held ashore for the visiting sailors; in return Beresford inspected a number of trawlers and held talks with their skippers. Most importantly, he held discussions with Councillor George Alward, a prominent trawler owner, and an author and authority on fishing matters. Alward had been a prime mover in the development of the steam trawler and the steam winches that were used in managing their nets.

Between them, they agreed that there were similarities between the technical needs of minesweeping as now perceived and the work of trawlermen in working their nets, cables and other tackle. As Beresford himself put it, 'our fishing fleet will be rendered inactive in time of war, and will in consequence be available for war service. Fishermen, by virtue of their calling, are adept in the handling and towing of wires and trawls, more so than naval ratings.'[3]

From these comparisons, it was but a short step

3. Built in Goole in 1908, *Seaflower* was one of the six trawlers delivered to the Admiralty in 1909 for evaluation as minesweepers and later became a training ship for the RNR(T), based at Chatham and Sheerness. At the outbreak of war, she was allocated as a minesweeper.
(© National Maritime Museum N04404)

to consider the utility of the strong, sturdy, steam trawler in minesweeping operations. Beresford pressed the Admiralty to undertake a trial of the idea and in early 1908 his fleet navigator, Commander Edward L Booty, was despatched from the flagship to Grimsby to collect two suitable vessels and return with them to Portland, where the North Sea trawlers *Andes* and *Algoma*, built in 1899 and belonging to Alward himself, arrived on 5 February, complete with their skippers and crews of nine men to each boat.

Beresford had formed a Channel Fleet Mining Committee to oversee the testing, headed by his Chief of Staff, Captain Frederick C Doveton Sturdee, and for eight days the little vessels, just over 100ft long, were put through their paces sweeping dummy mines. The first attempts proved less than satisfactory, but at the trawlermen's suggestion the use of improved kites rather than the original net otter boards gave every promise of success. Indeed 'the trawlers found that they could spread the sweep over two cables maintaining a sea-going sweeping speed of 5–6 knots according to weather'.[4] This was in fact never improved on during the war, as the additional weight of more wires impeded speed and efficiency. Six further trawlers were ordered 'off the stocks' by the Admiralty for continued research and development, to be conducted under Captain Clement Greatorix; and the official report into the *Andes* and *Algoma* experiments noted that 'the results achieved were

considered sufficiently satisfactory to call for tactical considerations of the value of minesweepers in general and estimates of the personnel and materiel requisite to form an adequate force'.[5] This was later calculated at 100 trawlers and 1,000 skippers and ratings to man them. It would prove to be a considerable underestimate.[*]

The first four of the six Admiralty trawlers were received in April 1909; they were billed as necessary for 'subsidiary services', their true intention being kept quiet. Named *Seamew*, *Seaflower* (plate 3), *Spider* and *Sparrow* (the other two were christened *Rose* and *Driver*) all but *Spider* would survive the coming war.[†] They proved that such vessels had the advantage of being able to function in heavier weather than, say, a destroyer and with their fish holds full of coal they were able to stay at sea for three to four weeks at a time.

Nonetheless, in July 1914, the Admiralty owned only sixteen trawlers, including the original six purchased from Alward. These were still used for minesweeping training and the remainder were employed towing targets. There were also two survey vessels, converted from trawlers, *Daisy* and *Esther*, both built in 1911. They were additionally fitted as minesweepers.

---

[*] It is possible that the idea of using trawlers came about prior to Beresford's epiphany and his subsequent claims to parenthood of the concept. Admiral George Ballard related after the war that the idea had come up in discussion at the Admiralty in 1906 and was submitted to First Sea Lord Sir John Fisher. He ordered that the next time the Home Fleet was cruising in the vicinity of Grimsby it should call in and inspect some trawlers and report on their suitability for minesweeping (Taffrail, *Swept Channels*, p40).

[†] She was wrecked off Lowestoft on 21 November 1914.

The Royal Naval Reserve – Trawler Section

Having identified the type of ship which would serve their purpose, the Admiralty had to face the question of how to obtain and man them.

Manpower

The Royal Naval Reserve (RNR) was created by the Naval Reserve Act of 1859, itself a product of the invasion scare of the same year. For one month a year, merchant sailors and fishermen were given gunnery training on drill ships stationed around the coast. When war was declared they were liable to be drafted to the fleet or reserve ships. As first created, the RNR consisted of up to 30,000 merchant seamen and fisherman who the navy could call on in times of crisis. By 1914, membership was drawn from professional officers and ratings of the Mercantile Marine, the fishing fleet and ex-naval ratings. For the former, it was voluntary but many major steamer companies encouraged their employees to join. After basic training, further periodic training with the fleet was undertaken.

In 1910, it was decided to expand the naval reserve through the creation of a special reserve for fishermen, the Royal Naval Reserve – Trawler Section. The first skipper to join the RNT(T) signed on in Aberdeen on 3 February 1911 (his name was Peter Yorston) and approval was given to recruit 1,278 men to crew 142 trawlers.[*][6] By April 1912, forty-two were ready but Commander Plunkett noted that 'in war we shall have 140 trawlers available [for minesweeping]'.[7]

Trawlers taken up by the Admiralty in time of need usually came complete with their pre-existing crews. Skippers were given warrant officer rank. Crewmen signed on under a T-124 agreement (see appendix 2) whereby they consented to serve under Admiralty rules (specifically it bound them to the Naval Discipline Act) in any commissioned vessel but retained certain aspects of their civilian pay and benefits. The ship's complement was supplemented by the addition of a signals rating and/or W/T operator and sometimes a regular navy sub lieutenant or other officer. And by the end of 1910, permission had been given to employ petty officers from the Royal Fleet Reserve (RFR)[†] in trawlers; they were intended to act as third in command and offer advice on 'proper' naval signalling, record keeping and other procedures. Additionally, annual courses for officers on the retired and emergency lists, provisionally assigned to unit-command of minesweepers, had begun. 'Certain retired lieutenants do a mining course yearly and are ready to take charge, one lieutenant to six trawlers', confided Reginald Drax.[8]

Initially, skippers received £3.6s for their four days' training and a retainer of £10 per annum. Second hands and engineers were paid £2.4s for four days' training and a retaining fee of £8. Deck hands were given £1.6s and an annual fee of £5 and coal trimmers received the same training rate but only £4 per annum.[9]

When war came, there was an enthusiastic response to the call for fishermen volunteers, at least if the *Fraserburgh Times* is to be believed. In its edition of 4 August, the newspaper noted that:

> the calling out of the Royal Naval Reserve[§] created great excitement in Fraserburgh, where hundreds of Highland hired men, engaged meantime on the herring fishing boats, are members of the Reserve. During Sunday forenoon, 257 men presented themselves at the Custom House, and received their warrants. In the afternoon at 1530 a special train, carrying 233 reservists, left Fraserburgh for Portsmouth. Unparalleled scenes were witnessed at the railway station, where several thousand assembled to give the men a hearty send-off. They marched from the Custom House to the station, headed by the Fraserburgh pipe band, under the charge of Leading Seamen Alexander Sim and Noah Killoh, both of Fraserburgh. For fully half a mile along the railway thousands of spectators lined the embankments on both sides, and tumultuous cheers were raised.[10]

Once at war, further financial incentive was provided. Wages were based on normal expectations for the fishing trade less 20 per cent; but a sum of £200 was offered to any trawler or auxiliary vessel which sank or captured a U-boat. This was raised to £1,000 in January 1915; at the same time £200 was awarded for damaging a U-boat and a bounty of £5 offered for each mine destroyed.[11] Salvage and prize money were sources of additional income for trawler crew. Over 400 trawlers received such payments during the course of the war.

Initially, there was no uniform provided; but concerns grew that men captured in such a state of undress in time of war would be executed as pirates. It was agreed that a badge would be produced which identified the fishermen as part of the Royal Navy. This comprised the letters 'RNR' above the letter 'T' embroidered in red or gold onto a dark blue rectangle all surmounted by a gold and red crown.[ß] And for skippers, as Lieutenant Maitland Walter Sabine Boucher, navigating officer of the Lowestoft trawler depot ship and torpedo gunboat *Halcyon* noted, 'enough officers' uniforms could not be produced at short notice for so many skippers. Each therefore was given an officers' cap and a set of uniform buttons, which he was told to sew onto his best suit.'[12]

---

[*] In fact, on mobilisation in August 1914 there were only sufficient crewmen available to man ninety-four trawlers.

[†] Founded in 1905, initially to provide civilian-manned coaling ships for the fleet in home waters or abroad, it was a force drawn from former naval ratings and petty officers who, after completing their contractual service with the Royal Navy, were liable to recall in times of emergency. The liability lasted for a specified number of years after leaving active service in the navy.

[§] The RNR was activated at 0125 on 2 August 1914 after a meeting of the Army Council, chaired by Prime Minister Asquith.

[ß] For a second hand. There were many variations, such as the letters embroidered in red on a blue ground and no crown for crewmen.

Throughout the war, recruitment into the RNR(T) continued. By the Armistice, the strength was 39,000 skippers and ratings, about a quarter of whom were employed on minesweeping duties. 'The institution of the Trawler Reserve', wrote the author of an official post-war report, 'will always rank as a monumental achievement in naval administration and the scheme devised three years before the war stood the test of rapid expansion to a degree far beyond expectation at the time of its inception.'[13]

Ships

So, men could be had; but what about vessels for them to crew? Captain Bernard Currey RN suggested that a contract between the Admiralty and fishing boat owners be drawn up that would allow the navy to take up sufficient vessels as necessary during a conflict. With First Sea Lord Jacky Fisher's approval, the Admiralty entered into negotiations with the Board of Agriculture (Fisheries Department), the local Fisheries Boards and trawler owners to agree terms for the hire of their vessels.

Those owners who accepted the terms offered had their vessels entered on a 'specialist list' which rendered them subject to release on request by the Admiralty. Lease terms were based on the boat's tonnage. The hull and outfit were valued at £18 for each unit of gross tonnage and at £40 per each unit of nominal horsepower. The value so calculated was depreciated for every full year of the trawler's age. The hire then paid was 12 per cent of this annual valuation. The Admiralty had the right of inspection at any time and the owners could withdraw vessels from the list, subject to notification of the authorities. Vessels needed to be less than ten years old and able to steam 1,000 miles at 8 knots. One hundred and forty-six trawlers were covered by these agreements when war came.

Mobilisation Officers were appointed for each key port in November 1911. When mobilisation occurred, this officer was to receive a telegram informing him which vessels were to be taken up and had then to work with the port Registrar of Shipping and Seamen to prepare crews to man the trawlers. The Mobilisation Officer had also to provide each skipper with the requisite charts and sailing orders. On arrival at his destination, the skipper was to draw naval stores, a White Ensign, paint his vessel grey and obliterate his registry port number. In reality, when the time came some of these activities were obeyed only in the breach; and indeed, within the first month of the war Admiral John Jellicoe, CinC Grand Fleet, ordered that all his patrol trawlers should retain their civilian livery and markings in order to persuade the enemy that they were unarmed.

For war purposes, trawlers would be formed into groups of six, each unit to be placed under the command of a (previously trained, see above) RN or RNR officer, the latter holding a master's or mate's 'Foreign-Going Certificate'.

But the call up of trawlers was not a simple process, for demand soon exceeded supply. On 9 November 1914, the First Sea Lord,

Jacky Fisher, recalled to the position on 30 October, instructed the CinC Home Fleets that he should 'arrange to take up as many trawlers as you require from the Scotch fishing ports, the local SNOs undertaking this'. The reason given was that 'it is very difficult to obtain more trawlers and man them in the southern ports and the men aren't so well suited to the local conditions as in the north'.[14] And by September 1916 only 500 trawlers remained in private hands, with over 1,300 being taken up by that stage in the war.

The navy's first priority had been to secure hired vessels. But the need for these hardy fishing vessels had outstripped all possible calculation and by mid-1916 it seemed that all those trawlers suitable for naval work had been gathered up. As a partial remedy, the Admiralty built their own vessels, the so-called 'Admiralty trawlers'. Between 18 August and 26 September, a series of conference and meetings with trawler operators resulted in a recommendation on 26 October for three classes of Admiralty trawler. By the end of the war 453 were commissioned, either purpose built, purchased from foreign sources or taken as prizes (see appendix 3).

The major fishing ports of Hull and Grimsby contributed heavily to the cause; from the two combined, 9,000 fishermen and 829 hired trawlers served.[15] Lowestoft and Aberdeen were also large contributors, with approximately 300 fishing vessels each.

The navy had not initially considered the mobilisation of drifters in their agreements with the fishing industry and owners. But the drifter proprietors proved anxious that the Admiralty should take the boats off their hands after they found themselves precluded by the needs of war from their most productive fishing grounds. It was perhaps just as well, for the humble herring drifter was to play a significant role in the Great War at sea as well. Some 1,372 were requisitioned during the conflict and additionally the Admiralty, as with trawlers, built their own to provide sufficient numbers, constructing 318 drifters, both wooden and steel (see appendix 4).

Losses were significant and continuous throughout the conflict. The second and third Royal Navy vessels to be sunk in the war were both trawlers, *Thomas W Irvin* and *Crathie*. They went down on 27 August 1914, sweeping mines off the mouth of the River Tyne, laid the previous day by German cruisers. They had swept seven mines when, at 1625, *Thomas W Irvin* hit one and blew up, killing three crewmen. Forty minutes later, *Crathie* – which had already snagged two mines in her sweep wires – caught a third which went unseen and exploded under her. Two men lost their lives. All the dead were members of the RNR(T).

The penultimate RN vessel to be sunk in the war was also a trawler, the former Grimsby-registered vessel *Renarro*. On 10 November 1918, one day before the war ended, she was minesweeping in the Dardanelles where she snagged three mines in her tackle. Her crew tried surging the wire and steering an 'S' manoeuvre to free them but as they were doing so, the mines detonated and she rapidly sank. All twelve of her crew died with her.

3: Materiel

Trawlers and drifters were thus rather unexpectedly a key component of the Royal Navy's battle for Sovereignty of the Seas. But what were the characteristics of each type that made them so valuable?

Fishing trawlers were particularly suited for many naval requirements because they were robust boats designed to work heavy trawls in all types of weather, and boasted large, clear, working decks. A minesweeper could be created simply by replacing the trawl with a mine sweep. Commander Archibald Bruce Campbell RNVR,[*] working with a group of minesweeping trawlers in Scotland, noted that 'the gallows on these little vessels, normally in use with trawls, were easily adaptable for the sweep wire and the otter boards which kept the net mouth open for fishing served admirably in controlling the depth at which the sweep wire worked'.[1]

Steam-powered, steel-built with high upstanding bows, they were typically 115–38ft long, 215–325 gross register tons (grt) and drew about 13ft of water. Seldom capable of more than eleven knots, and more usually having a top speed around ten, their range fitted them for long-distance patrols as well as work closer inshore. Crew size was normally around twelve men including the skipper, although under war conditions more crewmen were often squeezed aboard. A mizzen sail was generally carried, which was used to help steady the boat when its nets were out.

Their heavy trawls were usually conical nets held open by otter boards (kites) and dragged along the bottom of the sea or at a specified depth. And their winches were powered by a steam donkey engine, which was also suitable for reeling in minesweeping cables.

Trawlers were built to withstand the worst of North Sea or Arctic gales and had a long cruising range by virtue of storing coal in the fish holds. (This was not a wartime expedient, but a fisherman's trick designed to extend their productive time at sea; when the hold was emptied it was cleaned and used for fish!) These attributes fitted them, apart from minesweeping, for anti-submarine patrol work, work as Q-ships[†] and, later in the war, for convoy escort. Trawlers also served as boom defence vessels, despatch boats and a host of other day-to-day dogsbody duties.

The difference between a trawler and a drifter was primarily that trawlers pull their nets through the water to pick up schools of fish whereas drifters lower their nets into the water to collect up fish which swim into them and are trapped by their gills. Drifters were essentially a product of the herring trade. Usually wooden-built they were small steam- or motor-powered vessels used in fishing for the 'silver darlings' with drift nets, which were often some two-and-a-half-miles long and supported at regular intervals by floats. Smaller than trawlers, they were normally less than 100grt, used less powerful steam capstans to pull in their nets and carried a crew of ten or fewer men.

Their capability to manage long lines of nets made them ideal for laying and maintaining anti-submarine net defences, which were used to protect harbours, anchorages and sometimes whole channels, such as the Folkstone to Cap Gris Nez cross-English Channel U-boat barrier. The navy found these vessels extremely useful in other roles too, as fleet tenders, despatch boats, minesweepers, and harbour and coast patrol. Not the least of the attraction was that these smaller and cheaper boats could free trawlers from these duties.

Trawlers and drifters' lack of speed rendered them unsuitable to work with the battlefleet. Theirs was a more quotidian, and often solitary, existence of sweeping and patrolling in the dolorous waters of the North and Irish seas or the Atlantic coast.

The fishing boats taken up on hire by the Admiralty were of necessity of an heterogenous character. But, as noted in the previous chapter, the Admiralty ordered a large number of their own vessels. To start with the Admiralty acquired the ten-strong 'Military' class, purchased while building, and nine trawlers from Portugal. But by 1916 it was clear that the demand for trawlers in naval operations had outstripped the fishing fleet's ability to supply them without severe threat to the supply of fish for public consumption.

The Admiralty therefore placed their own orders on British (and foreign) shipyards. These embraced three main classes, based on their builders' mercantile prototypes. In total, 167 *Strath*-class were requested, of which 89 were delivered before the end of the war; 217 *Castle*-class were ordered, of which 127 came into use; and 156 *Mersey*-class, 69 of which were deployed during the conflict (see appendix 5). All of these vessels were given names drawn from the muster rolls of *Victory* and *Royal Sovereign* at the time of the Battle of Trafalgar. Additionally, a small number of fishing boats under construction at the time were requisitioned and added to each class as 'non-standard units'.

From Canada came the *Festubert* group (six), *Armentières* group (six) and another *Castle* class (sixty); in addition, fifteen trawlers were acquired for Indian naval waters. And twenty-nine prize trawlers

---

[*] During the Second World War, Campbell was a popular member of the panel on the BBC radio programme 'Brain's Trust'.

[†] A Q-ship was a seemingly defenceless and harmless vessel which actually concealed a powerful armament. They were intended to draw an unsuspecting U-boat to surface near them before revealing their true colours and attacking the enemy.

were given names with a '-sin' suffix. Finally, Russia provided seventeen trawlers which were assigned names ending in '-axe'.

Of the 'Military'-class boats, ten vessels of three different types were purchased in the UK while building, in December 1914 and April 1915, for a sum of £93,800. They served as minesweepers, equipped with a single gun, 3pdr, 6pdr or 12pdr. The exception was the appropriately named *Gunner*, which was fitted out in February 1915 as a Q-ship with a veritable arsenal comprising a 4in, two 12pdrs, two 6pdrs and two 14in torpedo tubes.

The nine Portuguese-built trawlers were acquired in September 1915 for a consideration of £80,788. These had all been intended as minesweepers but in fact seemed to have been deployed as patrol and anti-submarine vessels. All but one carried a 6pdr weapon, the exception (*Antares*) having a 3pdr.

The 115ft long *Strath* class were the smallest of the Admiralty trawlers, typically 215grt, and were largely launched in 1917 and 1918. Based on a design suitable for home waters, they were usually armed with a 12pdr gun and were used in minesweeping and anti-submarine roles. A typical example of a *Strath* vessel is shown in plans I and II. Two *Strath*s, *Henry Jennings* and *George Ireland*, were fitted with an experimental centrifugal-pump water jet propulsion, which delayed their receipt by the navy until after the war was over. The intention had been to assess whether engine noise reduction could be obtained to improve hydrophone performance (see chapter 5). The

4. A nice model of the *Mersey*-class Admiralty trawler *William Leech*. Of 324grt, and armed with one 12pdr, she was delivered too late to take part in the war and was sold on in 1922. In the Second World War, she served in the French navy as *Excellent*. (© Imperial War Museum Q 20434)

experiments were not a success and the vessels were refitted conventionally. Some of the class, such as *James Bentole*, sold in 1922 to become *Fort Robert*, survived to be requisitioned in 1939 for another world war.

The extensive *Castle* class of around 275grt and 125ft long was another pattern intended for home use but was also capable of foreign service. They carried 12pdrs and were used in both anti-mine and anti-submarine roles (an example of the type is shown at plan III).

Plan IV shows an illustration of a *Mersey*-class vessel. These were based on a design which pre-war had voyaged into the White Sea and Icelandic fisheries and had even reached Newfoundland and Morocco. They were the largest of the Admiralty builds (324grt) and also carried 12pdrs. At 138ft long and capable of 11 knots, they seem to have been considered very versatile, covering all sorts of duties, including training roles (see plate 4).

Of these three main classes, the most expensive to build were the *Mersey*s at £22,000 each. *Castle*s cost around £21,000 and *Strath*s £18,000. Each carried around fifteen crew, eighteen if wireless was fitted.

The main modifications made by the Admiralty to the original

5. *TR-9*, depicted here, was one of the sixty Canadian-built *Castle*-class trawlers ordered by the Admiralty in January 1917. Built by Collingwood Shipbuilding of Ontario, she was not delivered until May the following year. She was fitted with a 12pdr gun and served as a minesweeper for the rest of the war before being sold in 1920. (author's collection)

commercial designs of these three classes were the addition of a magazine and shell room in the fish hold, and extra accommodation for an increased crew, also in a fish hold. Depth charge chutes and stands, and a gun platform, were the obvious external alterations.

As for the *Festubert* group, they were larger units, around 320grt and designed to carry two 12pdrs, although in fact each ship only received one such gun. The *Armentières* class were larger still at around 350grt. They were specifically designed for patrol work in the rough conditions of the Atlantic coast and were armed with a single 12pdr. After the war, some of them became lightships. The Canadian *Castle*-class vessels were used as minesweepers. All three of these latter classes were manned almost entirely by Royal Canadian Navy sailors (see plate 5).

The Indian vessels were specifically ordered in 1917 to provide minesweeping capability around the Colombo area, where German minelaying had become more than the two harbour tugs, previously used as minesweepers, could cope with. Six trawlers were purchased in Japan[*] and another nine were ordered on builders in India. None

of these latter were launched in time to take part in hostilities.

Of the twenty-nine prize trawlers, all but two were captured German vessels, usually taken in cruiser or destroyer sweeps across the North Sea. Prize trawlers had been a useful additional resource from the beginning of the war. In November 1914, the Inspecting Captain of Minesweepers, Captain Thomas Parry Bonham, was apprised by some Aberdeen trawler owners that six captured German trawlers were in their port, ordered to be detained by a prize court. He requested the procurator fiscal to release them to the Admiralty and the prize court promptly gave orders for them to be delivered to the navy 'forthwith' but 'required an affidavit to be filed'. The steam trawlers *Elekunkel*,[†] *Dr Robitzsch*,[§] *Hummiel*, *Wardon*, *Elsflotte* and *Willis Vegesack* (actually a drifter) thus came into the Royal Navy's possession, despite the protestations of one Colonel Leslie of the Admiralty Coasting Trade Office who had had his eye on them for his own department.[2]

Most captured vessels were originally sent to Grimsby and later assigned for service in the Mediterranean. They were fitted with 6pdr guns.

[*] They were named *Kumarhami*, *Lankdy*s, *Lakshmi*, *Parvati*, *Ranmenika* and *Sarasvati*, and operated under the control of the Colombo harbour master.

[†] Renamed *Chirsin* and used as a minesweeper.

[§] Renamed *Clonsin* and used as a minesweeper.

6. The Canadian-built Admiralty wood drifter *CD27*. She was ordered in January 1917, built by Davie's of Quebec, and commissioned the following November. Of 99grt, she carried a single 6pdr gun and could manage 9 knots. After the war, the vessel was loaned to the Grenfell Mission, which provided medical and social services to people in the rural communities of northern Newfoundland and Labrador. (author's collection)

7. The Lowestoft-registered hired drifter *John Mitchell* was taken up in February 1915 and fitted with a 3pdr weapon. She was typical of the drifter type, used mainly for anti-submarine net management. She was sunk in November 1917 in a collision off St Alban's Head, Dorset. (author's collection)

As for the Russian vessels, they were seized or handed over in the White Sea in August 1918. All were British built, six by the Smith's Dock company; these had prominent forecastles, bows especially strengthened for sailing through ice and a sharply cutaway forefront below the waterline.

Orders for Admiralty trawlers were still being placed right up to the last moments of the war, although at the Armistice some 82 orders were cancelled and another 133 were completed as mercantile trawlers.

From 1917, the Admiralty also constructed ninety-eight wooden drifters, having recognised that a drifter could be as capable as a trawler in some roles, were cheaper to build and used different shipyards to trawlers. Typically, these were of 94grt, at a unit cost of around £11,500. Building commenced in May 1917 and most were delivered for the final year of the war, or later. A typical example is *Eddy* depicted in plate 9.

There does not appear to have been a consistent programme to arm them, although individual skippers no doubt acquired what weaponry they could. One hundred more wooden drifters were sourced from Canada (see plate 6). Most were delivered in 1918 and, where fitted, armed with a 6pdr gun in the bow together with two depth charges.

One hundred and twenty-six steel drifters were also built to Admiralty orders but most did not come into use until 1918.

Builders

The plans for the three main Admiralty trawler classes were based on successful commercial designs from three shipbuilders, who then went on to build much of 'their' class.

Cochrane's *Lord Mersey* created the template for the *Mersey* class; Smith's Dock's *Raglan Castle* was the pattern for the *Castle* class and Hall, Russell's *Strathlochy* was the template for the *Strath* class.

Cochrane's was founded by Andrew Cochrane at Beverley in 1884, establishing Cochrane & Sons in 1896. The company moved to Selby, on the tidal River Ouse, in 1898 and made a reputation for building trawlers and coasters for the Hull and Grimsby fishing fleets. During the war, the yard made ninety steam trawlers for private owners and seventy steam trawlers for the Admiralty. They were able to achieve such an output by building the trawlers ten at a time in five pairs. Additionally, the firm laid out their yard in such a way so that ships could be launched two at a time and construction could take place rotationally with members of staff working on one task at a time for a couple of weeks before the next task was taken in hand. Other *Mersey*-class vessels were constructed to Cochrane's designs by Lobnitz (of Renfrew), Goole Ship Building and Ferguson's (Port Glasgow).

Smith's Dock had its company origins in Newcastle upon Tyne in 1810 but became associated with the South Bank in Middlesbrough on the River Tees after opening an operation there in 1907, having moved from North Shields. By 1914, a contemporary *Whitaker's Red Book* listed them as 'dry-dock owners, engineers, shipbuilders, makers of steam trawlers, steam drifters and tugs'.

During the course of the war, they built 160 small ships. Other shipyards involved in building *Castle*-class trawlers included Cook, Welton and Gemmell (Beverley), Bow McLachlan (Abbotsinch, Renfrewshire), J P Rennoldson (South Shields), George Brown

8. Steam drifter *Inverboyndie*, originally from Banff, was built in 1910 and hired in 1916. She was fitted with a 6pdr gun and used as a net vessel. (author's collection)

(Greenock), Ailsa (Troon) and Fletcher, Son and Fearnall (Limehouse, London).

Aberdeen-based Hall, Russell had been formed in 1864 to build steam engines and boilers but in 1867 launched its first ship, *Kwang Tung*, for the Imperial Chinese Navy. As steam trawling took off in Aberdeen in the 1880s, the yard capitalised on its location and built many of the new trawlers required. When war came, the yard's main output was *Strath*-class trawlers and Admiralty drifters as well as vessels for the local fleets of the Aberdeen Steam Trawling and Fishing Co.

The *Strath* class was also built by, inter alia, Fullerton (Paisley), Fleming and Ferguson (Paisley), Montrose Ship Building, Hawthorn Leslie (Tyneside), and Murdoch and Murray (Port Glasgow).

Admiralty drifters were constructed by a wide range of shipbuilders. The steel-built vessels were based around the template of the Scottish drifter *Ocean Reward*, from the yard of Alexander Hall of Aberdeen in 1912. Of around 94grt, they undertook a range of work including minesweeping (see plans V–VIII) Where carried, they had a 6pdr weapon.

Wooden vessels were to the designs of John Chambers of Lowestoft and their drifter *Boy Roy*, at a cost of £10,800 each. The Canadian boats were to the same general plan.

Engines

The standard power plant was a variation on machinery which would typically be found on any steam trawler of the time. This was a single, coal-fired, vertical triple-expansion* reciprocating engine having one boiler, one shaft, and generating something in the order of seventy nominal horsepower. Typical manufacturers of engines

---

* A triple-expansion engine is a compound engine that expands the steam in three stages, having three cylinders at three different pressures.

9. The drifter *Eddy* was an Admiralty-built steel drifter, launched in August 1918 and intended for us as a minesweeper. She survived to fight again in the Second World War but was mined and sunk off Malta on 26 May 1942. (© National Maritime Museum N04453)

for trawlers would include, inter alia, Amos and Smith of Hull, Charles D Holmes and Co, also of Hull, Blair and Co from Stockton-on-Tees or Hawthorns and Co in Leith; Smith's Dock built their own engines, as did Hall Russell.

Hired vessels

The hired trawlers and drifters taken up by the Admiralty were an assorted group, in terms of both age and design. They came from forty-one different fishing ports of registration and a wide range of build dates. For example, the Grimsby-registered trawler *Angelus* was launched in 1914, taken up in May 1915 and sunk by a mine in February the following year at Dover. Her sister Grimsby boat *Balmoral II* was laid down in 1916 and joined the navy in June 1917. Whereas Hull-based *Columbia*, of 1886 vintage, was requisitioned at the start of the war and sunk on 1 May 1915 by a German torpedo boat.

A characteristic hired armed trawler is shown at plate 10 with a 12pdr in her bows. The vessel is probably *Regardo*, serving as a minesweeper at Dover.

Drifters too covered a range of types and ages. *Budding Rose* was built in 1914 and taken up as a boom defence vessel in the following year and the Banff boat *Cornstalk* was launched in 1916, immediately taken into the navy and, with a 3pdr gun fitted, used for net management. Very few of the hired drifters date from before 1900, the *Lillian Maud* from Wick being a rare exception in her

1890 construction. She was used for 'miscellaneous services'.

Typical of the drifters taken on for net and other duties was the wooden construction Lowestoft vessel *John Mitchell* (plate 7). Launched in 1913, she was taken up in February 1915, fitted with a 3pdr weapon and became part of the Dover Barrage net management force. By 1917, she was based at Poole and there came to grief off St Alban's Head in a collision with the Norwegian cargo vessel SS *Bjerka*, bound for Newport from London, at 0145 on 14 November. All her crew were rescued.

Another such craft was the steam drifter *Inverboyndie* (plate 8), originally from Banff, built in 1910 and hired in January 1916. She gained a 6pdr gun and was also used as a net vessel; *Inverboyndie* did not escape her naval bondage until 1920.

Other types

There were two other types of fishing vessel that were either requisitioned by the Admiralty for war use, or specifically designed and built for that purpose – whalers and *Kil*-class gunboats.

In 1915, the Admiralty became interested in the type of commercial vessel known as a whaler, used for hunting cetaceans.

10. This picture, taken in Dover harbour, shows an armed trawler with its sisters in the background and its 12pdr visible in the bows. Although unidentified in the original, the vessel is probably the hired trawler *Regardo*, serving as a minesweeper. (© Imperial War Museum Q 18226)

The benefits of the type were seen as high manoeuvrability and a low draught to avoid minefields. There was even talk of using them in conjunction with an anti-submarine harpoon (see chapter 5, lance bombs). The Smith's Dock company had designs already prepared, originally meant for the Russian government, and in March 1915 the Admiralty ordered fifteen such vessels. No more were purchased for the rest of the war. A small number of additional whalers did come into service, however. Three were German vessels seized in South Africa in 1914/15; two were hired; and twelve were purchased from their owners in 1917.

However, the type was a dead end. By the time they were in service the anti-submarine harpoon concept had been discredited. They were far less handy in rough waters than a trawler of the same tonnage, could not tow an anti-submarine sweep and were not fast enough to run down a surfaced submarine. Three squadrons of them were formed at the Humber, Peterhead and Stornoway, fitted with 12pdr guns and used primarily as escorts for the Scandinavian convoys.

The besetting problem regarding the use of the Auxiliary Patrol's trawlers for anti-submarine warfare was their lack of speed. With a maximum of 9–11 knots, sometimes less, trawlers and drifters were

no match for the later types of U-boat such as the *UB-III* class of 1916–17, which could reach 13.5 knots surfaced, or the *U-93* type, rated at 16.8 knots.

In mid-1917, the Admiralty issued a requirement for a vessel of roughly trawler size but not intended for fishing and specifically designed for anti-submarine and convoy escort work. Six trawler building companies were invited to submit designs and the Teesside-based Smith's Dock company's was evaluated as the best. Orders were placed with all six builders for eighty-five 'fast trawlers' and some ordinary trawler orders were cancelled to make room on the manufacturing schedules.

The most interesting design feature was that the ships were constructed to look the same at either end, the intention being to confuse a U-boat commander as to the direction of travel. They had two apparently identical superstructure blocks fore and aft, a single mast and a funnel dead amidships.

The type was named the *Kil*-class and the first vessel came into service at the end of 1917. They were described as 'fast trawlers' until 18 January 1918, when they were renamed 'patrol gun boats' (and later still 'sloops'). *Kils* were 182ft long, with a design speed of 13 knots and carried one 4in gun and twelve depth charges. (see plate 11) At least eleven of them were equipped as minesweepers. Thirty-eight were completed before the Armistice and post-war they were sold into private ownership for use as cargo vessels.

Major armament

The trawlers and drifters that the navy took from civilian life were obviously unarmed. And to start with they remained that way. A couple of rifles, perhaps a pistol or two, were the limit of their warlike stores. A rifle could be used to sink a swept mine but it was not much use against U-boats, which from early 1915 were pervasively found with deck guns. These might be 3.7cm (1.5in) in the early days of the war, ranging to 5cm (2in) firing a 3.9lb shell in early 1915 or 8.8cm (3.5in) with a 15lb projectile. And German tactical doctrine in the first years of the war was to attack with guns if possible, as torpedoes were expensive and often only six were carried on board. Clearly, a rifle was of doubtful utility in such circumstances.

Shortage of suitable weapons was the rate step preventing universal armament. Old, decommissioned guns from stores or from scrapped vessels were quickly sought out. Large ships demounted their smaller weapons. Anti-submarine and patrol trawlers were given priority for arming, but it was not until August 1915 that the hired minesweepers and drifters could be armed in quantity. When obtained by the trawler, guns were mounted aft over the engine casing or in the bow; this latter position was initially less common as it required reinforcement and the building of a gun platform. However, experience demonstrated that the forward siting was much the better and guns became pervasively mounted in the prow of the ship, on the forecastle, commanding a good field of view but somehow looking aesthetically unbalanced. Minesweepers were

11. HMS *Kilbride*, a *Kil*-class gunboat or 'fast trawler', seen here in 'dazzle' camouflage. This particular vessel is best known for a mutiny on board on 13 January 1919 while the ship was docked at Milford Haven. Eight men were court-martialled on charges of non-violent mutiny and sentenced to between ninety days and two years hard labour followed by dismissal from the service. (author's collection)

fitted with 3pdrs and then 6pdrs, patrol and anti-submarine (A/S) trawlers with (mainly) 6pdr and 12pdr weapons (when they became available), as the smaller guns were inadequate to inflict serious damage to a U-boat. Enterprising skippers 'acquired' machine guns and other unofficial armaments.

The 12pdr (see plan IX) had started life in 1904 as an anti-torpedo boat weapon on pre-dreadnought battleships. Of 3in/40 calibre (the Mark I was 3in/50), it fired a 12.5lb shell with a 3lb charge to a range of around 8,500–9,000 yards. It became the standard armament for pre-war destroyers and as they were retired there were so many on hand that, from April 1912, as existing ones wore out no more were ordered. However, the wartime demand to arm auxiliary craft, including fishing vessels, was such that from May 1915 large quantities were once more requested of manufacturers

and guns were taken from larger ships to be used in their smaller brethren.

The 6pdr gun most likely to be found in a trawler was the Hotchkiss-made version, its use in the RN dating from 1890. It was widely fitted to destroyers and other small craft. Of 2.24in/40 calibre it fired a shell of 6lb. In the latter part of the war, some were installed on high-angle mountings for use against Zeppelins and Gotha bombers, as for example on the 'Military'-class trawler *Highlander* and most of the prize trawlers. A scale drawing can be seen at plan X. There was also a Nordenfelt version of 42.3 calibre.

The 3pdr (1.85in/40 calibre) was a product of both the Nordenfelt and the Hotchkiss companies, first ordered for the Royal Navy in 1885. With a calibre of 1.85in/50 it delivered a 3lb 3oz shell over a range of 7,500–8,900 yards. They were often used as saluting guns and when war came the battleships surrendered their 3pdrs for mounting in trawlers and drifters, particularly minesweepers, where they were used to sink swept mines.

With a high muzzle velocity, they were considered a better anti-aircraft gun than the Hotchkiss 6pdr and began to appear in high-angle mountings from 1915.

In total, estimates suggest that 239 3pdr guns were deployed in

12. An unusual view of a whaler. HMS *Ramna,* taken up by the navy in January 1915, is pictured stranded on the sunken German battle cruiser *Moltke*, on 23 June 1919 after the scuttling of the German fleet at Scapa Flow. (US Naval History and Heritage Command NH 49918)

trawlers during the war, 849 6pdrs and 771 12pdrs.[3]

Of hired drifters, it is calculated that, where a weapon was mounted, 369 3pdr guns were used. Drifters also utilised 796 6pdrs, with all of the Admiralty-built drifters using this calibre where a gun was in place. Only five drifters carried a 12pdr.[4]

Organisation

Trawlers taken into the RN were known as auxiliaries,[*] and initially joined either what became known as the Auxiliary Patrol or the Minesweeping Service.

At the outbreak of war, the defence of the coastline of Britain was the responsibility of the admiral of patrols.[†] Under his aegis were twenty-seven patrol areas, each under a senior naval officer, often a 'dug out' (a retired senior officer recalled to duty) with a shore base. There were also eleven patrol areas in the Mediterranean, variously

[*] The term also applied to any vessel co-opted into the navy which was not a purpose-built warship.

[†] The post of admiral of patrols was originally created in May 1912 to protect the coasts from invasion or raid. It was abolished in 1915 and patrol vessels then came under the direct control of the admiral commanding the district.

under British, French or (after 1915) Italian control. A random assortment of vessels was entered into the organisation – hired yachts, trawlers, drifters, tugs and motor launches.

At first all the requisitioned trawlers were sent to Lowestoft for conversion to naval vessels. Most also needed basic equipment such as stays and a general refit. Then they would sally forth looking for U-boats or other enemy vessels.

The Dover Patrol, responsible not just for the cross-Channel net and mine barrier but also for the command of the Narrow Seas around it, had a heavy reliance on both trawlers and drifters. On 6 July 1918, as the war entered its final phase, Vice Admiral Roger Keyes, commanding at Dover, could call upon 131 drifters, primarily to manage the barrage, 70 patrol trawlers and 19 minesweeping trawlers. The versatility of the fishing vessels was attested to by Captain Taprell Dorling who wrote after the war that 'every one of the trawlers … at Dover was used as a minesweeper as well as a patrol or escort vessel. A dozen were even fitted out as minelayers.'[5] (Overall, the navy converted a total sixteen trawlers for minelaying. They carried twenty-four mines each.)

To maintain and service these craft, the Dover Engineering Works, famous pre-war for the manufacture of steam-isolating valves, iron fittings and waterproof, airtight inspection covers, became the reserve base workshop for the Dover Patrol.

Another command heavily reliant on fishermen and their boats was the Coast of Ireland, under Vice Admiral Sir Lewis Bayly. This encompassed Areas XV through to XXI in which, by January 1918, were deployed 162 armed patrol trawlers, 11 minesweeping trawlers and 194 drifters out of a total force of 461 auxiliary vessels.

Then there were Patrol Areas VI and VII, based on Granton in the Firth of Forth. Granton, now a part of Edinburgh, was a fishing port hosting some eighty trawlers pre-war. But from 1915, under the command of the irrepressible 'dug out' Commodore James Startin RNR, it became a major base for anti-submarine patrols and, from 1917, convoy escort.

Startin was a 'character' and in his earlier days was noted as a fearless horseman, a gymnast and an athlete. As a vice admiral he had been placed on the retired list on 14 September 1914, aged sixty, but was reactivated into the naval reserve four days later. Admiral Jellicoe described him as 'the life and soul of the patrols and minesweepers working from Granton, frequently at sea with decoy ships fitted out there'.[6] With his headquarters named after his 'Military'-class trawler *Gunner*, converted to a Q-ship and in which he frequently went to sea, Startin whipped his eclectic collection of RNR(T) fishermen, RNVR personnel and (after mid-1916) conscripts into a disciplined fighting force, a navy within a navy. Noting the fishermen's eye for a quick profit, he arranged financial rewards for the gun crews of the armed trawlers based on their success at target practice. Competitions were held with prizes for those ships which could lay their modified sweeps (see chapter 5) in the shortest time. Startin also arranged for British submarines to play the role of U-boats while he trained his crews to recognise and attack them.

He was an early adopter of the Q-ship concept and converted twenty-nine boats into disguised U-boat hunters, thirteen of which were Q-trawlers, which fished with the fishing fleets while waiting to spring their hidden armaments into play. Apparently, a concealed 12pdr 'could be brought into action from the lying down position in five seconds'.[7]

By January 1918, Startin's broad pennant flew over a command of 400 officers, 8,000 men, 100 WRNS, 55 minesweeping trawlers, 37 drifters, 29 Q-ships, most of them trawlers, and 38 other auxiliary vessels of various types. And on land he ruled over a kingdom of a rambling accumulation of stone buildings and wooden huts that made up the shore establishment.

Further north, the Orkney and Shetland Islands, Areas I and II, boasted 159 trawlers and 221 drifters in January 1918. And there were ninety-six trawlers at the Humber, another seventy-three at Portsmouth and forty-seven at Area XV, Milford Haven.

Patrol was a long and often monotonous duty, with nothing more to assist in spotting an enemy vessel than eyesight and binoculars. Taking as an example the Tyne Auxiliary Patrol, Area VIII, the sea to be covered was divided into three zones. Operations involved each trawler group spending six days at sea followed by three in harbour for cleaning, refuelling and rearming and other basic tasks. Trawlers worked in pairs, and cruised out some fifty miles from land before working their way back to the coast. There was little or no spare capacity and the SNO Tyne frequently complained to his masters that his resources were overstretched.[8]

But the ubiquity of the fishing vessels can be seen in all these area deployments – trawlers were useful all around the coast.

4: Fishing for Mines

On 10 August 1914, 6 minesweeping trawlers were ordered to Dover and 100 additional trawlers were taken up to be commissioned as sweepers at Lowestoft; they had all arrived by the 21st.[1] It was the start of the trawler minesweeping war.

Those vessels intended for minesweeping duties on the eastern coast of Britain 'belonged' to the Minesweeping Division, headed from 4 September 1914 by Rear Admiral Edward Francis Benedict (Ned) Charlton, as Admiral of Minesweepers, with his flag in the hired yacht *Zarefah* (ex *Maretanza V*),[*] armed with two 3pdrs. Charlton was succeeded at the end of 1915 by Rear Admiral the Hon Edward Stafford Fitzherbert.[†] However, it was only in October 1917 that strategic minesweeping responsibilities for the whole British coast came under one officer, when Captain Lionel Preston was appointed to the Admiralty as firstly Superintendent, and then Director, of Minesweeping.

The minesweepers were locally organised under an SNO, known as the Port Minesweeping Officer (PMSO). And the force was a diverse collection of vessels. Apart from the trawlers and drifters, paddle-steamer pleasure craft, cross-Channel ferries, motor launches and other shallow draught craft would eventually join the original ten converted torpedo boats and, in time, specially designed naval vessels. However, the Admiralty believed that 'trawlers have shown themselves to be peculiarly suitable for minesweeping by reason of the powerful steam winches they carry and their seaworthy qualities, *and the fact that they are available in large quantities*'.[§][2]

That may have been so but at the commencement of the war fishing boat owners were somewhat reluctant to supply the numbers demanded by the Admiralty. To attempt to incentivise them, the Fourth Sea Lord suggested raising the charter rate to 18 per cent per ton but this was vetoed by the Treasury. Consequently, as early as six days after the declaration of war, boats were forcibly requisitioned as well as hired. The owners' desire to volunteer their vessels grew, however, as access to the fishing grounds became more restricted.

The standard British sweeping system was the A-sweep in which a single steel wire was towed between two parallel vessels. In trawlers, the sweeps were run through gallows mounted aft, originally used for dragging fishing nets. Gallows were thought better than davits because they kept the kites under better control when they were lifted out of the water. Kites were about 12ft in length and weighed around a ton, so hoisting them was no easy task (see plate 13).

The sweep could be extended over a distance of two cables (about 200 yards) and was passed by hand from ship to ship. Later, one sweeper would steam ahead of the other and trail a grass line and barricoe (a small barrel) astern to be picked up by its partner.

Kites kept the sweeping wire at a constant depth, usually six fathoms. On catching a mine, the pair of boats would haul out of the channel and slip their sweeps, with the designated 'A' boat responsible for marking the position of the dumped mine.

With the A-sweep, trawlers were able to sweep at 6 knots in sea state 4–5; drifters at 5.5 knots in a 3–4 sea.[3] But in rough weather it was difficult to tell manually whether or not a mine had been snagged in the wire. This problem was solved by fitting dynamometers which signalled a change in the wire's tension. And this development also facilitated night sweeping in fine weather where the instruments 'indicated mines or the fact that the sweep is bumping the bottom'.[4]

Mines were intended to be severed from their mooring cable by the strain of the sweep wire acting on them. This could take some fifteen to twenty minutes to achieve; often it was necessary to adopt a sort of sawing motion by having one sweeper increase its speed relative to the other and then slow down while its partner vessel surged ahead.

It took time to equip and train the new minesweeping trawlermen; and minesweeping was suddenly a hot issue. In the absence of sufficient trawlers with sweeping gear, it was proposed in August 1914 that drifters should be used to catch mines with their

13. An illustration of the A-sweep minesweeping process, showing two parallel trawlers towing a sweeping wire between them. (author's collection)

---

[*] She had been built in 1905 for Sir John Pender, was hired by the Admiralty in 1914, purchased by them in 1916 and sunk in 1917.

[†] Later 13th Baron Stafford.

[§] Author's italics.

14. The most common way of exploding a mine which had been swept to the surface by gunfire was to shoot at it, often with a rifle, as shown in this drawing taken from the French weekly newspaper *L'Illustration* in 1916. (Alamy BGP5FG)

nets. The hired vessel *Eyrie*, a Lowestoft craft, was detailed to sweep mines near the Outer Dowsing shoal on 2 September. Predictably the venture was not a success. That same day, at around 0920, *Eyrie* netted a mine off Cley-next-the-Sea which detonated, blowing off her stern. She sank rapidly with the loss of six men, including Skipper Thomas Scarll. Next day, the drifter *Lindswell*, also from Lowestoft, was attempting to catch mines laid by the German minelayer *Nautilus* (accompanied by the light cruiser *Mainz* and the torpedo boats of the 3rd Half Flotilla) in the entrance to the Humber estuary. She too pulled the mine against her stern, which was destroyed, and at 1100 she sank with five men killed, including Skipper Charles Woodgate. The minesweeper *Speedy* (launched in 1893, one of the converted torpedo gunboats) closed her to pick up survivors and herself hit a mine, destroying her rudder and propellers; she sank an hour later. The dead of both drifters were all RNR(T).

The experiment was discontinued. And the loss of three minesweepers in two days resulted in the Admiralty changing its policy for dealing with minefields. From now on, instead of attempting to clear entire minefields, clear channels would be swept through minefields to give a safe route for shipping.

In 1916 a serrated sweep wire was devised which improved the sweep's ability to cut through mine moorings. First developed by wire rope manufacturers Bullivant and Company in London,[*] it proved a very successful innovation; indeed, the *Staff History of British Minesweeping* deemed it 'one of the greatest improvements in the history of sweeping'.[5]

Pre-war, there had been experimentation with single-ship so-called B-sweeps, as used by the French throughout the war, but the Admiralty considered that these were 'too complicated to be successfully manipulated even in moderate weather'.[6] However, a single-ship system was eventually developed, the Actaeon sweep. This was a light wire, a depth float, a small kite and an explosive grapnel. One was towed on each quarter of the minesweeper and on encountering a mine, the explosive grapnel slid towards it, blew up and parted the mine's mooring. It was not considered a particularly effective solution for clearing minefields, rather for finding out where they had been laid.

[*] William Munton Bullivant was an early innovator in the stranded wire cordage field, invented in the mid-nineteenth century by German mining engineers in the Harz Mountains. Sometime after 1875, he formed his own wire rope manufacturing firm, Wm Bullivant & Co, at Millwall.

By 1916, a new and more effective single-ship method of mine clearance had been invented, the paravane (see plate 17). This was the brainchild of two naval officers, who initially worked separately, Lieutenant Charles Denniston Burney and Commander Cecil Vivian Usborne. Funding for the work was provided by Sir George White, founder of the Bristol Aeroplane Company.

A paravane was a torpedo-shaped device, strung out and streamed alongside a towing ship, normally from the bow. The wings of the paravane would tend to force the body away from the vessel, placing a lateral tension on the towing wire. If the tow cable snagged the cable anchoring a mine then the anchoring cable would be cut by a 'knife' on the sweep, allowing the mine to float to the surface where

it could be destroyed by gunfire. If the anchor cable would not part, the mine and the paravane would be brought together and the mine would explode harmlessly against the paravane. The cable could then be retrieved and a replacement paravane fitted. The lifetime of the invention lasted into the Second World War, where they were still in general use.

Trawlers were fitted with the device but not in great numbers as it was determined that the paravane worked best at a speed of 13 knots or more, beyond the reach of many trawlers and all drifters, and not at all under 10 knots.

As with many new ideas, paravanes had started life with a different object in mind. Burney's intention had been to produce an anti-submarine weapon and build on the use of the towed explosive anti-submarine sweep; he initially called his device a 'high speed sweep'. Further consideration led to it becoming a minesweeping tool.

15. Minesweeping was a dangerous business. Here is an armed trawler showing the extensive damage to her bow caused by striking a mine. (© Imperial War Museum Q 18276)

The Admiralty determined that Burney's work had occurred five months prior to Usborne's work with his similar idea. On 4 March 1916, he was appointed to HMS *Vernon* in charge of paravane construction; a month later he was promoted to acting commander for 'special & valuable services in in inventing and developing Paravane Gear and the High-Speed Sweep'.[7]

Independent of method, when cleared, channels were marked by danbuoys* and as the war progressed some vessels were specifically equipped as danbuoy layers to follow the sweepers and mark the safe route. The route was indicated by dans on one side, painted in the colours of the flotilla which had swept the channel, and flags on the other. Often, mines brought to the surface were simply sunk by gunfire using rifles, 3pdrs or even 6pdrs. Alternatively, swept mines were to be taken to a dumping ground which 'should always be chosen out of the way of shipping and marked by dumping-dans'.[8] These were fitted with a top mark in the shape of a St Andrew's cross.

On occasion the sweep wire would fail to do its job and the mine, or its mooring rope and sinker, would become entangled in the sweep. To cope with this crisis there were three potential solutions. Firstly, the sweep wire could be slipped immediately – both ends of the sweep were cast off from the towing ships so that the mine would sink and the position was marked by laying buoys. Secondly, the mine might be towed into shallow water away from the shipping lanes before slipping took place. And thirdly the mine could be towed to a designated dumping ground before being slipped. Generally, before attempting any of these approaches, the minesweepers would steam towards each other heaving in the sweep until they could be clear that it was a mine they had captured and not some other piece of jetsam.

Trawlers and the War Channel

The first German mines to be laid off the British coast were deposited by the converted passenger ferry *Königin Luise*, which had been requisitioned by the Kaiserliche Marine on 3 August 1914 to serve as an auxiliary minelayer, carrying 200 mines. Immediately on the declaration of war between Britain and Germany she sailed from Emden to place her mines close to the major trade artery of the Thames estuary.

On the 5th she was able to lay a field off the Suffolk coast, near Southwold, before being intercepted by the scout cruiser *Amphion* and destroyers of the 3rd Flotilla. The German vessel was scuttled by her crew to avoid capture, after being fired on by RN destroyers. The following morning, *Amphion,* heading back to Harwich, was mined on the very same field that the minelayer had left behind and sank with the loss of 142 men, plus 19 rescued German prisoners. She thus gained the unwished-for distinction of being the first Royal Navy vessel lost in the war.

But eight days later, trawlers from Harwich had swept and buoyed a clear channel inshore of this field. The channel was extended over the next months in the face of repeated mining of the east coast ports,† into a fairway known as the 'War Channel'. This was a marked traffic lane, which eventually extended from Dover to the Firth of Forth, and was swept daily for mines, mainly by trawlers based at the Nore, Harwich, Lowestoft, the Humber, the Tyne and Granton. Soon the channel was being swept each day by up to eighty minesweeping trawlers and patrolled at night by drifters, often armed with nothing but the White Ensign, to deter minelayers.

In all, the War Channel came to stretch for about 540 miles. British and German minefields intermingled on the east side of this channel and it was decided not to sweep them as they formed an almost impenetrable barrier protecting the ports themselves. Then, on 2 November 1914, the British government declared the North Sea a prohibited area. All neutrals were warned that, unless their ships complied with the regular routes laid down by the Admiralty (and also generally submitted to being searched for goods intended to aid the enemy – contraband – as part of this process), they sailed at their own risk. Only in the designated swept channels would they be safe, and these were known only to the navy. The need for sweepers was such that, by April 1915, a total of 218 trawlers were operating as minesweepers; the majority (62 per cent) of these were working in the War Channel.§

German mining was initially through the use of surface ships. But by June 1915, they were using submarine minelayers such as the large UC types. These had twelve cylindrical mines fitted into vertical tubes in the hull and were able to lay their mines while submerged. Many small and unobserved minefields appeared as a result of this technological advance and this greatly increased the workload of the sweepers.

Minesweeping trawlers largely worked in sixes with each group under the command of a Lieutenant RNR. These officers were often 'dug outs' or ex-large merchant ships and were regarded with some suspicion by the trawlermen. However, the little pods of minesweepers soon took on something of a 'family firm' feeling and there developed a friendly rivalry between each section.

They were considered to be 'routine sweepers', too slow to work with the fleet and drawing too much draught to clear minefields laid in shallow waters. Their quotidian job was the daily search for, and removal of, mines laid in the War Channel or the approach to harbours. Throughout the war, this responsibility fell mainly on the fishermen of the RNR(T).

With experience and increased weapons availability, by 1917 the trawlers, Admiralty-built and otherwise, had begun to assume a consistent fit-out and profile. Gone were the mixed armaments and

---

† 180 mines off Southwold on 5 August; 200 off the Humber on 26 August; and another 194 off the Tyne the same day, for example.

§ North Shields twelve, Humber thirty, Lowestoft forty-seven, Harwich eight, Nore twenty-seven, Dover twelve. There were another twenty-one at Granton (ADM 186/604, NA).

---

* A danbuoy was a small temporary marker buoy with a lightweight flagpole, 'used for all purposes connected with minesweeping' (ADM 186/382, NA).

16. A painting by Geoffrey Stephen Allfree of a group of drifters going out from Portsmouth to mine sweep in 1918. (author's collection)

assorted weapon positions of the early years of the conflict. Now a 12pdr gun adorned the forecastle, and was frequently supplemented by a high-angle 3pdr anti-aircraft gun, mounted on the quarterdeck. This weapon shared the space with a large trawl winch with two drums, each holding 750 fathoms of 2.5in steel wire. And right aft were the two gallows, for hoisting the kite in and out.

But the traffic using the War Channel grew and grew (as did the number of mines to be swept). In 1917, 30,000 vessels passed by Lowestoft using the swept channel. Off Harwich, a key Royal Navy port, 288 mines were swept up between January and May 1917, including 108 from five separate fields in April alone.[9] And it was the fishermen minesweepers that bore the brunt of this work.

A dangerous trade

Minesweeping was an occupation fraught with difficulty and no little danger. The slightest misjudgement could set off an explosion that could kill anyone in the immediate vicinity and sink the vessel

itself. By the Armistice, one whaler, 4 Admiralty trawlers, 140 hired trawlers and 32 hired drifters had been sunk by mines.[10] And for every trawler sunk by mines during the war, an average of half the crew was lost.[11]

Death could strike at any time. On 27 February 1916, the P&O liner *Maloja* (12,431grt) was outbound for India with 122 passengers and a crew of 301 officers and men when she was mined on her starboard quarter within two miles of the entrance to Dover harbour. She had run into a new minefield laid by *UC-6*; 155 people died as a result.

The following day, the hired minesweeping trawlers *Lord Minto* (ex-Harwich registered) and *Angelus* (ex-Grimsby) left Dover harbour at 0550 to attempt to find and clear the minefield. They did not have to wait long to do so, for at 0740 *Lord Minto* caught a mine in her sweep in the harbour's western entrance. Having exploded it, she caught another, entangled in her kite, at 0845; this mine detonated and carried away the kite, forcing the trawler to return to Dover to fit a new one. By 1430 she was back sweeping again, once more in partnership with *Angelus*. Around 1715 both vessels took in their sweeps. But as *Angleus* was doing so she hit a mine. She began to settle very quickly. *Lord Minto*'s skipper slipped his sweep and launched his small rowing boat, towing it into position to pick up the survivors. He saved six men, one badly scalded, and landed them ninety-five minutes later at Prince of Wales pier. *Angelus* lost two men, her skipper Richard Saunders and deckhand John Boyle, both RNR(T). That same day and sweeping the same minefield, the Milford Haven-registered trawler *Weigelia* was lost to a mine. Trimmer John Thompson RNR(T) was killed. Three minesweepers in one day and a liner the day before; mines were both indiscriminate and profligate in their victims.

Regular losses were not unusual. Two armed trawlers were lost in May 1917 in the Coast of Ireland command. *Senator* was a Grimsby-based boat taken up by the Admiralty in 1915, armed with a 3pdr gun and converted to minesweeping duty. On 21 May she was sunk off Tory Island by a mine laid by *U-80*. Eleven men were killed, including skipper Robert George; they were all fishermen. And on 30 May the *Ina William*, another minesweeping trawler, hit a mine from *U-50* and sank two miles south of the Bull Rock Light, Berehaven. Skipper Charles Slapp and eleven of his men died, all RNR(T) bar an RNVR signalman. Both boats were lost trying to defend the vital Western Approaches at the height of the German unrestricted U-boat campaign.

Or consider the Milford Haven hired trawler *Arfon*, working out of Portland naval base, sweeping German mines from the shipping lanes where they had been laid by UC-class minelaying submarines. Built in 1908 at Goole for the Peter Steam Trawling Company and of 227grt, she struck a mine off St Alban's Head on 30 April 1917 and sank in just two minutes. She had been taken up in August 1914, eventually fitted with a 6pdr gun, ploughed the waves for mines for three years, and then – in a flash – was gone, as were fifty-three-year-old Skipper John Abrams from Grimsby and nine of her thirteen-man crew. They were all RNR(T), except for William Babstock, rated 'qualified seaman', who had come all the way from Newfoundland to die.[*]

Mines were used in every naval theatre of the war. The trawler *Arctic Prince*, once of North Shields, was a modern vessel, built in 1915 and immediately taken up by the navy. In 1917 she was serving in the Barents Sea when, on 15 April, she hit a mine. Six of her crew were killed, four of them deckhands, but the ship was saved. One deckhand survived the blast, David H Cooper from Church Marsh, Wells-next-the-Sea, who had joined the RNR(T) in July 1915. He and the trawler both survived to the end of the war. Cooper was discharged on 1 January 1919; and *Arctic Prince* served again, as *Clifton*, in the Second World War.

Minesweeping in trawlers was an extremely dangerous trade. According to Dr Laura Rowe, a lecturer in maritime history at the University of Exeter, 'There was an extremely high mortality rate. You had a nineteen per cent chance of dying doing this work – which is higher than frontline infantry.'[12]

It should be remembered that these men, and all the other fishermen, were not trained combatants and their vessels were not ships of war. Both ships and men had been taken from the quayside, fitted with minimal equipment and sent to fight a foe they often could not even see. Such weaknesses as this created were visible in the course of the disastrous Gallipoli campaign.

Trawlers in the Dardanelles

The disaster of the Dardanelles campaign of 1915 is too well known to require repetition here. Sufficient to say that, in an attempt to knock Turkey out of the war and open up shipping routes to Russia through the Black Sea, First Lord of the Admiralty Winston Churchill pressed a plan for the naval forcing of the straits and subsequent advance to Constantinople.

Minefields and heavy artillery guarded the narrow mouth of the Dardanelles and forts lined the passage towards the Black Sea. Nevertheless, on 25 February British and French warships under Vice Admiral Sackville Hamilton Carden attacked the entrance, the Ottomans evacuated the outer defences and the fleet entered the straits to engage the intermediate batteries.

On 1 March, four battleships bombarded the defences but could only go a small distance into the strait owing to minefields, and little progress had been made in clearing them. In fact, there had been twelve attempts to sweep the Kephaz minefield at the entrance to the Narrows, of which only two succeeded in penetrating into the field. And if the mines were not removed, the battleships and other gunnery platforms could not move up to engage the Turkish defences.

The minesweeping force accompanying the fleet was comprised of twenty-one minesweeping trawlers.[†][13] But a strong current runs down the straits from the Black Sea as it empties into the Aegean and it was difficult for the trawlers to make much progress against it. Accordingly, it was decided to sail through the minefields and when above them, to turn and sail downstream, sweeping on passage. An endeavour was made to put this plan into action on the night of 8/9 March. It was a failure. The hired Grimsby trawler *Okino* struck a mine and only the skipper and four crew survived the explosion; ten men died, eight of them fishermen RNR(T).

The following night, another attempt was essayed with seven trawlers and some picket boats providing the minesweeping force. Again, it did not meet with success. It proved impossible to douse the Ottoman searchlights which illuminated the little sweepers; and on turning to attempt to sweep they were subjected to heavy fire from the on-shore artillery batteries. They 'became so agitated that four out of the six, the seventh was the leader, did not get their kites down and so swept the surface'.[14]

Carden himself noted that 'only one pair got out their sweeps and little was effected'.[15] Two trawlers were hit by 6in shells and one

---

[*] Discovered in 2014, the wreck was given protected status by Historic England in 2016.

[†] Carden's Chief of Staff Roger Keyes claimed in his memoir that there were thirty-five trawlers. Both may be correct, dependent on timing.

17. From the American Keystone View Company comes this image of the newly invented paravane sweeping device. The body copy tells that 'The latest invention gotten out to aid the Allies in cleaning up European waters of German mines, is the Paravane. Shaped somewhat on the style of a torpedo. It is dragged through the waters by a trawler. The sharp knife seen on top is used for cutting the chains that hold the mine in place. The mine, then floating to the top of the water, is exploded by rifle fire.' (US National Archives, 45511976)

trawler, the Grimsby-registered *Manx Hero*, was sunk. She had been one of the pair at the head of the sweeping line, ensnared two mines and was sunk when they detonated. Skipper Woodgate in the Milford Haven vessel *Koorah* managed to rescue all her crew.

Chief of Staff Commodore Roger Keyes was livid at what he deemed to be a lack of courage shown by the fishermen crews in the face of the Turkish gunnery onslaught. 'I felt', he wrote, 'it was time to get on with the business at all costs.' And Churchill had added fuel to the fire by telegraphing that he doubted that 'sufficient determination was being shown in the attack'.[16]

Another attempt was carried out on the night of 11/12 March. Again, it failed and for the same reasons. 'The searchlights were on the alert and as soon as the leading boat came in the beam and the shells began to fall, she turned sixteen points and began to steam back. Her behaviour infected the rest.'[17] And on 13/14 March the Grimsby trawler *Fentonian* and *Star of Empire* from Lowestoft collided while attempting to sweep, killing three crewmen, two from the Trawler Reserve, the other a pensioner chief petty officer from the RFR.

Keyes was once more unsympathetic. He told the officers in charge that they had had their opportunity and there were plenty more to replace them. It did not matter if all seven sweepers in the group were lost, he averred, there were plenty more where they had come from.

He called for volunteers from the warships and, entirely manned and stiffened by these regular RN resources, the minesweepers set out once more on 18 March; but they met with the same result. The trawlers were unable even to reach the minefield they were intended to clear. Four of them turned tail and fled.

And, as the then Lieutenant Commander Andrew Browne Cunningham* wrote, 'a dangerous impasse was reached. The minefield batteries prevented the minefields from being swept. But until the minefields were swept, the big ships could not get close enough to knock out the minefield batteries.'[18]

The facts of the matter were clear. The Admiralty had sent boys on a man's errand; the combination of small-engined trawlers, which with their sweeps out could barely stem the current, and their civilian crews, unused to – and unschooled in – facing artillery fire, were not fit for purpose. Bravery is not a natural human characteristic; as Captain Taprell Dorling has written, 'that trawlers manned by fishermen were ever put into the position which they were at the Dardanelles not only seems to imply a profound lack of imagination, but a lack of understanding of human nature'.[19] And the painter Norman Wilkinson, the inventor of 'dazzle' camouflage, wrote that 'the men running these vessels are in the majority of cases elderly and the ships themselves were never intended to come under fire'.[20] Lieutenant Commander Cunningham simply noted that 'in mid-March it was decided, and not before time, that the trawlers were unsuitable for minesweeping'.[21]

The essay at a purely naval solution was abandoned and Gallipoli was the end result. But if proper fast, naval-manned minesweepers had been available, perhaps the outcome would have been different. The lack of focus on mines pre-war, and concomitant lack of purpose-built minesweepers, was surely one cause of the catastrophic Dardanelles campaign.

By the end of the war, the Royal Navy had built up a minesweeping force of 726 vessels of which 412 were trawlers and another 142 were drifters.[22] Nor were trawlers and drifters confined to British waters. In 1918 there were thirty-nine trawlers and four drifters employed on minesweeping duty in the Mediterranean with another eighteen and five respectively on the North American/Caribbean station.[23]

The Germans laid some 1,360 minefields, comprising some 25,000 mines around the British Isles, 90 per cent of them released by U-boats, and 43,636 in all parts of the world. By the Armistice, 23,873 mines had been destroyed, of which approximately half were British, either moored or drifting.

---

* A future First Sea Lord and Admiral of the Fleet.

5: Fishing for Submarines

On 5 September 1914, the scout cruiser *Pathfinder* became the first warship in the world to be sunk by a locomotive torpedo fired from a submarine when she was torpedoed by Otto Hersing in *U-21*; 259 crew members lost their lives. And then on 21 September, in the space of an hour, Otto Weddigen in *U-9* sank three British cruisers, *Aboukir*, *Hogue* and *Cressy*, killing 62 Royal Navy officers and 1,073 men and boys.* If anyone had doubted the U-boat's ability in war beforehand, those misgivings were now completely dispelled.

Because the Admiralty had not taken the threat posed by the submarine entirely seriously, neither had it aggressively pursued means of countering it. True, an ad hoc anti-submarine committee had been formed by the navy in 1910 under the presidency of Rear Admiral Cecil Burney, and reported its views at least fifty-five times to the Admiralty Board. But it went through five presidents in four years and, although some future needs were identified, a number of blind alleys were comprehensively explored. As Admiral Percy Scott commented 'with regard to attacking submarines, as the Admiralty before the war regarded them as little more than toys, it was only natural that no progress had been made in the direction of taking measures for destroying them'.[1] Scott himself recommended putting rams on trawlers and destroyers, a measure harking back to the Greek wars in the Mediterranean of some 500 years BCE.

Scott also advocated 'a bomb which could be thrown down onto a submarine if she was on or near the surface'[2] from the deck of a ship. And indeed, one was developed, the lance bomb (see plate 18). This was a hand-thrown weapon comprising a 7lb charge of amatol attached to a wooden handle some 4ft 6in feet long. It was a contact weapon, designed to explode when it hit a hard surface, such as a U-boat's hull, and was to be swung around the head of a strong seaman and then hurled at the enemy; an effective range of seventy-five feet was claimed. The device was introduced in April 1915 and supplied to trawlers and other small craft. Lance bombs were not withdrawn from use until early 1917; in that time 20,000 units had been produced but no U-boat had ever been sunk by the method.

This was not the most farfetched idea foisted upon the trawler submarine-hunters. 'One scheme tried was for whalers to be sent away armed with the ship's blacksmith, his 40lb sledgehammer and some canvas bags. When a periscope was sighted, a canvas bag was

slipped over it … the blacksmith was to smash the periscope glass with his hammer.'[3]

So, equipped with such good ideas and a rifle or two, the trawlers were sent out to seek U-boats. In 1914, hunting patrols, based on the Admiralty patrol areas (see chapter 3), sought the foe. They generally comprised an armed yacht, furnished with wireless, four trawlers or drifters and possibly a motorboat or two. During 1914/15 the trawlers acquired 3pdr, then 6pdr guns. Such patrols continued throughout the war. Even in 1917 there were 150 such numbered auxiliary patrol groups, now made up of one yacht and up to six armed trawlers. The latter were often equipped for minesweeping as well and generally had 6pdr or 12pdr guns. One or more of the trawlers were also fitted with radio and named as second and third leader.

But trawlers were not ideally suited to this kind of work. A U-boat submerged was about as fast as most trawlers afloat; and surfaced, a U-boat could easily outstrip a trawler. The *U-31* class, for example, had a submerged speed of 9.7 knots, which was faster than many hired trawlers could make on the surface; surfaced the U-boat had a design speed of 16.4 knots. On 24 May 1915, the ex-Fleetwood-registered hired trawler *Norbreck* came upon a stationary barque under whose quarter lay a U-boat. *Norbreck* opened fire with its 3pdr, the submarine replied and then using its much superior speed made off. A week later, another hired trawler, the ex-Grimsby *Ina William*, patrolling off the Fastnet Rock, spotted *U-34* on the surface some three miles away. She made all speed and opened fire but then the gun jammed; by the time it was cleared the U-boat had dived to safety.

For here was another problem; under water the U-boats were invisible. A trawler skipper could patrol the waters all he wanted – if the submarine was submerged, it would not be found.

There was also a clear imbalance in armament at this time; *U-34*, as an example, was a *U-31*-class vessel, a type generally armed, apart from torpedoes, with one or two 7.5cm (3.0in) or 10.5cm (4.1in) deck guns. The latter fired a 38lb shell some 14,000 yards.

Not all senior RN commanders were convinced as to the trawlers' utility. Vice Admiral Lewis Bayly, newly appointed to the Coast of Ireland Command in July 1915, wrote of the armed trawlers he had inherited 'even as escorts they are of little use … I had no idea what poor things the armed trawlers were … to catch submarines they are wanting'.[4] Later he noted that 'our method of defence by trawlers [against submarines] does not seem to me to be a serious one, except

---

* Skippers Tom Phillips and George Jacobs from Lowestoft took their sailing trawlers *Coriander* and *JCG* into the midst of the struggling survivors to rescue them, with no regard to their own safety.

where they are situated near the coast … and in ordinary weather. On the open sea it is doubtful that they are much use; few have W/T and what there is, is weak. Their speed is absurdly slow; their gun is easily seen from a considerable distance so that they are easily recognised and avoided. I should imagine that they are bad gun platforms.'[5] But they were, in fact, all he had, so desperate was the shortage of, and need for, destroyers – most of which were assigned to the Grand Fleet at Scapa Flow.

Commander Plunkett shared Bayly's concerns. In December 1914 he wrote that 'hitherto the menace has only been met by ultra-defensive measures on the part of the coastal patrols. These measures have met with so little success that the large number of vessels so deployed have not justified their existence … the enemy submarine roams round our coasts absolutely undisturbed.'[6] And Admiral David Beatty, commanding the Grand Fleet battlecruisers, wrote in mid-1915 that 'the outer trawler patrols … on account of their slow speed … can only be considered defensive craft … with very limited offensive power'.[7]

What could be done to change this asymmetric situation?

Nets

The Royal Navy was a great believer in, and prolific user of, nets as an anti-submarine measure.

This meant that the drifters came into their own. Hired drifters plodded to and fro across harbour entrances or coastal trade routes, towing long nets behind them in the hope of entangling a U-boat. Next came indicator nets. These were a light steel wire net, sections of which were stopped by a jackstay buoyed with bottle glass floats and shot and laid by the drifters. They could be up to 100ft long, made into longer lengths by clipping together. Some were kept extended by a drifter proceeding at low speed, others permanently moored.

They were fitted with buoys which were released by the violent motion of the submarine manoeuvring against the net or by a hydrostatic trigger when the buoy was dragged under. When fouled, the buoy released a calcium carbide flare which allowed the drifter to track the victim's progress. The drifter was then supposed to attack with lance bombs, summon help or slip its equipment and give chase; given the drifter's slow speed, this latter tactic was unlikely to meet with success.

In April 1915, the Admiralty experimented with EC mine nets. These were nets fitted with small mines, which were powered from batteries carried on the drifters or, in the case of the EC II net mine, armed hydrostatically and fired when one of its eight contacts was pressed, exploding against a U-boat's flanks. Initially they were intended to be towed but this proved more dangerous to the drifter than to any U-boat and they were thereafter always moored, though tended by a fleet of drifters to maintain them in good repair.

There were still problems, however; bad weather often caused the little drifters to have to ditch their gear and run for shelter and so the maintenance of a permanent deterrent was problematical, compounded by the fact that there were often gaps between the nets laid by one vessel and another, even in calm waters. And by 1916, U-boats were being fitted with knife-edged prows and hydroplane guards to cut through nets.

Initially intended to protect the entrances to harbours, netting became an obsession, with the navy attempting to close large stretches of water to U-boats.

From 23 February 1915 a rectangular area thirty miles long and twelve miles wide, which extended from the Mull of Kintyre to Rathlin Island, was completely closed to navigation by the laying of nets. A small passage three miles wide was left between Rathlin and the coast of mainland Ireland through which all traffic, neutral and Allied, had to pass, and then only between the hours of sunrise and sunset, and where it could be stopped and searched as necessary.

One hundred and thirty hired drifters, managed this continuous net barrage across the North Channel, closing the northern entrance to the Irish Sea. They towed their nets back and forth, 1,500 men on board. In the deep waters, the aim was not so much to entangle the U-boats but to force them to dive and stay under the surface, thus exhausting their batteries. The drifters were deployed in nine sections with at first nine, and afterwards twelve, in each, together with an armed yacht squadron from Belfast and three armed trawlers, two destroyers and the armed boarding steamer *Tara*. But it was a failure, and the success rate of the barrier in terms of sinking submarines was nil.

Meanwhile, strenuous efforts were being made to close the English Channel to U-boats through the construction of a barrier some twenty-three miles long from Folkstone to Cap Gris Nez. Five different deterrents across the Channel were tried. There was a minefield laid in the early days of the war; a towed nets and indicator solution; an aborted wood baulk and net barrier of 1915; a net and mine barrier of 1916; and in 1917 a new deep mine barrier. All required patrolling by drifters and other small craft, and there was further strengthening at the beginning of 1918.[*]

The drifters did not play a completely passive role. *UB-38* was attempting to cross the barrier on the night of 8 February 1918 when she was illuminated by a flare and chased by the drifter *Gowan II*. After a twenty-minute pursuit, the submarine was forced to dive into the minefields where it blew up with no survivors. And a month later, on 10 March, *UB-58* suffered a similar fate, submerging into the mines when chased by a division of six drifters after having been caught in the light of an armed trawler, and blowing up with the loss of all hands.

The Germans did not take all this activity lying down and the hired drifters and their fishermen crews often came under raiding attack. On the night of 14/15 February 1918, for example, the Germans tried to put an end to the barrier with a decisive attack. Two half flotillas of destroyers were deployed in the attempt. In total

---

[*] See S R Dunn, *Securing the Narrow Sea*, Seaforth Publishing (Barnsley, 2017), for details.

18. At the outbreak of war, the requisitioned trawlers and drifters had little or no armament with which to attack U-boats. Amongst the weird and wonderful weapons issued to them was the lance bomb. Here a sailor practises throwing one from a drifter. (© Imperial War Museum Q 18231)

seven British drifters and a trawler were sunk, together with three drifters and a paddle-steamer damaged. British dead numbered eighty-nine officers and men, every single one of them RNR or RNVR.

Nets were also deployed to close the Straits of Otranto. A forty-five-mile-wide barrage to block the Adriatic Sea was laid in autumn 1915. The intention was to keep the Austro-Hungarian Fleet in its bases at Pola and Trieste and German submarines confined to their port of Cattaro. To maintain the barrier, lay and tow the nets, and intercept U-boat incursions, a force of over 120 hired drifters and (later) 30 motor launches was utilised. The combined Austro-German forces attacked the nets some twenty-five times but they never succeeded in breaking it and driving the drifters away.

There were successes, such as when, on 12 May 1916, the Austrian submarine *U-6* attempted to break out of the straits to attack shipping between Santa Maria di Leuca and Valona. Linienschiffsleutnant Hugo von Falkhausen, her commander, intended to pass underneath two of the drifters operating a part of the Otranto Barrage. While submerged, von Falkhausen heard an unexplained noise on the hull of the boat. *U-6* had in fact fouled the anti-submarine nets deployed by the ex-Londonderry boat

Calistoga. Alerted by the indicator buoys firing their flares, *Calistoga* burned signal lights that attracted the attention of two of her nearby sisters, *Dulcie Doris* and *Evening Star II*. In the meantime, *U-6* surfaced to try to cut loose the entanglement being dragged behind the submarine. This proving impossible, von Falkhausen tried to flee on the surface but now the port propeller shaft became caught up in the nets.

Evening Star slipped its gear and opened fire with her 6pdr Hotchkiss gun, followed by *Dulcie Doris*, similarly armed, hitting the submarine, at which point von Falkhausen ordered his crew to abandon ship and the confidential papers to be thrown overboard while he opened the sea valves and scuttled his vessel.

The U-boat crew were picked up by the drifters and the Admiralty, delighted with their success, awarded a £1,000 purse to be shared amongst them.

But in the end, the drifters could not beat an old enemy, the teredo worm. Receiving no maintenance for two years had led to a bad worm infestation and the vessels were becoming unseaworthy. Most had to be sent home and replaced with steel-hulled vessels.

Many attempts were made to place net barriers off the enemy's ports, in combination with mines, in the attempt to restrict egress, especially from the U-boat bases on the Belgian coast. One such operation in 1916 was to lay a coastal mine and net barrage off the Belgian coast, between Nieuwpoort and the entrance to the River Scheldt, aimed at restricting the movements of the Flanders U-boat minelayers.

Six divisions of net drifters from Dover (to lay the nets) were utilised, together with four large minesweepers (to clear the passage in and out) and escorting destroyers, six minelaying trawlers, two monitors (to provide a diversionary bombardment) with the addition of a division of Harwich Force destroyers and the Flanders coast patrol from Dunkirk. The ships were in position by 0400 on 24 April, and by 0730 had laid a fifteen-mile double line of mines and thirteen miles of mined nets, 5,077 mines in total, twelve miles off the coastline.

One of the participating drifters was *Clover Bank*, an Aberdeen-registered boat, hired by the Admiralty in January 1915. She and her skipper, Alonzo Strowger RNR, had been the recipients of a signal honour the previous year when King George V visited the Dover Patrol on 23 September 1915. The drifters of the Patrol were anchored in three long lines off the dockyard wall and the crews were paraded ashore for the monarch's inspection. *Clover Bank*, with her nets and all gear ready for shooting, was moored alongside the wall for the king's inspection. A keen sailor himself and ex-Royal Navy commander, the king went on board her, inspected the equipment and went down to the after-cabin with Strowger, taking a great interest in the life and work on board.

Nemesis often follows hubris. Owing to an error of placement, the line of nets which *Clover Bank* and her sisters were laying, and should have been laid seaward of a line of mines, had instead been positioned on the shoreward side. After fulfilling her net-laying tasks *Clover Bank* sailed towards home, detonated a newly laid British mine and blew up off Zeebrugge. Skipper Strowger and all seventeen of her crew were killed. All were RNR(T).

As late as 1918, the navy was still laying new anti-submarine net barriers. In March, Lieutenant Albert Robert Williamson RNR was ordered to Poole to train fifteen drifters in laying nets fitted with contact mines. Each drifter carried one mile of gear, wire frames, moorings and mines. Williamson formed a group of ten drifters to lay what was effectively a five-mile portable minefield of net and contact mines and a number of these were laid in various positions between the Owers Lightship (east of the Isle of Wight) and Start Point, not far from Dartmouth.

This was deemed so successful that Lieutenant Williamson was awarded the DSC for 'services in the Auxiliary Patrol, Minesweeping and Coastal Motor Boats, between the 1st January and 30th June, 1918'.[8]

In the absence of other tools, nets were the navy's principal anti-submarine weapon until 1916. But newer developments were beginning to take the fishermen's fight to the enemy

Sweeps

Explosive sweeps had been developed as an anti-submarine weapon in 1910. The initial design, used from the start of the war, comprised a 2in diameter cable to which were attached an 80lb charge and a hydroplane kite. The idea was to cross the U-boat's track with some part of the cable and then fire the charge electronically, but there is no recorded instance of it sinking a U-boat. The device was not fitted to trawlers or drifters.

This was followed by the Modified Single Sweep, first tested by the destroyer *Seagull* in June 1912. According to Captain Henry Taprell Dorling, 'it consisted of a loop of wire about 200ft long fitted at intervals with explosive charges. The upper leg of the loop was floated near the surface by a line of wooden floats, while the lower leg was kept well beneath the surface by a wooden water kite.'[9] An enormous loop of wire trailed 500yds astern, with the charges at around 24ft deep. Taprell Dorling disliked the equipment as '[it] was extremely cumbersome to handle, was supposed to be towed behind a destroyer when hunting for a submarine which had already been sighted … it took at least twenty minutes to get out and double that time to get in and the complicated system of ropes and charges were for ever becoming hopelessly tangled'.[10] The swept vertical area was 300yds long by 48ft deep, and when the wire was fouled by a U-boat it would trigger a signal to an operator on board the towing vessel who would trigger the charges. The kite kept the lower wire at a constant depth.

Another drawback for a destroyer commander, such as Dorling, was that the towing speed had to be maintained at around 8 knots. This was, however, ideal for trawlers, and from the outbreak of war the Modified Sweep was fitted to them, initially at Lowestoft.

The Modified Sweep claimed its first victim on 4 March 1915, when *U-8* was sunk by the Dover Patrol destroyer *Viking*. Rear Admiral the Hon Horace Hood, commanding at Dover, was so pleased with this success that he ordained one drifter in every four in his force should be furnished with one. The author is not aware of any resultant sinkings.

Use of the Modified Sweep System ceased in January 1918, by when it was evident that depth charges were a far more efficient weapon.

Q-ships and a 'tethered goat'

Q-ships were vessels of quotidian appearance, apparently unarmed and un-naval, going about their business on the seas but, in reality, concealing a heavy armament. U-boats, reluctant to waste expensive torpedoes on small merchantmen or fishing vessels, would surface with the intent of destroying the target by gunfire or by setting bombs on board and would then be attacked by the hidden weaponry. The idea was credited to Admiral Lewis Bayly at

Queenstown in the Coast of Ireland Command, hence the 'Q' in Q-ship, and was strongly advocated by younger officers such as Commander Reginald Drax. As early as 4 December 1914 he noted that 'to navigate a submarine needs to identify certain defined and prominent points … these should be patrolled by numerous trawlers which should be painted in their normal colours to look as peaceful as possible but be armed and ready to attack'.[11]

Q-ship crews required a great deal of courage and seven VCs were won in such actions. Many Q-ship trawlers were deployed, as were a smaller number of sailing smacks, both mixed in with the fishing fleets and sailing alone. In total, fifty-one fishing vessels were converted to Q-ships and eleven of them were sunk while so disguised. In return, disguised fishing vessels had a direct hand in the sinking of five U-boats.

On 5 June 1915, the trawlers *Oceanic II* and *Hawk* sank *U-14*, an action that is described in chapter 6.

Next came *Inverlyon*, a 93-ton fishing smack, which sank coastal submarine *UB-4* by gunfire on 15 August 1915 in the North Sea. She was an apparently ordinary sailing ketch, a Lowestoft boat of wooden construction with a flush deck, two masts, and no engine. Her sails were fore-and-aft rigged and may have been red ochre in colour, the traditional sail colour for British smacks. However, she also had a concealed 3pdr gun under the direction of Gunner Mr Ernest Martin Jehan RN. Her crew and skipper, Mr Phillips, were RNR(T) men and four naval hands from HMS *Dryad* assisted Jehan. The U-boat hailed the little craft and stopped to board her, at which point Jehan fired his revolver at the officer on the submarine's bridge, which was the signal to open fire. At a range of no more than thirty yards the 3pdr fired three shells, two of which hit and exploded in the conning tower, and crewmen with rifles, lying hidden under cover, joined in. Six more shells were loosed from the 3pdr, four of which hit home, and the submarine went down by the bow. In sinking, it fouled the trawler's nets which had to be cut free. There were no survivors, although Skipper Phillips did dive into the oil-covered water to attempt a rescue of one sailor, who nonetheless drowned. Ernest Jehan received the DSC for his achievement.[*]

Likewise, *Telesia* and *Energic*, two 59-ton fishing smacks, accounted for *UB-13* and her crew of seventeen on 24 April 1916 off the Belgian coast, using mined nets.

Another idea for using trawlers to hunt U-boats was the so-called 'tethered goat'. This variant on Q-ship methodology, first suggested by Admiral Beatty's secretary Paymaster F T Spickernell, used a trawler to tow a submerged submarine, the tow hawser looking like a trawl. When a U-boat appeared, the towing skipper would use a telephone wire down the hawser to call up the submarine to attack. The tactic succeeded twice in the first six months of 1915, but then no more.

The Aberdeen-registered hired steam trawler *Taranaki*, originally

taken up as a minesweeper but working as a tethered goat with submarine *C-24*, helped sink *U-40* in the North Sea on 23 June 1915. *Taranaki* was armed with one 12pdr and one 6pdr gun and was commanded by Lieutenant Commander Harrington Douty Edwards RN, who was acting as goat for *C-24* under Lieutenant Frederick Henry Taylor RN.

Their success was not without problems. The trawler was cruising off the coast of Eyemouth, when at 0930 Edwards spotted a U-boat on the surface, trimmed down for diving and about 2,500 yards distant. The submarine signalled him to stop and Edwards called for Taylor to attack; but the rig for casting off the towing gear from the submarine failed. The trawler had to keep way on, preventing entanglement of her tethered partner. Eventually Edwards was forced to ditch the tow at his end, causing 100 fathoms of 3.5in wire to drag the nose of *C-24* down; it took much skill to get her back to the correct angle for attacking.

In order to distract the U-boat from observing the British submarine's periscope, the trawlermen put on a show of panic and attempted abandonment, while Taylor manoeuvred into a position abeam and 500 yards away from the German vessel. His first and only torpedo hit under the conning tower, blowing two officers and a petty officer into the water and sinking the U-boat with all remaining twenty-nine hands. Both Edwards and Taylor were gazetted for awards, the DSO and DSC respectively, together with an 'Expression of Their Lordships' Appreciation'.

And the Hull trawler *Princess Louise*, with the submarine *C-27*, sank a U-boat on 20 July 1915, off Fair Isle between the Orkneys and Shetland. The trawler was in fact originally *Princess Marie Jose*, but had been temporarily renamed *Princess Louise* and was under the command of Lieutenant Colin Cantlie RN; she was in company with *C-27*, Lieutenant Commander Claude Congreve Dobson commanding. They were off the eastern entrance to the Fair Isle channel when they fell in with *U-23*.

This time the slipping of the tow worked perfectly. However, Dobson's first torpedo was spotted in the water and evaded; but not his second. The U-boat blew up and when the smoke cleared only three officers and seven men of her crew were alive in the water; the remaining twenty-seven were lost. Both commanders were again recognised for their skill, Cantlie receiving the DSC and Dobson the DSO

But in the light of such ploys, German U-boat commanders became more suspicious of surfacing and giving fishing vessels time to abandon ship. Less mercy was shown and the tactic gained no more victories.

Depth charges

So far, the anti-U-boat devices discussed have been improvisational and had limited effect. What was needed was a relatively cheap but efficient tool with which to kill U-boats from a multiplicity of naval platforms – the depth charge.

Primitive depth charges had existed for some time before the war,

---

[*] All hands were eligible for Admiralty bounty money, which was not in fact paid until April 1923. *Inverlyon* herself was sunk by *U-55* on 1 February 1917.

19. The invention of the hydrophone listening device transformed the trawlers' ability to hunt submerged U-boats. Here a sailor is listening on a hydrophone and an officer is using binoculars on board an anti-submarine armed trawler. Notice both the primitive equipment and the exposed operating position. (© Imperial War Museum Q 18989)

made from aircraft bombs attached to lanyards which would trigger their charges. A similar idea was a 16lb guncotton charge in a lanyard-rigged can; two of these lashed together became known as the 'depth charge Type A'. It was fired by a float and wire system but problems with the lanyards tangling and failing to function led to the development of a chemical pellet trigger, known as 'Type B'. These could be set to explode at a depth of 40ft or 80ft. But they were far from adequate.

In December 1914, Admiral John Jellicoe, CinC Grand Fleet, had asked HMS *Vernon* to develop a more powerful device. The resultant weapon was based on a standard Mark II mine, which was fitted with a hydrostatic pistol (ie actuated by water pressure) pre-set to fire at 45ft and launched from a stern platform. Weighing 1,150lb, this so-called 'cruiser mine' was, in fact, a potential hazard to the dropping ship as well as the putative enemy. But further development was swift. By January 1916, the first really effective depth charge, the Type D, became available. These were barrel-like casings containing a high explosive, TNT or Amatol. There were initially two sizes, Type D, with a 300lb charge for fast ships, and Type D-star with a 120lb charge for those ships too slow to clear the danger area of the more powerful charge. A hydrostatic pistol set to a pre-selected depth detonated the charge and they were supplied with two depth settings of 40ft or 80ft.

Trawlers and drifters were equipped with the Type D-star from July 1916; these were discharged over the stern from chutes. Production was limited and could not keep up with demand and, initially, the trawlers only carried just one D-star depth charge, together with four smaller G-type on racks on the upper deck aft. Only in May 1917 was a second D-star was added to their equipment

But by 1917, a new water-pressure-activated pistol could fire the depth charges at 100–200 feet, allowing use of Type D on most ships. Production was slow in 1917, however; only 140 per week in July, rising to 800 per week in December. Trawlers' fit-out of such weapons was not increased to four per vessel until June 1918 with two double launch rails, and by the end of the war at least 285 armed trawlers had been fitted with depth charges.

So far, so good; but what about circumstances where a submarine was suddenly sighted ahead and alongside, and the mine-carrying ship was unable to manoeuvre in time to get in an attacking position?

In July 1917 the navy introduced a ship-mounted anti-submarine howitzer (or bomb thrower) for the backs and sides of vessels. They were designed in various calibres ranging from 3.5in to 11in and were intended as a short-range weapon to be fired at a nearby periscope. The 7.5in howitzer was the first to enter general service. Over 750 were ordered in March 1917 followed by 250 in the May. Fitted on a non-recoil mounting, they fired a 100lb projectile. Other innovations quickly followed including a stick-bomb projector, a sort of mechanical lance bomb, for use when the submarine was close up, and another type of stick bomb that could be fired from a 12pdr gun. By October 1917, the trawlers of the Auxiliary Patrol had been allocated fifty 7.5in howitzers, three 6in and twelve 3.5in. And by the end of the war, 237 trawlers of all types had been fitted with bomb throwers, 142 with 7.5in, and 36 with 3.5in. One lucky trawler, the ex-Grimsby hired vessel *Flintshire*, was actually equipped with an 11in *and* a 7.5in as well as a 6pdr gun.*

But there was still the issue of finding the U-boat when it was underwater, where it was completely invisible to the Mark I eyeball.

Hydrophones

Some of Britain's greatest scientists were recruited to bring science to bear on the U-boat problem, not least Professor Sir William Henry Bragg who, with his son, William Lawrence, had been jointly awarded the 1915 Nobel Prize for Physics in connection with their work on crystal structure using X-ray spectrometry. During the war, William Henry worked on methods of submarine detection, initially at Aberdour (see below), then at Harwich and finally at the Admiralty itself.

Bragg was involved in the invention of the hydrophone, a device for detecting underwater sound and thus pinpointing the location of a submarine. Sir Ernest Rutherford (a Nobel laureate for Chemistry in 1908 and the man who first postulated the existence of a charged nucleus in an atom) had originally produced a paper suggesting that underwater microphones offered the best potential

for experimentation. Bragg, working for the Board of Invention and Research, co-operated with the navy's own Hawkcraig experimental research station at Aberdour, under the control of Commander (later Captain) Cyril Ryan RN. Here there were the hired drifter *Tarlair*, once of Scarborough, and a staff of RNVR officers.

Between 1,000 and 2,000 men were employed, a mixture of scientists and sailors. Starting with shore-based listening systems, they went on to develop the 'Portable General Service' (PSG) model of hydrophone listening equipment. This was a non-directional tool also known as a 'drifter' for its mode of operation. The operator dangled it over the side of a stationary ship and sat on deck listening. The device was lowered to a depth of twenty to thirty feet and the operator tried to 'centre' any sound he heard in his two headphones by turning a small control wheel. When centred, the plot gave him a bearing which, unfortunately, could be 180° out, as the device could not detect which direction along the bearing the submarine lay.

This was followed by the Portable Directional Hydrophones (PDH) which entered service in 1917. PDHs were directional and comprised two diaphragms carried in a larger ring-shaped body; they responded to sound approaching each plate broadside on. The Mark I version had a production run of 844 and Mark II, 2,586. The later Mark IV featured a diaphragm acoustically isolated from the hull and 499 were produced for surface ship use. PDH sets could be used at low speed and eradicated the possibility of a 180° error. But they were subject to interference from water noise.

Trawlers benefitted from the Mark II and Mark IV; in the latter, the version for trawlers had the microphone placed vertically in the hull, although the plates followed the hull contours.

From October 1917, trawlers were fitted with the 'Shark Fin' hydrophone. These carried the listening phones in streamlined bodies outside the hull. They were non-directional. It is interesting to note the comments made by a US Navy captain working with Shark Fin equipment: it was 'considered of so little value that they were only listened to as a matter of curiosity and at no time seriously considered or used'.[12]

In an attempt to eliminate the problem of water noise, a variety of towed devices were developed. The 'Rubber Eel' was a rubber-skinned bronze tube containing a 2in microphone at the front end. It was towed behind the hunting ship and the rubber coating acted to remove water noise; but it was non-directional. However, operators could use it in a vessel under way and 463 sets were issued to smaller patrol craft, including trawlers.

In 1918, 199 'Fish' outboard hydrophones, towed behind a submarine-hunting vessel, were added to the armoury. This was a wooden torpedo, containing one stationary microphone and one which was rotated by a motor controlled from the towing ship. The stationary pickup provided the U-boat's location and the moveable one gave a bearing to the sound's source. The microphone did not work close-in and so the device was useless for making the final attack.

---

* She served in the Second World War as well, renamed as *Taipo*.

Finally, there was 'Porpoise', in use from September 1918, a development of Fish in which a single microphone, which could be rotated, was mounted. For best results the ship's engines had to be stopped (of course rendering it vulnerable to attack), and only thirty-one units were issued before the war's end. By 1918, many hydrophone-equipped patrol vessels were carrying more than one type.

From November 1917, it had been intended to form a force of some 140 hydrophone-equipped trawlers, utilising the Fish-type towed listening device. But by the end of the war, only 117 trawlers, Admiralty or otherwise, had any form of hydrophone fitted (see plate 19). There were also eighteen hydrophone-equipped drifters and a further eight drifters were used as 'hydrophone tenders'.

But hydrophones were not a panacea. Hunting U-boats was still a very frustrating process. HMT *Saxon* was a Cardiff-registered hired trawler built in 1907 and fitted with a 12pdr gun and a 7.5in bomb thrower – and a hydrophone.

In November 1917 she was operating in an area bounded by Swansea, Cardiff and Ilfracombe, hunting submarines in the Bristol Channel. Her directional hydrophone (presumably a PDH) had been fitted the previous month and she had also acquired a new commander, Sub Lieutenant A G L Knapton RNVR.

On 17/18 November her log records that she 'put hydrophone over and drifted'[13] several times a day, demonstrating one of the problems with listening devices – the vessel had to stop in order that her own engine noise did not drown out the sound of a U-boat.

Shark Fin hydrophones* were fitted from 21 November and on 25 November the now retired Admiral Lord Beresford paid a morale-raising visit to Swansea and made an inspection of the trawlers and drifters operating there, examining the fruits of his 1907 Grimsby visit. On 8 December a submarine was spotted by *Prince George* and *Saxon* was sent to join the hunt. A day later she dropped a single depth charge over an 'oily patch' in the location, and a passing Q-ship joined in. Nothing was observed and *Saxon* departed for the Mumbles. By the 11th she was 'hydrophoning'[14] from 0400. Records show that no U-boat was sunk on the 9th or any other day that month in the area.

Success

Despite this growing range of anti-submarine capability, the actual U-boat sinkings which can be directly attributed to (non-Q-ship) ex-fishing vessels is limited, perhaps only five. That includes the third U-boat to be sunk by British forces, *U-18*, on 23 November 1914.

At the beginning of the war, no one had believed that German submarines could reach as far as the Orkney islands and Scapa Flow, the anchorage of the Grand Fleet. But when *U-15* was sunk by the cruiser *Birmingham* off Fair Isle, that notion was disabused. Various false sightings then caused panic in the fleet and on 22 November,

the Grand Fleet left Scapa. That same night, *U-18* (Kapitänleutnant Von Henning) noted lights in the direction of the Flow, and the Pentland lighthouse still lit, and dived to try to effect an entrance. At 1100, aided by the strong tides and the fact that the boom nets were open to allow a steamship to pass, *U-18* entered Scapa Flow. Von Henning raised the periscope and to his disappointment found the waters to be empty of targets. As he made his way back through the boom and to sea, the submarine's periscope was spotted by the trawler *Tokio*, acting as an examination vessel, which raised the alarm. The destroyers at notice raised steam.

In order to navigate out to sea, Von Henning had to again raise his periscope from time to time. At 1210, this was sighted by the minesweeping trawler *Dorothy Gray*, one and a half miles off Hoxa Head.

Built in 1908, *Dorothy Gray* was a 199grt Aberdeen-registered steam trawler, built by Hall, Russell and Co and owned by the Peterhead Trawling Company until she was taken up in August 1914. She carried a 6pdr gun, but Skipper Alexander Youngson RNR had no time to use it. Calling for the trawler's best speed, he drove his little boat straight towards the U-boat and rammed it. The *Dorothy Gray* shot three feet into the air; but the submarine was thrown on its beam-ends, her steering gear and hydroplanes were damaged and the periscope bent over at right angles. The trawler's crew seized anything at hand to throw at the submarine in an attempt to further damage it; indeed the engineer is reported to have 'appeared on deck with a sledgehammer in his hand, ready to deal with the enemy at close quarters'.[15]

Von Henning dived again, but *U-18* was uncontrollable and once more came to the surface, where she met HMS *Garry*, a River-class destroyer, haring in to the action in response to an exultant signal from the trawler. *Garry* rammed the submarine for the second time. This time the impact was terminal. With a fire on board and damaged propellers to add to his misfortune, Von Henning gave the order to surrender. Twenty-six German crew were rescued by the destroyer.

Skipper Youngson[†] and his crew received £500 from the Admiralty Prize Court for his bravery and quick thinking, perhaps £60,000 today – a profitable day's work.[§] First Lord of the Admiralty Winston Churchill telegraphed *Dorothy Gray*'s skipper 'hearty congratulations to trawler no 96 for brilliant service'.[16] And Germany lost a third U-boat.

Drifters were also utilised for anti-submarine work, with Ramsgate an auxiliary patrol base and home to an armed drifter squadron. For five weeks in July and August 1915, the drifters at Ramsgate were commanded by the oldest serving officer in the Royal Navy, William Balfour Forbes. Born in 1845, Forbes had retired

---

* Therefore, it would appear that *Saxon* was carrying both a directional and non-directional set.

[†] After the war, Youngson was awarded the MBE 'for valuable services in minesweeping operations' (*London Gazette*, no 31354, 24 May 1919).

[§] In 1940, *Dorothy Gray* was again called up, for use as an armed patrol vessel, until released in December 1944.

from the navy in 1888. He volunteered for service at the outbreak of war, was commissioned with the rank of commander RNR and given charge of a dummy battleship which, when torpedoed off Mudros, had successfully completed its intended function: whereupon he was appointed to Ramsgate and a brood of thirty armed drifters.

The seventy-year-old Forbes did not appreciate his new situation. 'Ramsgate seems a vile place,' he wrote to his wife, 'a horrible noisy place.'[17] He was accommodated at the town's Royal Hotel, which cost him 7s.6d a night for the privilege. As for his charges, Forbes thought that they were 'just little steam fishing boats with quick firing guns, most uncomfortable, except in fine weather'.[18]

His drifters spent four days out at sea, mostly inside the Goodwins, hunting U-boats and then two days in harbour. Submarines were not the only threat to them. 'One of the drifters … was attacked by a German aeroplane from very high up (7,000 feet) and bombs were dropped all round her, but the second shot from the drifter's high angle gun drove him off.'[19]

Forbes was taken suddenly ill on 12 August and shortly afterwards stepped down on the grounds of health. He was subsequently advanced to captain on the retired list for his pains.

Drifters were small and lightly armed but they could pack a punch. On 28 November 1917 at around 0630, the squadron sighted and engaged the German submarine *U-48* which, while waiting for the moon to set and recharging its batteries on the surface, had drifted aground on the Goodwin Sands. The drifters *Paramount*, *Majesty* and *Present Help* attacked and were joined by *Feasible*, *Acceptable* and *Lord Claud Hamilton*. A short sharp exchange of fire followed in which *Feasible* stood in so close that she bumped the sand some 30yds from the submarine. Armed only with 3pdr or 6pdr guns the small ships were outgunned by the submarine's heavier 88mm (~3.5in) weapon. Shells fell all around them and *Paramount* was hit; but just after 0700 the destroyer *Gipsy* arrived from the north and opened fire at 2,000yds range with 12pdr and 6pdr weapons, quickly achieving hits.

At this point *U-48* had sustained thirteen hits and was unviable. Her commander ordered confidential books destroyed, gave the orders to abandon ship and set scuttling charges. The crew leapt overboard and the submarine blew up, taking her captain and twenty men with her. One officer and twenty-one survivors were made prisoners. There were no casualties on the drifters. The Admiralty paid prize money of £1,000 and the destroyer captain and three drifter skippers, the latter all RNR, were awarded medals. Skipper Hemp of *Paramount*, Skipper Barker of *Majesty* and Skipper Lane of *Present Help* (all Lowestoft boats) were each presented with the DSC. Five ratings gained the DSM. The press entitled this success 'The Battle of Ramsgate'.*

---

* *Feasible* survived the conflict and in the Second World War took part in the Dunkirk evacuation. Amazingly, she still exists, privately owned and currently moored in Penzance, where it is intended to restore her.

Another fishermen's victory came in December 1917. The trawler *Ben Lawers* was an Aberdeen trawler, built in 1900, owned by the North British Steam Fishing Company and taken up in November 1914. She was fitted with one 12pdr and a 6pdr gun and used for minesweeping and escort. In the early morning of 9 December, the trawler was escorting a coal convoy across the English Channel to France and was passing near to Start Point, when *UB-18*, bound for the Western Approaches, inadvertently surfaced close to her. The trawler's skipper, sixty-two-year-old James Culling RNR from Londonderry, immediately gave the order to ram and *Ben Lawers* caught *UB-18* just behind the conning tower. The U-boat submerged or sank, it mattered not which for she was never seen again, and her twenty-four crew all perished with her. The trawler herself was so badly damaged that she barely made it back to port. Culling was awarded the DSC for his efforts.[20]

There was further success for the fishermen U-boat hunters on 17 April 1918 off Torr Head to the north of Ireland. This time it was the drifters to the fore.

About around 1730 the Lowestoft drifter *Pilot Me*, armed with a single 6pdr, sighted a periscope and dropped two D-star-type depth charges while zigzagging over the course the enemy appeared to be steering. She then stopped and used her hydrophone. Presently *UB-82* surfaced between *Pilot Me* and another drifter, the Lowestoft vessel *Young Fred*, at an angle of 45°. All the drifters on the scene opened fire at short range and *Young Fred* dropped her two depth charges right over the enemy's last position. This produced an explosion and a high column of water, which for a moment caused the other drifters to believe that *Young Fred* had blown up. Suddenly, the sea roiled with the detritus of wreckage, woodwork fittings, gratings and seamen's caps. The U-boat had sunk with all thirty-six crewmen; there were no survivors.

A number of DSCs and DSMs were presented to the participants, and the sum of £1,000 was awarded by the Admiralty to be shared amongst the attackers.

The final definitive success for the trawlers alone came on 13 August 1918. At about noon *UB-30* was preparing to attack a convoy proceeding southwards at a distance of some three and a half miles from her position, in the vicinity of the Tyne. The commander of the U-boat, Rudolph Steir, was so intent on observing the convoy's progress that he failed to observe the approach of the *Castle*-class armed trawler *John Gillman*, part of the Tyne auxiliary patrol, which had sighted a periscope and prepared to ram. Steir tried to dive but could not escape quickly enough to avoid the onrushing threat and the fishing boat grated over her hull, bending the periscope. As she passed over, the trawler dropped two depth charges, the explosion of which in such close proximity knocked many of her crew to the floor. The armed yacht *Miranda II*, fitted with two 12pdrs, joined and dropped two more depth charges and the hydrophone-equipped trawlers, *Viola* and another *Castle*-class vessel, *John Brooker*, steamed up to begin a listening watch. After two hours, a lookout discerned the shape of a submarine moving just under the

20. After the Dover barrier, the single largest employment of drifters was the Otranto Barrage. Here are some of the drifters which manged it in harbour. They were fitted with a 6pdr gun, carried depth charges and sometimes had primitive hydrophones on board. (© Imperial War Museum Q 63046)

surface. The trawlers fired their 12pdrs at the surface and again dropped depth bombs. Now the ex-Grimsby *Florio* arrived and, as the stricken U-boat surfaced leaking bubbles of both oil and air, both she and *John Gillman* attacked again, dropping six depth charges between them. This time it was fatal. *UB-30* sank once more, never to return to the surface. All her crew died with her.

Not all successes involved a sinking. Just two weeks after the destruction of *UB-82*, on 30 April, the drifter *Coreopsis*, registered in Kirkcaldy and now based at Larne, sighted the conning tower of *UB-85* at 0300. Lieutenant Percy Sutcliffe Peat quickly called for his gunner, who appeared on deck wearing only his shirt, and a 6pdr shell was fired as the U-boat ran across the drifter's bows, hitting the submarine's conning tower. The submarine made off on the surface and the much slower drifter lumbered after her. But suddenly the U-boat hove to and fired a Very light, the crew calling out that they surrendered.

Peat was suspicious, and manoeuvred to put the submarine in the moon's light and then fired several rounds at its gun, a weapon much more powerful than his own. There was no response. Other patrol vessels arrived on the scene and Peat sent his boat to bring off

the crew who were battened into the hold and taken as prisoners to Larne.

The surface patrols had caused *UB-85* to remain submerged for a long time and her air supply had become foul with chlorine gas from the batteries. Additionally, *Coreopsis's* shell had damaged a hatch, allowing in fifteen tons of water which set off more battery gas and made the hull untenable. Not a sinking then, but a drifter playing its part in the capture of a U-boat; Lieutenant Peat received the DSO for his pains and his skipper, George Stubbs, a Gorleston fisherman by trade, was awarded the DSC. Perhaps more welcome, the Admiralty gave a bounty of £1,000 to be divided amongst the crew.

In total, including Q-ship actions, fishing vessels directly accounted for sinking ten U-boats (and capturing one).* But this does not indicate the value of their efforts in suppressing the threat through assisting other ships, net management, depth charging in company with other naval vessels and, by their mere presence, keeping U-boats submerged or away from their intended targets.

But losses of trawlers to submarines were incurred in return for these partial successes. U-boats sank seventeen armed trawlers during the war and thirty-four drifters, and possibly accounted for some of another ten and eight respectively, lost to 'unknown causes'.[21]

* Some sources claim that trawlers were complicit in sinking *UB-3, UC-49, UB-103* and *U-74*, but modern scholarship disproves this.

6: General Duties

From the beginning of the war, trawlers and drifters found themselves undertaking a range of duties which owed nothing to anti-submarine or mine defence.

Drifters were regularly used as despatch vessels, delivering mail, messages, supplies and personnel around the fleet. On 5 June 1916, it was a drifter, the ex-Wick registered *Mayberry*, which carried Secretary of State for War Lord Kitchener and his party from Jellicoe's flagship *Iron Duke* to HMS *Hampshire*, immediately before their departure for Russia, a voyage which was terminated by a mine off the western coast of Orkney. Kitchener and 737 men died.

The Boom Defence Service utilised many trawlers and other fishing vessels alongside the specialist craft initially allotted to the task at the start of the war. These included unpowered 'dumb' vessels carrying (generally) a 12pdr gun and known as barrage or boom defence vessels, converted sloops and gunboats and a variety of other craft.

The typical defensive boom was a series of 40ft long timber baulks chained together and stretched across a harbour or river mouth to deny access to enemy surface craft. When any friendly vessel needed to pass through, the attending boom defence vessels (BDVs) had to draw the obstruction aside and, after passage, replace it in position. It was heavy, repetitive and hard work, often conducted by pairs or more of boom vessels.

Trawlers were always to the fore in this duty, their sturdy steadiness making them ideal for the task. Many of these vessels did not have commissioned status and operated under the Red Ensign. Others were fitted with armament in their role of protecting the fleet anchorages.

21. This plate and the next depict trawlers which served as boom defence vessels. *Kennet* was built in 1899 in Aberdeen and taken up by the navy in June 1915. Her gun mounting can be clearly seen on the forecastle. (© National Maritime Museum N04376)

One such fishing boat was the hired HMT *Orizaba* (plate 22); Grimsby registered and owned by a Mr Bannister, and carrying a skipper and nine men. She had been leased at the end of December 1914 and armed with a 6pdr weapon. The vessel survived to fight in the Second World War as well. And HMT *Riby*, the property of a Mr Grant and from the same port, with eight crew and a skipper. She had been taken up in June 1915 and fitted with a 12pdr gun. In 1916, these two trawlers had crossed the Irish Sea to be BDVs at Lough Swilly.[1]

A small number of fishing craft were also used as colliers and water carriers to service the other BDV vessels. By February 1916, there were 190 boom defence drifters in service and 100 more used for harbour service duties.[2]

Maids of all work

The drifter *Bracoden*, originally registered at Fraserburgh, was requisitioned in January 1915 and sent to Lemnos for service in the Gallipoli campaign in the June. Armed with a single 6pdr and intended for net-laying duty, she was soon at work setting anti-submarine nets around the British and French battleships bombarding the Turkish guns.

But her duties quickly became more varied. On 1 August she was sent to the beach at Cape Helles to pick up some soldiers. All the time she was under fire from Turkish guns but *Bracoden* was taken alongside the beached SS *River Clyde*, now utilised as a quay but four months earlier a landing ship on which six Victoria Crosses had been won in a single day. Here the drifter 'filled the vessel with men'[3] before departing, still with Turkish shells falling around her.

Five days later she was towing a lighter half full of coal to a collier for refilling and from there she went back to shooting her nets off Cape Helles. Through September, *Bracoden* alternated between patrolling her nets and towing lighters; and she was still doing so in December.

Drifters were also useful in a number of non-traditional ways, such as towing observation or anti-aircraft balloons, the former of which were used to spot ahead for enemy submarines on or just below the surface (see plate 23). Winching and rope-handling skills were important in this task and of course the fishermen had them. Later on, once convoy was adopted, balloons were widely used for convoy escort duty as well, towed by an assortment of craft including trawlers and drifters. A study by the US Navy Planning Section in 1917 noted that their advantages included the facts that 'the distance patrolled equals the distance advanced by the convoy during daylight hours – fog neglected' and 'a surface vessel can be directed with precision towards any object sighted'.[4]

Trawlers too proved to be versatile and useful outside of their originally intended functions. *Loch Broom* was an Aberdeen trawler built in 1907 and taken up at the outset of the war. She mounted a 3pdr gun and left England on 17 March 1915 for minesweeping duties at Gallipoli, arriving too late to take part in the inglorious failure described in chapter 4. But from the first day of the landing of the invasion force on 25 April, her primary duty was to ferry men and stores, often in towed lighters, to and from the shore at Gaba Tepe. On one occasion in May, deckhand James Clarke noticed that of the forty soldiers they were taking to the beach 'half of them were drunk'.[5]

The summer brought Clarke and his skipper, J T Burrell, a less salubrious challenge, for they were attached as a tender to a hospital ship and had to collect dead bodies from her for burial at sea. On 28 June they picked up three corpses but 'we are finished with the hospital job', Clarke confided to his diary, 'as we take it in turns and it is not a very fine job, we buried thirty-three altogether in the short time we had it'.[6] But they were soon back to their mournful duty. At the end of July, Clarke noted that 'it is not a good job but somebody had to do it'. However, things came to head on 24 August; they had to wait for five bodies, which the hospital ship wanted them to sew up and put weights into the shroud. The crew refused to a man, 'as it is not a very pleasant job'.[7] They went to the beach to pick up some wounded instead. And by October, the trawler was making a daily run from Anzac Cove to Imbros collecting rations, mainly beef and bread, 20,000 portions at a time.

Loch Broom's war continued in the Aegean, where she had been sent in 1916 on minesweeping and anti-submarine duties, as well as being used as an examination vessel. But here she took part in what was surely her most curious adventure. On the night of 24/25 July, Skipper Burrell and his crew were involved in a raid on a Turkish-held island. They towed two sailing vessels full of Greek soldiers, 50 men out of the 270 who formed the landing party. The assault captured over 3,000 head of sheep and cattle; and a fleet minesweeper, four minesweeping trawlers and four drifters took them all on board. At a stroke the Turks would go hungry and the Allied troops would feast well. At 1000 on the 25th, *Loch Broom* offloaded 400 head of sheep and goats, 11 donkeys and a bull. It must have been quite a clean-up job after that.

The Northern Patrol

The Northern Patrol was mounted by the 10th Cruiser Squadron from August 1914, from its base in the Shetland Islands. Its role was to intercept neutral or enemy cargo vessels to examine them for suspected 'contraband' – war supplies for the enemy. First utilising ancient cruisers, which were knocked to bits by the weather, it then became the responsibility of Armed Merchant Cruisers (AMCs), large civilian liners and merchant ships, converted to carry naval weaponry.

But they were unhandy for boarding purposes, and trawlers soon found themselves in the mix as well, used as examination vessels, as they were at most major ports around Britain.

One Northern Patrol trawler was the *Tenby Castle*, once of Swansea, now fitted with a 12pdr gun and a 7.5in bomb thrower and under the command of Lieutenant J S Randall RNR. On 8 July 1915 she sighted the German steamer *Friedrich Arp* off the Huso and Haran Islands on the Norwegian coast and, having fired a shot across her bows, ordered her to steer south-west by west. The

German captain ignored this order and steered towards the land. This time Randall fired a shot into the steamer's stern. That stopped the German but she still refused to steer as ordered. Randall informed her captain that he would be sunk unless he obeyed orders. Disregarding or disbelieving this, the German vessel again made for the shore. The *Tenby Castle* opened fire and sent sixteen rounds into the *Freidrich Arp*'s starboard quarter and she quickly sank. The crew and pilot were rescued and transferred to the AMC *India*. The German ship had been bound for Stettin from Narvik with a cargo of magnetic ore (magnetite, ferrous-ferric oxide), an essential commodity for the German war effort in a number of industrial processes. This was just one of many successes around the British Isles for armed trawlers policing the shipping lanes for enemy trade.

Convoy escort

The Royal Navy was late to adopt convoy, despite the rising toll of sunken merchant ships and the evidence from past centuries that convoy worked. Certainly, when trawlers were first taken up into the navy there was no expectation that convoy escort would become a general duty for the type.

There were essentially three reasons for the navy's reluctance to adopt such protection. Practically, they badly overestimated the number of movements that would have to be covered. Moreover, many merchant masters and owners objected to convoy as they felt it would lengthen sailing and turnaround times, costing them money. And culturally, the RN disliked convoy because it was defensive – their self-image was of an aggressive force, taking battle to the enemy battlefleet, not skulking around after a few merchant ships.

However, by early 1917 it was clear that Britain's losses of ships and cargos was far exceeding any ability to replace them. After Germany reintroduced unrestricted submarine warfare at the end of January 1917, losses shot up. In January British ships sunk totalled 153,666grt; in February 313,486; March 353,478; April 545,282.[8] On 27 April 1917, First Sea Lord Admiral Sir John Jellicoe told the cabinet:

> the real fact of the matter is this. We are carrying on the war at the present time as if we had the absolute command of the sea, whereas we have not such command or anything approaching it. It is quite true that we are masters of the situation so far as surface ships are concerned, but it must be realised – and realised at once – that this will be quite useless if the enemy's submarines paralyse, as they do now, our lines of communication.
>
> Without some such relief … the navy will fail in its responsibilities to the country and the country itself will suffer starvation.[9]

In fact, such relief was at hand. Under pressure from the French and the Norwegian ship owners, whose ships carried much of the cargo, protection of the cross-Channel French coal trade by convoy had started in January 1917 with markedly successful results. Trawlers played a key role in the escort, but it was a daily grind. For example, HMT *Sapper*, a 'Military'-class vessel, armed with a 12pdr gun, took colliers to France on a daily basis. On 11 March 1917, in company with another armed trawler *Rose*, she took eleven coal carriers to Caen. The next day she took ten; and on the 13th another eleven, this time with three others of her kind, *Myna*, *Tenby* and *Rose*. Between 9 March and the 20th, she took eleven convoys across the Channel. After a seven-day break for coaling, resupply and inspection, she was back with the colliers again for the last four days of the month. On the penultimate day, returning to Portsmouth at 0030 to pick up the next convoy, she came across a sinking collier from another group and sent her boat away to rescue the master and fifteen men, five more crew being missing.[10]

Nine months later, *Sapper* herself was sunk in the English Channel. On 29 December, she struck a mine in a field laid by the submarine *UC-71*, just off the Owers Light Vessel. Edinburgh-born skipper Charles Thomson and all eighteen of his crew lost their lives.

Meanwhile, in Scotland, and on their own initiative, Vice Admiral Frederic Brock and CinC Grand Fleet Admiral David Beatty had by April 1917 instigated convoying on the vital Scandinavian routes.* It met with immediate success.

The problem was that there was a marked shortage of suitable destroyer or sloop escorts able to handle the rough seas and crossings. Trawlers became the default option. And this put the ships and their fishermen crews in danger's way.

The armed trawlers *Elise* and *P Fannon* were part of the escort of a Scandinavian convoy on 17 October 1917. Both of the trawlers carried only a single 6pdr gun. *Elise* was a Peterhead-registered hired vessel, built in 1907 and taken up initially for minesweeping purposes; *P Fannon* was a 1915-built Aberdeen boat, also originally hired as a minesweeper. Neither was capable of more than around 9 knots. The convoy was attacked by the German light cruisers *Brummer* and *Bremse*. The convoy and its destroyer escorts were sunk and the trawlers fortunately survived to pick up survivors.

On the same route, on 12 December, four hired trawlers, three armed with one 3pdr gun, *Livingstone*, *Commander Fullerton* and *Tokio*, and *Lord Alverstone*, armed with a 6pdr, together with two M-class destroyers, formed the convoy escort. They were attacked by four *torpedobootzerstörers*, German destroyers. All six ships of the convoy were sunk; so were all the armed trawlers. They were there to protect the convoy from submarines or mines, not surface ships, and their armaments were pop-guns compared to the enemy's weapons. *Commander Fullerton*, Hull-registered, was hit near the gun platform, in the mess deck and then on the winch while it was being used to lower the lifeboat, causing the men in it to fall into the water. Her survivors were eventually picked up by the destroyer

---

* For the full story, see S R Dunn, *Southern Thunder*, Seaforth Publishing (Barnsley, 2019).

22. *Orizaba* served at Lough Swilly in a boom defence role. Built in Grimsby in 1908, she was taken up in December 1914 and equipped with a 6pdr weapon. She survived to serve in the Second World War as well, as pictured. (© Imperial War Museum FL 17122)

HMS *Sable* in the evening. The skipper, forty-year-old John William Whelan RNR, a native of Hull, was not amongst them. *Livingston*, another Hull vessel, was struck in the engine room, cabin and mess deck before foundering. Some of her crew were made prisoner by the Germans and three were fished from the water by another destroyer, *Sorceress. Lord Alverstone*, from Grimsby, was speedily sunk but all twelve members of her crew managed to escape in a boat, reaching Stolmen Island where they were collected by a Norwegian naval vessel. And *Tokio*, of Hull, was also sunk, slipping beneath the waves with little fuss or bother.

Not everybody was delighted with the use of trawlers for convoy escort. Their slow speed attracted criticism from some quarters, even in the House of Commons. On 29 January 1918 the perpetual self-appointed expert on matters naval, Commander Carlyon Wilfroy Bellairs, MP for Maidstone, asked the First Lord of the Admiralty whether 'he has considered the increased risk to a twelve knot ship when convoyed by eight knot trawlers, as in a recent case of a valuable refrigerating ship which was lost; and whether he will sanction the release of at least 200 of the eight knot trawlers and crews in order that they may assist the food supply of the country?'

Replying for the Admiralty, Dr Thomas Macnamara, Financial Secretary, tartly noted that 'the answer to the first part of the question is in the affirmative; but in the case quoted by my hon and gallant friend, the vessel referred to was unable to maintain a higher speed than nine knots. In arranging escorts, consideration is given to the actual sea speed of a ship and not to the nominal speed'. His answer to the second part of the question showed that the demand for trawlers was in no way lessening: 'the question of releasing the slower trawlers and drifters on Admiralty service is constantly before the departments concerned, but in view of the constant and growing demand for these vessels, it is not possible to release any of them at present without detriment to the naval service'.

Sir Robert Paterson Houston, MP for Liverpool West Toxteth, then joined in, asking 'is the right hon gentleman not aware of the many complaints which are made by masters of speedy vessels at being convoyed by trawlers, and having to reduce their speed to about six or seven knots to prevent them running away from them'? Macnamara flat-batted this away with 'we have had the advantage of the experiences and opinions of practical merchant seamen'.[11] But it remained a problem; they were nowhere near enough fast escorts.

Despite such criticism, losses, and the constant attrition of mines, U-boats and other causes, the trawlers kept at sea, and convoy proved successful; Britain never suffered shortages caused by a sea blockade in the way that Germany did.

The price of fish

When war was declared, hundreds of British steam trawlers were scattered either singly or in fleets across the North Sea fishing grounds and beyond. Additionally, the seasonal herring fishery was at its height and hundreds of drifters were working the herring which was shoaling off the north-east coast of England. The Admiralty immediately issued instructions to harbourmasters that no further fishing boats were to sail for the North Sea grounds and that all those at sea should be recalled. As none carried radios, this was problematic.

Very quickly, three conditions combined to create a sudden shortage of fish for human consumption. Firstly, trawlers were prohibited from visiting their traditional fishing grounds, a ban that was gradually relaxed over time. Secondly, men and vessels were called up for Admiralty service. And thirdly, volunteering to fight and (post March 1916) involuntary conscription severely reduced the ranks of men available to man the nets.

The only beneficiaries from this were sailing smacks, fishing boats which moved under wind power only, and those trawler skippers too old for combat. And the Irish. The Irish fishing fleet was still mainly sail powered; the removal of English and Scottish vessels from around the Irish coast, together with the political decision not to impose conscription in Ireland, led to a bonanza for the Irish fishing industry.

As a consequence, shortages led to demand-driven extra profits. While food prices nationally rose by 78 per cent between July 1914 and November 1916, those for fish rose by 132 per cent; even when, in 1918, the Fish (Prices) Order belatedly laid down maximum prices, those maximums quickly become minimums.

Boats which kept fishing, usually with skippers and crews too old even to be reservists, benefitted. Even the humble dogfish found a market. According to *Fishing News*, Scottish boats working herring from Yarmouth during the 1915 season 'only had to go to sea and put their noses in the fishing grounds to come back with at least a catch worth £100'.[12] In Dundee the previous December, the sprat fleet had been getting over £2 a cran* compared to six or seven shillings pre-war.

Some of these Scottish boats working from Yarmouth showed a little humanitarianism, however, donating a cran of herring each in 1914 to be sold for the Belgian Relief Fund in support of the many Belgian families who had fled to England after the German invasion. And the following year, they made the same donation to the British Red Cross Society.

Considerable financial returns were to be had; the boats the Admiralty didn't yet need were making fortunes. 'Here's an old salt' reported the *New York World*, '… who could now be making £100 a day in these times of high prices.'[13] By January 1916, the President of the Board of Trade, Walter Runciman, was forced to deny that there was a problem with excess profit. In the House of Commons on 17 October he pronounced that 'fish is not dear because there is any undue profiteering. It is dearer because there are not the same number of boats at sea, because they are engaged in trawling for mines.'[14]

But there was a cost to be paid for the continuation of domestic fishing and the super profits to be made. The Grimsby-based *Tubal*

Cain was a steam trawler of 227grt fishing off the coast of Iceland on 7 August 1914; she was captured by the German Armed Merchant Cruiser *Kaiser Wilhelm Der Grösse* and destroyed by gunfire, becoming the first British commercial fishing boat to be sunk in the war. Skipper William Smith and his crew of fourteen only discovered war had broken out when they were captured; and before sinking the trawler, the Germans took several good halibuts for themselves.

Then, between 22 and 26 August, fourteen Grimsby and ten Boston trawlers were sunk. From there on, there was a steady drumbeat of sinkings of fishing boats.

After the German declaration of unrestricted submarine warfare of February 1915, such sinkings became a regular occurrence. By the month of April, German submarines were making a particular play of destroying British fishing vessels, perhaps as some sort of retaliation for the food shortages now being experienced in Germany itself as a result of the blockade imposed by the Royal Navy. The commander of the German submarine *U-9* (Johannes Spieß[†]) recorded that 'we captured and sank scores of smacks off Dogger Bank. This was far less glorious than gunning for armed men-of-war, and less exciting. But it supplied many unexpected thrills.'[15]

On 19 April, the Admiralty Censor issued a communiqué to the press bureau (charmingly misaddressed as the 'bress bureau') reporting the loss of a trawler. 'Today a German submarine sunk by torpedo the trawler *Vanilla*. The trawler *Fermo* endeavoured to rescue the crew, but she was fired on and driven off. All hands on the *Vanilla* were lost. This killing of fisherfolk for no military purpose should not escape attention. It is the second murder of this character committed within a week.' Threateningly, the note went on to add that 'a careful record will be kept of these events'.[16]

However, the carnage continued; June 1915 was a very bad month for losses. Seven fishing boats were sunk by U-boats on 3 June and another five on the 5th. On 23 June, one U-boat, *U-38*, sank sixteen drifters east of the Shetland Islands. In total, there were sixty sinkings in the month. By the end of 1916, 378 such vessels had been destroyed by German submarines or surface vessels, mainly the former.[17]

Some fishermen were fortunate to meet with a U-boat skipper who was prepared to act in a humanitarian fashion, behaviour which became less and less common as the war wore on. At dusk on 24 September 1916, fifteen trawlers were fishing on the Whitby Fine Grounds, twenty miles to the north-east of Scarborough. Twelve were from that port, with one each from the nearby fishing towns of Hartlepool, Whitby and Hull. Most were fishing in close proximity, wearing oil lamps at their masts to indicate that they had their nets down (there were as yet no blackout restrictions at sea).

The crew of *Fisher Prince* were suddenly shocked to find a U-boat, *U-57* under the command of Kapitänleutnant Carl-Siegfried

---

* A cran, in use from at least the eighteenth century, was a unit of measure of landed uncleaned herring employed in the North Sea fishing industry. In 1852, it was defined as the equivalent of one standard box of about 37.5 imperial gallons – typically around 1,200 fish, but varying anywhere between 700 and 2,500.

† In his six months in command of *U-9*, Spieß sank fourteen vessels of which ten were fishing boats.

23. Drifters were multi-purpose units. Here one is towing an observation balloon (note the basket hanging beneath the inflatable) used to spot for enemy ships or a submarine at or just below the surface. (US Library of Congress LC-DIG-ggbain-25169)

von Georg, surface next to them. In a choreographed operation, the U-boat crew swung grappling hooks onto the gunwales and armed crewmen boarded the trawler, led by their commander.

Skipper Dave Naylor was told to stop the engines, and von Georg then demanded the ship's register as proof of his capture. A prize crew was placed aboard the trawler and the crew confined to the fish hold, the raiding party returning to their submarine.

Still surfaced, von Georg now moved to a nearby trawler, *Otterhound*, and repeated the exercise. This time the fishermen were taken on board the U-boat and the Germen submarines helped themselves to the trawler's provisions. *Otterhound*'s crew were then placed in *Fisher Prince*.

Throughout the night, acting with daring and skill, von Georg captured a further twelve trawlers, each of which was searched for

food and their luckless crews placed in the fish hold of *Fisher Prince*. Eventually, the little trawler held 126 captured men, under the guard of 4 German sailors, and 14 trawlers had been seized.

The U-boats now sank the trawlers, twelve by gunfire and the *Nil Desperandum* by a scuttling charge, placed in her engine room. And, as dawn broke, von Georg stopped a northward-bound Norwegian cargo ship and arranged with her captain to take the captured fishermen to a British port. Skipper Naylor was instructed to start up the engines of the trawler and manoeuvre her alongside the Scandinavian vessel. The trawlermen were allowed to board her, wished a cheery *Auf Wiedersehen* and watched as *U-57* sank *Fisher Prince* with her gun. They were later landed at South Shields and safety.

Only one fishing boat of the fifteen that had been peacefully at work twelve hours earlier survived. *Ben Hope*, skippered and owned by Dick Crawford, evaded capture as she was fishing away from the main body. Hearing the noise of gun fire, Crawford ordered his crew to haul in the nets and then steamed home with his catch at the best speed he could muster.

Not all attacks on fishing craft went unavenged. On 5 June 1915, *U-14* chanced upon a group of trawlers off the coast of Peterhead. In order to afford some sort of protection to such fishing vessels, the Admiralty had taken to putting armed trawlers or Q-ships amongst the genuine fishing boats. One such was the hired Hull trawler HMT *Oceanic II*, built in 1893, taken up by the Admiralty at the outbreak of war. Now she was fitted as a Q-ship and armed with12pdr and 3pdr guns.

Another such trawler was the Hull-registered *Hawk*. She had just rescued the crew of the fishing vessel *Lappland*, blown up by a U-boat, and taken them back to port. Now she returned to the scene and joined *Oceanic II*.

U-14's commander Max Hammerle surfaced and, identifying trawlers to attack, ordered the gun crew to fire two warning shots across the *Oceanic II*'s bows. It was a mistake; *Oceanic* returned the fire and was joined by *Hawk*, carrying two 3pdrs. *U-14* was hit and Hammerle ordered a crash dive. But something went wrong and the vents of the forward diving tanks jammed. The submarine sank stern first but its bows remained well above the water, a target which both trawlers shot at and hit repeatedly; *Hawk* additionally attempted a ramming run.

The panic-stricken U-boat crew abandoned ship and were rescued by their attackers; but twenty-nine-year-old Hammerle refused to leave his command and went down with his vessel, the only German casualty. Skipper John Cowie RNR(T) of *Oceanic* and Lieutenant Herbert James Ferguson RNR of the *Hawk* both received the DSC[18] while a number of other crewmen were awarded the DSM.

Mines were also a problem for fishermen. The example of the fishing trawlers *Angelo* and *Sabrina*, is typical of the many. Owned by Hellyers of Hull, they ran into a minefield off the Dogger Bank on 21 May 1915 and were sunk. All of *Sabrina*'s crew were killed. *Angelo*'s men, having fouled a mine in their nets and seen their vessel explode and sink stern first as they escaped in the rowing boat, had then to survive for twelve hours in the North Sea. Their little boat had been damaged in the explosion and leaked; so they stuffed their caps and other items of clothing into the holes. They were barely afloat when rescued by a Norwegian steamer.

By the end of 1916, the commercial fishing trawler fleet was a quarter of its pre-war size, uptake by the Admiralty[*] and high trawler losses the reasons. Fish catches were down and prices were inflated. Only ninety-three fishing trawlers were working out of Hull and all the fish and chip shops in the town had closed for the duration.

To prevent the industry collapsing, in May 1917 the remaining steam trawler fleet (and some smaller fishing vessels) were requisitioned and placed in the newly created Fishery Reserve (FR) under Admiralty control. Requisition was compulsory on all British trawler owners but the scheme was not extended to sailing trawlers and steam drifters (see plate 24).

The men of the Fishery Reserve signed an F124 agreement and were not members of the RNR; but they did come under section 90 of the Naval Discipline Act. However, 'it was not the original intention to apply the Naval Discipline Act to the Fishery Reserve, as it was realised that the Reserve was a tender plant'.[19]

Fishery Reserve trawler owners were only paid a nominal amount by the Admiralty[†] and the vessels were unarmed. However, the FR trawlers were considered as 'seagoing ships in commission and were entitled to duty free stores'. By the end of 1917, this was causing friction, for it had become recognised that the fishing was very profitable. '[As] they are earning a very high wage for their fishing,' wrote an anonymous naval administrator, 'it becomes a question whether they should continue to enjoy the privilege [of duty free].'[20]

Under the so-called 'Group System', all offshore fishing vessels were put under Admiralty control. The FR vessels only put to sea with the protection of one or more armed trawlers. Fishing vessels were required to sail in groups and an attempt was made to ensure that at least one escort had a radio, in order to call for support in the event of attack. All the FR craft were commissioned and flew the White Ensign and they came under the command of the senior naval officer of their base port, who decided when and where they could fish. In total, 388 vessels served in the Fishery Section of the Trawler Reserve.

There were still losses, and the armaments of the escorts were generally too light to defend against resolute attack by submarine. On 10 July 1917 a group of one Hull and seven Grimsby trawlers was destroyed by U-53 off Suðuroy, while sailing between the Pentland Firth and the Faroes. Such distant sailings were prohibited until more 12pdr guns could be fitted to the escorting trawlers; but

by September, the sailings were resumed. And in November the groups were standardised to contain six trawlers, five of which were armed in some fashion, two with 12pdrs and one carrying a wireless.

Yet, overall, the system seemed to work, not least when the armed trawlers *Conan Doyle*, under Skipper William Addy and section leader Lieutenant John Francis MacCabe RNR, and *Aisne*, were part of a group of six trawlers in the North Sea on 20 June 1918. Both were classified as working fishing boats and in the Fishery Reserve, but were also armed for escort purposes. While returning home from fishing in Icelandic waters, they were intercepted by U-53, commanded by the highly successful Kapitänleutnant Hans Rose,[§] and a running battle developed. The submarine was heavily armed, with three guns,[ß] but at 0545 *Conan Doyle* made a direct hit forward and the enemy ceased fire for ten minutes and increased speed to close the convoy's bow. Addy and MacCabe altered course, keeping the submarine more or less abeam. U-53 maintained a continual rapid shellfire from all its weapons at *Conan Doyle*. A thick rainstorm at 0700 hid the enemy for twenty-five minutes, but when weather cleared the submarine was sighted 7,000 yards off and it at once opened fire with shrapnel at the convoy of fishing craft. Trawler *Aisne* was hit several times.

By 0845, *Conan Doyle* had only fifteen rounds left; Addy and MacCabe hoisted the signal 'prepare to ram'. But *Aisne* now obtained a direct hit on the after part of the enemy and *Conan Doyle* scored a hit below the enemy's forward gun, which disappeared after a burst of flame and smoke. The submarine turned to port and fired its after gun until at 0900 *Conan Doyle* made another direct hit forward, and below the conning tower. At this point, Rose and U-53 had had enough and left the fishermen alone.

Sir Arthur Conan Doyle presented the skipper of his namesake with an engraved silver cigarette case in recognition of his deeds. MacCabe received the DSO and Addy the DSC, as did the five other skippers. One fisherman was killed and four wounded. But the fishing boats and their catch were protected.

Prisoners

The last fishing vessel to be sunk was on 7 November 1918, when the sailing smack *Conster* hit a mine. But apart from being sunk, there was a further threat to the fishing fleet throughout the war – that of being taken prisoner.

On 18 May 1915 the German cruiser SMS *Hamburg* was laying mines in the North Sea when her escorts came across four fishing boats, the *King Charles* from Grimsby, and *Euclid*, *Duke of Wellington* and *Titania* from Hull. They sank all four but instead of turning their crews loose in the lifeboats, they were taken to Germany as prisoners, presumably to keep the location of *Hamburg*'s minefield

---

[*] Some 1,400 of the calculated 1,900 steam trawlers available.

[†] A nominal rate of one shilling per month per boat and one shilling per crew member was paid by the Admiralty to the owners. Their owners paid the crew at RNR(T) rates plus 5 per cent of the catch profit bonus. Owners retained the fishing earnings.

[§] Rose and U-53 sank eighty-two vessels between July 1916 and August 1918.

[ß] Two of which were 8.8cm (3.5in), firing a 15lb shell, heavier than the trawlers 12pdrs. The third (non-standard for the class) may have been a machine gun mounted in the conning tower.

24. The trawler *Brisbane* was one of the trawlers taken into the Fishery Reserve in 1917. She was of 207grt and built in Grimsby in 1903. (© Imperial War Museum Q 19008)

a secret. The men were sent to Ruhleben internment camp, six miles west of Berlin, and there remained for the duration.

They were not alone. Some forty different fishing trawler civilian crews were captured during the war, thirty-five of them between 1914 and 1916, starting with the trawler *Marney*. She was seized by a torpedo boat E by N from Spurn Head on 22 August, just sixteen days from the commencement of hostilities.

The fishermen prisoners were initially kept at Sennelager, a camp notorious for its poor facilities. Here 600 men slept in tents on the uncovered ground. Later they were moved to the former racecourse at Ruhleben. 'Letters from the camp were subjected to severe censorship and reports suggested that pressure was placed upon prisoners to describe conditions better than they were in reality. The US ambassador, James W Gerard, described the barracks as overcrowded.' Six people were cramped together in a horse's stall and conditions in the haylofts above the stables were even more crowded. 'Sixty-four men lived in that confined space with light so faint that prisoners' eyes will be seriously injured' stated the ambassador, 'if their sight is not permanently lost.' They slept on sack mattresses, stuffed with wet and mouldy straw. Many of the horse stalls still had manure clinging to the walls and concrete floors. Food was scarce

and of bad quality, often just cabbage soup, and Gerard further noted that he thought that 'prisoners were at risk of starvation'.[21] For ablutions, twenty wash basins, all filled from one cold tap, were provided for 250 men.

The prisoners' long-term health suffered and on their final release, at least three men found that they had been presumed dead and life insurance monies paid to their wives.

By the end of hostilities, only 14,000 men were left commercially fishing, of whom 8,000 were over military age. A large number of underage boys also helped man the fishing craft, with 4,000 of the fishermen being under the age for conscription.[22]

Over the course of the war, 675 British fishing vessels were destroyed or captured due to enemy action and 434 fishermen lost their lives.[23] But despite the drain of manpower and the losses incurred, Britain never ran out of fish to eat, even if the price in lives and suffering was high.

7: Life on Board

Sea fishermen were (and are) a tough breed, used to harsh weather, difficult conditions and hard lying. 'As hard and as rugged as granite,' thought one naval commentator 'tough in body and spirit … fearless, inured to discomfort, contemptuous of danger.'[1]

This was no more so than at the beginning of the war. The men who began to flow into the RNR(T) and then go to war were not navy men; they were unused to drill and discipline, spit and polish, and taking orders. And the cultural, social and attitudinal gulf between working fishermen and many Royal Navy officers was enormous.

Even seafaring technique was different; fishermen used knots to join a wire, whereas the navy spliced them and many trawlermen had to learn this new (to them) method. Knots were in fact dangerous in minesweeping for the mine might catch on one in the sweep; and the sweep could break several times in the course of a day's work.

Moreover, subjecting them to fierce naval discipline raised very considerable resentment, in both directions. Captain Humphrey Wykeham Bowring, in charge of the Dover Patrol drifters for most of the war, thought that 'the skippers, as a whole, are good competent men … the mates on the contrary are mostly unreliable, ill-educated … who are evidently in their current position owing to want of ambition or ability'.[2] And the SNO at Jarrow reported that some skippers of the Tyne auxiliary patrol 'do their best to get into harbour on the slightest pretext'.[3]

Nor were they keen on uniforms. Some skippers went to sea wearing a bowler hat and a tweed suit, as they had in civilian life, but adorned with navy-issue brass buttons (see chapter 2).

Largely uneducated, many skippers and crews could not read navigational charts; like the natives of far off Samoa – once called the Navigation Islands after the almost superhuman facility of their natives to navigate at sea without any external aids – they used their senses and long familiarity to sail to and around their fishing grounds. Indeed, more than a few fishermen were illiterate, unable even to tell the time from a clock. The flag captain to Admiral Sir Hedworth Meux, CinC Portsmouth, Richard Greville Arthur Wellington Stapleton-Cotton, observed that no more than a tenth of his skippers and mates 'knew anything about charts'.[4] But, as one senior skipper, admitting he could not read a chart, told his CO, Commander Charles Courtenay Bell, 'I'll go anywhere in the North Sea if you give me its bearing and distance from somewhere I know.'[5]

Skippers were by and large experienced sailors and fishermen, and with master's certificates. 'Top skippers were hunters at heart: but more than hunters, they were also resourceful leaders who combined an intimate knowledge of the sea and of the fishing grounds with an ability to get the best out of the ships and crews under their command. … they also needed to return to port with a catch that made money for owners and crew alike. Every trip was heavily dependent upon their expertise and leadership skills.'[6]

But such qualifications did not necessarily bring status with it when these men joined the auxiliary patrol or minesweepers. James Milne, John Main and David Ralph, all of Nairn, were qualified skippers and Milne was in fact in charge of a boom defence trawler. All were members of the RNVR (Section Y), in which fishermen were enrolled for service in the RNR(T) when required.[*] In 1918 they were ordered to join up but were forced to serve as ordinary seamen. This caused them no little displeasure and their case was raised in the Commons by Sir Archibald Williamson, their local MP. He received the response '[It] is not the practice to enter such men direct in the Trawler Section as skippers, as they must first be tried under service and war conditions, but their qualifications are noted at the time of entry, and if found suitable they receive early advancement'.[7] Command still had to be earned.

For the very best skippers, a new rank was introduced in 1917, that of chief skipper. The very first person to be so advanced was Peter Yorston,[†] who had been the first skipper to be enrolled in the RNR(T) back in 1911. These men were put in charge of groups of trawlers, commands which previously had been the preserve of retired officers or senior grades from the RNR or RNVR. Only 60 men were given the rank, while 120 were appointed temporary chief skipper,[8] but it was nonetheless a recognition of the abilities of men from the trawling trade.

Trawler life

A trawler did not provide a luxurious living environment in peace time. In war, with extra personnel aboard, it was worse for the 'fisher-jacks'.

In civilian life, crewmen provided all their own equipment and

---

[*] Section Y of the RNVR was a method whereby professional seamen, when conscripted for war service, could continue their occupation provided that they accepted a liability to be called up for sea service. It reduced the likelihood of skilled seafarers being conscripted into the army and kept men out fishing to provide food for the country's tables.

[†] Chief Skipper Yorston was awarded the DSC in September 1918 for 'Services in the Auxiliary Patrol, Minesweeping and Coastal Motor Boats, between the 1st January and 30th June, 1918' (*London Gazette*, no 30909, 17 September 1918).

25. Conditions on board the trawlers were cramped in the extreme. Here sailors wash their clothes on deck using a bucket and a basin. (© Imperial War Museum Q 18998)

there was generally nowhere to stow it. Typically, deckhands and trimmers slept in the tiny forecastle with a small stove to keep them warm and dry their gear. There was no water supply and no toilet facilities. The second engineer, firemen, cook and galley boy (if carried) bedded down in the coffin-like spaces around the edge of the saloon, over the propeller. The mate and chief engineer each had a miniscule cabin off the same saloon. Neither cabin nor saloon had washing or WC facilities. The skipper had a small room under the bridge, with water and other means of easement. But this usually doubled as the chart room. The sole lavatory for the crew was right aft on the main open deck. It also housed the liver boiling plant. The most important man aboard was the cook, who produced barely edible food from a miniscule central galley stove, which smoked and stank all day and night.

In short, it was not a pleasant life.

It became even less salubrious when the fishing boats joined the navy. Firstly, there was the danger. Captain Wilfred Montague Bruce RNR (Senior Naval Officer Lowestoft in 1919) commented that 'as a general rule there was little to disturb the monotony of the grim

routine … twelve days at sea and four in harbour, in all weathers. The prospect of death and mutilation must always have been in the minds of the crew.'[9]

Indeed, coming under fire for the first time was a frightening experience. Trawler *Loch Broom* came under Turkish artillery fire at Gabe Tepe on 3 June 1915. One shell struck their small rowing boat, carried on through the trawler's deck and was brought to rest by the stern post – 'which was a good job or we would have been sunk', thought deckhand James Clarke.[10] One crewman was wounded in the leg by shrapnel but there were no fatalities. 'It was the first time we have been hit with a shell', wrote Clarke, 'and I hope it will be the last.'[11]

Then there was the pressure of accommodation to consider. All trawlers had to carry additional men, signalmen, gunners and the like. Often a fish hold was converted into a living and sleeping space, airless and dark, while the second hold would contain extra coal.

And there were often additional passengers to care for. The drifter *Bracoden* had a crew of twelve men. But there were also a Jack Russell terrier, a kitten and a caged bird on board; two of them were probably useful in keeping rats at bay.

Initially no wireless telegraphy (W/T) operators were carried and communication to land was by homing pigeons kept on board for the purpose. At Grimsby, a special loft was established where local pigeon fanciers could donate their birds which were then allocated out to each trawler as required. From 1915, W/T operators began to join the burgeoning crews, usually young RNVR men who had been especially trained up in wireless telegraphy. There was a shortage of such qualified personnel throughout the war.

The *W S Bailey* was a 200-ton ex-Hull trawler H546, fitted out as a Q-ship and based at Granton, with three hidden guns, including a 4in and a 12pdr. She carried a crew of thirty, all of whom lived in the only large cabin which was filled with sleeping bunks. In the room's centre stood an iron stove, always red-hot and on which men cooked their food as they came off watch. As part of her disguise she had to trawl for real and the crew ate fish for breakfast, lunch and dinner, the cooking smells of which filled the room. Signalman Harry Chadwick-Smith RNVR recalled that the 'atmosphere was hot and fuggy and saturated with the smell of cooking fat. Most of the bunks were tenanted by loathsome bed-bugs and then jumping fleas.'[12] Ventilation was provided by a small, yard-square, opening in the ceiling against which rested a ladder, the only means of entrance or exit.

At least they had ready access to food, unlike the men on the destroyers and other small naval ships. A reporter quoted the master of a (trawler) minesweeper who was asked whether he was not anxious to get back to his fishing. '"Fishing?" he exclaimed, "why we fish all the time!"'[13] Sweeping for mines, it appeared, was no bar to handling the usual trawl net at the same time.

Cooks were a troublesome breed. No sort of naval discipline seemed to regularise the relationship between a skipper and his cook. Lieutenant Boucher recalled many occasions of *Halcyon*'s doctor patching up cook or skipper or both after a fight. 'The galleys of trawlers are small and not easy to move about in', he recollected, 'so the cook, being on his own ground usually won … never assault a cook in his own kitchen. Have it out with him on deck.'[14] And one officer recalled attempting to shame his cook in the Aberdeen-registered trawler *Dreadnought II*. While firing at an overhead Zeppelin he 'double-shotted the [6pdr] gun with his suet dumplings which we had been unable to eat for dinner'.[15]

And it should never be forgotten that these crews were human beings with human failings, and the ordinary desires and behaviours of mankind. The Hull-registered, 12pdr-armed, trawler *Lord Minto*, in harbour at Dover, recorded in her log book for 25 June 1915; 'R Lewis, cook, left ship by Skipper's orders to fetch provisions; failed to return on board till 5.00am Saturday morning; spent night in guard ship; reported to base, and ordered by Commander Rigg RN

to refund £1–15s* from his wages to crew, which he had spent and wasted from crew's money with which he had been entrusted to buy provisions.'[16]

Another sort of human frailty was shown by two deckhands on the hired drifter *Girl Annie*, based at Dover though Yarmouth registered and fitted with a 6pdr high-angle anti-aircraft gun. Tiring of an evening's entertainment at the Dover Hippodrome they saw, through the window of the gallery, a cask of beer sitting temptingly below them. Scrambling out and sliding down the drainpipe they opened the door of the yard and were able to roll the barrel towards the harbour and their vessel. This proved thirsty work and so about halfway there they tapped the cask and, in the absence of glasses, drank up from an old paint tin. Their pleasure was considerably reduced by the arrival of the local constabulary and the evening ended in the police station cells.[17]

And there was the weather. Chadwick-Smith also served on a smaller Grimsby trawler, 'a mere cockleshell of a boat', escorting convoys from Scotland across the North Sea; 'gales blew most of the time force 8, force 9, force 10 and waves up to forty feet in height, and all this had to be endured on a 100 ton fishing trawler' he recalled.[18]

Trawlers and their crews often served away from Britain. It was policy that they should be rotated home after two years' foreign service. That this did not always happen was evidenced in a question asked in the House of Commons in 1918 by Sir Frances Blake MP, member for the fishing community of Berwick-upon-Tweed. He noted that 'many men of our trawler crews have been serving in foreign waters for two and a half to three years without home leave' and asked 'whether some consideration can be shown to them and their families and arrangements made to enable them to come home'. In reply, he was informed that 'none of the men referred to have been on a foreign station for three years. A certain number have been abroad for two and a half years, and in these cases reliefs have been detailed. As far as circumstances permit, however, every effort is now made to relieve trawler crews regularly as soon as they have completed two years abroad.'[19]

Nontheles, in practice the rule seemed to be often ignored. William Oliver, in peacetime a trawler skipper from Hull, served three years and four months in Malta, commanding a minesweeping Dundee trawler, *Marion* (mined and sunk off Malta in February 1918), and then another anti-mine vessel, *Kymric,* ex-Grimsby. He was there for so long that he sent for his wife and children to join him on the island.

Most of the fishermen just wanted the war to end and to go home. On New Year's Eve 1915, James Clarke of *Loch Broom* confided to his diary 'that finished another year with the navy blue and I wish it was finished all together, fed up'. He didn't get his wish; a year later to the day resignation had set in: 'still here but they have been very good today and let us stop at anchor'.[20]

---

* Around £175 in 2020 money!

8: Fishing Heroes and Memory

'During the whole of my time at Dover, the officers and fishermen of the trawler patrol … showed great fortitude and a fine spirit by implicit obedience to orders, zeal, and devotion to duty. No call was made to them without obtaining their most willing and ready response, and it is with pride that I recall the memory of having had such a splendid body of officers and men under my command.'[1] Thus spoke Admiral Reginald Bacon of his time commanding the Dover Patrol. The fishermen of the minesweeping and anti-U-boat forces were not militarily trained or necessarily so inclined. They were ordinary men who, on occasion, did extraordinary things.

In 1917 alone, eleven skippers were awarded the DSC, while forty-eight second hands, engineers and deckhands received the DSM. Seventeen skippers and forty-four other ranks were mentioned in despatches. Two more skippers received the DSC for actions with submarines, one deckhand the DSM for the same and five skippers were mentioned in despatches for anti-U-boat activity. All were RNR(T). And two fishermen were awarded the country's highest decoration for bravery, the Victoria Cross.

'This mad united resistance'

The Otranto Barrage (see chapter 5) comprised 120 net drifters and some 30 motor launches. Although history proves that it was of limited value in the prevention of U-boat movements, it was a clear and present irritation to the Austro-Hungarian forces who repeatedly picked at it with small raids; four such attacks were made in March and April 1917.

But on the night of the 14/15 May, the Austrians made a more determined assault. Three light cruisers, *Novara*, *Saida* and *Helgoland,* of modern construction and mounting twenty-seven 10cm (3.9in) guns between them, were detailed to attack the barrage, which was comprised that evening of forty-seven steam drifters arranged in eight divisions of six. Each cruiser took a third of the drifter line and opened fire on it, having first given the crews the opportunity to escape in their boats. Some did; but unbelievably, most chose to stand and fight with their motley collection of 3pdr, 6pdr and the occasional 12pdr, guns.

Admirable's crew only abandoned ship, and their one 3pdr pea-shooter, after the boiler blew up and the wheelhouse had been shot away. Even then her second hand, Adam Gordon, went back aboard and fought their weapon until he was killed. Meanwhile, the Austrian *Novara* came to within 100 yards of the Fraserburgh drifter *Gowan Lea*, mounting a 6pdr gun, and ordered her to abandon.

Gowan Lea's captain, Skipper Joseph Watt RNR, had other ideas.

Thirty-years-old and born in Gamrie, Banffshire, his father had been drowned at sea when Joseph was only nine. His mother moved to Fraserburgh and Joseph went to sea to earn his living. At the outbreak of war, he was skipper and part owner of the motor drifter *Annie*. The sea was his trade and in his blood. And he was not to be bullied around. As soon as he heard the firing, Watt slipped his nets, ordered full speed ahead and called for three cheers from his crew before engaging the shocked cruiser with his 6pdr. Under heavy fire from their opponent, the drifter's crew struggled to get their weapon to fire again, the breech having been struck by a round from the cruiser, and another caused a box of ammunition on deck to explode, shattering the gun layer's leg and peppering his face with splinters. *Novara* steamed on through the line, convinced that the little drifter was sinking after being hit by four of her rounds. But she was still under way and put alongside another drifter, Great Yarmouth-based *Floandi*,* many of whose crew were already dead or dying. Watt's men rendered what assistance they could, taking off the wounded, and eventually limped into Otranto harbour. Fourteen drifters were lost in the attack, and three damaged, with seventy-two men taken prisoner and thirteen men killed. But the barrier was protected and held. The Austrians called the defiance of the drifters 'this mad united resistance'.[2]

The driftermen won five DSCs, a bar to a DSC, five CGMs, eighteen DSMs and a bar to a DSM in the action. And Skipper Joseph Watts was awarded the Victoria Cross, receiving his medal from King George V at Buckingham Palace on 6 April 1918. The citation read; 'For most conspicuous gallantry when the Allied Drifter Line in the straits of Otranto was attacked by Austrian light cruisers on the morning of the 15 May 1917'.[3] Watts and several other fishermen were also invested with the Italian silver and bronze medals by King Victor Emmanuel III of Italy.†

After the war, Watt returned to herring fishing in his own steam drifter, *Benachie*. A quotidian fisherman, but a hero too.

'I'm done, throw me overboard'

Throughout the war, German U-boats preyed on the small fishing smacks which plied their trade around the British coast. Sail powered and generally defenceless, they made easy targets and their loss or harassment served to deplete the nation's food stocks. Somewhat

* Six of whose crew died.
† Watts died in 1955. His medals were sold at auction in 2012 by Spink of London for £204,000.

reluctantly, the Admiralty started to hide armed vessels amongst the sailing smacks, small Q-ships generally only armed with a 3pdr and some rifles. One such vessel was *I'll Try*, commanded by Skipper Thomas Crisp RNR, a forty-one-year-old Lowestoft man, and a fisherman and sailor since boyhood. In company with *Boy Alfred*, Skipper Walter Samuel Wharton, Crisp had his first taste of action when, on 1 February 1917 (the day the Germans once more declared unrestricted submarine warfare), the two vessels came upon a U-boat which ordered them to abandon ship; and another U-boat surfaced nearby. When one of the U-boats was close enough, Wharton opened fire and hit the conning tower; both submerged and Crisp stalked the wounded submarine and then pretended to turn for home. At this point, as Crisp had hoped, the U-boat again surfaced and *I'll Try* opened fire, claiming a probable hit. Thomas Crisp was awarded the DSC for the presumed sinking of the submarine and Wharton a bar to his pre-existing one. But in fact no U-boat was lost on that day.

Both smacks were renamed to try to preserve their anonymity and *I'll Try* became *Nelson*, its crew augmented with two regular navy seamen and a Royal Marine rifleman, making ten, including Crisp's son Tom. *Boy Alfred* became *Ethel and Millie*. They were again working together on 14 August, near the Jim Howe Bank,* and had just pulled in a catch when at 1445 Skipper Crisp sighted a submarine some three to four miles away, emerging from the afternoon mist. He just about had time to shout 'sub oh, clear for action' when the first shell fell 100yds off *Nelson*'s port bow. German submarine commanders were by now aware of Q-ship decoy tactics and no longer stopped British merchant shipping before sinking them, it being expedient and safer to sink such vessels from a distance with gunfire.

The range was too great for Crisp's boat to reply and he held his fire hoping to draw the submarine in. But the U-boat's fourth shell holed *Nelson* below the water line and the seventh hit Thomas Crisp himself, shattering both his legs at the hips and partially disembowelling him. Somehow, the skipper still managed to give the order to open fire anyway and release the ship's carrier pigeons with the message '*Nelson* being attacked by submarine. Skipper killed. Jim Howe Bank. Send assistance at once.' The U-boat turned away and fired at *Ethel and Millie* while *Nelson* shot off her ammunition locker; when there were only five shells left, Crisp ordered the crew to abandon ship as *Nelson* settled by the bows.

Son Tom asked his father if they should take him to the life boat. 'No, Tom, I'm done,' Crisp replied, 'Throw me overboard.'[4] He died in his son's arms moments later and was left to go down with his ship. After two days drifting at sea, the survivors were picked up by the fishery protection vessel *Dryad*, alerted by the arrival of one of the messenger pigeons, named Red Cock.

The crew of *Ethel and Millie* then abandoned their battered boat and were taken aboard the German submarine, where the *Nelson*'s

* Shoals off the Norfolk coast.

26. The memorial to Skipper Thomas Crisp VC in Lowestoft Cemetery. (author's collection)

survivors last saw them standing in line being addressed by a German officer. The seven crew were never seen again. Opinion at the time was that they were killed and dumped overboard by the U-boat crew or abandoned at sea without supplies.

Skipper Crisp was awarded the VC, gazetted on 2 November 1917.[5] Son Tom received the DSM. It was a time of great concern regarding the progress of the war, and on 29 October 1917, Earl Curzon of Kedleston, Lord President of the Council, used Crisp's sacrifice in a wide-ranging morale-boosting speech in the House of Lords. He noted that Crisp's actions were representative of the Royal Navy's commitment and in his encomium stated that 'though armed only with a 3pdr gun and outranged by her opponent, she refused to haul down her flag even when the skipper had both his legs shot off and most of the crew were killed or wounded. "Throw the confidential books overboard and throw me after them," the skipper said; and, refusing to leave his ship when the few survivors took to the boats, he went down with her.'[6] It made Crisp into a posthumous celebrity whose story ran in all the major papers for a week, an uplifting story of personal sacrifice, filial devotion and probable German barbarity.

And the pigeon Red Cock had place of honour at the East London Federation of Homing Pigeons Show in December 1921.

Understatement

Courage comes in many forms and trawlermen and their vessels took part in countless deeds of bravery and selflessness, of which a very small number are related below.

Understatement typified much of the heroism displayed in the war. Fifty-two-year-old Lieutenant Herbert Basil Boothby RNR, the great-grandson of the 7th Baronet Boothby of Broadlow Ash, was in command of the minesweeping trawler *Orianda*, once of Grimsby, sweeping for mines off Scarborough where the light cruiser *Kolberg* had laid them on 16 December 1914, under cover of the infamous 'Scarborough Raid'. On the 19th, at 1100, the *Orianda* struck a mine while travelling at her full speed. She immediately filled with water and sank like a brick; but Boothby managed to get all his men safely off the ship bar one RNR(T) deckhand.

By 6 January 1915, Boothby was back at work, in command of another ex-Grimsby trawler, *The Banyers*, when it too was shattered by an exploding mine. Boothby was thrown against the wheelhouse roof by the blast and stunned. He owed his life to the ship's cook who put his own lifebelt on his recumbent captain and helped him leave the sinking ship by the wheelhouse window. Two of the crew were lost, fifty-nine -year-old RNR(T) Second Hand Thomas Strickland from Boston and Albert William Thirkettle, a deckhand.

Boothby survived to return once more to minesweeping, which he stuck at for the rest of the war. He was awarded the DSO for his service in the February after his second sinking[7] and afterwards wrote that he got it 'for losing two ships'.[8]

As for the Scarborough minefield, sweeping operations by the trawlers continued over the next month and some fifty-three mines were swept from the area; but twenty others succeeded in claiming victims.

Runo

On 5 September 1914, the Wilson Line steamer *Runo* was mined off the Tyne with 237 passengers and 33 crew on board. As she settled by the head, the passengers rushed the boats, which were launched. At 1810, her second officer and members of the crew returned to the ship and she was taken in tow by the trawler, *Euripides*. Only six of her nine lifeboats had been lowered; some capsized due to overcrowding and many passengers remained on board the stricken liner. But *Runo* was clearly doomed and the tow was abandoned. Instead, skipper Ambrose Fisher of *Euripides* and Frederick Woolaston of *Cameo*, both Hull vessels, took their little ships to the starboard and port quarters of the sinking vessel and took off the passengers, including all the women and children. In this they were assisted by the trawlers *Silanion*, *Straton* and *Prince Victor*, all from Grimsby. Only twenty-nine souls were lost in the sinking; it would have been so many more without the intervention of the fishermen. *Runo* sank at 1830; the rescue had been carried out in less than twenty minutes.

Their selflessness was rewarded with the presentation by King George V of the Silver Medal for Saving Life at Sea to all the skippers involved. Both *Euripides* and *Cameo* were taken up by the Admiralty, as patrol vessel and minesweeper respectively in 1915.

Providence

Not all fisherman heroes became so through direct encounter with the enemy or his weapons of war. On 1 January 1915 the pre-dreadnought battleship *Formidable* (1898) was torpedoed by *U-24* off the Jurassic coast of Lyme Bay. From her crew of 780, 583 men and boys died. Of the survivors, seventy-one owed their lives to the courage of a fisherman and his sail-powered fishing boat.

They were in the battleship's 34ft cutter; most of the oars had been smashed and a gale force storm was raging. With great difficulty the men on board managed to get clear of the sinking battleship before she sucked them down with her and they used the remaining oars to keep the boat's head to the wind. For hours they were rowing incessantly. The waves constantly threatened to swamp the boat. They sang 'Tipperary' but could not keep it up for long. It seemed that at the end of every line a giant wave would wash over them.

The boat became badly holed. The mast had been carried away so the boathook was pressed into service as a substitute and a black silk muffler attached to the top as a makeshift signal flag. One sailor clung to it like grim death for several hours to keep it erect. But their small vessel, battered by gale force winds and massive waves, continued to drift to the south and west until at approximately 0930 they were 15 miles from Berry Head where providence intervened. They were spotted by a Brixham sailing trawler, *Provident*, seventy-five feet long and weighing fifty tons, skippered by William Pillar with his crew of four (see plate 27).

Pillar, thirty-years-old, married and the owner of *Provident*, was an experienced seaman and second coxswain of the Torbay lifeboat. He had participated in many rescues. Now he would face his biggest ever challenge. *Provident* had been running for shelter in the teeth of the gale and in mountainous seas and had hove to when his third hand, John Clarke, sighted the cutter. In flailing wind Clarke shinned up the rigging to get a better look and then reported to Pillar that there was a boat in trouble. As a lifeboat man, and as a fellow sailor, William Pillar knew that he had no choice but to attempt a rescue.

As *Provident* approached the boat Pillar could see that it was full of water and leaking badly. He had to act quickly and in doing so showed magnificent seamanship. With upmost difficulty he gybed his trawler and manoeuvred to windward, trying to get the cutter into the shelter of his lee. Eventually, after four attempts and nearly three hours of trying, he managed to get a line on board the little boat. Using his capstan, Pillar was able to haul the launch round to the trawler's stern, enabling the sailors to begin to jump on board. Constant waves, some thirty feet high, made the task both extremely

dangerous and difficult; it took half an hour to get all the men onto the trawler, but he did it. As the last man left the cutter, it broke up and sank. But for William Pillar, all seventy-one men would have been dead.

Still, the fight was not yet over for Pillar. He and his crew then battled for six hours through the horrendous weather, reaching Brixham at 1900. There he anchored in the outer harbour and rowed ashore to report the rescue to the coastguard and arrange for the tug *Dencade* to help him reach the landing stage, where the survivors were put ashore.

Pillar's magnificent seamanship was recognised through the award of the Board of Trade Sea Gallantry Medal for Bravery and a sum of £250 from the Admiralty. He felt he was doing what any fisherman would have done, stating 'we only did our duty as every Englishman would do and I think that every Brixham fisherman would do the same'.[9]

It was not the end of Pillar's encounter with the dogs of war. On 28 November 1916 he and the rest of the Brixham fishing fleet were attacked off the South Devon coast by a German submarine. *Provident* was the first ship to be brought under fire of the surfaced vessel's gun and the initial shot brought down her jib and a second cut her topsail halyards. Pillar and his crew hastily launched a small boat and fled as twenty further shots and some sort of grenade from close range completely destroyed his trawler. The Germans next turned their fire on Pillar and his men in their tiny craft but fortunately missed.

Pillar was made a temporary skipper in the RNR(T) and later commanded the armed trawler *Concord II*. He survived the war.

Tribute

Throughout the war, the exploits of the fishermen warriors gained public approbation. Speaking in the House of Commons on 7 March 1916 in a debate regarding the Naval Estimates, First Lord Arthur Balfour paid tribute to the work of the armed trawlers and drifters:

> the mine sweepers, the armed trawlers, the vast numbers of men who, alone and unsupported in circumstances of great difficulty, often of great peril, have done work of incalculable value for the country. I am afraid I cannot do justice to all that I feel about the work of these men. Necessarily it is little known to the public. They do not work in the presence of great bodies of men, who can admire and applaud them for their gallantry. Small crews, in stormy seas, suddenly face to face with unexpected peril, they never seem to me to fail. No danger, no difficulty, is too great for them to overcome. To them the debt of this country is almost incalculable.[10]

(Left) 27. A typical Brixham fishing smack, very similar to William Pillar's *Provident*. (author's collection)

A year later Earl Curzon included the fisher-jacks in a tribute to the minesweepers and patrol vessel naval forces in general:

> Equally wonderful is the record of the auxiliary naval services, which have been expanded to an extraordinary degree to meet the changes that have occurred in maritime warfare by the development of the mine and the submarine. I allude more especially to the mine-sweepers and the patrol vessels. Over 3,300 vessels are now engaged on these duties. At the beginning of the war there were twelve. They are out in all weathers, day and night, searching and sweeping for mines, patrolling the coastal routes, escorting merchant traffic, hunting the enemy submarines. It is impossible to imagine a more arduous or a more dangerous duty. Never a day but they may be in contact with a mine or torpedo; never a week but some of them are sent to the bottom; yet in all this time of stress not a single man has asked to be relieved, and if one man is lost scores leap forward to take his place'.[11]

But perhaps Admiral Reginald Bacon, who had command of many fishermen when in charge of the Dover Patrol, and who was always unshakably certain that his own opinions were ironclad truth, put it best:

> Someday, the people of this country will realise, not merely repeat as they do occasionally, parrot-like, in vague platitudes, the debt they owe to our irregular sea forces. Then they will never pass a merchant sailor or deep-sea fisherman except with a warming of the heart, and a genuine feeling of pride in their brotherhood with the sea-faring population of these islands.[12]

Service and memory

By the end of the First World War, 1,467 steam trawlers, had been hired or requisitioned for naval service, as had their crews.[13] Some 83 per cent of them were estimated by the navy to have served as minesweepers at one point in their wartime career.[14] The Admiralty themselves built 453 trawlers and 300 vessels were taken into the Fishery Reserve.

Additionally, 1,502 steam drifters and 118 motor drifters (the latter largely from Scottish ports) were hired by the Royal Navy, primarily for use in anti-submarine net duty. Lowestoft (323), Banff (299), and Yarmouth (181) provided the highest numbers but altogether thirty ports supplied vessels.[15] Admiralty-built drifters added another 318 to the total.

And seventeen hired or seized whalers, together with fifteen Admiralty purchased ones, served.

Between 1914 and 1919, 54,000 warrant skippers and men passed through the RNR(T) and at the Armistice its strength was 37,145 men.[16] Apart from the two VCs, 2,238 officers and men of the Trawler Section were granted honours and awards by the British and Allied Governments.[17]

During the course of the conflict, 246 hired trawlers and 18 Admiralty-built vessels were destroyed, together with 130 hired drifters, representing a total of 71,828grt.[18] Additionally two whalers were sunk. The worst year for sinkings was 1917, the year of the greatest German U-boat and mining efforts, when ninety-one Admiralty and hired trawlers together with forty-two hired drifters were lost* (see appendix 6).

The human cost totalled 3,338 skippers and men.[19] This understates the deaths of all fishermen, for many had joined the general RNR and served and died on ships other than armed fishing vessels.† They are remembered on many war memorials up and down the land. Amongst them is the magnificent Merchant Sailors and Fishermen Memorial at Tower Hill, London, dedicated on 12 December 1928 and designed by Sir Edwin Lutyens, with sculpture by Sir William Reid-Dick. It commemorates the almost 12,000 Merchant Marine and fishermen casualties who have no grave but the sea.

The trawlermen minesweepers have a share in a memorial at Dovercourt, near Harwich too. It was unveiled on 20 December 1919 and is dedicated to the officers and men of the Royal Naval Reserve, Royal Naval Volunteer Reserve, Auxiliary Reserve and Minesweepers. Three large bronze panels have the names of the fallen and their vessels embossed onto them, while a fourth carries a dedication, which reads: 'To the Glory of God and in proud memory of the officers and men of the Royal Naval Reserve & Royal Naval Volunteer Reserve serving in the Auxiliary Patrol & Minesweepers at Harwich who died in the performance of their duties that the sea might be made free …'

In Grimsby, the artist Arthur Sherwood Edwards designed a memorial tablet for the Bethel Mission at Tiverton Street. It recorded 1,043 names of fisherfolk and minesweeper crews who perished, inscribed on a large marble tablet divided into three sections. The central section bears a bas relief carving of a widow and her child, and the outer sections carry the dedicatory inscription and list the names of the fallen. In the background a trawler was carved. It was unveiled on Remembrance Day 1920.

At the other end of the scale, The Fishermen's Bethel at Lowestoft installed an arched-shaped brass plaque with black lettering on a wooden mount with just eleven names, fishermen members of the congregation who fell in the war.

Even in the twenty-first century, a First World War RNR fisherman was honoured, if only transiently. Giant sand portraits of people who died during the Great War were created on thirty beaches across the UK's coastline as part of film director Danny Boyle's 'Pages of the Sea' project, only to be washed away again when the tide came in. One trawlerman was included. On 11 November 2018 at Ynyslas Beach in Ceredigion, Wales, the image made was that of Richard Davies RNR, from the Welsh coastal town of Borth, one of fifteen men killed when the minesweeping trawler *Evangel*, once from Grimsby, hit a mine and sank in the St George's Channel on 25 March 1917.

The contribution to the war effort made by British fisherfolk and their vessels between 1914 and 1918 was enormous and their impact on the outcome of the war at sea should not be underestimated. They were the main part of the so-called Auxiliary Patrol and the minesweeping forces – yachts, fishing boats, whalers, paddle steamers, ferries – all taken up by the navy and used to protect the seaways of empire.

---

* As noted in chapter 6, there were also 675 unarmed British fishing vessels lost or captured due to enemy action and 434 fishermen killed (*British Vessels Lost at Sea*, Section 2, p163).

† In 1937 the Admiralty estimated that 53,160 fishermen had served in all branches of the RNR (ADM 116/3367, NA).

Part Two

The Second World War

9: Between the Wars, 1919–1939

The First World War ended on 11 November 1918; except that for many of the trawlers, drifters and fighting fishermen it didn't.

Amongst the first priorities was the clearance of the many minefields that surrounded the British coastline, and elsewhere. Britain was one of twenty-six countries represented on an International Mine Clearance Committee dedicated to clearing 40,000 square miles of sea of leftover mines. Each power was allotted an area to clear. Around Britain, 'during the war no less than 1,360 minefields or groups of mines were laid by the Germans in proximity to our coast, … in waters abroad to be cleared by the British about sixty fields or groups, totalling some 1,200 mines, … while British mines, which had also to be swept up, numbered about 65,000 in home waters and 8,000 in the Mediterranean'.[1]

Experienced minesweeping sailors were asked to volunteer for another twelve months' service with the promise that they would only be engaged in peaceful mine clearance, not martial activities. A special 'Mine Clearance Service' was formed to this end with its own badge – 'His Majesty the King's Mine Clearance Badge'* – which was presented to each volunteer, and an increased weekly pay supplement was awarded. This was particularly necessary for the fishermen as they would otherwise have returned to fishing where, for the moment, they could earn four times as much as a rating in the RNR(T). Some 600 officers and 15,000 men served in this fashion, including many trawlers and fisherfolk, with service to expire automatically on 30 November 1919.

One of the key clearance priorities was the North Sea Mine Barrage, laid in 1918 at American insistence and largely using American mines and minelayers. Over 70,000 mines had been laid and these now had to be swept up. The mission was under US control but the British chartered twenty minesweeping trawlers to the Americans, all Admiralty-built vessels. These were the *Strath*-class *William Ashton*, *George Burton*, *Pat Caharty*, *John Clay*, *John Dunkin*, *John Fitzgerald*, *Thomas Graham* and *Thomas Henrix*; the *Castle*-class *George Clarke*, *Thomas Blackhorne*, *Thomas Buckley*, *William Caldwell*, *George Cochran*, *John Collins*, *William Darnold*, *Sam Duffy*, *John Graham* and *Thomas Laundry*; and the *Mersey*-class *Richard Bulkeley* and *William Johnson*.

George Cochran was typical of the twenty. She was commissioned into the USN on 28 May 1919 at Grimsby Naval Base, with Lieutenant (junior grade) R C Thompson, USNRF, in command. Departing Falmouth 29 May, *George Cochran* commenced her minesweeping duties with the North Sea Minesweeping Detachment, based in Kirkwall Bay. She and her sisters swept behind the main line, picking up stray mines and dropping danbuoys to mark safe channels for five weeks.

But the trawlers' hulls had not been designed or built to withstand repeated underwater shocks from the exploding mines, and leaks

28. An example of a Mine Clearance Service badge. (author's collection)

and damage soon became apparent. Proving unsatisfactory for the task, most of them were returned to the Admiralty. *George Cochran* departed Kirkwall for Brightlingsea, arriving 9 August, where she was decommissioned and returned to the Royal Navy on 11 August 1919.§

Nor did the dying end with the conclusion of the war. On 4 January 1919, the hired trawler *Glenboyne*, from Fleetwood, was clearing a minefield off Folkestone when she struck a drifting mine, broke up and sank in less than a minute. Two men were killed, a stoker and an engineman. Those working below seldom survived a rapid sinking. A month later, on 1 February, the Great Yarmouth drifter *John Robert* sailed from Mersina (south-east Turkey) and was never seen again. Skipper John Stewart and his eight crew were lost, all RNR(T) bar an RNVR signalman. In April, the ex-Russian *Frostaxe* was sunk in a collision in the Mediterranean when nine men were lost.

And the Admiralty steel drifter *Catspaw* was lost in a dreadful storm on 30 December. After service in the Baltic campaign against the Bolshevik navy and under the command of twenty-one-year-old Acting Lieutenant Rowland Reynolds she left Reval on 28 December, bound for Copenhagen and then back to Blighty. On passage she picked up two sub lieutenants, Geoffrey Williams and

---

* A mine in the centre of a circle surrounded by laurel leaves, surmounted by a crown, motto on lower badge 'Mine-Clearance Service'. It was worn on the left sleeve (see plate 28).

§ She was sold out of the navy in 1920.

Frederick Vallings, and some ratings, all of whom had been manning a forward signalling station. During the night of the 30th, in the midst of appalling weather, *Catspaw* disappeared. All fourteen men on board died, three officers and eleven ratings. They died when the Baltic campaign was effectively over, returning to the home they so desperately wanted to see.

The RNR(T) was finally wound up on 30 April 1920 as part of the downsizing of the post-war navy which would be accelerated from 1921 onwards by the so-called 'Geddes Axe' of government expenditure cuts. By then, most of the Admiralty-built trawlers had been sold into trade and all of the requisitioned vessels returned to their owners.

But trawlers still had a part to play. At the 1921 Imperial Conference, two Admiralty-built trawlers became the foundation of a nascent South African navy. It was agreed that South Africa should cease to pay its £85,000 contribution to the cost of the Royal Navy and instead build its own naval force on a permanent basis. The Admiralty loaned the trawlers *Foyle* (Goole-built *Mersey*-class, originally *John Edmund*, one 12pdr) and *Eden* (Cochrane-built, *Mersey*-class, originally *Thomas Johns*, 12pdr) which were renamed HMSAS *Sonneblom* and *Immortelle*,[*] to form the beginnings of His Majesty's South African Navy, based at Simonstown.

As replacement for the RNR(T) the Admiralty created the Royal Naval Reserve Patrol Service (RNPS). A limited number of fishermen were involved and attended for training purposes the 'stone frigates' HMS *Boscawen* and HMS *Osprey*,[†] both at Portland. The Director of Torpedoes and Mining at the Admiralty expressed the need for 400

29. HMT *Cornelian* had been built as the *Cape Warwick* fishing trawler in 1933 but was acquired by the Admiralty in 1935 in the wake of the Abyssinian Crisis. She and nineteen other such acquisitions formed the Admiralty 'Gem' class. She was fitted out with a 4in gun, depth charges and ASDIC and served as a Liverpool-based convoy escort through much of the war. *Cornelian* also took part in D-Day and was sold off in 1948, becoming *Lincoln City*.

vessels and 454 skippers, together with 3,733 ratings, to be the trained establishment; this number was never reached in the inter-war years. For example, in November 1936, the Patrol Service stood at 2,457 men of which 1,518 were fishermen.[2] RNPS-enrolled skippers were paid an annual retainer of £20,[§] or £25 for chief skippers.[3] But both trawler owners and the Admiralty were lukewarm towards committing to a standing reserve trawler force, the latter for reasons of cost as much as culture.

The 1920s and 1930s were dominated by cuts in naval budgets and international treaties to limit the proliferation of naval forces. The Washington Treaty of 1922 and the Treaty of London in 1930 enforced reductions in materiel on the Royal Navy and successive governments used these to effect deep naval budget reductions. Spending money on auxiliary minesweepers, convoy escorts and the like was not considered a good use of funds; far better to ignore the learnings of the First World War and build, within the treaty limits imposed, nice shiny battleships and cruisers.

Additionally, the late 1920s and early 1930s were a time of deep economic depression ('The Great Slump') with many out of work and a sluggish economy.[β] Fishermen suffered along with everybody else. In 1932, an Aberdeen trawler skipper wrote that 'our business has been such a heart break these last few months that it is almost

---

[*] In 1992, they both featured on a specially produced South African postal cover, celebrating seventy years of the South African Navy.

[†] *Osprey* was also home to ASDIC training.

[§] Perhaps £1,400 at today's prices.

[β] Real GDP growth was negative in 1930 and fell by nearly 5 per cent in 1931. In 1932 it grew by only 0.44 per cent. Unemployment peaked at 15 per cent in 1932 and remained in double figures until 1936.

(Above) 30. The 'Gem'-class trawler HMT *Agate*, ex-*Mavis Rose*. Acquired in 1935 and fitted out as an anti-submarine vessel, she became a total loss on 6 August 1941, when she grounded off Cromer. Note the 4in gun mounted prominently forward. (author's collection)

(Right) 31. HMT *Tourmaline*, a 'Gem'-class trawler originally named *Berkshire*, was purchased in November 1935, and sunk off the North Foreland by German bombers on 5 February 1941.

32. A rather dramatic photograph of the 'Gem'-class trawler HMT *Turquoise*, launched in 1935 as *Warwickshire* but purchased by the Admiralty in the same year. In 1942 she achieved a brief moment of fame by sinking a German E-boat, for which her CO received the DSC and four crewmen were mentioned in dispatches.

impossible to take an interest in anything. What with weather, slack fishing and if we got home with a decent catch, we have nothing for it. It has been a case of set your teeth and bear it.'[4] And on New Year's Day 1937, the Fleetwood Fishing Vessel Owners Association wrote to Lord Stanley (Edward George Villiers Stanley, 17th Earl of Derby), Lord Lieutenant of Lancashire, asking for his intervention with government over their perceived plight. 'I desire to draw your Lordship's attention', wrote their president, 'to the parlous state in which the fishing industry of the country at present finds itself.'[5] In a follow-up letter three weeks later he added 'in the case of trawler owners, for the most part profits are either absent or negligible'.[6] Indeed, by the end of that year, 20 per cent of distant water trawlers were voluntarily laid up.[7]

And over the same period large numbers of herring fishermen were thrown out of work, few new drifters built and the fishing often shut down before the season ended. An Admiralty report noted that the 'drifter fleet is to be allowed to diminish until it is on an economical

and self-supporting basis … [it is] largely a poor man's industry'.[8]

Trawler owners would have welcomed some naval interest in their underutilised vessels. Sir Alec Black, who owned large trawler fleets in Grimsby and Hull, attempted to stimulate Admiralty attention in 1936. He stated that he was willing to acquire fourteen new trawlers, of a faster and more modern design, powered by diesel engines. He suggested that, if the Admiralty paid him a subsidy of £1,000 per vessel per year, he would ensure that they were built in such a way as to be readily convertible to naval operations and would incorporate any features that the Royal Navy saw fit. The discussions dragged on until 1937; but Black eventually withdrew his offer in a huff when the Admiralty proposed involving other operators, via the British Trawler Federation (with which Black had some sort of beef), in the discussions.

In general, 'approaches from trawler owners for subsidy to enable their ships to carry out escort duty were coolly received', according to Captain Stephen Roskill,[9] although by the mid-1930s the Admiralty did inspect and earmark certain trawlers, especially fifteen of those of the Mac Line of Fleetwood, for potential requisition. And other fishing vessels such as drifters were considered for minesweeping duties. Additionally, some steps were taken to reserve anti-submarine and minesweeping equipment.

In fairness, the criticism that the Admiralty has subsequently received for the decision to neglect smaller vessels could be construed as misplaced, at least to some degree. As Professor Norman Friedman has noted, 'escorts and minesweepers had little peacetime function. The battlefleet had a very real function, to deter possible attackers.'[10]

The coming to power and prominence of the dictators of Germany and Italy did not immediately change the government's or the Admiralty's stance regarding small ships. Appeasement was seen as the best policy; there was no support for rearmament until post 1935. One trigger which, at least in naval terms, changed this position was the Abyssinian Crisis.

The Abyssinian Crisis and the 'Gem'- and 'Tree'-class trawlers

Between 1934 and 1936, Mussolini's Italy planned and actioned an invasion of Abyssinia (The Empire of Ethiopia), despite objections and mild sanctions imposed by the League of Nations. Italy ignored the sanctions, resigned from the League, made special arrangements with Britain and France and ultimately annexed and occupied Abyssinia after defeating the nation in the Second Italian-Ethiopian War. The League of Nations was terminally discredited through this process.

France's motivation for caving in to Mussolini was prompted by her fear of Germany, which in March 1936 had marched into the Rhineland. Britain's reluctance to stand against the Italian dictator was the product of the fear of a two-front naval war, in the Mediterranean and in the Far East, where a bellicose Japan was thought to be waiting to take advantage of any Mediterranean distractions to attack Britain's Asian colonies, and which resources did not allow for.[*]

However, the crisis proved to be the catalyst for increases in the Naval Estimates, of 1935 and 1936. Amongst the additional items now allowed for in 1935 were twenty modern trawlers, the first time since the Great War that such expenditure had been authorised.

These trawlers, which were all purchased from trade, were named the 'Gem' class (for the anti-submarine vessels) and the 'Tree' class (for those ships intended for minesweeping duty). The classes were not homogenous, and the trawlers came from a variety of builders and sources. All were of recent construction and of an average 600grt, substantially bigger than their First World War equivalents. Originally, there were ten of each class but in 1936 a further trawler was added as a depot ship (*Vulcan*) and in 1939 they were supplemented by another twenty acquisitions, of which fifteen were designated 'Tree'-class minesweepers. Three of these, *Punnet*, *Quannet* and *Rennet* were actually used as boom defence vessels.

HMT *Cornelian* is a good example of the type. She was built by Cochrane's in Selby for the Hudson Steam Fishing Company of Hull

33. 'Gem'-class HMT *Ruby* (1933) was originally named *Cape Bathurst* and was purchased by the Admiralty in 1935. During the Second World War *Ruby* served as an anti-submarine unit. She was sold back into civilian life in 1947 as *Carella*.

in 1933 and named *Cape Warwick*. After successful trials, *Cape Warwick* was sold to the Admiralty in November 1935 and her Hull registry was closed. Renamed *Cornelian*, she was fitted with a 4in gun, depth charges and ASDIC[†] and became an anti-submarine vessel.

Cornelian and her 'Gem'-class sisters *Agate*, *Tourmaline*, *Turquoise* (ex-*Warwickshire*) and *Ruby* are depicted in plates 29–33. The plans for *Quannet* are shown at plan XI and those for the 1935 'Tree'-class *Laurel* at plan XII.

Six whalers (the 'Lake' class) were also purchased in 1939. One of these, *Ellesmere*, is pictured at plate 34. They were building at Smith's Dock when war broke out. This seems a strange decision in retrospect, given that this type had been discredited for naval use in the 1914–18 war. However, they had some advantages; they were oil burners, not coal as were all the trawlers. Additionally, they had a couple more knots of speed and a rudder like a barn door, which made them extremely manoeuvrable.

The *Bassets*: HMT *Basset* and her kin

During the 1930s, scant attention was paid to the provision of small escort vessels, as noted above. But in 1934, the Admiralty did design an ASDIC-equipped anti-submarine trawler to its own specifications 'with a view to rapid construction in an emergency'.[11] This was HMT *Basset*. Launched in 1935, she had a larger forecastle than her commercial sisters and the bridge was placed slightly more amidships. The perceived success of the type can be seen in the fact

---

[*] This fear persisted up to the outbreak of war. In January 1937, ex-First Sea Lord Admiral Ernle Chatfield wrote that 'we have to stand unsupported in both hemispheres … war simultaneously in east and west would be fatal and it must not happen' (Roskill, *Naval Policy Between the Wars*, vol II, p324).

[†] An underwater, active sound detection apparatus first fitted to RN warships in 1923 and which had been approved in the 1939 Naval Estimates.

that 250 Admiralty trawlers followed in her path with very little change to the basic design.

Built by the firm of Henry Robb Ltd (Robbs) at Leith Dock, *Basset* (plate 35) was bigger than her Great War predecessors, at 460 tons displacement, 160ft long, capable of 12 knots and home to a crew of thirty-three. Coal fired with cylindrical boilers and the sort of reciprocating machinery that would be familiar to fishermen reservists, she could make 12 knots. A generalised layout of the type is at plan XIII. The 'Tree'* and 'Dance' classes that followed her were variations on her theme.

Three years later, in May 1938, the Admiralty commissioned a larger version of *Basset*, also built by Robb, named *Mastiff*. She was a longer and heavier vessel at 163 feet and 520 tons and had an extra knot of speed. *Mastiff*'s war was to be short, for she was mined and

34. The 'Lake'-class whaler *Ellesmere* is shown her, displaying her pretty flared bow and gun. This was a six-ship class, purchased in 1939 while building at Smith's Dock (she was originally ordered by the Norwegian company Kosmos A/S a Jahre, Sandefjord), and fitted with one 12pdr, three 20mm (two superfiring ones can just be seen aft) and two 0.5in machine guns. She also carried two depth charge throwers and fifty depth charges, twice a trawler's amount. *Ellesmere* was sunk by a torpedo fired by *U-1203* on 24 February 1945, west of Brest. Thirty-seven sailors lost their lives, twenty-eight of them RNPS.

sunk in the Thames estuary on 20 November 1939, with six crew dead and nine wounded.

Also in 1938, four *Basset*-type vessels were constructed for the Royal Canadian Navy, *Comox*, *Fundy*, *Gaspé* and *Nookta*. Two were built on Canada's west coast and two on the east. They were known as the *Fundy* class and were commissioned as minesweepers, armed

* Confusingly, not the same 'Tree' class as the 1935/39 purchases.

35. Designed and built in 1935, HMT *Basset* was the Royal Navy's prototype 'ideal trawler'. Her 4in gun and subsidiary anti-aircraft armament (aft) can clearly be seen, as can the minesweeping cable drum astern. She was the model for the future Admiralty-built trawler classes. (© Imperial War Museum FL 1555) .

36. The Canadian navy HMCN *Fundy*, a *Basset*-type trawler built by Collingwood Shipbuilding of Ontario in 1938. (author's collection)

with a single 12pdr gun and two 20mm Oerlikons. Later they were also to be equipped with twenty-five depth charges. *Fundy* is depicted at plate 36.

Moreover, it became clear that better training facilities than existed at Portland were necessary. In 1938, the old destroyer base at Port Edgar, HMS *Columbine*, which had closed in 1928, was reopened – firstly as a hospital in 1938 and shortly thereafter as a naval training centre. It was specifically intended for minesweeping and trawler training and it became HMS *Lochinvar*. During the early war years, 13,000 men and 4,000 officers were to be trained here (and at nearby Granton, an old friend to naval trawlers) in minesweeping skills.

The revived interest in fishing vessels evident in the late 1930s extended to fishermen crews as well. In time of war, the Admiralty decreed, it would take a large number of fishermen into the navy, as part of an extended RNPS. The Board of Trade and the Ministry of Agriculture and Fish, however, thought fishing should be a reserved occupation, to protect the nation's ability to feed itself. This discussion continued until the Second World War had actually started.

In the end, the first Schedule of Reserved Occupations excluded all classes of fishermen from conscription, except for service in the navy. Quite a number joined the Merchant Navy or the Royal Navy of their own accord, but the policies pursued throughout much of the Second World War meant that most fishermen continued fishing until required for naval service, and those recruited were generally sent to the RNPS.

37. HMT *Fort Robert* was built in 1917 as the Admiralty *Strath*-class trawler *James Bentole*. Armed with a 12pdr gun and with a crew of 15–18, in the First World War she served as a minesweeper and then hydrophone vessel. Sold into civilian life in 1922, she was requisitioned by the navy in November 1939 and in 1940 was converted to an magnetic minesweeper. She is depicted here after her conversion back to a war footing.

September 1939

War was declared against Germany on 3 September 1939. The total trawler strength available to the Admiralty was small. Forty 'Gem'- and 'Tree'-class vessels made up the bulk of the force together with six *Basset*s; but the navy had not been completely denuded of its Great War trawlers. There were still on the books four *Axe*-class ex-Russian vessels; one *Strath*-class; two *Castle*-class; fourteen *Mersey*-class; and three *Armentières*-class belonging to the Royal Canadian Navy. The Royal Navy went to war with just seventy trawlers,[*] of which twenty were fitted with ASDIC underwater detection gear. Additionally, twenty-four Great War Admiralty-built drifters remained in service, three of which were wooden hulled. Thus, the Royal Navy had a total of ninety-four trawlers and drifters; in contrast to the approximately 3,000 that eventually served in the First World War.

The limited resources available were used to establish the 1st Anti-Submarine (A/S) group of five trawlers at Portsmouth, the 2nd A/S group of three trawlers in the Western Approaches, the 3rd A/S group of three trawlers at Rosyth and the 4th A/S group of five trawlers in the Mediterranean.

And recognising the urgent need for more small ships, the Admiralty immediately requisitioned 140 trawlers[†] and commenced fitting them out for anti-submarine service. These were joined by 30 First World War vintage ex-*Mersey*s, 125 former *Castle*s and 75 quondam *Strath*s, sold into private ownership after the first war and largely renamed, which were requisitioned back to the colours in 1939 and 1940. One such, HMT *Fort Robert*, originally built in 1917 as the Admiralty *Strath*-class trawler *James Bentole*, is shown at plates 37 and 38 in her naval and civilian guises. Another, which was not completed in time for the First World War, was the *Mersey*-class Admiralty 324grt trawler *Robert Cahill*. Delivered in 1921, too late for the war for which she was intended, she was immediately sold on into French ownership and named *Pierre Andre*, before being taken up as a minesweeper in July 1940 (see plate 39). Older ships were deployed as minesweepers, the more modern ones in the war against the U-boats.

Once again, trawlers, drifters and fishermen went to war.

---

[*] Forty *Basset* derivatives (Tree- and Dance-class) were under construction in September 1939.

[†] Thirty-five of them were requisitioned on 23 August 1939, just before war was declared (Roskill, *Naval Policy*, vol II, p482)

38. And here is *Fort Robert* in
her fishing days for comparison.

39. Shown here at anchor in the Clyde, the 'Mersey'-class Admiralty 324grt trawler *Robert Cahill* was delivered in 1921 and was immediately sold on as a fishing vessel, named *Pierre Andre*. Taken up as a minesweeper in July 1940, she was fitted with a 12pdr and a single 20mm Oerlikon, whose 'bandstands' can be clearly seen fore and aft. At one point during the Second World War she was crewed by Free French forces.

10: Of Men and Ships

Conscription applied from the beginning of the war. The 1939 Military Training Act required young men to undergo six months' training and on the first day of the war the National Service (Armed Forces) Act extended it to all men between eighteen and forty-one (although universal registration of all men and their occupations took until June 1941). By the end of 1939, over 1.5 million men were in the regular armed forces.

So, unlike the first war, the fishermen of the RNPS and RNR were joined from the start by factory hands, clerks, shopkeepers and businessmen who had to be trained in the ways of the seas.

Sparrow's Nest

As war loomed, the Admiralty urgently needed a place of assembly, training and kitting out for the trawlers and drifters it was about to requisition and the men who would crew them. After much havering, their selection was Lowestoft, and the Admiralty surveyor of lands was duly despatched there to acquire a base. His choice fell on a municipal park on the littoral, known as 'Sparrow's Nest'.

Sparrow's Nest originally formed the grounds and formal gardens of the early nineteenth-century thatched summer residence of one Robert Sparrow, a local wealthy landowner. The town council purchased the gardens in the 1890s and they became a popular venue for concerts, such that the Borough of Lowestoft commissioned the 1,300-seat Pavilion Theatre in the grounds in 1913. Now the park was to become the headquarters of the RNPS.

In the event of mobilisation being ordered the Admiralty's choice of commander for the base fell on fifty-seven-year-old Captain Basil Hamilton Piercy, a retired naval officer who had left the navy in 1926 and whose main qualification for appointment seemed to be that he lived close by. Nonetheless, it proved to be an inspired decision.

On 23 August 1939, the Admiralty issued the 'preparation for war' telegram; Piercy packed his bags and appeared at the stage door of the theatre to interrupt a show by 'Gert and Daisy'[*] and take over the buildings for the navy. From 24 August, trawlers earmarked for naval service were intercepted as they returned to port from fishing and workmen swarmed aboard to begin fitting them out for warfare. Fish holds became mess decks; magazines were constructed and filled; deck beams were strengthened to receive guns; and an officers'

cabin, no more than twenty feet square and situated below the wheelhouse, gained two bunks, a table and two each of upright and easy chairs. Time would show that they would get little use. On 29 August Britain mobilised for war and on the 31st all naval reserves were called up. The White Ensign flew over the Sparrow's Nest. And in this new command, Basil Piercy largely had to make it up as he went along.

One immediate problem was accommodation. This was solved by Lowestoft's now guestless boarding-house landladies. Piercy co-opted them to take as many sailors as they could house and feed, and some 963 of them operated as surrogate mothers, wives and caterers to the trainee matelots, braving the 20,000 bombs which Germany dropped on the town to do so.

However, the accommodation was not always of the best. Fisherman Sid Kerslake from Hull, a naval reservist, reported to his Mercantile Marine office in his home town after the declaration of war and was sent to Sparrow's Nest. Here he was allocated a billet in a house on London Road South. 'I am certain there were about a hundred sailors already in digs there,' he wrote, 'if not there certainly appeared to be so. The liveliest things in the place were the other occupants of my bed. I was covered in flea bites when I woke up that first morning.'[1]

Later, Nissan huts were built over the grassy open spaces and the trainee Sparrows lived under their shelter.

Skippers awaiting an appointment or in training were housed at a large house named 'Briar Cliffe'; and local schools were pressed into service for a different type of education, that of fighting seaborne threats. An orphanage and a convent were amongst the buildings requisitioned for naval use. But perhaps the most important of Piercy's innovations was a naval cookery school. The cook is a key man on any naval ship and especially a trawler. But the experienced ones were already out at sea and the new recruits generally had no idea how to even make tea. Captain Piercy called upon Miss Grace Musson,[†] principal of the Lowestoft Technical College. And she established, in the Lowestoft Church Road School, an RNPS cookery school. She recruited eleven domestic science teacher helpers and fitted out coal-fired ranges in the premises, such as would be found at sea. Over a five-week course Miss Musson turned dross into, if not gold, then at least good British sterling silver, 160 men at a time.

---

[*] Florence Elsie Waters and Doris Ethel Waters, a British female comedy act. Their brother Horace was better known as Jack Warner, aka 'Dixon of Dock Green'.

[†] College principal between 1923 and 1946. Miss Musson was made a Knight (Dame) Commander of the British Empire in the New Year's Honours List of 1941 for her efforts (*London Gazette*, no 35029).

40. Plates 40–45 show six Admiralty-built 'Isles'-class trawlers, fitted with a variety of armaments. *Ensay*, launched in 1942, carried a 12pdr forward and a single 20 mm Oerlikon aft. The 'bandstand' for both can be clearly seen. She was sold off in 1965 and sunk in 1983 by the Italian navy, who used her as a target ship.

41. *Hascosay*, of 1944, was an 'Isles'-class vessel modified as a danlayer and fitted with three 20mm Oerlikon cannons, one aft, two forward.

42. A starboard-quarter view of the 'Isles'-class *Unst*, built in 1942 and seen here painted in the Western Approaches camouflage scheme. Her crew can be seen 'manning the rails'. In 1946, *Unst* was one of sixteen Admiralty trawlers transferred to the Italian government for minesweeping purposes.

43. The 'Isles'-class *Gairsay* (1943) was a combined anti-submarine and minesweeping unit, armed with a 12pdr and an Oerlikon mounted aft. She was sunk off Normandy by a German explosive motor boat on 4 August 1944, with the loss of thirty-one lives, twenty-eight of them 'Sparrows'.

44. HMT *Biggal*, 'Isles'-class, launched in December 1944. Of 545 tons displacement, like all her sisters, she carried a single 12pdr gun and three 30mm anti-aircraft weapons, two of which can be seen mounted behind her main gun and in front of the bridge.

45. Finally, Canadian-built *Texada* (1942) was equipped with a 12pdr and no less than four high-angle Oerlikons for anti-aircraft work. She mounted a Type-291 search radar, almost universal amongst the RN's smaller ships by the war's end. Its antennas can be seen at the masthead.

46. *Butser* was an Admiralty 'Hill'-class vessel, armed with a 12pdr gun and two 20mm Oerlikons on her bridge wings and used for anti-submarine duties. She spent much of the war in the 2nd A/S Group, based at the naval base of Freetown, Sierra Leone, a staging post for Allied traffic in the South Atlantic and the assembly point for SL convoys to Britain.

Piercy's flair and improvisation and Grace Musson's organising ability ensured that the RNPS at sea would not starve.

By February 1940, the RNPS fishermen were mostly at sea. But Sparrow's Nest was busier than ever; for now they had to train conscripts to be seamen. In navalese, the base was termed *Pembroke X*; but as the numbers of men and ships continued to grow, it was raised to the status of a port division for the whole fishermen's fleet, becoming *Ramola* for eight weeks from 15 February to 14 April 1940 and then HMS *Europa* with the motto *In Imis Petimus* (We Search the Depths). By December 1940, 22,900 men had passed through the Nest, of whom 5,600 were the naval reservists.

The first WRNS arrived in January 1940 and by end of 1945, there were 740 on site. On 13 August 1941, HRH the Duchess of Kent[*] visited the camp and dispensed regal charm.

During its existence, the base had three commanders; Basil Piercy until April 1941; Commodore Daniel de Pass, captain of HMS *Cossack* immediately before the war and reputedly a 'terrible sailor',[2] until March 1944; and then Commodore Robert Gordon Duke until the base was closed in June 1946, when its residual functions were incorporated into Royal Navy Barracks, Chatham.

'Graduates' from HMS *Europa* were known in the navy as 'Sparrows' and the whole Royal Naval Patrol Service gained the ironic nickname of Harry Tate's Navy, named after a comedian popular between the wars and referring to the perceived 'make do and mend' nature of the RNPS.[†]

One Sparrow who passed through *Europa* was the Rt Hon Lord Callaghan of Cardiff, prime minister of the UK from 1976 to 1979. In keeping with the rather chaotic nature of the mobilisation, he had thought that he was volunteering for the fast and sexy motor torpedo boats, only to find himself in Lowestoft, billeted above a fish and chip shop, and eventually serving on the anti-submarine trawler *Cape Argona*.[3] By the end of the war, Callaghan had been one of 66,000 men who had served with the RNPS, Sparrows every one.[§]

At First Lord of the Admiralty Winston Churchill's urging, the men of the RNPS gained the distinction of their own insignia, an exclusive silver badge. Officers and men of the RNPS were awarded this badge after a total of six months' service at sea. It could also be presented beforehand to those showing worthy conduct while engaged in action. Roughly the size of an old shilling (*c*.0.93in diameter), the badge was designed by George Kruger Gray, best known for his designs of coinage and stained-glass windows, and symbolised the work of both the minesweeping and the anti-submarine personnel. It depicted a shield upon which a sinking shark (representing a U-boat), speared by a marline spike, was set against a background made up of a fishing net with two trapped enemy mines. This was flanked by two nautical knots and, at the top, a naval crown. Beneath the device was a scroll bearing the letters

[†] The expression had been used as jargon for anything clumsy and amateurish. Harry Tate (d1940) was a music hall entertainer who would play a clumsy twit who could not get to grips with various contraptions. His act included a car that gradually fell apart around him.

[§] Other famous Sparrows included the pianist Russ Conway, the dance band saxophonist Freddie Gardener and the actor Eric Barker.

[*] Princess Marina of Greece and Denmark

47. A 'Hill'-class vessel, *Inkpen* (1942) was equipped with a single 12pdr and three 20mm Oerlikons, one aft and one on each bridge wing. She too served from 1942 as part of the 2nd A/S Group based at Freetown, for which purpose she could carry up to fifty-five depth charges.

M/S-A/S (Minesweeping, Anti-Submarine).

The route to command of an armed trawler was not necessarily through Sparrow's Nest. Colin Warwick, for example, was a qualified merchant officer who had left the sea to work in advertising. On the outbreak of war, he volunteered for naval service and was sent to HMS *Osprey*, the anti-submarine warfare school at Weymouth, for what was meant to be a six to eight-week course but which, under the exigency of wartime, was being completed in nine days. From there he went straight to be number one in the trawler *Cape Passaro* and shortly afterwards to command his own vessel, HMT *St Loman*, as a lieutenant RNR.

And Michael Thwaites, a twenty-five-year-old Australian academic, Rhodes Scholar, Newdigate Poetry Prize winner at Oxford

and later winner of the King's Medal for Poetry, arrived at HMS *King Alfred* in 1940, to discover it was a converted seafront resort centre in Hove where the underground car park had been transformed into a dormitory. He underwent a six-week training course at the end of which he found himself apparently a qualified Temporary Acting Sub Lieutenant in the Royal Navy and was posted to HMS *Fortitude*, another 'stone frigate' at the port of Ardrossan. Here he was liaison officer to the 29th Group of anti-submarine trawlers; and before long found himself posted aboard one, *Northern Dawn*.

Sheen

Another example of the haste and somewhat extemporaneous nature of the mobilisation of the small craft can be seen in the story of the drifter *Sheen* in the days leading up to war.

The Admiralty-built steel drifter *Sheen* was a First World War veteran, launched in May 1918 at the Lowestoft yard of J W Brooke and Co. Fitted then with a 6pdr gun, she saw little service but unlike many of her sisters, was retained within the Royal Navy in the inter-war years.

As Europe raced to another conflict, *Sheen* was taken out of reserve in Portsmouth and recommissioned for service at Scapa Flow. She was under the command of twenty-year-old Acting Sub Lieutenant Geoffrey Astley-Cooper, a linear descendent of Sir Astley Paston Cooper, 2nd Baronet, nephew of the noted surgeon and identically named anatomist. Eighteen-year-old Midshipman W David Scott was posted from the battleship *Revenge* to be his number one. The contrast between these two postings must have been considerable for Scott, who noted only that the wardroom sported just four tiny bunk beds.[4]

Sheen was coal fired; designed for 9 knots, she could now do no more than seven. In company for the trip north was the drifter *Mist*, another Admiralty steel vessel, built by John Lewis and Sons of Aberdeen and intended as a minesweeper but completed after the Armistice, and like her half-sister retained within the service. Unusually, she was now fitted with diesel engines and could attain 10 knots, with a range of 600 miles. Her commander was Sub Lieutenant Radford RNR with two naval cadets to assist him.

The pair of drifters departed on 25 August 1939 and immediately ran into problems. *Sheen* had to stop every two days for water, on the 26th her cook fell ill and could not make any food, and then both drifters collided with some trawlers in fog.

On arrival at Scapa they were put to anti-submarine work. *Sheen* was now fitted with a 3pdr gun; but she also carried two depth

48. HMT *Coverley* (1940) was a 'Dance'-class trawler used for minesweeping and A/S duties. The class closely resembled the 'Isles'-class vessels but carried a heavier deck armament of one 4in gun mounted behind a shield forwards and three 20mm Oerlikon cannons, two on the bridge wings (the starboard one can be clearly seen in the picture) and one aft.

charges, two boxes of grenades and four spanking new rifles. They had indented for a heavy machine gun but none had been forthcoming. Nonetheless, Scott was 'confident that no enemy submarine would be able to resist the large quantity of HE we were carrying'.[5]

The first three days of patrol were eventful. *Sheen*'s young officers manged to ram the old battleship *Iron Duke*; crush a man's hand (requiring amputation); get the propeller foul of some moorings; get lost at night in the middle of the Flow; lose one of their crew; and run into a boom.[6] Astley-Cooper must have been pleased when he was posted to a destroyer. But it gives some indication of the hurried preparedness and the lack of experienced manpower available for patrol duty at that time.[*]

---

[*] Scott became an admiral and eventually the controller of the UK's Polaris programme. Astley-Cooper was killed when the old destroyer *Wren* was bombed and sunk off Aldeburgh in July 1940. *Mist* and *Sheen* were both sold into trade in 1946.

49. The following ten plates (49–58) depict the multi-purpose trawlers of the `Military' class, the largest Admiralty-built trawlers of the war, similar in size to a corvette. They carried a 4in gun plus up to four 20mm Oerlikons together with sixty-five depth charges and were capable of 12.5 knots. *Bombadier* (1943), shown here, was primarily used for A/S convoy escort. (Taken on 23 May 1943, this picture shows a pennant number which is not that originally assigned, T304. To date, no records have been found which show an F flag superior assigned to trawlers. But the pictorial evidence is clear and suggests she was on escort duty when photographed.)

(Right) 50. The 'Military'-class trawler *Fusilier* (1943) in coastal waters.

(Above) 51. HMT *Grenadier* (1942) was a convoy escort and A/S trawler. She and her skipper became famous for the rescue of the crew of the SS *Inger Toft* in 1945, three miles off the Isle of Skye.

(Below) 52. The 'Military'-class HMT *Guardsman* (1944). Her aft Oerlikon gun shield can be clearly seen. In 1948 she was sold and became the Grimsby trawler *Thuringia*.

(Above) 53. HMT *Home Guard* (1944). This interesting picture shows a different fit-out to her sisters' with a twin Oerlikon 'bandstand' placed forward of the bridge, behind the 4in gun, and a twin Oerlikon mounting at the rear. She was intended to provide extra anti-aircraft cover for her convoys. In March 1945 *Home Guard* rescued thirty-five survivors from the torpedoed freighter *Alcedo*.

(Below) 52. *Sapper*, 'Military'-class, like her sisters a large trawler of 750 tons displacement, was launched in 1942 and fitted with a 4in gun for anti-submarine patrol work. She carried four 20mm anti-aircraft weapons, the rearmost mounting for which can be clearly seen.

(Above) 55. Another `Military'-class trawler, *Lancer* (1943). She was sold off in 1946 as the Hull-based *Stella Orion*. (This vessel has been positively identified as *Lancer* but wears the pennant number originally assigned to the `Isles'-class *Lindisfarne*).

(Right) 56. The bridge layout of the 'Military'-class Admiralty trawler *Grenadier* showing telephones and voice pipes (and an empty beer bottle).

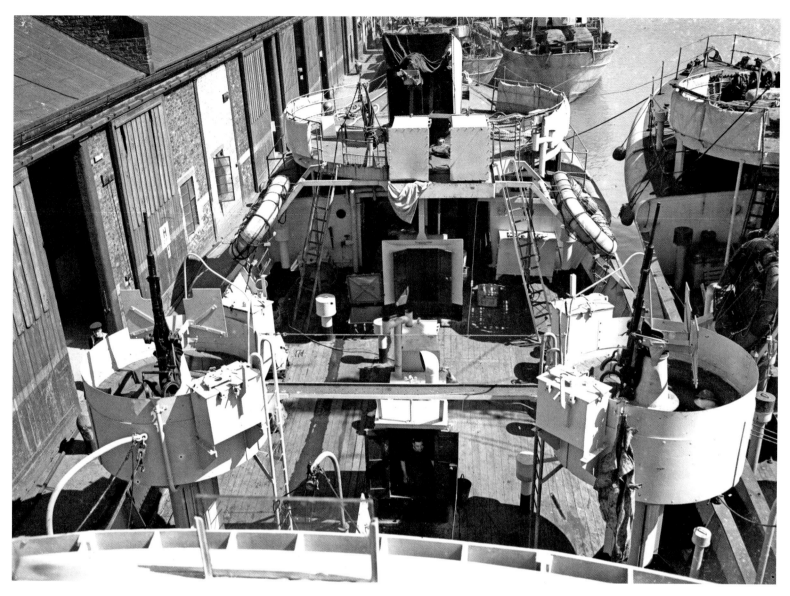

(Above) 57. The 'Military'-class trawler *Grenadier* is shown here whilst moored. The photograph gives an excellent impression of the crowded nature of the deck space. The forward 'bandstand' for her 4in gun and the smaller elevated positions for her 20mm Oerlikons mounted in front of the bridge are obvious.

(Right) 58. Finally, the 'Military'-class *Royal Marine* (1944) in an excellent side-on view which displays her forward 4in mount and aft Oerlikon.

59. *Star of Orkney*, built in 1936 and requisitioned in 1942, was used as a minesweeper and was fitted with LL acoustic sweep gear. She was the progenitor of the 'Round Table' class.

Trawlers and drifters

The Royal Navy started the war with twenty-five First World War vintage Admiralty-built trawlers, forty-one 'Gem'- and 'Tree'-class and two *Basset*-class, as per chapter 9.[*]

But construction of improved *Basset* types swiftly followed. The (second) 'Tree' class and 'Dance' class came into service in 1939–41. These and their successors departed from standard trawler (and *Basset*) practice by stepping the mast abaft instead before the bridge. Air-warning radio direction finding (RDF) was fitted at the mast head and all-steel bridgework replaced the former mattress-protected wood or canvas structures.

Another difference compared with the First World War Admiralty trawlers was the size. 'Tree'- and 'Dance'-class vessels were of 530 tons displacement compared to the largest surviving Great War vessels, the *Mersey*s at 438 tons or the Canadian navy's *Armentières* at 440 tons. Moreover, the later vessels had a much bigger complement, thirty-five compared to around twelve to fifteen, reflecting the increased level of technical equipment carried. Twenty 'Trees' and twenty 'Dances' were eventually constructed.

Next off the slips were the 'Shakespearians', a class of twelve, larger still at 545 tons displacement and built in 1940/41. They seemed to have been deployed primarily as minesweepers.

But by far the most numerous of the Admiralty-built trawlers were the 'Isles' class, 145 strong (of which 16 were built in Canada). These again were mainly used against mines and were launched between 1940 and 1943.

Three 600-ton, Robb-designed, 14 knot trawlers were constructed for the Royal New Zealand Navy in 1941, which also gained a further fourteen First World War designed *Castle*-class trawlers in 1941–43, built in the Antipodes.[†]

Eight Hill-class vessels were added in 1941. They were followed between 1942 and 1944 by ten Fish-, eight Round Table- and nine 'Military'-class, the latter the largest Admiralty trawlers yet built at 750 tons displacement and specifically intended for anti-submarine duty (see appendix 7).

Additionally, in 1942 six wooden-hulled and six steel-hulled trawlers were purchased from Portugal for the RN. Further afield, orders were placed in Brazil for six vessels but these were turned over to the Brazilian navy on their entry into the war in 1942.

A general plan of the 'Shakespearian'- and 'Isles'-class vessels can be seen at plan XIV and the 'Isles'-class A/S trawler *Lindisfarne* is featured at plan XV. Detail and general layout for the 'Round Table' class is shown at plan XVI and the 'Round Table'-class *Sir Galahad* is drawn at plan XVII. HMT *Coldstreamer*, a 'Military'-class A/S vessel,

---

[*] There were also forty-eight *Basset*-class vessels ordered for the Royal Indian Navy during 1941–3, with the contracts placed in India and Burma. Of these, twenty-five were later cancelled and four were lost incomplete.

[†] Seventeen ordered, fourteen delivered.

60. Depicted here is *Northern Gem*, 655 tons, German built in 1936 and requisitioned in 1939. She served as convoy escort in both of the notorious Arctic convoys, PQ17 and JW51B. Based at the Wallasey trawler base, in 1943 she was refitted as a Convoy Rescue Ship, with a small sick bay and medics on board.

is detailed at plan XVIII.

And photographs of the various classes are shown at, inter alia, plates 40–45 ('Isles'), plates 46–47 ('Hill'), plate 48 ('Dance') and plates 49–58 ('Military').

In contrast to the First World War, the Admiralty did not build any drifters in the 1939–45 conflict. At the start of the war there were twenty-four Great War Admiralty-built drifters still in commission, both of wooden and steel construction. The navy made up the rest of its requirements by requisition and hire.

Builders

Of the trio of builders who dominated the design and construction of the 1914–18 trawlers, Hall Russell and Cochrane's continued to be important constructors for the Admiralty. Smith's Dock, however, were now wholly focused on the production of corvettes and frigates. Smith's position was taken by Cook, Welton and Gemmell (CWG). Founded in Hull in 1883, CWG built vessels there between 1885 and 1904 and then at Beverley from 1902. They developed a reputation for high-quality trawlers and had prospered between the wars. All

eight 'Hill'-class boats were built by CWG. They were based on the design of the Grimsby-registered trawler *Barnett*,[*] part of the 'cricketers' fleet owned by Herbert Crampin. Likewise, all nine 'Military'-class trawlers were constructed by CWG, again following one of their standard designs. And 59 of the 129 British built 'Isles'-class vessels came from CWG's yards.

Cochrane's designed and built the ten Fish-class trawlers, based on their plan for the commercial trawler *Gulfoss* of 1929. And Hall Russell's *Star of Orkney* from 1936 (see plate 59) supplied the template for all the 'Round Table' class.

Unlike 1914–18, the Admiralty regulated the ordering of their trawler requirements well and very few orders were cancelled at the end of the war.

Hired trawlers and drifters

As in the first war, the requisitioned and hired vessels comprised a very mixed bag. Around 500 drifters were taken up by the navy, of which sixty had been Admiralty-built in the First World War and subsequently sold into trade. Requisitioned drifters ranged from the elderly *Aberdour* of 1908 to many others dating to the first twenty years of the century. Herring fishing had been much affected by the economic conditions of the inter-war period and the loss of the

---

[*] Crampin's ships were all named for famous cricketers. *Barnett* was after the Gloucester and England batsman, Charlie Barnett.

Russian trade, and few new vessels had been commissioned or constructed.

Trawlers ranged more fully across the years. *Akita* had been launched in 1939 and was immediately taken up for minesweeping purposes; whereas *Star of Britain* dating from 1908, was requisitioned in 1940, also as a minesweeper. But she was the exception. Modern trawlers such as *Northern Gem* (1936), *Stella Pegasi* (1935) or *Stoke City* (1935) were more the norm and gave stalwart service. In the photograph of the latter, she certainly shows hard usage (see plates 60–66).

Before a hired trawler could be taken in hand for conversion to a war footing, it was necessary for the owners and the Admiralty to inspect the ship and agree on her current condition in order that, at the end of her war service, she could be handed back in at least as good a condition as she was when taken up.

The process of conversion of hired or purchased trawlers was sudden and brief. As an example, the 1935 Grimsby-registered trawler *Vascama* was sold by her owners to the Admiralty on the

61. Stern view of *Northern Gem*, showing her single Oerlikon together with twin 0.5in Vickers machine guns on a Mark IV mounting. Also visible are her smoke pots (perforated drums) and empty depth charge rails

outbreak of war and immediately put in dockyard hands. Her huge fish hold was converted into crew accommodation. And extra bridge structure was added above the wheelhouse and a 4in gun platform erected forward of the foremast and straddling the forecastle. The mizzen mast was removed to improve the field of fire for the anti-aircraft weapons and other gun positions were created on the bridge veranda. A short tripod was welded to the funnel to carry wireless aerials and signal hoists while depth charge racks were fitted aft (and throwers amidships) and her huge trawling winch completely taken away. Finally, the pendant number FY-185 replaced her fishing number. *Vascama* the fishing boat was now a warship. And she had a long war, which included use as an armed boarding vessel, A/S duties, loan to the Portuguese navy between 1943 and 1944 and final disposal to trade in April 1945.

(Above) 62. Plates 62–65 show four excellent images of the trawler *Stella Pegasi* which demonstrate clearly how the forward gun position sat high on the flared bow like an old-fashioned mediaeval 'fore castle'. Built in 1935, she was requisitioned at the start of war and used for anti-submarine duties

(Below) 63. *Stella Pegasi* side-on view in 1943, with her 'bandstands' fore and aft clearly delineated.

64. The aft 'bandstand' of *Stella Pegasi* in 1943, with her twin 0.5in Vickers anti-aircraft guns elevated.

65. The twin depth charge racks (loaded with four bombs each) at the stern of *Stella Pegasi*, depicted in 1943. A rating is signalling to the bridge that a depth charge has been dropped. (© Imperial War Museum A 17181)

The armed trawlers were supposed to be painted overall in navy grey when taken up; but this instruction was seldom observed except in the breach. In 1940, the 28th Anti-Submarine group of *Lord Essendon, Lord Middleton, Lord Nuffield* and *Lincolnshire*[*] proudly wore their fishing colours of green hulls, buff upper works and red funnels.[7]

One of the differences between Admiralty-designed vessels and those taken up from trade was that in the former case, the aft mast was placed immediately behind the wheelhouse, giving a clearer space on deck for weaponry.

This was not always the case in the converted trawlers, which can clearly be seen in the two plans of HMT *Thuringia* (plans XIX, XX and XXI). Built by Cochrane's in 1933 for the Great Grimsby and East Coast Steam Fishing Co Ltd, she was taken up in 1939 and fitted out for anti-submarine activities with a 4in guns, anti-aircraft (AA) weapons and ASDIC. Her career was to be short. Working with the 21st A/S Group from Dover, she struck a mine on 28 May 1940, 25 miles east of Margate, and quickly sank. Out of a crew of eighteen

only four people survived; all the dead were Sparrows, as was forty-four-year-old Chief Skipper David William Leon Simpson RNR from Swansea. Simpson had been awarded the DCM in the previous war[8] and the DSC in the New Year's Honours List 1940 'for, unfailing courage, endurance and resource in HM Trawlers, Drifters and Minesweepers in their hard, arid, perilous task of sweeping the seas clear of enemy mines and combating submarines'. The task was indeed perilous.

Surprisingly, the terms of hire had not been agreed between Admiralty and owners when the war started, despite the growing interest in trawlers and the increase in world tension. Even in December 1939 it was still a matter of debate. Replying to a question in the House of Commons from Labour MP William Adamson regarding the terms for taking over '200 steam trawlers and drifters for mine-sweeping duties by his department; and if there is any contract for the future restitution of the fishing fleet in the event of losses or by excessive depreciation of the vessels', the Admiralty's representative, Geoffrey Hithersay Shakespeare, could only respond that 'final terms of hire have not yet been arranged for requisitioned trawlers and drifters. It is hoped that these and other financial matters, including compensation for loss or damage to the vessels, will be settled by agreement with the owners, but in the absence of agreement, compensation will be payable under the Compensation (Defence) Act, 1939. In the meantime, advances on account of hire are being made.'[9]

---

[*] The first three vessels had been requisitioned from Pickering and Haldane's of Hull.

66. Both anti-submarine and minesweeping duties were hard on men and ships. Pictured here, the quondam Consolidated Fisheries 422-ton trawler HMT *Stoke City*. Launched in 1935 and requisitioned in September 1939, she appears rather weary and non-descript. *Stoke City* mounted a 4in gun, clearly visible, and three 20mm single Oerlikons. For most of her naval career she was based around the coast of Scotland on anti-submarine duties.

In the end, approximately 1,409 trawlers were taken up from trade by the Royal Navy, a similar number to that of the first war. Generally speaking, the larger, faster trawlers were fitted out for ani-submarine work and the older and smaller vessels were used as minesweepers and for general duties.

These included foreign vessels, mainly from Belgium and France. Belgium had no navy before the war, but when it capitulated in 1940 hundreds of Belgian fishermen, many in their own fishing vessels, escaped to Britain. Here they were formed into a *Section Belge*, with some of them given commissions in the RNR and RNVR. By 1942 the Belgians were operating minesweeping trawlers, drifters and boom defence vessels and, at its peak, the *Section Belge* totalled nearly 500 officers and men. They sailed in craft such as the trawlers *Adronie Camiel* and *Adriatic*, both of around 140 tons, diesel powered and with their bulky shape, very distinctive. They were often operated

as ferries. *Andre Monique* was another, larger, Belgian trawler used for general patrol work (see plates 67–69).

As well as the trawlers and drifters, some 150 whalers were hired or acquired,[10] in addition to the pre-war Admiralty 'Lake' class. These were all intended as anti-submarine craft. Many of them were from South Africa and others were originally Norwegian.

Motor fishing vessels

From 1942 onwards the Admiralty also took responsibility for the building and hire of a large number of motor fishing vessels (MFVs) which were meant for use as tenders and for other small vessel purposes, such as ferry services, boom management, in river estuaries and for harbour defence and patrol (see plate 70).

There were four main Admiralty-built types, and two groups of hired MFVs, all of which were diesel- or petrol fuelled. The Admiralty MFV 1 series of 50 tons displacement had a Kelvin diesel and a crew of six. They were armed with a .303 machine gun. The 28-ton series 601 used Atlantic diesels or Chrysler petrol engines with four men on board and a single machine gun, while series 1001 of 114 tons had a Lister diesel, a .303 gun and a crew of nine. The 200-ton 1501 type used a Crossley diesel engine, again had a single gun and carried a crew of eleven.

67. Plates 67–69 picture three Belgian trawlers. They escaped from the Belgian coast and were taken into the Royal Navy as ABVs, and sometime ferries, in 1940 and based at Milford Haven and Fishguard. Shown here *is Adronie Camiel*.

68. The Belgian trawler HMT *Adriatic*.

69. And the *Andre Monique*, built in 1937 and taken up in June 1940. The protected bandstand for the gun can be clearly seen. She was a large example of her sort, and was used for general patrol work.

Of the hired vessels, one group of eleven was requisitioned in 1942; it was a mixed class and unarmed, at least officially. The other hired class was a set of French vessels, none larger than 120 tons and taken up from 1940. Altogether there were at least eight of them.

More MFVs were ordered than completed and in total, from builders in the UK, Australia, South Africa and Bermuda, 850 Admiralty-built craft entered service,[11] together with perhaps 19 hired vessels. Five were lost in the course of the war.

Main gun armament

The experience of the First World War had shown that lighter calibre guns were both ineffective and under-ranged against submarines and their deck guns, and as a consequence the Admiralty trawlers intended for anti-submarine work were armed with 4in guns from the outset (see plate 71). These were largely the QF Mark IV and Mark V models, taken from First World War destroyers and the like. They fired a 31lb shell and could also be modified for high-angle (HA) work against aircraft, with a maximum altitude (Mark V) of 30,000ft.

The majority of U-boats armed with deck guns carried the 8.8cm or 10.5cm weapon. The 8.8cm gun fired a 12–14kg round with a 9kg (nearly 20lb) warhead and the usual ammunition fit-out was 250 rounds. Larger submarines, such as the Types I, IX, and X, had a more powerful 10.5cm gun, firing a 17.4kg (38lb) projectile with 110 rounds on board. The trawlers' 4in was thus a reasonable match for the German U-boat weapons while on the surface.

But post the massive anti-submarine efforts of the Allies in 1942 and 1943, German deck guns were removed from almost all U-boats and from 1943 the deck gun was, for most of them, a thing of the past.

Minesweeping trawlers were equipped with the 12pdr weapons familiar from the last war (see plates 72–74). Requisitioned trawlers had initially to make do with antiquated 3pdrs and 6pdrs but they were quickly brought into line with the Admiralty builds and a much greater uniformity of gun armament prevailed than in 1914–18.

Protection

Although mainly built of steel, trawlers were unarmoured with highly exposed decks and wheelhouses. The Admiralty builds now sported steelwork around the bridge but the hired trawlers came as they were. In order to provide some protection from shell splinters etc, additional protection (known as splinter matting) was carried around the command area and down the vessel's sides. There was also a canvas screen around the top bridge, although these additions probably provided scant comfort either psychologically or practically (see plate 75). Indeed, Wireless Operator Jack Law remembered 'we were on the top bridge which had a rail round it which was covered in canvas, mainly to keep the sea from getting under the bridge. This time we hear a plane coming at us with all guns blazing. We dropped flat on the bridge, taking cover behind the canvas. The first lieutenant looked at me and said "Sparks, don't tell the men that you and I were lying behind the canvas."[12]

70. Two series 1 Motor Fishing Vessels shown at sea; they were the only war vessels in the Royal Navy still to use sails in all conditions. The sails were for steadying purposes. (© Imperial War Museum A 16909)

71. The breech mechanism of the 4in gun on board HMT *Cornelian* and some interested crew members.

(Opposite) 72. The 12pdr gun armed many trawlers in both world wars. Plates 72–74 show the weapon close up. Here a 12pdr gun crew on a trawler go through a drill. The next round is in fact an empty shell case. The ship's mascot is an interested observer.

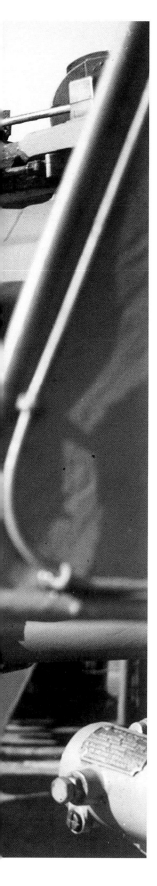

(Above) 73. Here is the same crew with the gun trained to port aft and at a high angle.

(Left) 74. Aircraft attack was feared and success against bombers much desired. This picture shows the 12pdr (Mark V) gun crew of the trawler minesweeper *Lovania* re-enact for the cameras their success in shooting down a Junkers Ju 88 bomber in October 1942. L–R, Seaman J Cooper, Leading Seaman F Wood, Seaman E Westall and Seaman A Hart.

Lovania, Grimsby registered and built in 1912, was requisitioned in 1940 but had already served in World War One as *Ninus*, when she carried two 12pdrs and was fitted out as a hydrophone vessel.

(Right) 75. A front-on picture of an unidentified armed trawler which clearly shows the additional protection (splinter matting) carried around the command area and down the vessel's sides as well as the protective canvas screen over the top of the bridge.

11: Keeping the Seas – Anti-Submarine Warfare

In the Great War of 1914–18, the U-boats were practically undetectable when under water until late into the war; and even then, the primitive hydrophone systems deployed were less than fully effective.

The potential game changers in the hunt for U-boats in 1939 were ASDIC[*] and shipboard radar. The navy had placed great faith in the former, but, as historian Stephen Roskill has noted, 'its fine performance in the hands of skilled operators had led the naval staff to believe that the submarine menace had to a great extent been overcome'.[1] This proved patently not the case. As for radar, in 1939 very few ships were fitted with it.

ASDIC

Early forms of ASDIC had been developed at HMS *Tarlair* in 1917 (see chapter 5) but the system was first tested (in the cruiser *Antrim*) only in 1920 and entered production in 1922. The 6th Destroyer Flotilla had ASDIC-equipped vessels by 1923 and the following year an anti-submarine school was established at HMS *Osprey* for ASDIC operations and a training flotilla of four vessels based there.

The most secret part of the ASDIC device was the oscillator, hand built from small pieces of quartz and fixed to a steel plate or diaphragm. Upon an electric current of 1,000 volts being passed through it, the diaphragm oscillated and when submerged in an ASDIC dome mounted forward, under the trawler, produced a very narrow beam of reverberation through the water for some 2,500 to 3,000 yards. When this beam struck a submerged object, it produced an echo, sounding rather like striking an empty tin can. The response was also shown as a dark mark made by a moving stylus on a sensitised paper roll.

The ASDIC operator sat in a high chair and tuned into his equipment through headphones; a small wheel turned the direction of the oscillator and allowed for a sweep with the beam. The direction of any contact was given a bearing from the trawler by a lighted line on a compass rose. To attack the target, the trawler then ran down the indicated line at its best speed of 10–12 knots and the echoes became shorter and closer together as the range decreased. On impulse and echo becoming simultaneous, depth charges were fired.

ASDIC could not track a U-boat on the surface but often a hydrophone effect could be obtained. This used ASDIC in listening

mode; the propeller noises of the U-boat would sometimes be heard and underwater the operation of various machinery and its use of compressed air in the ballast tanks to change depths was audible on occasion.

But the system was far from perfect. Above 18 knots, there was too much ship-generated noise and good contacts were difficult to identify in the din. The same issue also resulted from bad weather when the ships were rolling, pitching and heaving.

A further problem was that often U-boats could not be detected due to water conditions. ASDIC was not very reliable in rough water, nor when layers of different temperature deflected the sound waves. U-boats could dive beneath such layers to avoid detection.

Not all A/S trawlers were fitted with ASDIC; but for those that were it was a significant advantage.

Anti-submarine radar

ASDIC could not easily detect U-boats on the surface. But the development of radar solved this problem. Detection of a surfaced U-boat required RDF systems operating at higher frequencies than the sets that existed in 1939 because of a submarine's smaller physical size. It also required antennas which could generate a narrow beam capable of maintaining contact as the tracking ship rolled. The development of short (50cm and 10cm) wavelength equipment (known as centrimetric radar) resolved this issue and once available the Admiralty rushed to fit them in ships as quickly as possible.

Designated the Type-271 radar, the first such sets were tested in March 1941, identifying the periscope of a submerged submarine at almost a mile range. The system commenced deployment in August 1941 and on 16 November the first German submarine was sunk after being detected by a Type-271.

The 271 was mainly used on smaller vessels and was eventually replaced by the Type-272 (which also had some utility against aircraft). However, this system was not considered particularly successful. Plate 76 shows the danlayer *Sandray* sporting a Type-272 in its Perspex radome above the bridge. It could pick up a surfaced U-boat at around three miles range and its periscope alone at 900 yards. Plate 77 also shows a trawler mast-mounted radar array. From mid-1942, both these early systems were replaced by the Type-291 which became the default radar for all Royal Navy small ships. Plate 45 shows a Type-291 installed at the mast head of the 'Isles'-class *Texada*.

Such radar sets required an additional three ratings to man them, creating yet more pressure on accommodation. One of their less

---

[*] Not named after a (mythical) Anti-Submarine Detection Investigation Committee but a way of making A/S Division into a catchy word

76. *Sandray* (1945), a danlayer, carried three Oerlikons together with four .303 machine guns. She was fitted with the unsuccessful Type-272 centimetric radar for detecting surfaced U-boats; its Perspex housing can be seen above the bridge.

helpful traits was to pick up 'contacts' which were in fact wave tops. Another issue was that the extra top hamper could cause the trawlers so fitted to roll quite badly.

Depth charges

The main anti-submarine weapon of the war remained the depth charge, largely unchanged from that used at the end of the 1914–18 conflict. Essentially, Second World War depth charges were a simple steel drum containing 250–300lb of explosive with a metal tube in the centre. Here a water pressure-actuated detonator was inserted, on which was a key for marking the required depth settings, from 50ft to 500ft. Typically, at the outset of the war, trawlers were fitted with twenty-five charges in each of two stern rails (see also plate 65).

A trawler's standard firing pattern of depth charges was five. Three would be rolled off the stern rails while two were fired from a sort of mortar, not unlike the First World War bomb throwers, mounted amidships on either side (see plate 78). For these weapons, the depth charge was held on the end of a T-shaped steel stalk, the other end of which was inserted into the thrower. After firing, the 'T' was manually reloaded and the new depth charge fitted using a hoist situated next to the mortar. The idea was to create a 'five of clubs' pattern; during an attack, the command 'fire one' caused one stern charge to be rolled into the sea; 'fire two', activated the amidships bomb throwers and a further depth charge from the aft

rails; and 'fire three' a final stern rail discharge.

If trawlers suffered from a lack of speed in attack, they also had a hidden edge. An attacking ship could be easily picked up by the hydrophone operators of a U-boat; and the quick beat of a destroyer's propellers was readily identifiable. But a trawler's single screw was identical in sound to that of a merchant ship and in this the trawlers possessed an advantage; often U-boats did not recognise them as a threat until it was too late. Moreover, a turn to starboard, combined with the right-handed thrust of the trawler's single screw meant that a trawler could turn in its own length to re-acquire the target and launch a new attack. Destroyers carried their oscillator diaphragms higher up than in an A/S trawler and this exposed them to a greater turbulence when reversing their course; they also had a larger turning circle.

In terms of economy, the depth charge was a very cost-efficient weapon. Each one cost, complete with pistol, £22.10s (£1,130 in today's money); together with the T-thrower and cartridge it was only £5 more expensive.[2] It was a very cheap way to kill a U-boat.

Trawlers hunting U-boats

Trawlers were used to hunt for, and protect from, U-boats throughout the war. At least six U-boats were sunk by direct action from trawlers and two were captured.

HMT *Visenda*, ex-Grimsby registered, 455grt and built in 1937, had been taken up by the Admiralty at the outbreak of the war. On 23 March 1941 she was escorting a convoy south of Iceland when she received an alarm call from the Belgian freighter *Ville de Liège* which was about to come under surface attack by *U-551*, which was on its first patrol and sailing into the North Atlantic from Bergen.

Working up to her full speed of 13 knots, *Visenda* spotted the

U-boat some four miles ahead. The submarine dived but *Visenda* managed to get an ASDIC contact and hold it while she fired off eighteen depth charges over the period of an hour and a half. During this time, the ASDIC broke down and was repaired and the port side bomb thrower packed up. But one depth charge hit the bows of the U-boat and is thought to have detonated a torpedo in its tube. The U-boat exploded under water and all of the forty-five-man crew perished. It was the first U-boat kill by an A/S trawler in the war, a proud honour for *Visenda* and her largely RNPS crew. Her commander, Lieutenant Ralph Spearing Winder OBE RNR received the DSO for the action, his number one Sub Lieutenant Anthony Charles Rumney the DSC and Able Seamen Alfred Hutchinson the DSM. Two RNPS Sparrows were also recognised; Leading Seaman Charles Henry Ball was awarded the DSC and Engineman Bert Stage Smith was mentioned in despatches.

Unfortunately, thirty-four-year-old Lieutenant Winder's DSO was awarded posthumously. On 22 June, while still in command of *Visenda*, he was killed in action; the medal was presented to his next of kin.

A combined air and sea attack accounted for *U-452*, a German Type VIIC U-boat. Setting off on her first, and only, patrol from Trondheim, Norway, on 19 August 1941 she was caught on the surface, south-east of Iceland, by an RAF Catalina flying boat six days later. *U-432* dived but was damaged by four depth charges dropped from the aircraft and forced to resurface, where she was attacked with further depth charges by the A/S trawler *Vascama*, built in 1935 by Cochrane's

(Above) 77. The German-built convoy escort *Northern Pride* (1936) was requisitioned in September 1939. Depicted here escorting convoy RA-53 (Kola Inlet to Loch Ewe) in 1943, she clearly shows signs of the hard work and difficult conditions that were the norm for the Russian convoys. Her radar equipment can be seen on the foremast and above the bridge. She was another vessel eventually fitted with a fully equipped sick bay for convoy rescue work.

(Right) 78. Depicted here are *Northern Sky*'s crew lowering a boat on the starboard side. The lowering davits and a sideways firing depth charge thrower can be clearly seen.

of Selby for the Atlas Steam Fishing Company Ltd of Grimsby.

The U-boat sank by the stern, taking with her all of her crew, forty-two men in total.

HMT *Lady Shirley* was a CWG vessel, built in 1937 and registered pre-war at Hull. Taken up in 1939 as an A/S trawler and fitted with a 4in and ASDIC, in September 1941 she was serving with the 31st Anti-Submarine group out of Gibraltar.

On the 29th she was ordered to search for up to three crippled merchant vessels which were trying to reach Las Palmas in the Canary Islands, especially SS *Silverbelle** which was under tow by the French sloop *Commandant Dubac*.

* *Silverbelle* sank before reaching safety.

On 4 October, still looking for the *Silverbelle*, *Lady Shirley* encountered *U-111*, also seeking the damaged ships, south-west of Tenerife. Mistaking the trawler for her target (though *Lady Shirley* was small, the U-boat commander thought she was far away), the U-boat was caught at periscope depth when Lieutenant Arthur Callaway RANVR, the Australian commander of the trawler, spotted the submarine and attacked with depth charges, forcing the U-boat to the surface. *Lady Shirley* then engaged with her 4in and began a gunnery duel which the trawler comprehensively won. With their vessel sinking the German crew surrendered and forty-five were picked out of the water by their opponent. When the trawler re-entered Gibraltar, she was given a rousing welcome from all the warships there assembled. Callaway received the DSO, and there were two DSCs, six DSMs, a CGM and five mentions in despatches awarded for the action.

But just two months later, Nemesis came calling. On 11 December, *Lady Shirley* was torpedoed by *U-374*, sinking in the Straits of Gibraltar. All thirty-three crew went down with their ship, including Lieutenant Commander Callaway. Twenty-five of the dead were RNPS.

The Mediterranean proved a lucky hunting ground for trawlers in 1944. HMT *Mull* was an 'Isles'-class Admiralty-built trawler launched in 1941 and generally intended for minesweeping purposes. Her sisters can be seen at plates 40–45.

On 10 March 1944, *Mull* was in the Mediterranean, south of Sardinia, when she came upon the German submarine U-343. *Mull* attacked with depth charges and the U-boat went down with the loss of all fifty-one hands aboard.

Then on 15 May, two Catalina flying boats identified a U-boat on the surface, attempting to force a passage through the Straits of Gibraltar. It was *U-731*, on its fourth patrol of the war. The Catalinas attacked with depth charges and called for support; up came the American-built patrol vessel HMS *Kilmarnock* and the armed trawler *Blackfly* (in fact the renamed *Barnett*, see chapter 10). They attacked with depth charges and the U-boat was sunk north of Tangier, taking all her crew with her.

U-732 was part of the 8th U-boat Flotilla based at Danzig. On her third (and what transpired to be final) war patrol she was spotted off Tangiers in the afternoon of 31 October 1944 by the British anti-submarine trawler *Imperialist* (built in 1939 and immediately taken into the navy). The U-boat dived but came under depth-charge attack from the trawler and was forced to surface, whereupon *Imperialist* engaged her with her deck guns, forcing her to dive once more. *Imperialist* again attacked, throwing a total of twenty-eight depth charges over the course of the action but was unable to destroy the U-boat.

U-732 had managed to dive and lie on the sea bed, hoping to escape when darkness fell; but the oxygen level in the submarine became critically low and the batteries were almost discharged. Any remaining hopes of evading the continued attentions of the trawler were shattered by the arrival of a destroyer, HMS *Douglas*, and at 2230

the U-boat commander decided to order the crew to abandon ship and scuttle his craft. Although all crew members made it off *U-732*, the heavy swell in near total darkness meant that only nineteen were picked up out of a complement of fifty.

In the history of the anti-submarine war, there was only one example of a U-boat seeing service in both the German and British navies; and trawlers played a key role in the events that led up to it. On 27 August 1941, the German submarine *U-570* was attacked while on the surface by an RAF Hudson A/S patrol. She dived but on surfacing found herself under attack from a second Hudson. As *U-570* dived for a second time she was caught in a pattern of four depth charges dropped by the aeroplane and damaged. Remaining on the surface, the submarine was strafed from the air until the crew held up a white board, indicating that they surrendered. Here was a remarkable opportunity to seize an intact U-boat and 100 miles away Lieutenant Norman Leslie Knight RNR in the 655grt German-built trawler *Northern Chief* (her sister ship *Gem* is at plate 60) was instructed to make for the submarine, which was kept under constant air observation, and capture it.

Knight arrived around 2200. Just after dawn another trawler, *Kingston Agate*, commanded by Lieutenant Henry Owen L'Estrange RNR, joined, followed by two 'Lake'-class whalers, *Windermere* and *Wastwater* (see plate 34 for the class). Two destroyers also stood by. L'Estrange formally accepted the German submarine's surrender.

But the German crew had remained on board *U-570* overnight; they made little attempt to scuttle their boat, especially as *Northern Chief* had signalled that she would open fire and not rescue survivors from the water if they did so.

At daybreak, the Allies and Germans exchanged signal lamp messages, with the Germans repeatedly requesting to be taken off as they were unable to stay afloat, and the British refusing to evacuate them until the crew secured the submarine to prevent it from sinking. To further complicate the situation, a small Norwegian floatplane appeared and bombed and fired on both the submarine and *Northern Chief*.

In worsening weather, several attempts to attach a tow-line to *U-570* were unsuccessful. Losing patience, the RN ships fired on the submarine and then an armed boarding party of an officer and three men from *Kingston Agate* paddled a Carey raft to the U-boat, boarded, and spent a tense five hours persuading the Germans to come up on deck. It was thirty hours after their surrender that the crew were finally taken off onto *Northern Chief*.

U-570 was slowly towed to Iceland and beached; she gave up her secrets to forensic examination and was then commissioned into the Royal Navy as HMS *Graph* and carried out three combat patrols before being scrapped as she was difficult to maintain, especially her MAN diesel engines. Lieutenant L'Estrange was awarded the DSC for his part in the capture.

These were cheering successes for the trawlermen. But it was not one-way traffic; at least eighteen armed trawlers were sunk by U-boats, as were three whalers.[3]

12: New Threats from the Air and the Sea

Maréchal Foch famously described the Treaty of Versailles as 'a twenty-year armistice'. He was only wrong by twelve months. But in the time between the end of one world conflict and the start of the next, technology, driven in part by the locomotive of war, had advanced significantly; and nowhere was that more true than in the field of aviation.

In the First World War, trawler minesweepers and drifters on net duty had been required to deal with aircraft attacks. However, except in the Dover/Calais area, these were not a daily occurrence and the armaments available to the aviators meant that their effectiveness was usually limited. But from 1939 the fast, well-armed, German fighter-bombers took a regular and deadly toll of the RNPS's ships and men.

Indeed, such was the pressure on the minesweeping forces, and the perceived lack of recognition for their attainments, that in 1940 the Admiralty instructed its senior officers that 'in view of the hazardous work being carried out by the minesweepers and the fact that they are continuously operating in the zone of intensive air attack it is desirable that no cases of gallantry or special devotion to duty should pass unnoticed'.[1] The threat from air attack was such that night sweeping was introduced in the Nore Command in August 1940 to reduce sweeper losses.

Over the course of the war, aircraft sank 71 armed trawlers and 6 whalers out of a grand total of 271 Royal Navy victims directly attributable to aerial assault. Losses were particularly bad in 1940 and 1941. To highlight one of many, *Tourmaline* (see plate 31), was a 'Gem'-class trawler originally named *Berkshire*, purchased by the Admiralty in November 1935. Air attack accounted for her when she was sunk off the North Foreland by German bombers on 5 February 1941. Three men died, all RNPS.

Lowestoft suffered from repeated air attack. Almost visible from the Sparrow's Nest, the trawler minesweeper *Ben Gairn*, built by Hall Russell in 1916, was sunk by a parachute mine on 4 May 1941, sinking in Waveney Dock with one stoker killed. Four days later, the drifter *Uberty* was sunk by bombing just outside Lowestoft harbour. Skipper R H Alexander RNR and all twelve ratings were lost; all but two were RNPS. And the old (1900) trawler *King Henry*, in use as a boom defence vessel, was sunk by German bombers in the same area a month later, on 13 June. Overall, the RPNS lost on average a vessel every two days during that terrible May.

The threat to shipping from aircraft was reflected in the AA armament installed on the trawlers. At the start of the war, most vessels carried machine guns, often two or three of them. These were generally First World War vintage .303 Lewis guns, usually mounted on 5ft-high cylinders of about 12in diameter and sited either side of the bridge.

Later, these were either replaced or complemented by 20mm Oerlikon cannons. From the 'Dance' class of 1940, Admiralty trawlers were fitted with two or three 20mm AA as standard. The large 'Military' class carried four.

The Swiss Oerlikon 20mm cannon (many plates, plan XXVII) came into the navy partly as a result of a sustained crusade by the

79. An early Holman projector being tested in March 1940; note the crude aiming sight mounted on the barrel. (author's collection)

then Captain Lord Louis 'Dickie' Mountbatten. He campaigned on behalf of the weapon's designer, Anton Gazda, and even introduced him to Admiral Sir Roger Backhouse, the First Sea Lord.[*] The RN gunnery school preferred the British-made Vickers multi-barrel 2pdr pom-pom but eventually, during the first half of 1939, a contract for 1,500 guns was placed in Switzerland. However, due to production delays and then the German invasion and takeover of France, only 109 guns had reached the United Kingdom by mid-1940.

In June 1940, the Oerlikon Company licensed and approved manufacture of their gun in the United Kingdom. The Royal Navy managed to smuggle out the necessary drawings and documents from Zurich and the production of the first British-made Oerlikon guns started in Ruislip at the end of that year, reaching the Royal Navy in March and April 1941.

The Oerlikons (and often machine guns) were mounted in 'bandstands', which bore more than a passing resemblance to oil drums. Indeed, enterprising skippers who had acquired extra weapons over and above those fitted by the dockyard, would sometimes cut down old oil drums to make a rostrum base for their new weapons.

Prior to the arrival of these highly effective Swiss guns, the problem of defence against aircraft brought into being one of the more unusual weapons of the war, the Holman projector (see plate 79, plan XXIX). As originally designed, this was a pneumatic mortar, with an upward-pointing steel pipe bearing a simple sighting mechanism, mounted on a heavy metal baseplate. Ammunition was made from hand grenades (Mills bombs) wedged in small metal canisters, and dropped down the pipe by the projector's operator. On striking the pipe's bottom, compressed air would fling the bomb skyward where it might hopefully hit or deter an aircraft.

The navy asked for a version powered by steam, of which trawlers had a-plenty. The design had to be changed since the harsh weather experienced by the trawlers invariably rusted the valves of the pneumatics (when steam was used in such a system, the water would condense in the pipes and prevent firing of the weapon). The naval version was given a pedal-operated firing trigger which actuated the device. When a ship found itself under attack, the crew would pull the pin and drop a hand grenade down the barrel of the projector. Then, the gun crew would aim at the enemy aeroplane and tramp on the pedal to release boiler steam. The rush of steam would propel the grenade aloft and, if all went according to plan and the fuse timing was correct, knock it out of the sky. This seldom happened.

The device was much unloved by the trawlermen. The coxswain of HMT *Northern Gem* commented that 'if the steam pressure applied to the projector wasn't correct, the grenade and its container had a

nasty habit of just managing to climb out of the end of the pipe, and drop onto the deck where they separated, rolling about until they either exploded where they were, and fragmented amongst those of the crew who were panicking to throw them over the side, or in the sea out of harm's way if the crew had been successful in doing what they had set out to do. Most ships' crews found as time passed by that the best use for the Holman projector was for throwing potatoes at chummy ships as they passed by them in a channel.'[2]

Another far from satisfactory device for deterring aircraft was the PAC (parachute and cable) rocket. In essence this was a system whereby a rocket would lift a cable into the air and hopefully into the path of an enemy aircraft. The bottom end of the cable carried an explosive device and there was a parachute at the top. Once the rocket burned out the parachute slowed the cable's fall and if the cable was intended to catch an attacking plane's wing or other surface; then the drag from the parachute would pull the cable across the target until the explosive made contact and detonated.

They were fitted to some trawlers in 1941 and phased out quickly afterwards, as being too slow to reload and generally ineffective. HMT *Pearl*, a 'Gem'-class purchased in 1935 carried one, fired by a lanyard along the deck head of the top bridge. On at least one occasion the officer of the watch fired one off in error while reaching for the siren lanyard.

Trawlers were armed on conversion with a main gun and light AA weapons. But crafty skippers were always seeking ways to expand their armament, particularly against the threat from the air. By 1941, *Pearl* carried a First World War 4in on the whaleback with an Oerlikon 20mm on either wing of the bridge (increased to twin Oerlikons later), twin Vickers 0.5in machine guns down aft above the wardroom (plus, later, twin Browning machine guns on either side of the well-deck forward) and Lewis guns on the top bridge. She also had PAC rockets and a Holman projector for a short time.

The 'Military'-class *Home Guard* and *Sapper* (plates 53 and 54) carried four Oerlikons each to provide additional anti-air cover for convoys.

Trawlers did score the occasional success against attacking aircraft. On 5 June 1941, for example, the German-built, 656-ton anti-submarine trawler *Northern Sky*, shot down a Heinkel 111 with its twin 0.5in Vickers Mark III machine guns, obsolescent at this time but fitted to trawlers for close-in AA work. The gunner was Steward Ernest William Boakes who was mentioned in despatches, as were Seaman Joseph Webber Harris and Temporary Lieutenant Allan Wright RNVR,[3] for their 'good services when an enemy aircraft was destroyed' (see plate 80). At a time when the country was sorely pressed, the government made sure that Boakes was feted in the newspapers.

Northern Sky (built in 1936), first of Fleetwood and then Grimsby, had been initially taken up in 1939 as an auxiliary boarding vessel (ABV) but changed to escort and anti-submarine duties later. She distinguished herself when, operating off Iceland,

---

[*] Although this is a commonly accepted claim, it was disputed by the naval historian Captain Stephen Roskill who stated 'I have recently disproved his claim to have been responsible for the adoption of the Swiss Oerlikon gun' (see Lownie, *The Mountbattens*, p372).

80. A trawler anti-air success came in June 1941 when Steward E Boakes (pictured) of *Northern Sky* shot down a Heinkel. He is seen manning a twin 0.5in Vickers Mark III machine gun, obsolescent at this time but fitted to trawlers for close-in anti-aircraft work. Boakes was mentioned in dispatches (2 September 1941) for 'good services when an enemy aircraft was destroyed'. German-built *Northern Sky* (1936) had been initially taken up in 1939 as an ABV but changed to escort and anti-submarine duties later.

she made the last attack on a U-boat of the war.

In 1942, the A/S 'Gem'-class trawler *Cornelian* (plate 29) made the headlines for shooting down not one but two German planes. Commanded by Lieutenant S Correll RNR (and his dog Sally) she accounted for German bombers on 4 February and 5 March. Their first victim was a Junkers Ju 88 attacking a convoy. Then the following month they came upon a Heinkel 111 which was dropping mines near the Eddystone Rock, 20ft above the waves. At

a range of 200ft, the skipper engaged the German with the port Lewis gun while the gun crew blazed away with the 4in forward until, when the Heinkel was dead ahead, they scored a direct hit.

The progenitor of the Admiralty-built trawlers which would serve between 1939 and 1945 was *Basset* (plate 35). On 20 April 1942 she too scored a success against air attack. *Basset* was attacked off Harwich by no less than four Messerschmitt Me 110s; but she returned such a blizzard of machine gun, Oerlikon and 4in fire that one of the aircraft exploded in mid-air. A second was so badly damaged that the machine turned half a loop before the pilot could recover control and bits of the plane fell into the sea as it began to lose height. The pilot tried to make a landing on the English coast but instead was observed to crash into the sea. The remaining two aircraft fled. *Basset* could thus legitimately claim two Germans downed and, moreover, without damage to the ship or her crew.

Twelve-pounder guns on high-angle mounts were also sometimes successful against German planes. The trawler *Lovania*, Grimsby registered, built by Cook, Welton and Gemmell in 1912 and once owned by Sir Alec Black, was requisitioned in 1940. She had already served in the First World War as *Ninus*, when she had carried two 12pdrs and was fitted out as a hydrophone vessel. On 19 October 1942, now equipped for minesweeping duty, *Lovania* and her crew, commanded by Temporary Skipper T A Edmund RNR, shot down a Junkers Ju 88 with their Mark V weapon (see plate 74). Acting Leading Seaman Frederick James Wood received the DSM for his role in the action. The aircraft had been part of a bombing raid on coastal towns of the south and south-east of England. Guns from a nearby naval base destroyed a second aircraft.

Air search radar

Radar changed the nature of warfare compared to 1914–18. In the Second World War it became increasingly possible to spot an aircraft or surfaced U-boat before it suddenly appeared next to your ship.

The most common air search radar carried by British vessels was the 140cm wavelength Type-291, which can be seen at plate 45. Introduced from early 1942, by 1944 it had been fitted to nearly all British destroyers and lesser escorts. The equipment could be installed in a week.

The initial model of the radar had separate transmitting and receiving antennas, but they were soon combined. Originally, a rather primitive hand-steered antenna was used but later variants had power training and a plan position indicator was developed. An aircraft at 10,000 feet could be detected thirty-five nautical miles out and, as an added benefit, the system could also spot a surfaced U-boat three nautical miles away.

The antenna was located at the top of the foremast and the operator's office was fed the signal by a Pyrotenax* cable. This coaxial-type cable consisted of a centre conductor surrounded by a powdered, ceramic-like compressed insulating material. The copper conductor and the insulation were enclosed within a hollow copper tube. If moisture entered the cable, its insulation properties fell below acceptable limits and the radar feed was compromised. Canny operators used treatment with a blow torch to drive out the moisture.

E-boats

The trawlers and drifters operating along Britain's east coast, and particularly in the English Channel, were a regular target for German E-boats operating out of Belgian or French ports.

E-boat was the Allies' designation for the Kriegsmarine's fast attack craft (*Schnellboot*, or S-Boot). The most popular type was the S-100 class, a very seaworthy design, heavily armed and capable of sustaining 43.5 knots. They were powered by three marine diesel engines, were about 114ft long and carried three 20mm guns, with a 37mm mounted aft, together with two torpedo tubes.

But sometimes the trawlers could hit back hard. In 1942, HMT *Turquoise* (see plate 32), a 'Gem'-class vessel built and purchased by the navy in 1935, was escorting a convoy off Sheringham in an area of sea where E-boat attack was so prevalent it was known as 'E-boat alley'. It was a coastal convoy of over seventy ships and was under fierce attack by German Heinkel He 115 floatplanes. The escort was blasting off at the enemy when suddenly the lookout on *Turquoise* sang out 'E boat Green 10'. As one of her crew, CPO William Davies RNR, recalled:

the angle was too acute for us to see the German but our forward guns were letting fly. In the starboard wing, manning the Lewis gun was the steward, a Cockney veteran of World War One. He was a four foot nothing man and had a beer crate to stand on, and we could see him up on his crate blazing away. Now the E boat was in sight at eighty yards, the whine of bullets was loud in the air and the thud of them finding a home in the padding round the bridge sounded clear above the turmoil. Our little steward raked the German gunners at their guns and, doll like, they fell over and firing ceased from her. She was now running broadside on to us and our guns methodically raked her, then as she sheered away from us one had the impression that she was finished.'[4]

They then had to fight off renewed air attack before making it to harbour, where the crew were given twenty four hours excused duty and a bottle of beer each. The commanding officer of the trawler, Lieutenant C M Newns RNVR, received the DSC and there were four others mentioned in despatches, including the steward machine-gunner.

---

* Initially named after the manufacturer.

13: Clearing the Way – Minesweeping

At the outbreak of war, the Royal Navy only had about forty fleet minesweepers. Over half of these (twenty-three) were aging 'Smokey Joes' – First World War coal-burning sweepers laid up at Malta and Singapore. The requisition of trawlers and drifters would be key to swiftly boosting these numbers.

Requisitioned trawlers had to proceed to one of several ports designated for fitting them out as minesweepers. This process in itself could be dangerous. The old (1909) Cochrane's-built trawler *Washington* had been taken up on 27 November 1939 for minesweeping purposes, at a hire rate of £52.5s.0d per month. On 6 December, she was sailing from her home port of Grimsby to Great Yarmouth to receive her equipment. She never made it. The previous night *U-59* had laid mines near the Outer Dousing Light; and *Washington* became their first victim. Off the coast of Caister, Skipper Joseph Anson Jennison RNR and six crewmen were lost, all fishermen; there was just one survivor.

The Admiralty moved quickly to get a new minesweeping (M/S) organisation in place to cope with the sudden surge in numbers that the uptake of fishing boats would cause. Officially, command of the minesweeping trawlers fell to the admirals or other senior naval officers responsible for the area where the craft were in operation. In locations where large numbers of auxiliary craft were in use, the Admiralty saw fit to appoint a Captain (Minesweepers). Five were assigned to Great Yarmouth, Dover, Sheerness, Harwich and the Nore for 'ongoing command of those auxiliary minesweepers operating from the ports'.[1] Port Minesweeping Officers (PMSOs) were appointed to Plymouth, Portsmouth, Harwich, Chatham, Tynemouth, Leith, Lyness, Ardrossan, Larne, Birkenhead and Milford Haven, while the Lowestoft minesweeping fishing boats were placed under the operational command of a local Commander M/S and came ultimately under the authority of the Captain and PMSO Great Yarmouth.[2]

81. The advent of the magnetic mine brought with it the countermeasure of new methods of sweeping. Here a minesweeping skid, a wooden dumb lighter with a magnetic coil on top, used in the early days of magnetic mines, has capsized and is being towed into harbour by the drifter *Silvercrest*, which served as both a minesweeper and a Fleet Air Arm safety vessel.

As an example, at Hartlepool there were usually twenty-six trawlers plus two drifters; in early May 1940, these were organised for minesweeping into six groups of trawlers, Groups 1, 22, 23, 24, 26 and 41, each of four vessels. The two drifters were also used for minesweeping. All reported to a 'dug-out' officer, fifty-five-year-old Commander Fredrick Neville Eardley-Wilmott in the base ship *Paragon*. Elsewhere on the east coast there were forty minesweeping trawlers and three drifters on the Humber; forty-three trawlers and nine drifters at Yarmouth; and twenty-four trawlers and six drifters at Harwich. In total, by this stage in the war, 280 trawlers and 75 drifters were employed minesweeping, nearly all of them manned by the men of the RNPS.

The Oropesa sweep

The navy confidently expected mining to be as it had been in the previous conflict – mostly moored, contact mines. It had, however, developed different thinking regarding the sweeping of them. The classic A-sweep, strung between two trawlers, was now considered less than optimum as the sweepers' freedom of movement was dangerously restricted, especially under air attack.

It had been replaced by the single-wire Oropesa* sweep, initially used with fleet sweepers only. But a lighter Mark II version was developed with trawlers in mind; at first this did not work well as the otter board it required had too high resistance to water. But a Mark II-star was produced in 1937 and was found satisfactory.

The Oropesa comprised a single wire, which had a steel torpedo-shaped float attached to its outer end. The float was stored right on the outer quarter of the minesweeping vessel, next to the minesweeping davit. There was also an otter, attached to the outer end and connected to the float by a wire, which equalled the required sweeping depth. When the sweep wire was running the Oropesa float would be racing through the water so to keep it visible it had a vertical steel pole which carried a small flag or steel pellet painted red or green. The wire was serrated and required leather gloves to handle it. The serrations acted as a saw against the mine's mooring wire. Usually, special cutters, sometimes fitted with explosives, were also attached to the wire at intervals. These were metal clamps in the shape of a V fitted to the sweep wire and which would snag the mine mooring cable as the sweep wire dragged across it. Each clamp held a small explosive charge designed to detonate when snagged. When the cable was winched back in, the clamps were removed one by one otherwise they would explode when they came into contact with the winch. At all times an axe was stored by the winch in case of a sudden need to cut the cable.

As in the first war, the swept channel was marked with danbuoys. Trawlers were expected to sweep at around 5–6 knots, have a maximum draught of 14ft and work in no more than a force 5 sea. The key to sweeping contact mines was to cut the mooring cable and destroy the mine when it came to the surface, either with rifle fire, aimed at the horns, or machine gun, which targeted the area below the surface, to puncture the mine and cause it to sink to the bottom.

As soon as the war started the Germans began laying contact mines from their estimated stock of 200,000. Destroyers, torpedo boats and even seaplanes laid mines off the English east coast and in the Thames estuary. This was as had been expected. But, the navy's confidence in the type of enemy they would face was soon undercut. Suddenly ships started to be sunk without any contact mines being observed; the destroyer HMS *Blanche* on 13 November 1939; the cruiser-minelayer *Adventure*, badly damaged in the Thames estuary, also on the 13th; and HMS *Gypsy*, entering Harwich, on the 21st were all early victims. What was going on?

New enemies

The answer was the magnetic mine, a new foe for the minesweepers to counter. Except there was no solution. It was hoped that countermining with depth charges would work; it didn't. Then a destroyer, HMS *Douglas*, was ordered to steam at full speed over the new mines in an attempt to trigger them yet escape the explosion. Fortunately for the crew, that didn't work either. The drifter *Ray of Hope* from the Mine Recovery Flotilla caught one on 10 December; but it exploded, sank the vessel and killed nine men, all RNPS.

Hence, as more magnetic mines appeared in the Thames estuary during November and December, there came an impassioned radio appeal† for wooden-hulled trawlers and drifters to volunteer. They were equipped with towed magnetised iron bars to attract the mines. Known as the 'Bosun's Nightmare', this invention was an A-sweep between two vessels with thirty-four magnetic bars attached to it.

By late December 1939, Germany's mining focus shifted from the Thames to the Norfolk coast to try and close the east coast War Channel which eased the pressure on the Nore Command at the mouth of the river. Additionally, German magnetic mine stocks were now running low, but 470 had been laid by the end of the year, causing heavy losses.

Eventually, HMS *Vernon* (the navy's mining school) discovered the mines' secrets and countermeasures were developed§. One of the first was a 'skid' – magnetic coils mounted on a barge and towed behind a trawler or drifter (see plate 81). This was followed by the LL-sweep,β which proved to be the final answer to the magnetic mine. Two long, buoyant, electric cables of unequal length were streamed from the stern of a trawler or other vessel. By pulsing the electrical power on and off a magnetic field was created which detonated the mine (see plate 59).

---

† Specifically, the Admiralty asked for 200 'drifters' and 2,000 men aged 18–35, especially enginemen and stokers.

§ In November 1939 a magnetic mine was dropped on land and was dissected with great courage by Lieutenant Commander John Garnault Delahaize Ouvry. This allowed for an understanding of the mine's workings. Ouvry received the DSO for his action.

---

* Named after the trawler it was first tested in.

β Short for 'Longitudinal line'.

82. Drifters were used for minesweeping purposes too. This is the steel-sided herring drifter *Ocean Vim*, built in Aberdeen in 1930 and registered at Yarmouth. During the war she was based at Barrow and converted to a minesweeper with an LL reel sweep.

Trawlers used the Mark II LL-sweep, towing one long leg of 525 yards length and a shorter one of 125 yards. Each cable finished with a 50ft copper electrode emitting a five second pulse at sixty second intervals; sweeping speed was 6–8 knots.

By April 1940, the Germans were once again air-laying magnetic mines in the Thames estuary and off the Downs. On the 17th, aircraft of the 9th Flieger Division dropped twenty-four mines and

their Junkers Ju 88s came again on 21 and 22 April to sow their spheres of death. The latter two lays sank three motor vessels. And the first magnetic mine to be successfully swept in the Humber area was on St George's Day 1940, when the ex-Grimsby requisitioned trawler *Sisapon*, using an early version of the LL-sweep, bagged one. Less than two months later *Sisapon* herself fell victim, mined off Harwich on 12 June; twelve crew were lost including Skipper Frederick Henson and eight RNPS men.

Drifters were also used to hunt magnetic mines with the LL-sweep. Later in the war they mounted acoustic sweeps (see below) in the bows too (plate 82 depicts this well). The drifter *Ocean Vim* was too small to accommodate the large reel aft for the LL electric sweep, so it was laid along both sides of the upper deck, and was manhandled to the stern for streaming. There was also an A-frame at the bow for the acoustic sweep drum. A deckhouse and a small open upper bridge completed the fit-out and she was armed with two .303 anti-aircraft Hotchkiss machine guns aft.

Magnetic mines required the north–south polarity field created by a steel hull to trigger them. So next came a programme of de-Gaussing hulls, demagnetising them by wrapping a long electric cable around the hull and energising this from a generator; soon all the ships operating around the coast had these cables installed, initially wrapped around the side of the ships, later fitted internally.

Another technique was 'wiping' whereby a strong electric current was passed through wires dragged up and down the ship's hull to give some temporary protection; wiping stations were constructed around the coast of the British Isles.

But magnetic mines did not replace contact mines in the German armoury; daily sweeping against those continued, as did frequent losses.

Then, in 1941, another new mine type appeared, the acoustic mine. These were detonated by the sound of the victim's propellers reacting on a diaphragm built into the weapon. After much Heath-Robinson experimentation (which included rattling tennis balls in a box) it was found that the best counter was a 'pneumatic hammer'; this was a commercial 'Kango' road drill which emitted white noise without gaps in the sound range. The hammer was fixed inside a conical steel box mounted on a boom at the trawler's bows and lowered down below the sweeper's forefoot when the sweep was being operated. HMT *Sir Kay*, a 'Round Table'-class vessel, was modified for acoustic and magnetic sweeping, as were all of her sisters except *Sir Galahad*, and is shown in plan XXII (note the boom at her prow).

Finally, in 1944, there came the pressure mine, detonated by changes to the water pressure around them and first used by Germany at the D-Day Normandy beach approaches. Known to the navy as 'oysters', they proved practically unsweepable right up to the end of the war.

There were constant improvements to the technology of mines

83. Built in 1911 at Beverley, HMT *Wardour* served in two world wars. She is here pictured at Queenborough, with the Isle of Grain in the background. She detonated a mine in 1940 but did not sink and was repaired to serve throughout the remainder of the war.

as the war progressed. For instance, mines might sometimes include a 'ship counter' function which could set the mine to ignore the first (say) two ships passing over it (which might be minesweepers deliberately trying to sweep or trigger the mines) but detonate when a third ship passed overhead, hoping it to be a higher value target.

And there were bottom or ground mines, used when the water was no more than 200ft deep or for anti-submarine measures down to a depth of 660ft. They were much harder to detect and sweep and could carry a much larger explosive charge than a simple moored mine.

Finally, mine obstructers, devices laid in combination with mines to hinder or damage minesweeping equipment, became a commonplace danger for the sweepers to deal with.

Sweeping

It was not just German mines that posed a danger to the fishermen minesweepers. The armed trawler *Firefly* was taken up in December 1939. Built in 1930 by Cook, Welton and Gemmell to fish from Hull, she was firstly based at Great Yarmouth where she was immediately in the thick of things, playing a key role in the rescue of survivors from the Norwegian ship SS *Rudolf* which was torpedoed by *U-46* on 21 December and sunk thirty miles north-east of St Abbs Head. (Norway was still neutral at this time.) The *Rudolf* lost nine of her crew but *Firefly* and another trawler, *Cardew*, rescued fourteen survivors.

Less than two months later it was *Firefly* herself that needed help. On 3 February 1940 she was despatched from Leith to neutralise a mine which had broken away from a British minefield and was floating in the Firth of Forth. As the crew attempted to deactivate the mine it exploded. The entire upper structure of the trawler was destroyed and twelve of her crew were killed with the rest wounded, including Second Hand Edward Barker, born in Cleethorpes, living in Grimsby, a fisherman all his life, who died two days later. Amongst the dead were four RNVR officers and seven RNPS seamen. *Firefly* didn't sink, however, but was towed back to Leith, and would later be rebuilt to serve again. To die in war is a risk that must be accepted; but to be killed by one's own weapons is a tragedy.

A luckier fate awaited HMT *Wardour* (plate 83). Built in 1911 at Beverley, *Wardour* served in two world wars. She was first requisitioned by the Admiralty in 1915, when she was known as *St Malo*, fitted with a 12pdr gun and used as a minesweeper. Returned to her owners in 1919, in 1932 she was registered at Grimsby and renamed *Wardour*. In August 1939 she was once again taken up by the navy as a minesweeper, based firstly at Great Yarmouth and then Queenborough. On 31 October 1940, *Wardour* detonated a mine. Her crew took to the lifeboat and were rescued. However, she didn't sink and was repaired at Sheerness before serving at the naval base *Wildfire III*, Trawler Group 3 (Queenborough) for the remainder of the war.

The most successful minesweeper of the whole war was a fishing boat, and her skipper a fisherman. In 1906 Cochrane's built and launched the 238-ton trawler *Hercules*. She served all through the First World War as a hired minesweeper. At some point afterwards her name changed to *Woodbury* and then to *Rolls Royce*, under which appellation she was taken up by the navy in March 1941, at the height of the German mining campaign.

Her skipper was thirty-nine-year-old Leopold Dickson Romyn, an experienced fisherman from Bridlington, who with his very first sweep on 9 March detonated three mines. Part of the 110th Minesweeping Group, operating out of Grimsby, keeping the East Coast Channel free for use, by 13 November Romyn and his *Rolls Royce* crew had swept 100 mines in just eight months. As it was the custom for the minesweepers to mark up their 'kills' by painting a ring around the funnel; her funnel must have been either a very pretty or a very messy sight.

The Rolls Royce company adopted the trawler and her men, and their representatives were on board for her very last minesweeping mission, when Romyn captured yet another mine

Over the course of the war, Leopold Romyn, who was advanced in rank to skipper lieutenant in January 1943 and twice awarded the DSC,[*] swept up 197 mines; he also attained the distinction of finding the largest number of lost anchors. *Rolls Royce* returned to fishing in January 1946, as did her skipper.

When shipping lanes were swept clear, the safe route was marked by danbuoys, laid by specially converted and equipped vessels. Plan XXIII shows the converted 'Isles'-class trawlers *Bryher* and *Farne*, both modified to be danlayer channel-marking boats. Their uncluttered stern area, suitable for the dropping of dans, can be seen clearly.

Plates 40 and 76 also depict danlayers.

Surely one of the oldest trawlers to be employed as a danlayer was *Elk* (181grt), a small trawler built by Cook, Welton and Gemmell in 1902. Fitted with a 3pdr gun, in the First World War she served as a minesweeper before reverting to her quotidian fishing life at Grimsby. In November 1939, she was once more taken up by the navy, converted for danbuoy work and armed with a 6pdr weapon. Her thirty-eight-year life came to an end nearly twelve months later when she was sunk by a mine south-east of Penlee Point, off Plymouth, on 27 November. Fortunately, there was no loss of life.

Comforts

It was recognised by many on the home front that the work of the minesweeping trawlers was difficult and dangerous and that conditions were poor. In some towns and villages people set up 'Minesweeping Trawlers Comfort Funds'.[†] A typical example was that at Dore and Totley, just outside Sheffield. In November 1941, chairwoman Mrs Duffy and secretary Mrs Grayson arranged for

---

[*] DSC January 1941, bar to the DSC January 1942, mentioned in despatches October 1941.

[†] These included, inter alia, the Dover Patrol (Minesweepers) Comforts Fund and the Royal Scottish Motor Yacht Club Minesweepers Comforts Fund.

eleven packing cases of 'goodies' to be sent 'to provide comforts for the men who keep the sea lanes open'. The articles supplied included two gramophones, hand-knitted socks, 144 writing pads, footballs, dartboards, magazines and so on, all paid for by fundraising events organised by the Dore and Totley ladies.

The CO of *Artegal* (a 1918 *Strath*-class vessel built as the *Robert Harding* and sold into trade, only to be re-requisitioned by the Admiralty in November 1939) wrote fulsomely in reply, noting that 'it is good to know that we have kind people who are doing everything to make life on board the trawlers a little more pleasant' and going on to remark that his pleasure was increased by the fact that he was a 'Sheffield lad'. And Skipper Lieutenant John Watson RNR of *Rehearo*, another First World War vessel, built as the *Castle*-class *John Burlingham* in 1917, thanked the Yorkshire ladies for the games and magazines sent to them for 'they help to pass away a spare hour or two in these dark days'.[3]

Chairperson Mrs Freda Duffy made certain that the residents of Dore and Totley would put their hands in their pockets a little later in the month, writing to one and all on the 24 November that:

> the third Xmas day of the war is drawing near and to the men of the Minesweeping Trawlers – those little ships that go out every day to clear the sea lanes – it will be a day of duty. They can't relax because contact mines, magnetic mines and acoustic mines may sink ships on that day as on any other day. But, in brief spells below deck, there must be some Xmas Cheer to keep alive their thoughts of the past and their hopes for the future, when officers and ratings will once again be re-united with their families on Xmas Day. To provide good cheer and woollen comforts for the fleet of minesweeping trawlers which we have adopted as our special care is the purpose of this appeal. Several hundred men … have to be provided with extra good things, to eat, to drink and to smoke, that will make their Xmas Day a day of festivity.
>
> A sum of £200 is needed to provide these comforts. Already their anticipatory thoughts are warming the cockles of their hearts. They must not be disappointed. Please put your donation in the enclosed packet.[4]

In every major naval port, the Admiralty appointed a Port Amenities Liaison Officer, often the base chaplain, whose role was to ensure the fair distribution of these heartfelt donations.

Other well-wishers adopted specific vessels. The Rotary Club of Frome (Somerset), in combination with the town's Inner Wheel, adopted the minesweeping trawler *John Cattling*. Every month they sent the crew a parcel consisting of groceries, toiletries and cigarettes, together with home-knitted warm wear such as gloves and scarves.

During the Second World War, the Germans laid over 120,000 mines and 30,000 minesweeping obstructers in north-western Europe alone, plus many more in the Mediterranean. All of these

had to be identified and then swept. But despite the best efforts of the RNPS, Axis mines are calculated to have sunk 281 British warships of all types and 296 British merchant vessels (521 Allied merchant ships altogether).[*]

And of a total of 745 minesweeping fishing vessels employed throughout the war, mainly requisitioned, 402 were trawlers, 287 drifters and 56 whalers.[5] The contribution of the fishing fleet and RNPS fishermen and conscripts to retaining Sovereignty of the Seas cannot be underestimated.

Of the 402 trawlers, 111 were completed before 1914 and 134 during the First World War. It was the old that bore the brunt of the sweeping effort, and of the losses. Three were lost in 1939, thirty-three in 1940, and twenty-three in 1941. Thereafter the rate of loss slackened, partly because other types of vessel took over some minesweeping duties. But eighty-four minesweeper trawlers were sunk in the war.[6]

Regarding drifters, of the 287 sweepers, 55 were lost, 39 of them in 1940 and 1941.[7]

---

[*] For comparison, the British laid over 185,000 mines for protective purposes in all theatres of war and over 76,000 mines in enemy waters (nearly 55,000 by aircraft, 11,000 by fast minelayers and destroyers, 5,500 by Coastal Forces and 3,000 by submarines). These are estimated to have sunk 1,050 Axis warships and merchant ships and damaged a further 540.

14: Convoy

Germany started the war with thirty-nine U-boats, more than at the commencement of the First World War. This total quickly grew to 250 in commission at the end of December 1941, 358 by May 1942 and 420 a year later. Moreover, unlike the first war, by mid-1940 the French coast was in German hands thereby making it much quicker for U-boats to get to the Atlantic shipping lanes. One hundred of them were operating there in early 1943.

Unlike in 1914, the Royal Navy introduced some limited form of convoy from the beginning of the war. Indeed, the first coastal convoys, mainly coal for London which needed 40,000 tons per week, began on 6 September 1939. However, exactly akin to 1914, there were nowhere near enough purpose-built convoy escorts. Thus, the system was far from comprehensive and most convoys had minimal escort.

Indeed, initially, the main use of the anti-submarine trawlers was in submarine-hunting groups (hunter-killer groups) which sounded suitably glorious but largely failed to deliver and took resources away from the duty of convoy escort. These 'A/S striking forces', primarily based around Scapa Flow, consisted of groups of four trawlers, usually with a 'dug-out' retired RN officer in overall command.

However, as losses mounted and the demand grew for convoy everywhere, it was to the armed trawlers that the navy turned for trade protection in the early years of the war. Their weatherly qualities, so often demonstrated in civilian life, often meant that they were the only form of attendant vessels which could operate in heavy weather and they could stay at sea when other types of escorts were compelled to seek shelter. But with their slow speeds, if a trawler left station to investigate a contact or rescue the crew of a torpedoed ship, it could take hours for the vessel to regain station on the moving convoy. Nonetheless, the burden of ensuring that war materials could flow from the USA, and from the Empire, fell disproportionately on the trawlers and the men of the RPNS. They played a key role in protecting the convoys and cargo ships involved; and statistics proved convoy's worth. During the first six months of the war, out of 164 ships sunk by U-boats, only 7 were sunk in convoys escorted by A/S vessels.[1]

But there were other demands on the resources available. One was the use of trawlers around the coast as an anti-invasion task force: '[A]ll around the coasts were some hundreds of armed trawlers, motor-torpedo boats and minesweepers which could take part in the melee, if invasion were attempted', Churchill told the War Cabinet in July 1940.[2] And again, on 15 October, he insisted that the Royal Navy could not be allowed to detach ships for convoy escort as they were still needed for anti-invasion.[3]

As but one example, the A/S trawler *Northern Dawn* was escorting convoys around Scotland when she was urgently recalled to Dartmouth as part of the counter to the invasion of Britain.[4] And on 15 September 1940 CinC Western Approaches, Admiral Sir Martin Dunbar-Nasmith VC, warned all his ships that there was 'every indication that the enemy is about to attempt the invasion of our country' and hoped that the foe would be given 'a smashing blow from which he will never recover'.[5] By trawlers, apparently.

Indeed, Churchill was curiously willing to incur considerable losses in the Atlantic in the early years of the war, preferring to use his resources in a more aggressive fashion to the east. As a result, 1.3 million grt of British shipping were lost between Northern America and Canada and the UK in 1940. It was only when the sinkings became unsustainable, such as 2.76 million grt in 1942, that the navy was allowed to give serious attention to running heavily escorted convoys.

Moreover, in the early months of the war, there was no method for sharing good practice between those escorts and commanders who evolved successful tactics versus U-boats and those who desperately needed to learn them. This gap was eventually plugged in mid-1940 by the establishment of an anti-submarine escort school at Tobermory, HMS *Western Isles*.

HMS *Western Isles*

The Royal Navy has a long and distinguished tradition of throwing up 'characters' who live in the memory long after their bodies have shuffled off the mortal coil. One such was Vice Admiral Sir Gilbert Owen Stephenson.

Stephenson had been a member of the 'Fishpond' in the Mediterranean – one of Jacky Fisher's hand-picked coming men – pre-1914. Aged just twenty-three, he was given command of the destroyer *Scourge*. He then took the torpedo course at Royal Naval College, Greenwich and was posted to the staff of HMS *Vernon*, the Royal Navy's torpedo school. During the war Stephenson had gained wide experience both in the Admiralty and in command positions at sea and ended up as one of the controlling brains behind the Otranto Barrage, undertaking early experiments into the use of hydrophones to detect submarines. Post-war, Stephenson was director of the anti-submarine division of the Admiralty. He left this role in 1921 to command the cruiser *Dauntless*, and then in 1923 the battleship *Revenge*, where he had the young Louis Mountbatten as one of his junior officers. In other words, Stephenson was a highly qualified officer who, when he retired from the navy in 1929 in the rank of rear admiral, could look back on a successful career.

On retirement, the unmarried Stephenson involved himself in Boys Clubs and the Navy League. Heavily bearded, he was nicknamed 'Monkey Brand' by the boys after a famous make of hand soap. Recalled to the colours on the outbreak of war as a commodore RNR, in 1940 the sixty-two-year-old Stephenson was tasked with setting up HMS *Western Isles*, the Royal Navy's new Anti-Submarine Training School.

He proved both an inspired and controversial choice. He emphasised strict discipline in his training combined with encouraging a willingness to adapt quickly to various situations, with surprise inspections and orders to trainees, as well as creative wargames to simulate difficult situations at sea. A frequently recounted, although possibly apocryphal, tale is that when inspecting a corvette and its crew, he suddenly threw his hat on the deck and called it an unexploded bomb. A trainee immediately kicked it into the water. After Stephenson commended him for quick action, he suddenly shouted that the hat was now a man overboard and the crestfallen trainee had to dive in to retrieve it.

He was also a martinet, and gloried in the reputation of a man unafraid to fire anyone who came to his school, from commanding officers downwards. On one occasion, he dismissed Commander, the Earl of Carrick,[*] in charge of a trawler A/S group. At a dinner later in the war, he delighted in telling the assembled company that 'I had him out like that' jerking his closed fist over his shoulder. On being informed that the earl was now British Naval Liaison Officer in Norfolk, Virginia, he exclaimed 'God Bless My Soul. He was absolutely useless.'[6]

But whatever, his personal peccadillos, Stephenson beat, frightened, or otherwise inculcated effective A/S tactics into a large number of trawlers, their crews and skippers and other small escort craft, and he played no small part in winning the Battle of the Atlantic.

The Atlantic convoys

There were at least two enemies to be faced by the trawlers in the Atlantic. German aggressors for sure; but also the weather. 'The weather in the North Atlantic could be anything, from being like a mill pond, to a savage and ruthless killer, with huge mountainous seas, flinging ships all over the place with no regard for their size. They could overwhelm a large and well-founded merchant ship suddenly without warning, and without any other vessel in the vicinity being aware of what had taken place … the sea could be at times more dangerous than the U-boats and the mines, it could be tranquil and also treacherous – a proper Jekyll and Hyde.'[7]

And if it was hard on ships, the weather was equally tough for the crews:

hurricanes seemed to be abundant and prolific, especially in the middle three years of the war, '41, '42, and '43, with howling winds and huge rolling seas seemingly miles high accompanied by frequent rain hail and snow which felt like bullets as it hit you. On watch one was constantly wet through even though you had on several layers of clothing, on the top of which you had oilskins and sea boots and a sou'wester on your head, with a towel wrapped around your neck to keep out the water and stop it from getting down to the inner layers. Coming off watch proved to be just as bad. Trying to get your wet clothing off while being thrown from one side of the cabin or mess deck to the other was a nightmare at times, and on many of these occasions you just could not be bothered to try. You just turned in to your bunk as you were, oilskins and all.[8]

However, the trawlers fared better than the regular navy ships. Lieutenant Colin Warwick recalled that his trawler *St Loman* and her sister ships 'made light of the worst of the North Atlantic weather despite their low freeboard amidships. The fleet destroyers with their shallow draught and knife-like bows made heavy going in the usual rough weather, severely reducing their cruising speed to avoid taking heavy seas forwards.'[9]

Escort groups for the Western Ocean convoys were initially based at Greenock and those for the Gibraltar convoys at Liverpool. But soon Liverpool became the nerve centre for transatlantic convoys and the largest convoy port in Britain. The escorts for the Atlantic convoys took the merchant ships halfway across, to the so-called CHOP line, where Canadian escort vessels based at Halifax, Nova Scotia and Argentia, Newfoundland, took over; these Canadian ships had brought out with them ships making the return journey which were now handed over to the British-based escorts.

As better-equipped escort vessels became available, the role of the trawlers changed. Many now were used for 'unbuttoning': they provided an escort for groups of cargo ships which had to break off from the main convoy upon arrival at its terminus and head for smaller or more distant secondary ports. Likewise, they collected vessels from these ports to escort them along the coastline to the convoy assembly point; perhaps unsurprisingly, this was called 'buttoning'. This was the role played in 1941 by the Admiralty 'Dance'-class trawlers *Gavotte*, *Saraband* and *Foxtrot* (see plate 48 for the type). Based at Belfast, they ushered small convoys from the major assembly port of Oban around the top of Scotland to Edinburgh.

Trawlers were also invaluable for the escort of so-called 'coastal convoys', often coal from Wales or the north-east to southern ports, especially London. These became a particular target for E-boats; in 1940, they sank 47,985grt of merchant vessels (twenty-three ships).

Russian convoys

The Atlantic convoys were dangerous and difficult. But the Arctic

---

[*] Theobald Walter Somerset Henry Butler, 8th Earl of Carrick, an RNR officer.

convoys, seventy-eight of them in total between August 1941 and May 1945, were loathed and detested by Royal and Merchant Navy sailors alike. Sailed at Churchill's insistence in order to keep Russia supplied and fighting Germany on the eastern front, the route skirted German-occupied Norway, where significant anti-ship air forces were based. On passage to the Soviet ports, the dangers included the proximity of German air, submarine and surface assets, the likelihood of severe weather, the frequency of fog, and the strong currents and the mixing of cold and warm waters, which made ASDIC use difficult. Drift ice and the alternation between the difficulties of navigating and maintaining convoy cohesion in constant darkness in winter convoys, or being attacked around the clock in constant daylight during summer months, were other issues to be faced.

Trawlers were no strangers to this environment, however, having been regular peacetime visitors to the fishing grounds of Iceland and the White Sea. In this respect, if no other, they were suited to escort duty in the North Atlantic and Arctic waters. And one such, the ex-Fleetwood and Grimsby trawler *Northern Gem*, had the misfortune to be part of two of the most difficult of the Russian convoys.

Northern Gem was built in Germany in 1936, ordered by Leverhulme Limited to absorb frozen credits in Germany, and on the outbreak of war was taken up by the Admiralty for anti-submarine duties. Of 655grt, she carried the usual depth charge equipment together with a 4in gun and three .303 Lewis guns, one on either side of the bridge and one astern on top of the galley. Later she gained a 0·5in Vickers machine gun and an Oerlikon 20mm as well (see plates 60 and 61). She was also fitted with smoke-laying equipment.

On 27 June 1942, she departed from Hvalfjord, Iceland, for the port of Archangel in Soviet Russia as part of the close escort for a convoy PQ17. Three other trawlers sailed with her, *Lord Austin* and *Lord Middleton*, both ex-Hull, and *Ayrshire*, ex-Grimsby. *Northern Gem* had by this time acquired a motley collection of additional weapons, some of which can be seen with her crew members in plate 84.

In total, there were thirty-four merchant ships, an oiler for the escort and three rescue ships. The escort was made up of six destroyers, four corvettes, three minesweepers, four trawlers, two AA ships and two submarines. There was also a distant escort of an aircraft carrier, two battleships and a medium-range group of four British and American cruisers.

The convoy suffered from the usual air attacks, in which three cargo ships were sunk, but was making fair progress when, on 4 July at 2133, the Admiralty ordered the convoy to scatter and ships to make their own individual way to Russia. They had received (erroneous) intelligence that the battleship *Tirpitz*, together with its battle group, was at sea and planned to attack the convoy.

Coxswain Sidney Kerslake remembered the stunned reaction on board *Northern Gem*: 'to say that all of us on the *Gem* were stunned would be putting it mildly. I can remember the words that I said at the time, "What are we splitting up for, we're better off as we are,

on our own we have no chance at all". The more we thought and talked about it, the more horrified we became. I was only twenty-two, and like many others of my age, was still young enough to want to live and come through this war, but now I felt that my time had come. It was probably only because I had a responsible position that I was able to keep my worst thoughts to myself.'[10]

Northern Gem and her sisters eventually made Russia; but of the thirty-four merchant vessels which had left Iceland, twenty-three were sunk and only 35 per cent of the tonnage consigned to the Soviets actually arrived. It angered the Russians and left a bitter taste with Britain's American allies.

For the *Gem*, there was now the return journey to face. On 13 September, she departed Archangel as part of the escort of a twenty-ship convoy, QP 14, bound for Loch Ewe in Scotland. The Germans set up a patrol line of seven U-boats to intercept them and aircraft continuously attacked and bombed the convoy.

On 20 September, the minesweeper HMS *Leda*, part of the close escort, was torpedoed in the Norwegian Sea, south-west of Spitsbergen, by *U-435*. Skipper Mullender of *Gem* saw the explosion and immediately set course to effect a rescue. When *Gem* got to within about a hundred and fifty feet of her, and was beginning to ease round to go alongside, *Leda*'s crew started to abandon ship by jumping over into the sea on her port side; Mullender had to go full astern to stop, making sure that he did not run some of the faster swimmers under. One of the first to be picked up was a lieutenant, and he was followed by some eighty of the crew. Eventually, Mullender came right alongside *Leda* as the stricken minesweeper lay stopped in the water, so that the crew could step on board without getting their feet wet.

Coxswain Kerslake was on *Gem*'s wheel:

We had the rescue nets over the side for them to climb up as quickly as was possible and as they did so a destroyer came up our starboard side and shouted through her loud hailer for our skipper to get back to the convoy, for we were not supposed to stop to pick up survivors on the run back. Our skipper told him to "f*ck off", whereupon the destroyer's CO said he would report him when we arrived in port, … It was all go, just backing and filling with the engines on slow to save men who were in danger of drifting past ahead or astern of the *Northern Gem*. Having picked them all out of the water, we came hard to starboard and made our way back to our station, and astern the *Leda* turned on to her starboard side and slid under the cold waters of the Arctic ocean. … we had three dead onboard, an SPO, a PO and an ordinary seaman, all having been injured in the torpedo explosion which I think hit her in the forward boiler room.[11]

They had manged to save all but fourteen of the minesweeper's crew. Eighty-one men had been rescued, a total which included nine men previously sunk on the way out.

84. The villainous looking crew of the escort trawler *Northern Gem*, with an assortment of weaponry, at the start of the infamous PQ-17 convoy in June 1942. Front L–R, Leading Seaman Tim Coleman, Seaman Johnny Wardle, L/Asᴅɪᴄ Operator Jack Sullivan; Back L–R, Gunner Bill Reed, Officers Steward Jimmy Budd, Coxswain Sidney Kerslake.

QP 14 finally reached Loch Ewe on 26 September 1942. In his report, Acting Commander Arthur Hugh Wynne-Edwards of *Leda* wrote that 'the large majority of those who got away from the ship were picked up in spite of the low temperatures and the fact that most of them were immersed in fuel oil. This largely due to the excellent work performed by *Northern Gem* … I cannot speak too highly of their efforts in picking people up.'[12] And far from being reported, Skipper Mullender and three crewmen were mentioned in despatches.

But *Northern Gem*'s adventures in the Arctic were far from over. On 22 December 1942, she departed Loch Ewe for Murmansk as part of the close escort for the fifteen-ship convoy JW51B. *Gem* was accompanied by the minesweeper *Bramble,* two corvettes and one other armed trawler, *Vizalma* (ex-Grimsby). The close escort was supported by six Home Fleet destroyers led by *Onslow.* A cruiser cover force, comprising *Jamaica* and *Sheffield* and two destroyers, was also at sea to guard against attack by surface units.

The German navy planned a sortie to intercept JW51B, code-named Operation Regenbogen. This required the heavy cruiser *Admiral Hipper*, the pocket battleship *Lützow* and six large destroyers to attack and destroy the convoy. On 31 December 1942, the Germans commenced their assault but, despite being heavily outgunned, the destroyer escort, under the command of Captain R

St Vincent Sherbrooke in *Onslow*, beat off the attack in the so-called 'Battle of the Barents Sea'; not one merchant vessel was lost.

At 1115, at the height of the encounter, the destroyer *Achates* was laying smoke to protect the merchant vessels when she was hit by gunfire from *Admiral Hipper*, killing the commanding officer, Lieutenant Commander Arthur Henry Tyndall Johns and forty crew. First Lieutenant Loftus Peyton-Jones took over command and, despite having sustained severe damage in the shelling, *Achates* continued to lay her smokescreen. But she was clearly in a bad way and *Northern Gem* was ordered to take her in tow. When *Gem* approached it could be seen that *Achates* was well down by the stern and had a considerable list over to port. Within minutes of the trawler's arrival the destroyer went further and further over, until she lay completely on her port side.

Sidney Kerslake remembered the scene:

I could see the figures of men, some with red lights on their life jackets and some even smoking, clambering through the rails and on to her starboard side which had now become her deck. As she went further over until she was floating completely bottom up, the men slid down her side and into the water, her keel now pointing to the heavens. Then as the men in the water started swimming towards the *Gem*, we stood on our deck and listened in amazement as we heard their voices giving out with a rendering of "Roll out the Barrel". Here they were in dire peril, not only from drowning, but freezing to death if we could not get them out of the water within a few minutes, singing at the tops of their voices. Those who had survived the action and the struggle to keep their ship the *Achates* afloat, were now fighting for their own lives, to save themselves in those cold and freezing waters of the stormy Arctic Ocean. Their agony was our agony, … until the gallant *Achates* slid beneath the surface of the disturbed seas, taking with her the dead and the badly wounded who could not be moved … we had got safely onboard all that was possible of those who were still alive.[13]

Gem's crew each took a spell for a few minutes over the side on the rescue nets. They entwined their legs in the nets to leave arms and hands free, additionally making sure that they should not be pulled away by the suction of the seas rolling under the ship's hull, or by the weight of the men in the water. Then they grabbed for the floating bodies and hauled them up high enough for others of the crew to pull them over the ship's rail and onto the deck, from where they were taken below to the warmth of the seamen's messdeck.

Coxswain Kerslake saw a young lad drifting past the stern with his arm outstretched to catch a line; as he threw it to him it dropped over his shoulders, but he seemed to have lost all the feeling in his body due to the cold. 'I screamed at him to hold on, but he could do nothing to help save himself, so I tried to throw several loops of the line around his arm, but in those last few seconds "Mother" was the last word I heard as he disappeared below the surface. I know that I was crying myself with helplessness and frustration as I saw him go.'[14]

Any hope of further rescue was snuffed out by a huge underwater explosion which lifted *Gem* bodily out of the water. The depth charges on *Achates* had exploded; the surface of the sea shivered for a few moments then burst into a boiling cauldron of confused froth. When it returned to its former state, there was no one left alive in the water. *Northern Gem* went to full speed to catch up with the convoy. One hundred and thirteen men from *Achates* died that night; but *Northern Gem* rescued a further eighty, a remarkable achievement in the dark and under attack.

And the trawler's work was not yet done. She carried no doctor and the injuries to many of the rescued men were beyond the elementary first aid that her crew could offer. Surgeon Maurice Hood was transferred by jumping across from the destroyer *Obdurate* while *Gem*'s skipper edged his trawler towards her. Once

aboard, the forward mess deck became the operating theatre, and the mess-deck table the operating table. This had to be held firmly in place by several other members of their crew, so that it would not be thrown on to the deck by the wild movements of the ship.

Given the frequency with which *Gem* was involved in such work, it was perhaps appropriate that in 1943 *Northern Gem* was refitted as a convoy rescue ship,[*] with a small sick bay and medics on board, as was her sister ship *Northern Pride* (plate 77).

The Arctic convoys delivered 700 shiploads of cargo, 4 million tons of goods, to Stalin's Russia, sailing round Norway in appalling weather at Churchill's insistence.

And in total, some 9,000 convoys were escorted to and from Britain, roughly one every two days for five years. In all these enterprises, trawlers and their fishermen crews played a key role.

---

[*] The genesis of the convoy rescue ship came in 1940 when the losses of merchant vessels and the drain on experienced Merchant Navy personnel became a grave concern to government and Admiralty alike, as did the effect on the morale of the sailors involved.

On 22 September 1940, the CinC Western Approaches, Admiral Sir Martin Dunbar-Nasmith VC, wrote to the Admiralty expressing his worries regarding such issues and advocated introduction of enhanced specialised 'picking up' ships, aka Convoy Rescue Ships (CRS), to follow astern of convoys and to transfer from an outbound to an inbound convoy along with the convoy escorts at the CHOP point. Initially the CRS accompanied outbound ships for three to five days before switching over to an inbound one. This often involved the CRS loitering at the meeting point and during one such case, the first CRS, the coastal steamer SS *Beachy*, was sunk.

15: *In Imis Petimus*

Life on board

A sailor is a slave to his stomach; so unsurprisingly, food and drink were a key preoccupation amongst the men serving in Harry Tate's Navy.

Coxswain Sid Kerslake of *Northern Gem* noted, 'I found myself ordering all of the food, and doing all of the victualling, the issuing of the rum ration, making sure that the ship was kept clean at all times, at sea or in harbour, weather permitting of course; in fact I was doing all the things that a coxswain of a ship was supposed to do, and many others that he was not.'[1]

But the food still had to be cooked and served. On the 'Gem'-class anti-submarine trawler *Pearl*, the galley, which comprised a coal range and oven, was right aft. There was no below-deck communication, so all meals had to be collected from the cook and carried along the open decks and down the steep ladders into the mess decks. It was both a dangerous and difficult job in heavy weather and the food was often soaked with sea water before it reached anyone's stomach, given the low freeboard. In rough weather, seas swept aboard and put out the cooking fires.

Conditions often mitigated against decent grub. 'Food was one of the biggest problems. We would have fresh meat and veg when we left base but when that ran out it was tin stuff and hardtack … I went along to the galley and the cook had a piece of beef. He was just going to put in a saucepan of boiling water to kill the maggots … bread was as hard as a rock and mouldy. Cook's method was to soak it in a bucket of water and then cut the mould off and then soak it longer and put it in the oven to dry out.'[2] Surprisingly, the result of this treatment was found palatable.

Another problem was the dreariness of the food available. Generally, a meal would include one or more of red lead (tinned tomatoes), tinned sausage, bully beef (corned beef), pilchards or Chinese wedding cake (rice). Sid Kerslake thought that 'meals got monotonously repetitive at times, though this was no fault of the cook's; he always did his best with the food he had, and we often got freshly baked bread'.[3]

And, when on duty, the days often seemed to merge into each other. Christmas Day 1942 aboard the A/S trawler *Northern Gem* was spent escorting convoy JW51B to Russia. The event 'had come and gone, with dinner consisting of corned beef sandwiches for those who felt like eating'.[4]

But occasionally, fresh food could be obtained while at sea. Plate 85 shows the crew of HMT *Northern Sky* anxiously awaiting the return of their ship's boat which had gone to a working fishing trawler to get some fresh food – cod, ling, haddock and skate were obtained, enough to last for five days. The ship's boats seen here were to a design specified by the Admiralty for both trawlers and drifters. In the case of the former, this was a 16ft 'Admiralty pattern trawler's boat'. For drifters, a slightly smaller version at 14ft 6in was specified in 1934, as shown in plan XXX.

On the A/S trawler *Kingston Agate*, 'the messdeck was alive with small red beetles of the cockroach strain. There were tens of thousands of them; they were everywhere, on the deck, the bulkheads, the deckhead, the tables, the bunks and even on the occupants of the messdeck, who seemed supremely indifferent to their presence. The whole place seemed alive with crawling, scurrying insects. They ran over the food on the plates and had to be brushed off before a mouthful was eaten; they dropped on to your hair and shoulders as you sat at the table.'[5]

Sometimes there were unexpected benefits to the hard graft of minesweeping. Frank McGovern was serving on an Oropesa-equipped small trawler, *Maretta*, built in 1929. While sweeping in the Channel they spotted an object in the water which, on closer inspection, turned out to be a barrel. Ascertaining it was full, the skipper ordered it hoisted aboard where it proved to be a cask of Guinness – 'and the CO told us to keep quiet about it. We didn't need telling twice … we had a good time while it lasted and a lot of pints were consumed.'[6]

Accommodation was 'challenging' on board. In *St Loman*, the seamen's and stokers' messes and sleeping quarters were converted from the former fish holds underneath the foredeck. Wash basins and 'heads' were on the deck, under the forecastle head. The officers' cabin and mess deck were an aft extension of the seamen's mess, separated from the lower orders by wooden panelling. Heating was provided to both messes by a potbellied stove with a chimney poking out on deck, whose smoke joined with that of the engine room funnel. An American naval officer who was given a tour of the *St Loman*'s crew accommodation commented that 'that place has all the comforts of a dank, dark prison. Your officers' wardroom and sleeping area are as bare and inviting as a baboon's bottom.'[7]

The relationship between the fishermen and the regular navy was not always a smooth one. There were conflicts between the more formal navy and merchant officers and the trawlermen, who were used to a more unstructured environment. 'I've heard that lots of strange things happened on other HM trawlers that had RNR officers in command, and ships with Wavy Navy Officers [RNVR]. The majority who at the early part of the war had little or no authority

85. Carrying enough food to keep all the crew supplied during voyages of indeterminate length was a problem. Pictured in May 1942, the crew of HMT *Northern Sky*, part of the Northern Patrol, anxiously watch the progress of their boat towards a Grimsby fishing trawler to collect some fresh fish.

of the sort required were, I am told, sticklers for naval protocol. Some seemed to think that trawlers were destroyers, manned throughout by three badge killicks.* It's surprising how when some people get a bit of authority thrust upon them, they take on the mantle of the Almighty.'[8]

And Commodore Duke noted that '[the fishermen] were fine seamen and they were doing good and efficient work at sea. The discipline of the sea they understood but the ordered and disciplined life of the navy on harbour was beyond their ken.'[9]

---

* Leading seamen with three good conduct badges.

Wages were much less than a fisherman might expect to make in a good season. All this discomfort and danger was endured for the princely sum of 2s.5d per day; but at least the Admiralty recognised that the job was tough; RNPS men at sea received an extra 6d a day hard-lying money.[10] And for officers, service in trawlers brought with it an extra 2s a day hard-lying money and 3s command money for the commanding officer.[11]

Nearly all trawlers carried some sort of animal, usually a cat or a dog, sometimes both. They were useful as companions and more so as moggies and terriers would keep down the ever-present rats. This was not a wartime peculiarity; in peacetime, fishermen did the same and were very superstitious about the behaviour of their animals.

Cloughton Wyke was an old trawler, launched as the Admiralty-built *Mersey*-class *John Johnson* in 1918, sold in 1922 and then taken up again by the Admiralty in June 1940 for duty as a minesweeper. She had a cat which lived on board.

On 2 February 1942, the trawler was preparing to leave

Gorleston (near Great Yarmouth) to sweep in the War Channel. As the lines were being cast off the cat, sitting on the gunnels, jumped ashore. She was passed back. Again, she jumped ashore and was once more returned to the deck. Finally, as the trawler left the quayside, she gave a mighty jump and was last seen crossing the nearby fields at speed. She had even left her kittens aboard. If this had been in ordinary times, many fishermen would have refused to sail, seeing this as a bad luck omen. But it was war, and they set off to sweep.

Out at sea, off Cromer, *Cloughton Wyke* developed a problem, and was ordered to break formation, haul in the sweep, and stay to one side until the problem was resolved and she could restart her progress. The men relaxed and made a brew. Then, out of nowhere, the little minesweeper was attacked by two German planes, bombed and sunk. Four men were killed. The cat had been right.

Service overseas

The trawlers and men of the RNPS did not just serve in the waters around the British coast or on Atlantic convoy escort. Many trawlers and drifters were sent to the Mediterranean, others to Africa and some to America. Even in New Zealand, British trawlers played a part.

The Mediterranean, 1940

In September 1939, the Mediterranean Fleet had five trawlers of the 5th A/S group and another two trawlers and four drifters for general purposes. A year later there were twenty.

One of the Mediterranean minesweepers was the trawler *Moonstone*, a 'Gem'-class purchased by the Admiralty in 1939 and previously named *Lady Madelaine*. Because she had been part of the navy before the war, her crew were Royal Navy general service ratings, commanded by a boatswain, with an RNR second-in-command. *Moonstone* was part of the 4th A/S group, now serving in the Med. In June 1940, Italy joined with Germany in the war against Britain and the Italian navy, the Regia Marina, commenced operations against the Royal Navy and Allied shipping. Within a few weeks of starting minelaying operations on 6 June 1940, the Regia Marina had laid over 10,000 mines in dozens of fields.

On 16 June 1940 *Moonstone* rescued the crew of the Norwegian tanker *James Stove* which had been sunk by the Italian submarine *Galileo Galilei* earlier that day. Two days later, the Regia Marina's submarine was sighted and attacked by RAF Blenheim aircraft after she had fired a warning shot at a neutral steamer. *Moonstone* heard the gunfire and headed to the area. When darkness fell, the submarine resurfaced to recharge its batteries but was discovered by *Moonstone*, forcing it to crash dive. Early on the 19th, Boatswain William Joseph Henry Moorman RN obtained an ASDIC contact and attacked with two depth charges. This triggered the release of poisonous fumes in the submarine and the symptoms of methyl chloride poisoning appeared in some crew members. Her commander, Corrado Nardi, decided to fight it out with his smaller opponent on the surface, where he would have the advantage of speed (up to 17 knots) and particularly firepower, with his two 100mm (3.9in) guns.

Breaking the surface, *Galileo Galilei*'s crew manned her guns and got off the first shot, but this missed; meanwhile, Moorman ordered speed and course to close. *Moonstone* bore down bows-on to give the smallest profile to the submarine's gunners and she continuously fired her bridge-side Lewis guns, before opening up with the 4in, hitting the submarine's bridge and forward gun position and killing or wounding the bridge crew, including Nardi, who died in the attack.

Leaderless and with the remaining gun jammed, *Galileo Galilei* surrendered and was boarded by the trawler. *Moonstone* was joined by the destroyer *Kandahar* and between them they towed their prize to Aden. The Italians had twelve men killed and four wounded; *Moonstone* had no casualties. Petty Officer Frederick Quested, in charge of the gun crew, received the DSM. William Moorman was awarded the DSC; his citation noted that he was 'awarded the Distinguished Service Cross on July 5th, 1940, for daring, enterprise and skill in capturing an Italian submarine, [and] has been specially selected, in further recognition of these services, to take courses with a view to his promotion to the rank of Lieutenant'.[12]

The utility of a well-handled trawler had been proved again. And by May 1944, the three Mediterranean commands possessed a total of 138: western – 11; central – 73; east – 54. A slight majority were operating as minesweepers, a few for boom defence and the remainder on A/S patrol.

Whalers too played a part in the Med. The South African Navy sent the 22nd Anti-Submarine Group of four former whalers,[*] which deployed to Alexandria in June 1940. Two of these ships sank the Italian submarine *Ondina* on 11 July 1942. In November 1941, the South Africans also despatched eight minesweepers;[†] one of these was the whaler HMSAS *Boksburg* (see plate 86), built in 1926 and requisitioned by the South African naval authorities in 1940 as a minesweeper. She served in the Mediterranean in 1942/3 and was part of the minesweeping force which kept the entrance to the port of Tripoli free to supply the 8th Army. The Durban-based Union Sealing and Whaling Company's whalers *Albert Hullet* and *Sidney Smith* were also requisitioned in South Africa and became HMSAS *Langlaagte* and *Parktown* on 8 August 1940.

They were found to be in such bad condition after years of hard usage in southern waters that it took until February 1941 to put them right, when they were deployed to the Mediterranean equipped as LL minesweepers. On 20 June 1942, *Parktown* was sunk after a one-sided fight with a flotilla of E-boats, off Tobruk. She had defended herself with a single Oerlikon and AA machine guns, until a direct hit to the bridge killed the captain, Lieutenant (SAN) Leslie James Jagger, as well as the coxswain. Within fifteen minutes, *Parktown* was stationary with a hole in the boiler, half of the crew

---

[*] *Southern Isles*, *Southern Floe*, *Southern Maid* and *Southern Sea*; all 350-ton equipped with one 4in gun. One was lost.

[†] *Boksburg*, *Bever*, *Gribb*, *Seksern*, *Imhoff*, *Treern*, *Parktown* and *Langlaagte*; all 260-ton with a 3in weapon. Three were lost.

86. Requisitioned vessels were not taken solely from the UK. This unusual vessel is the South African Navy's *Boksburg*. She was a whaler, built in 1926 and requisitioned by the South African naval authorities in 1940 as a minesweeper, later serving in the Mediterranean.

casualties, out of ammunition and with the upper deck on fire. She was abandoned and later sunk by a British MTB.

The USA, 1942

After Germany declared war on the United States on 11 December 1941, German U-boats quickly became a serious threat on America's eastern seaboard. The United States Navy was ill-prepared to defend against submarine warfare as – like Britain – it had failed to provide for and build sufficient small craft for escort and anti-submarine duty. U-boats enjoyed easy pickings in the German Operation Paukenschlag (Operation Drumbeat) when 121 Allied ships were sunk between January and May 1942, including 35 in March. The U-boat commanders called this period the 'American Shooting Season'.

The Admiralty offered to loan A/S trawlers and crews to ameliorate the lack of escorts and, commencing on 14 February, it sent twenty-one mainly ex-Grimsby and Hull trawlers[*] and two 'Lake'-class whalers, the trawlers almost entirely crewed by British RNPS men, calling first at St John's Newfoundland to refuel. After a rough crossing, here the little ships were painted in camouflage colours and had their boiler tubes cleaned or replaced, before sailing for the US coast to be based at Boston, New York, North Carolina and Norfolk Virginia. As the whaler *Wastwater* sailed up the lower Hudson for New York harbour, her Lieutenant Jones announced 'Courage, America. Help is on the way.'[13]

---

[*] Some sources give twenty-four as the number sent, others (*vide* Warwick, *Really Not Required*, p116) twenty-six. Lenton and Colledge are specific that it was twenty (Lenton and Colledge, *Warships of World War II*, p438). But the author's reconciliation (see appendix 9) gives twenty-one. That is the figure used here, as it is provable.

It proved to be a difficult assignment for the fishermen warriors. Commencing in March, the trawlers patrolled United States waters. HMT *Le Tiger* was one of Sir Alec Black's vessels, a fine, fast ship of 516 tons and capable of 14 knots. Built in 1937, she was sold to the Admiralty in December 1939 and fitted out as an anti-submarine vessel. She achieved a rare success in US waters when, on 3 July, she depth-charged and sank *U-215* with all forty-eight hands, 130 miles south-south-west of Shelburne, Nova Scotia.

But in return, six of the trawlers were lost and 125 mainly RNPS sailors died.

The German-built *Northern Princess* (1935) was torpedoed and sunk by *U-587* off Newfoundland on 7 March; thirty-eight men were killed. HMT *St Cathan* was lost off Charleston on 11 April in a collision with a Dutch cargo vessel; thirty men died. Less than a month later, the huge Hall Russell-built French trawler *Senateur Duhamel* (913grt) was rammed by USS *Semmes*, a destroyer, off Wilmington. The Americans later claimed that they had been dazzled by an interrogatory light flashed from the trawler; the fishermen said that they had mistaken her for a U-boat and intended to ram. The *Semmes* had its side ripped open to the bridge but there were no casualties on either side.

The 1935 Smith's Dock-built *Bedfordshire*, in company with HMT *St Loman*, had been sent to look for a U-boat thought to be in the vicinity of Ocracoke Island, South Carolina. In the early morning of 11 May, *Bedfordshire* sent the message 'have sighted something suspicious'; she was never seen again. She had, in fact, been torpedoed at the second attempt by *U-558*. Four days later, a total of four bodies had been washed ashore on Ocracoke Island. The Williams family of Ocracoke requested that they be allowed to bury the men in cemetery land donated by Alice Wahab Williams; a memorial service is still held there in May each year.* Thirty-seven crew died; the thirty-eighth, a young stoker named Sam Nutt, had been detained at Morehead City by local police and thus missed boarding the ship for her last patrol.

In June, the trawler *Kingston Ceylonite*, built in 1934 by Cook, Welton and Gemmell, together with USS *Bainbridge*, was escorting the American tankers *Esso Augusta* and *Robert C Tuttle* when, on 15 June, all four ships ran into a minefield laid by *U-701* in Chesapeake Bay, off Norfolk, Virginia. *Kingston Ceylonite* struck a mine and sank with the loss of twenty crew; fourteen were rescued. One tanker was damaged by a mine and one sank but was salved.

And finally, another 1934 CWG vessel, HMT *Pentland Firth*, was rammed by the minesweeper USS *Chaffinch* and sunk a few miles west of Ambrose Light Tower. Again, it was thought that the USN vessel had mistaken her for a submarine.

Two of the loaned trawlers had been lost to torpedoes, one to a mine, one in a collision and two fell victim to US Navy rammings.

The survivors were redeployed to South Africa in October.

Anti-submarine trawlers were also despatched to Canada to fight off German U-boat depravations in the St Lawrence River area. In spring 1942, six vessels were sent to Sydney, Nova Scotia, to patrol the mouth of the river and escort ships upstream to Montreal and Quebec. *Cape Mariato*, *Cape Argona*, *Everton*, *Middleton*, *Northern Wave* and *Wolves* were assigned to the task. The first two vessels, taken up from Hudson Brothers Trawlers of Hull in 1940 and 1939 respectively, were large ships at nearly 500grt and almost 200ft long. Originally built by Cochrane's in 1936, they now sported a 4in gun forward, three 20mm Oerlikons (one each side of the bridge and one aft), twin 0.5in machine guns aft, four depth charge rails plus an additional four throwers, and had the capacity for 100 depth charges to be carried. *Cape Mariato* was fitted with both ASDIC and radar, the latter having an operator's cabin bolted onto the port side of the well-deck.† There was a wardroom of four and another forty-three men aboard.

They had been at Dunkirk, served in the Russian convoys and would return to northern waters after nearly twelve months in Canada. *Mariato* was also present at D-Day; she had a long and hard war.

Freetown

The port of Freetown, Sierra Leone, had been a Royal Navy port since 1808 when, until 1870, the navy maintained a permanent squadron there, at times up to one-sixth of its operational strength, to intercept slavers off the West African coast. It had a fine harbour, built by 25,000 African labourers, which could hold up to 150 ships.

The fall of France had resulted in an escalated danger to merchant ships passing through the Mediterranean. It was now a hostile environment for any vessel trying to reach the Suez Canal. Hence those headed east were routed via the Cape of Good Hope, which suddenly made Freetown an important base again; for fifty-eight ships per day passed by, and this attracted the attention of German U-boats.

Convoys headed east assembled at one of Avonmouth, Clyde, Liverpool or Swansea. And their first port of call was at Freetown, where the shorter-legged Atlantic liners and the coal-burners required fuel and the whole convoy water, both for boiler feed and drinking purposes.

This placed an enormous demand on the limited resources of Freetown and it was always a major problem leading to delays both in the troop convoys, caused by the heavy demands upon local labour in coaling ship, and in the homeward-bound trade convoys by the depletion of coal stocks, which were of necessity shipped out from Britain. Furthermore, Freetown was also an anchorage where all supplies had to be loaded by hand from lighters (in the case of coal) or by water boats, which were also in short supply. Thus, U-boats could guarantee that there would be targets in the area.

---

* A lease for the 2,290sqft plot, where a White Ensign flies at all times, was given to the Commonwealth War Graves Commission for as long as the land remained a cemetery. The US Coast Guard station on Ocracoke Island maintains the property.

† A well-deck is a space lower than decks fore and aft, usually at the main deck level.

The whalers *Southern Pride* and *Southern Gem* were used as escorts on at least two of the convoys (WS18, WS24) but the main use of fishing vessels was with the 2nd Anti-Submarine Group, based at the port. For example, the South Atlantic Command, which included Freetown, boasted five A/S and six minesweeping vessels in May 1940, before the impact of the fall of France, but twenty-two A/S and two minesweeping trawlers in May 1944, together with nineteen trawlers and thirty-seven minesweepers from the South African naval forces.

Amongst the trawlers deployed there were the Admiralty 'Hill'-class *Butser* and *Inkpen*, large (750 tons displacement) anti-submarine trawlers capable of carrying as many as fifty-five depth charges (see plates 8 and 9). They were painted white or light grey for tropical service but, given that the crew spaces were – as usual – in the fish holds, must have been uncomfortably hot ships to serve in.

Inkpen was part of the escort for the French merchant ship *Saint Basile*, off the coast of Greenville, Liberia, alongside her fellow 'Hill'-class *Birdlip* and the hired trawler *Turcoman*. At 0136 on 14 June 1944, *U-547* attacked the convoy and sank *Birdlip* with a Gnat acoustic homing torpedo. The other two trawlers rushed to save their fellow sailors but thirty-seven men out of a crew of fifty-one died. The dead included Skipper Temporary Lieutenant Iorwerth Brian Evan Humphrey RNVR, from Newton-le-Willows, Cheshire, a chartered accountant in peacetime. The submarine sank the Frenchman too.

New Zealand

British trawlers reached as far as New Zealand. *Humphrey* was the ex-*Strath*-class First World War Admiralty-built trawler *Robert Farecloth*, purchased in 1928 by the Kiwi fishing company Sanford.

When war broke out, the New Zealand Division of the Royal Navy had only one minesweeper in commission, HMS *Wakakura*, and was ordered to take up vessels for sweeping with despatch. *Humphrey* was first leased, and later purchased from her owners in November 1940 for £22,500 to reduce the cost of the charter. As in Britain, the civilian crew of *Humphrey* was kept on and the skipper given a temporary naval rank, while volunteer reservists were posted to the ship to complement the fishermen.

She was joined by two other Admiralty-built First World War trawlers, *James Cosgrove*, a *Castle*-class vessel which saw service from March 1918, and *Thomas Currell*, another *Strath*-class, delivered to the Royal Navy in May 1919.

Humphrey, armed with one 4in and two machine guns, served until 1944 when she was first intended for conversion to a boom defence vessel and then sold back to her previous owners; but she did have one small moment of fame. The German raider *Orion* laid mines in the Hauraki Gulf. These claimed the RMS *Niagara* which sank taking a consignment of gold with her.* *Humphrey* and her sisters

swept the approaches to Auckland and swept up the remaining mines.

By the war's end the New Zealanders had three Robb-designed trawlers, together with fourteen locally built using First World War *Castle*-class plans, as their fishing boat minesweeping force.

Versatility

Trawlers and drifters fulfilled all sorts of unexpected duties during the war. Jimmy Grey served in the drifter *John Alfred*, of 1913 vintage, taken up in November 1939 and now based at Sheerness. He later recalled that 'she was bristling with guns. Her job was to lie in the path of the 'doodlebugs'[†] and shoot them down.'[14]

And then there was the rather odd mission given to the armed fishing boats, Operation Quixote, which involved cutting the six submerged telecommunication cables between Britain and German-occupied Norway, which all departed land from the east coast, at Lowestoft, Baton and Mundesley.

Screened by four destroyers, six minesweeping trawlers, *Cape Melville*, *Grampian*, *Pelton*, *Milford Queen*, *Milford Princess* and *James Lay*, all with RNPS skippers and under the overall command of Lieutenant Albert Longmuir RNR, left Great Yarmouth on the night of 18 May 1940 and paired off with an escorting destroyer before sailing to find 'their' cable. At around 0330 on the 19th they threw their grapples over the side and began to 'fish'. When a cable was snagged, it was drawn to the surface, hacked in two and thrown back over the side again.

The action was not without incident. An escorting destroyer, HMS *Jackal* (1938), sighted and intercepted an unknown vessel. It was a Dutch tug, *Hector*, without a soul on board, a genuine *Marie Celeste*. The same ship also came across a dinghy and found it contained the shot-down crew of a Whitley bomber, all fortunately still alive.

By nightfall, two of the three cables had been cut; on 28 May they located and severed the third and one of the RNPS vessels' less obvious tasks was completed.

Rarely, trawlers were used for laying mines. But four 'Isles'-class vessels were converted to a very specific type of minelayer, the 'controlled mine vessel'. HMT *Blackbird* was one of them, originally launched in 1943 as HMT *Sheppey*, and intended for work as a minesweeper, she was renamed *Blackbird* in that same year and converted into a controlled minelayer, pennant number M15, as shown in plate 87. All four of the 'Isles' class so treated were given new bird-related designations and a letter 'M' pennant number.

Controlled mines were a circuit-fired weapon used in coastal defences. They had been used for harbour defence before the First World War when responsibility for them was vested with the Royal Engineers. A controlled-mine minefield location was chosen so that it could be under observation from the shore and the exact placement of the mines was required to be available to the observers so that they could be fired from the control position when a target vessel was plotted to be within the mine's effective range.

---

* There were 295 boxes, each containing two ingots of gold, valued at £2.5 million (perhaps £150 million at 2020 values).

† German V-1 flying bombs.

Mines were laid by specialised vessels (known in the USA as 'mine planters') in predetermined locations with electrical connections made through cables to the firing position. The complex collection of mines, cables and junction boxes required regular maintenance and this, together with the laying of the mines, was the task of vessels like *Blackbird*.

Some fishing boats joined the army! The Great Yarmouth drifters *Ocean Breeze* and *Boy Phillip* were hired to work with the Royal Army Service Corps (RASC) and link up with their heterogeneous collection of launches, water carriers, target towers and coasters used to support the land forces.

Manned by civilian crews and under the overall control of the Inspector of Shipping, they sailed as part of a 340-ship task force supporting Operation Torch,* leaving Milford Haven on 4 December 1943 with their fish holds full of coal for the voyage.

On passage they helped rescue a Greek ship of 8,000 tons, which had broken its moorings in a heavy gale, and eventually joined up with a motorboat company in Algiers.

Trawlers too played a part with the RASC. The service numbered nine large vessels loaned out by the Admiralty, including the 'Isles'-class *Copinsay*, *Inchcolm*, *Mull* and *Oxna*, and the 'Dance'-class *Foxtrot* and *Valse*. Generally, these trawlers served as mother ships to launches and motorboats.

Dynamo and Overlord

There were many trawlers involved in Operation Dynamo.† Amongst the minesweepers keeping open the three cleared routes back to England were HMT *Thomas Bartlett*, *Our Bairns* and *Inverforth*. On 28 May they were all sweeping for magnetic mines in the Dunkirk Roads using LL equipment. In the morning, the trawlers came under fire from the shore and, in trying to escape from it, *Thomas Bartlett* ran into a British minefield, detonated a mine and sank. Eight men were killed and Stoker Joseph Collinson RNPS died the following day. She had been built as an Admiralty *Castle*-class in 1918 and had survived that war. But not a second one, or British mines.

Thomas Bartlett was not the only blue-on-blue loss amongst the fishermen in the melee of Dynamo. In the early hours of 29 May, the destroyer *Wakeful* had embarked 640 Allied troops at Dunkirk, but in the course of departing she was torpedoed by the German E-boat *S-30*. Another destroyer, *Grafton*, came alongside to pick up survivors but she too was sunk, torpedoed by *UC-62*. The danlayer motor drifter *Comfort*, just 60 tons, built in 1903 and previously of Fraserburgh, came alongside *Grafton* to assist; but for some inexplicable reason the former thought that *Comfort* was the E-boat which had sunk *Wakeful* and started firing on her. This attracted the minesweeper HMS *Lydd* which, coming to *Grafton*'s support, rammed the little drifter and sank her. *Comfort*'s skipper, forty-nine-year-old

Aberdonian John D Mair, and five of his fisherman crew were lost, all RNPS. There was only one survivor.

HMT *John Cattling* was at Dunkirk on 29 May 1940. Built in Paisley in 1918, she was another *Castle*-class Admiralty trawler and had served in the previous war. Now she was again conscripted into conflict as a minesweeper. Alongside the harbour wall, attempting to take off the retreating army, she was bombed by Stukas; next to her, one other trawler was sunk and one badly damaged* and a destroyer, HMS *Grenade*, hit by two bombs and left mortally wounded and foundering. Skipper George William Aldan, in peacetime a fisherman as were his twenty-strong crew, towed the stricken *Grenade* out of the harbour so that it would not block the entrance, and shortly afterwards it exploded.

Later, Aldan and *John Cattling* took off seventy-seven soldiers from the shore and got them safely back to England. For his actions he was awarded the DSC[15] and subsequently, in another command, would receive a bar to his medal and be mentioned in despatches.

Many trawlers made repeat trips to Dunkirk to bring men off. Others performed notable acts of rescue. On 2 June, three trawlers, *Blackburn Rovers*, *Westella* and *Saon*, were on A/S picket, trying to keep the seaway clear for boats departing from France. *Blackburn Rovers* thought they had an ASDIC contact but instead had wandered into a British minefield. Her bows were blown completely off by an explosion and her depth charges detonated in the water amongst the survivors. *Westella* tried to manoeuvre to help, but she too hit a mine and also lost her bows. Chief Skipper William Mullender, on *Saon*, knew he had to try to rescue his fellow fishermen. 'We saved thirty-two men in all from the two crews,' he later reported, 'many of *Blackburn Rovers* survivors were suffering from internal haemorrhage as a result of being caught in the depth charge explosions. The mess deck of *Saon* was like a slaughterhouse, with blood running everywhere.'[16]

And then there was *Cambridgeshire*, an ASDIC-equipped anti-submarine trawler. Built by Smith's Dock in 1935 and operating from Grimsby in peacetime, she had been taken up by the Admiralty in August 1939, fitted with a 4in gun and depth charges, and sent off to war. On 17 June 1940, she was off St Nazaire when there was a tremendous explosion and the huge troopship *Lancastria* blew up under sustained aerial attack by German aircraft.† There were more than 6,000 men crowded aboard her and she seemed on the verge of sinking. Without hesitation, the trawler's skipper, Lieutenant Commander Arthur Blewett, RNR, took *Cambridgeshire* close to the stricken ship and her crew began pulling men out of the water. Despite constant air attack, she took 1,009 survivors on board, so many that the vessel was in permanent danger of capsizing on the way back to England. The troopship went down in 30 minutes; at least 4,000 men died,§ but it

---

* The Anglo-American invasion of French North Africa.

† The evacuation of the British army from France, via Dunkirk.

* *Polly Johnson*, which sank on the way back to England.

† During Operation Aerial, the evacuation of Allied forces and civilians from ports in western France from 15 to 25 June 1940

§ Modern estimates range from 3,500 to 6,000.

87. HMT *Blackbird*, originally the 'Isles'-class *Sheppey*, was converted to a controlled mine layer and given the new pennant number M15, the 'M' reflecting her new mine-related role.

would have been much worse except for a courageous reservist skipper and crew. Blewett received the DSC for his actions.[17]

In total, 113 trawlers and drifters took part in Operation Dynamo and seventeen were sunk with two badly damaged (see appendix 8). Three were French and five were drifters.

There were trawlers at Operation Overlord – D-Day – four years later too; but by this time many of the sweeping duties had been taken over by newer, purpose-built, often shallow-draught, naval minesweepers. Twenty trawlers were used as specialist LL sweepers[*18] and another thirty-eight as danlayers in the minesweeping groups, twenty-five on the British landing beaches and thirteen in the American sector.[19] Within each of ten designated landing channels, eight fleet minesweepers took part, supported by (usually) four danlaying trawlers. The fleet minesweepers were preceded by small harbour-defence motor launches and each sweeping route also

utilised two trawlers equipped with LL-sweeps, specifically to deal with magnetic mines.

And trawlers were also important on D-Day in other roles. *Cape Mariato*, for example, escorted sections of the Mulberry Harbour to Normandy, after which she worked in an anti-submarine role, standing offshore behind the landing vessels. In total, thirty trawlers were used as A/S escort or defence and a further sixty-two were involved as smokescreen-layers.[†]

But a trawler skipper's fisherman's profit instinct was never far from the surface. Operating close to the invasion beaches, Sub Lieutenant Brendan Maher RNVR, in the Fairmile B-type motor launch minesweeper *ML137*, saw a trawler hove to next to an abandoned jeep which was underwater. The trawler had its boom out and was lifting the vehicle out of the water where it hung precariously from the hook, dripping water from all surfaces. The ML's commander hailed the trawler; 'You don't have to rescue that you know,' he yelled across. 'I'm not rescuing it,' rejoined the skipper, 'I've never had a car in my life; now I've got one. This is coming home with me.'[20]

---

* They were the 131st, 139th, 159th, 181st Minesweeping Groups, each of five vessels. Altogether there were 351 minesweepers, danlayers and support vessels involved in clearing the channels (*Administrative History of US Naval Forces in Europe, 1940–1946*, vol. V, pp301ff).

† As far as the author can assess, only two trawlers were lost supporting the D-Day landings between 6 June and the end of August. They were the 'Isles'-class *Gairsay* (thirty-one killed) depicted in plate 43, and the requisitioned *Lord Wakefield* (twenty-eight dead).

Commercial trawling during the war

In 1914–18 the government had failed to act quickly to offset the impact that the Admiralty's appetite for trawlers, combined with the German predation of the fishing fleets, was having on the supply of fish. The creation of the Fishery Reserve was the eventual answer.

In the Second World War, the strength of the English and Welsh trawler fleet actually available for fishing during the conflict was generally at about 25 per cent of pre-war levels, but its catching power was much less for the Admiralty deliberately requisitioned most of the larger and more efficient modern vessels.

The numbers of trawlers available to fish fell markedly; Scarborough had seven trawlers fishing in July 1939 and five in December 1940, then down to just four by the close of 1944.

Hull had 191 at the beginning of the war but just 66 in December 1939. A year later there was just one. Grimsby had 381 at the start of the war and never went below 66. The extensive mining of the North Sea made Fleetwood the premier British fishing port for some time and the principal grounds fished during the conflict were off Iceland, the Irish Sea, the west coast of Scotland and the Hebrides, as well as north-west Ireland and off that country's south-western coasts.

As in the first war, the Germans targeted the unarmed fishing boats. In the early months of the second war, a number of trawlers were again sunk by gunfire from U-boats. The first Grimsby vessel to be so lost was the fishing trawler *Lynx II* (250grt), built by Cochrane's in 1906. She had served in the first war and on 29 October 1939 was on passage from Grimsby to her fishing grounds when she chanced upon the Hull-registered modern trawler *St Nidan* (565grt), a Cook, Welton and Gemmell-built vessel operated and owned by Thomas Hamling and Co. *St Nidan* had been stopped by *U-59*; her crew took to the boats and the submarine fired twenty-three shells into the fishing vessel, sinking it. Skipper Arthur Cressy of *Lynx II* picked up the *St Nidan* men from their boats; but then his vessel was also shelled by *U-59* and both crews took to the sea once more. They were finally rescued by the Hull trawler *Lady Hogarth* and taken to safety in Scotland.

This was the beginning of the main U-boat phase of the fishermen's war and lasted for about three and a half months. But after that, aircraft attacks became the problem.

For self-defence against air and surface attack, from late September 1939 the fishing fleets were formed into sections of between four and eight vessels of which two were armed with 12pdr guns, similar to the programme eventually adopted in the first war. But in May 1940 Dunkirk called for all available boats and those trawlers which had been fitted with weapons were swiftly requisitioned and sent there. After these 12pdr trawlers had been taken, various armaments were used to equip the fishing fleet including Lewis guns and other types of automatic weapons, rockets and eventually Oerlikon guns as and when they could be spared.

This lack of defensive ability manifested itself in heavy losses. The years 1940 and 1941 were probably the worst of the war for the British trawling trade. Nearly two-thirds of the English and Welsh trawlers lost through enemy action while fishing over the six years of war were sunk in 1940 and 1941. But it was mines that were the fisherman's worst enemy. Sea mines sunk more fishing vessels than any other weapon and were much feared by fishermen; but they still went out. An eye-witness reported:

> here in the north east we felt the first brunt of war. Hardly a ship is sunk in any part of the world without our men being on it. Ours were the men who with our trawler men felt the first cruel blow of the magnetic mines. They never flinched. I remember visiting a convoy of five trawlers which had put into the Tyne after one of its number had been blown to pieces on a mine. The men told how the boat and its crew – their mates – went up like a puff of smoke. Yet an hour later what remained of the convoy went out to sea again without a word of protest.[21]

There was some official recognition of the dangers inherent in the job. Each member of the crew of a fishing trawler during the war years received £10 in war risk money.[22] It probably didn't seem enough.

The war had a considerable impact on the British fish supply. The total supply from all sources, fresh or frozen, amounted to 22,417,780 cwt in 1938 but by 1941 this had slumped to 7,771,016 cwt or 35 per cent of the 1938 total.[23] Thereafter there was a gradual improvement and by 1944 supplies were running at 48 per cent of the pre-war total. But fish remained unrationed although it rose sharply in price until price controls were implemented in mid-1941. And the nation never lost fish from its dinner plates throughout the conflict.

16: Heroes and Memorials

Unlike in the First World War, there were no fisherman VCs awarded in the 1939–45 struggle. But there was a Victoria Cross won in a fishing boat. HMT *Arab* was a 531grt trawler built in 1936 and taken up into the navy at the outbreak of war. In April 1940 she was part of the splendidly named 15th Anti-Submarine Striking Force, which in reality comprised four armed trawlers. *Arab*'s commander was Richard Been Stannard, a thirty-eight-year-old RNR lieutenant, pre-war a second officer with the Orient Line, with a crew of RNPS fishermen.

In early April 1940, German forces had invaded Denmark, and then Norway during Operation Weserübung. British ships landed soldiers to attempt to repel the Norwegian invasion, including landings at Namsos, about 100 miles north of Trondheim and it was here on 28 April that *Arab* and her sisters arrived. Their role throughout the campaign had been to carry out the essential sweeps of the approaches to the fjords by day and troop landing and evacuation by night. German Stuka and Heinkel bombers concentrated on their elimination. Churchill stated that the trawlers were the 'little ships which went through hell'.[1] In fact, the Norwegian campaign demonstrated for the first time that air cover was essential to maintain an army expedition overseas or even to operate ships off an enemy-occupied coast.

Arab was initially ordered to ferry stores to the shore. But between her arrival and 2 May she was subjected to thirty-one bombing attacks. When the Namsos jetty was hit and ammunition set on fire (next to an ammunition ship), Stannard ran *Arab*'s bows against the wharf and endeavoured for two hours to extinguish the fire with hoses from the forecastle. He succeeded in saving a part of the jetty which was invaluable in the evacuation of Namsos. After fighting off air attack, Stannard established an armed camp under shelter of a cliff where off-duty seamen could rest under cover from air attack. When another trawler was hit and about to blow up, he with two others re-boarded *Arab* and moved her 100 yards to safety. And when, finally leaving the fjord, his trawler was attacked by a German Heinkel bomber which ordered him to steer east or be sunk, he kept on his course, held his fire till the enemy was within 800 yards and then shot the aircraft down. By now, his ship had a

88. *Kingston Onyx*, built in 1927, was requisitioned in August 1939. In 1941, she rescued the entire crew of the torpedoed cargo ship *Empire Thunder*.

damaged rudder and propeller and cracked main engine castings; but he still sailed her back to England.

Richard Stannard was advanced to Lieutenant Commander RNR on 29 June and presented with the Victoria Cross by King George VI at Buckingham Palace on 3 September. His citation noted that his medal was awarded 'for outstanding valour and signal devotion to duty at Namsos'.[2]

There were many other acts of bravery by trawlermen, a few well known, many understood only by those involved. Some required moral not physical courage.

On 9 February 1940, for example, Heinkel 111 bombers sank two minesweeping trawlers off the coast of Aberdeen, *Fort Royal* and *Robert Bowen*. A total of twenty-two sailors were lost, including both skippers and eleven RNPS men. The following day another would join them. The 1915 Hall Russell-built trawler *Theresa Boyle* had already served in one world war when in August 1939 she was called up as a minesweeper for a second. On 10 February, she was working about 115 miles off Aberdeen when she was attacked by Heinkels and sunk. But this time no lives were lost. Skipper Oliver Bell got his men into the lifeboats; and for two days he kept them together and in fair spirits until an RAF aircraft spotted them and alerted the ex-Hull trawler *Almandine* and the 1918-built ex-*Castle*-class *Brabant*. Both trawlers found the survivors and took them on board after fifty hours adrift in the North Sea. All were suffering from exposure but alive. Skipper Bell's moral courage had saved their lives. And *Brabant* achieved some sort of revenge in August 1941 when she shot down a German bomber, an act which earned Lieutenant James Henry Alexander Winfield RNR a DSC, Signalman Jack Hurst a DSM and two mentions in despatches for other crew members.

In the same Norwegian campaign in which Lieutenant Stannard gained his VC, another trawler and her largely fisherman crew showed their mettle. On 8 June 1940, the 'Tree'-class Admiralty-built trawler *Juniper* was taking part in the evacuation of Allied troops from the ill-fated Norway campaign, escorting the oil tanker *Oil Pioneer*, the empty troopship *Orama* and a hospital ship *Atlantis* on passage through the Norwegian Sea and back to Britain.

The trawler's captain was forty-two-year-old Lieutenant Commander Geoffrey Seymour Grenfell. He had fought in the First World War as a midshipman and sub lieutenant before leaving the navy with the rank of lieutenant in 1920. In 1938 he had married the Countess of Carnarvon, Anne 'Catherine' Tredick Herbert who had divorced the 6th Earl of Carnarvon two years previously.[*]

Unbeknown to Commander Grenfell, a German naval squadron (comprised of the battleships *Scharnhorst* and *Gneisenau*, heavy cruiser *Admiral Hipper* and four destroyers) under Vizeadmiral Wilhelm Marschall had received Luftwaffe reports of two groups of ships; Marschall decided to attack the southernmost group. This sealed *Juniper*'s fate.

It was dawn when Grenfell sighted a group of heavy ships. He quickly sent off a sighting report and challenged the nearest large vessel by light, receiving the reply that it was the Royal Navy cruiser *Southampton*. In fact, it was the German *Admiral Hipper*, 18,200 tons, eight 8in and twelve 4.1in guns, against which *Juniper* opposed one 12pdr, three 20mm AA and depth charges.

Grenfell didn't hesitate. He ordered the ships in company to run for it and, White Ensign proudly flying, turned to engage the German; and was blown to pieces. Twenty-three men died, including Commander Grenfell, with only four survivors. Nor did Grenfell and his crew's sacrifice save their charges; the hospital ship was spared but tanker and troopship went to the bottom (as later that day did the aircraft carrier *Glorious* and the destroyers *Ardent* and *Acasta*, again sunk by Marschall's forces).

Juniper might just have escaped if she had run for it. But she stood to fight; and Lieutenant Commander Geoffrey Seymour Grenfell died facing the enemy, as had his father, Captain Riversdale Nonus Grenfell, killed on the Western Front in 1914, and his uncle,[†] Captain Francis Octavius Grenfell, who fell on 24 May 1915, having won the VC in August the previous year. Their maternal grandfather was Admiral John Pascoe Grenfell and their uncle was Field Marshal Francis Grenfell. Moral and physical courage ran in the family.

Or consider the case of the 'Military'-class *Grenadier* (see plate 51). On the morning of 16 March 1945, she was close escort to convoy RU-156 from Loch Ewe to Russia, sailing alongside the Norwegian cargo vessel *Inger Toft*. At 0900, the merchantman was struck by a torpedo fired by *U-722* and quickly began to sink. Her crew abandoned ship.

Naval practice required the commanding officer of *Grenadier*, Acting Skipper Arthur George Day RNR, to go to full speed and drop depth charges. But as a former merchant officer himself, Day knew that meant certain death for the survivors from *Inger Toft*, now floating in, and awaiting rescue from, the sea.

Instead, Day turned his trawler in the direction of the sinking vessel. *Grenadier* managed to save the entire thirty-man crew, including the master, from the freezing waters. Skipper Day had disobeyed standing instructions but showed great moral bravery; his humanitarian instincts earned him a mention in despatches, gazetted on 14 June 1945.

But often it was just quotidian seamanship and hundreds of uncounted and largely unknown acts of daily mercy. Merchant Navy sailors had good cause to be happy if trawlers were part of their convoy escort, for the fishing vessels were often designated as rescue ship and proved very good at it. A typical example occurred in early 1941.

SS *Empire Thunder*[§] was a brand-new merchant vessel of 5,965grt, built by Pickersgill's of Sunderland. Her maiden voyage was in January 1941 as part of convoy OB-269, sailing in ballast for

---

[†] Riversdale's twin brother.

[§] An *Empire* ship was a merchant ship owned by the Ministry of War Transport and contracted for operations to various British shipping companies.

[*] And whose family seat was Highclere Castle, the fictional Downton Abbey.

Washington; but on the 6th she developed engine trouble and began to straggle behind her companions and the escort. Here she was easy prey for *U-124* which sank her with a single torpedo, about 100 miles north-east of Rockall.

Empire Thunder's entire crew managed to get off in the ship's boats but one of them was then hit by a torpedo. Nine men, mainly from Sunderland, died; the remaining thirty crew, including the master William Dowell, were picked up by the A/S trawler *Kingston Onyx* (see plate 88) and taken to safety. They were the lucky ones; as were many more merchant sailors, plucked from the sea by trawlers.

The war ends

The last two trawlers to be sunk in the Second World War were *Ebor Wyke* and the 'Shakespearian'-class *Coriolanus*.

Ebor Wyke was built in 1929 by Cochrane's and sold to the Admiralty in 1939 by her owners, West Dock Steamship Co of Hull. In 1945 she was serving as part of 137th Minesweeping Group, based in Reykjavik. On 2 May 1945, with Hitler dead and the Russians entering Berlin, she was torpedoed by *U-979*, seven miles north of Skagi. Of her forty-eight-man crew, only one survived, Coxswain John Milnes; thirty-nine of the dead were RNPS. Five days later, Germany formally surrendered. *Ebor Wyke* was the last British warship to be sunk by a U-boat in the war.[*]

But on 5 May, *Coriolanus* (1940) gained the unwanted honour of becoming the last armed trawler to be lost in the war when she was mined in the North Adriatic while minesweeping. Fortunately, all of her crew were saved.

It is estimated that around 66,000 men passed though HMS *Europa* and became 'Sparrows'. And so did some 6,000 ships, including trawlers, whalers, drifters, MFVs (Motor Fishing Vessels), MLs (Motor Launches), MMs (Motor Minesweepers or 'Mickey Mouses'), American-produced BYMs (British Yard Minesweepers) and numerous requisitioned vessels. Lowestoft became a Royal Navy town. Eventually five bases were established there, HMS *Europa* (RNPS Headquarters), HMS *Martello* (the local Auxiliary Patrol and Minesweeping base), HMS *Minos* (the Port of Lowestoft, harbour defence and other craft) and later HMS *Mantis* (Coastal Forces Motor Gun Boats and Motor Torpedo Boats) and HMS *Myloden* (Landing Craft Training for Royal Marine Commandos and Combined Operations).

Some 1,409 trawlers were taken up from trade to serve with the Royal Navy during the course of the war and Admiralty-built vessels added another 338 to the total. Around 500 drifters entered the navy as did 150 whalers, which joined the six pre-war 'Lake'-class.

Losses were heavy: 251 trawlers; 17 boom defence vessels, mainly trawlers; 35 whalers; 107 drifters.[3] At a minimum, 410 RNPS fishing vessels were sunk during the conflict. Of the trawler losses, seventy-nine were to mines and seventy-one to aircraft; for drifters, the numbers were twenty-one and fourteen, with another twenty-one just recorded as 'wrecked'.[4]

And although it is not possible to calculate exactly how many fishermen died while serving with the Royal Navy, it is estimated that some 2,385 officers and men of the Royal Naval Patrol Service, aged from sixteen to over sixty, lost their lives and have no grave but the sea.

The commercial fish trade as a whole, and working fishermen in particular, also paid a heavy price. At least 1,243 British fishermen died while following their livelihood during the war and 136 active fishing vessels were lost to enemy action.[5] The effect can be gauged a little more accurately at certain ports: Hull boasted a fleet of 191 trawlers in July 1939 but, by VE Day, 96 – just over half – had been lost. Grimsby lost over 600 fishermen while on naval service during the same period.[6]

Memorials

On 7 October 1953, Lowestoft hosted a gathering which included First Sea Lord Sir Rhoderick McGriger, Admiral Sir Philip Vian, Lord Stradbroke[†] (the Lord Lieutenant of Suffolk), Lord Carrington and the Bishop of Norwich, Percy Mark Herbert.[§]

They were assembled to dedicate a memorial to the men of the Royal Naval Patrol Service. Erected high above Sparrow's Nest and with a clear view of the North Sea, it comprised a tall fluted stone column surmounted by a gilt bronze lymphad.[ß] Intended solely for the memory of those serving RNPS personnel who died between 1939 and 1946 and who have no known grave, seventeen bronze panels bear their names.[Φ] There is also a small addenda stone set into the ground, listing those who died on land but have no known resting place (see plates 89 and 90).

Most of Sparrow's Nest was demolished after the war. Only a small amount of brickwork and a veranda remain of the original construction and now house a Royal Naval Patrol Service museum, run by volunteers. The grounds are a public park once more and contain an open stage/bandstand, rebuilt in 1994 and dedicated to the RNPS.

A further memorial to the men of the Royal Naval Patrol Service was erected in the National Forest, near Litchfield. In 2009, an upright rectangular stone of remembrance was raised on a square stone base. The monument comprises a roughcast grey/white column with polished black granite tablets affixed to each face. The principal tablet has an engraving of the insignia of the RNPS; the other tablets have depictions of minesweepers and fishing vessels

---

[*] Payment for her loss from the Ministry of War Transport was made to the sum of £14,342.

[†] Who had been educated at Osborne and the Royal Naval College, Dartmouth.

[§] A mason, he was also the Provincial Grand Master of Norfolk.

[ß] A lymphad or galley is a charge used primarily in Scottish heraldry. It is a single-masted ship propelled by oars. In addition to the mast and oars, the lymphad has three flags and a basket.

[Φ] The memorial is maintained by the Commonwealth Graves Commission

with further inscriptions. Atop the stone is a naval mine.

It was dedicated on 23 August in the presence of Commander Garry Titmus (President of RNPSA), John Street (National Chairman of RNPSA) and Reverend Jim Izzard (National Padre of RNPSA), together with RNPSA members.

The inscriptions on all four faces are rather prolix; but the most telling phrase is surely:

the trawler, the drifter, the smack
we fought our war the hard way
and many of us ne'er came back.

89. Two views of the Royal Naval Patrol Service memorial, situated above Sparrow's Nest in Lowestoft. (author's collection)

Envoi

In two world wars, without the fishing fleet and the fishermen who manned it, it is possible, even likely, that Britain would have lost control of the seas and with it the ability to secure victory in the conflicts. In both conflagrations, nearly 1,500 trawlers (and a similar number of drifters in the first war) were pressed into service as warships and filled a multitude of roles which had been overlooked or neglected in peacetime. Whether as convoy escort, anti-submarine vessels, minesweepers, ABVs, boom defence, despatch vessels or countless other roles, trawlers and drifters helped Britain retain Sovereignty of the Seas.

But in both world wars, the use of the fishing fleet was not a strategically planned exercise. Both the RNR(T) and the RNPS were to some extent extempore. Estimates of numbers of vessels and men needed were wildly incorrect; provision of training was slow to start, scanty, brief and something of a 'wing and a prayer' exercise, viz 'Harry Tate's'. Fortunately, fishermen were generally consummate seamen and had little to learn about day-to-day ship handling.

In a navy whose admirals placed a premium on having as many battleships and cruisers as they could afford it was not easy to justify the maintenance of a large numbers of escort or patrol vessels outside of war, or the men to man them. This was especially true in the inter-war years when there was so much pressure to reduce the costs of defence and strong 'peace at all costs' and pro-appeasement political movements. Only in the mid-to-late 1930s did the message that Britain could not rely on the League of Nations, or on the good will of dictators, finally get through and by then it was nearly too late. And although by 1939 Britain's mighty fishing fleet of the early 1900s was no longer the force it had been, it was still strong enough to serve the country's need.

In two world wars, at least 5,723 men died in service with the RNR(T) and the RNPS; most of them fishermen, most of them in armed trawlers or drifters. Another 1,667 fishermen were killed while engaged in commercial fishing. These are large sacrifices from a small part of the community.

However, looking around such ports as Grimsby, Hull, Brixham, Fleetwood, Aberdeen in the 2020s one sees no sign that the fishermen could once more rise to the call. The UK's fishing industry has been wilfully destroyed by joining the EEC* and by successive governments' inaction and neglect. A report by the House of Commons Library estimated that in 2016 only 7,940 people were engaged in the UK fishing industry and 62 per cent of those were in Scotland. The once mighty Humber district had only 1,500 persons so employed; and, to make matters worse, these figures included people working in aquaculture, such as fish-farming.[1] And according to Seafish Economics, there were 4,512 active fishing vessels in the UK in 2018. Of these, around 1,600 were 'low activity'† and 74 per cent were under 10 metres, meaning vessels which only operate inshore.[2] In other words, there were only 1,173 open sea fishing boats registered in the whole of the UK.

Compare this with the totals immediately before the First World War when there were 45,382 British fishermen across the country catching 800,000 tons of fish a year in 7,271 fishing craft, excluding the smallest ones (see chapter 1).

The post-Second World War Royal Navy has been diminished through government policy to the point where it hardly exists; and nowadays it can be seen that the navy could expect little or no help from a severely reduced fishing fleet.

Except that …

Plus ça change, plus c'est la même chose.§

When Argentina invaded the Falklands in 1982 and a Royal Navy task force was sent out to regain the islands (Operation Corporate), history repeated itself. Minesweeping forces would be absolutely vital for the task force. But the elderly *Ton*-class coastal mine countermeasures vessels (MCMVs) in service at the time were unsuited for the long passage and heavy seas expected in the South Atlantic; moreover, the first two of the new 'Hunt'-class MCMVs were not yet operational. The Admiralty turned to the very vessels which had provided such stalwart service in two world wars – the fishing trawlers.

Five Hull-registered trawlers were requisitioned and quickly converted for minesweeping duty, including fitting Oropesa sweeping gear. The vessels were commissioned into the Royal Navy

---

* Before joining the EEC (European Economic Community) in 1973 (which became the European Union in the early 1990s) Britain – like most other countries in the world – controlled its own fishing waters. This was a zone extending 200 nautical miles from a country's coastline an area known as a country's Exclusive Economic Zone. With EEC membership Britain could only control a zone of only twelve miles from the UK coastline, with the rest of Britain's waters now part of Europe's combined Exclusive Economic Zone and controlled by the EEC, which could set quotas for all EEC members to fish in ex-British waters.

† Fishing income less that £10,000.

§ 'The more it changes, the more it's the same thing'.

and crewed mostly by the ships' companies of the *Ton*-class MCMVs based at Rosyth: The trawler *Cordella* (1,238grt), built in 1973 by the Clelands Shipbuilding Company of Wallsend, was manned by HMS *Upton*; and her sisters *Farnella* by *Wotton*; *Junella* by *Bickington*; *Northella* by *Soberton*; and *Pict* by *Bildeston*.

The group was designated the 11th Minesweeping Squadron and sailed from Portland on 27 April 1982 with Lieutenant Commander Martyn Holloway as senior officer in *Cordella*. Just as in 1914–18 and 1939–45, they became Jacks-of-all-trades. Arriving at South Georgia, they spent day after day transferring troops, stores and ammunition in atrocious Antarctic weather with wind speeds in excess of 100 knots, often for several days at a time, before heading on towards the Falklands.

And on reaching the Falklands, they were able to sweep ten of the twenty-one naval mines which had been laid in Port Stanley harbour (the remaining mines failed to deploy or had broken adrift) as well as assisting in the landing of covert operations.

Once again, the fishing fleet had saved the navy's blushes. It was another triumph of improvisation, of filling the gaps left by political inaction or ignorance. The few remaining fishing boats of Britain did not let the nation down.

The Plans

I. L/S/44/A HM *Strath*-class Admiralty trawler, general arrangement, 1917

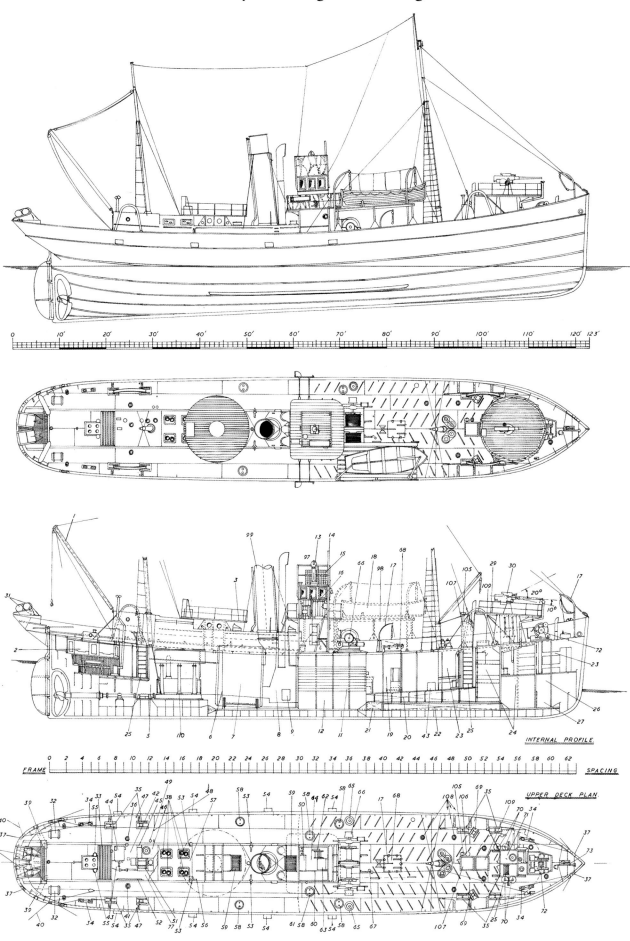

INTERNAL PROFILE

FRAME   SPACING

UPPER DECK PLAN.

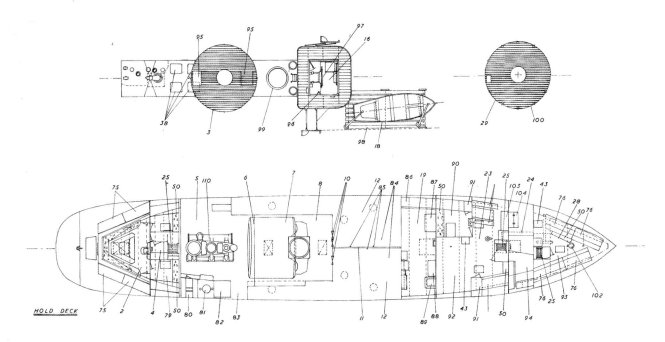

HOLD DECK

CLASS DATA:—

MOULDED DIMENSIONS.——115 FT. x 22 FT. x 13 FT.	1
EXTREME LENGTH & BREADTH—123 FT. x 22 FT. 5 INS.	2
LIGHT DISPLACEMENT.——310·7 TONS.	3
LIGHT DRAFT FOR'D.——6 FT. 3·25 INS.	4
LIGHT DRAFT AFT ——11 FT. 10·75 INS.	
LIGHT MEAN DRAFT——9 FT. 1 INCH.	
LOAD DISPLACEMENT.——429 TONS.	
LOAD DRAFT FOR'D.——8 FT. 4 INS.	
LOAD DRAFT AFT.——14 FT. 0 INS.	
LOAD MEAN DRAFT.——11 FT. 2 INS.	
DEADWEIGHT.——118·3 TONS.	
TONS PER INCH AT LOAD DRAUGHT.—4·8	
GROSS STEEL & IRON.——133·25 TONS.	
WEIGHT OF MAIN MACHINERY——92·5 TONS.	
COAL CAPACITY.——102 TONS.	
FEED WATER.——19 TONS.	
FRESH WATER.——1·3 TONS.	
MAIN MACHINERY	
DIAMETER OF CYLINDERS.—12 INS, 20 INS, 34 INS.	
STROKE.——23 INS.	
REVOLUTIONS.——110.	
DESIGNED I.H.P.——430.	
DESIGNED SPEED APPROX.—10 KNOTS.	
CONDENSING SURFACE.——500 SQ. FT.	
BOILER	
LENGTH & DIAMETER——10 FT. 0 INS x 12 FT. 6 INS	25
WORKING PRESSURE——180 LBS. PER SQ. INCH	26
No OF FURNACES——3.	
DIAMETER OF FURNACES—2 FT. 11 INS.	
HEATING SURFACE.——1,347 SQ. FT.	
GRATE SURFACE.——40 SQ. FT.	
PROPELLER:—	
PITCH.——11 FT. 6 INS.	
DIAMETER.——8 FT. 4 INS.	
SURFACE.——29 SQ. FT.	
AVERAGE SPEED ON TRIALS —10 KNOTS.	
AVERAGE TOTAL COST [HULL & MACHINERY]	
£18,200.	
No OF STRATHS ORDERED UP TO ARMISTICE.	
No ORDERED FOR ADMIRALTY SERVICE.—103	
No ORDERED AS FISHING VESSELS.—46	
TOTAL——149	

HISTORY - FORT ROBERT.

ORIGINAL NAME — JAMES BENTOL.
BUILDER ———— HALL RUSSELL.
DELIVERED ———— 10 | 8 | 17.
DISPLACEMENT ——— 203 TONS - AS BUILT
1922—SOLD OUT OF SERVICE ~
RENAMED FORT ROBERT.
24|11|39 — REQUISITIONED — AUX PATROL VESSEL.
4|40 — CONVERTED TO MINESWEEPER.
8|45 — RETURNED TO OWNERS.
6|9|60 — ARRIVED ST DAVID'S FOR SCRAPPING.

CLASS DATA:~

AT A CONFERENCE HELD 26|9|16 IT WAS STATED
THAT SINCE WAR BEGAN THE ADMIRALTY HAD
REQUISITIONED 1300 OUT OF SOME 1800 TRAWLERS
IN THE UK & THAT THE STRENGTH OF THE AUXILIARY
PATROL HAD TO BE INCREASED. IT WAS PROPOSED THAT
STANDARD TRAWLER TYPES BASED UPON COMMERCIAL
DESIGNS FROM THE PORTS OF HULL GRIMSBY &
ABERDEEN BE CONSTRUCTED AS THEY WOULD HAVE A
COMMERCIAL VALUE AFTER HOSTILITIES.

DETAIL:—

FIXED AIS DERRICK.	
MESS ROOM.	
GUN PLATFORM PARALLEL TO W/LINE	
WHEN SHIP TRIMMED 7' 0" BY STERN.	
PANTRY.	
ENGINE ROOM.	
SCREEN BULKHEAD.	
CYLINDRICAL BOILER	
STOKEHOLD.	
SLIDING DOOR — 27"x 21".	
TRIMMING DOOR — 18"x 18".	
WOOD DIVISION.	
COAL BUNKER.	
STANDARD COMPASS.	
STANDARD FOR LIGHTS.	
FLAG LOCKER — STBD SIDE ONLY.	
WHEELHOUSE.	
AMMUNITION DAVIT.	
BOAT — 18' x 6' 0"—STBD SIDE.	
MAGAZINE & SHELL ROOM.	
20 TONS BALLAST - CEMENT 3" THICK.	
SLIME TANK.	
BOILER FEED TANK — 19 TONS.	
ACCOMMODATION	
STORE.	
LADDER	
FORE PEAK.	
CHAIN LOCKER.	
CREW SPACE.	
GUN PLATFORM PARALLEL TO W/LINE	
WHEN SHIP TRIMMED 5' 0" BY STEM.	
12 POUNDER 12 CWT P MARK I* GUN.	
'D' TYPE DEPTH CHARGES.	
STRAIN INDICATOR BOX.	
WOODEN GRATING.	
MOORING BITT.	
GALLOWS FEET.	
7" DEAD LIGHT TO ENGINEERS CABIN.	
FAIRLEAD.	

DETAIL ARMAMENT DRAWINGS AVAILABLE:~

L10103	·303" LEWIS GUN.
L10107	4" MK. IV GUN ON P.IX MTG
L10121	TWIN ·303" HEFAH GUNS.~[W W II]
L10122	3 PDR. HOTCHKISS GUNS.
L10123	Q.F. 3" 12 PDR's. ON MK. V & VI MTG's.

STEEL SKYLIGHT WITH 7" DEADLIGHT.	38
TOWED AIS CHARGE STOWAGE.	39
POSITION WHEN TOWING CHARGE~[ALL	40
CABLE OUT].	
7" DEAD LIGHT TO OFFICERS CABIN.	41
GALLEY.	42
COAL BOX.	43
GALLEY RANGE.	44
VENT.	45
OFFICERS W.C.	46
SCUPPER.	47
OIL FILLING PIPE~ [LUBRICATING OIL].	48
4" HAND PUMP TO ENGINE ROOM.	49
SEAT.	50
ENGINE ROOM ENTRANCE.	51
HAND RAIL	52
TRAWL LEADS.	53
WASH PORT.	54
TYPE 'C' CHARGE.	55
AIR & FILLING PIPE TO F.W. TANK.	56
ENGINE ROOM SKYLIGHT ~STEEL COVER	57
WITH TWO 8" BULLSEYES.	
COALING SCUTTLE.	58
STEEL GRATING.	59
CURTAIN.	60
BUNK WITH DRAWERS UNDER.	61
RADIATOR.	62
FOLDING TABLE.	63
CHART ROOM.	64
STEAM TRAWL WINCH.	65
4" HAND PUMP TO SLIME TANK.	66
W.T. HATCH COVER TO MAGAZINE.	67
GALLOWS LEAD BLOCK.	69

AIS STICK BOMBS.	70
CREWS W.C.	71
STEAM WINDLASS.	72
CHAIN STOPPER.	73
DONKEY PUMP.	74
1 BUNK BED.	75
2 BUNK BEDS.	76
PASSAGE.	77
DRESSER.	78
OFFICERS CABIN.	79
ENGINEERS STORE.	80
GAS PLANT.	81
FRESH WATER TANK — 300 GALLS.	82
SPACE FOR DYNAMO—IF FITTED.	83
COAL BUNKER - CAPACITY 45 CUBIC FT.	84
PER TON = 100 TONS.	
2½" DIA. PILLARS.	85
OPEN BIN.	86
12 POUNDER AMMUNITION BOXES.	87
BIN FOR SMALL ARMS AMMUNITION.	88
BOX FOR BLANK AMMUNITION.	89
COMMISSIONED OFFICERS CABIN.	90
WARDROBE.	91
SPACE FOR WIRELESS ROOM~IF FITTED.	92
MESS~FOR 8 MEN.	93
LAMP ROOM.	94
PORTABLE GRATING.	95
ENGINE ROOM TELEGRAPH.	96
WHEEL	97
SIDE FAIRLEAD.	98
FUNNEL.	99
GUN PLATFORM.	100
CHAIN PIPE.	102
FOOD LOCKER.	103
VEGETABLE LOCKER.	104
STOVE FUNNEL.	105
6" MUSHROOM VENT.	106
COMPANION WAY.	107
7" DIA DECK LIGHT.	108
STORE ROOM HATCH.	109
MAIN ENGINE.	110

SHEET ONE OF TWO
SHEETS

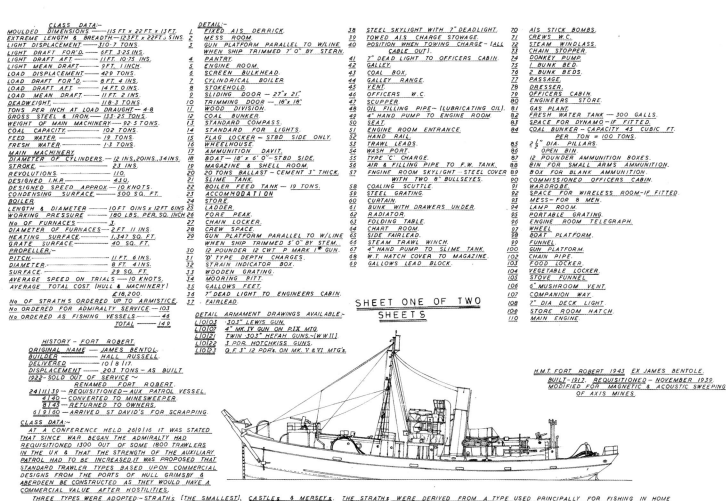

H.M.T. FORT ROBERT 1943 EX JAMES BENTOLE.

BUILT—1917. REQUISITIONED – NOVEMBER 1939.
MODIFIED FOR MAGNETIC & ACOUSTIC SWEEPING
OF AXIS MINES.

THREE TYPES WERE ADOPTED ~ STRATHS [THE SMALLEST], CASTLES & MERSEYS. THE STRATHS WERE DERIVED FROM A TYPE USED PRINCIPALLY FOR FISHING IN HOME WATERS. IT WAS BASED FROM THE TYPE OF VESSEL BUILT BY HALL, RUSSELL & CO GENERALLY FOR THE ABERDEEN "STRATH" STEAM TRAWLING & FISHING CO. LTD.

DESIGN~ A FLUSH DECK HULL WITH 3 WATERTIGHT BULKHEADS. A CHARTHOUSE, WITH WHEELHOUSE & NAVIGATING VERANDAH ABOVE, BEING FITTED AT THE FOR'D. END OF THE BOILER CASING. AFT ARE A DECKHOUSE ENCLOSING, OFFICER'S W.C. GALLEY & COMPANION TO A CABIN SPACE BELOW. FOR'D. IS A LAMP ROOM STORE & MORE ACCOMMODATION. A SINGLE SCREW, DRIVEN BY A TRIPLE EXPANSION ENGINE DEVELOPING ABOUT 430 ihp. A CROSS BUNKER FOR'D OF THE BOILER SPACE & SIDE BUNKERS GAVE A COAL CAPACITY OF ABOUT 102 TONS. FOR'D OF THE CHARTHOUSE A TRAWL WINCH WITH 2 DRUMS EACH TAKING 750 FATHOMS OF STEEL WIRE ROPE WAS STANDARD. ALONG WITH A STEAM WINDLASS ON THE FOX'L. ADDITIONAL FITTINGS PROVIDED FOR ADMIRALTY SERVICE INCLUDED~ MAGAZINE & SHELL ROOM IN THE FISH~HOLD. ACCOMMODATION FOR 3 ADDITIONAL CREW. IN THE FISH~HOLD AS WELL AS A GUN PLATFORM OVER THE ENGINE CASING DEPTH CHARGE CHUTES & STANDS, KITE M/S RACKS & TOWED AIS CHARGE GEAR. SOME STRATHS CARRIED A 4" GUN. THERE WERE 149 BUILT ALL BEING NAMED AFTER THE OFFICERS & MEN WHO FOUGHT IN THE VICTORY & ROYAL SOVEREIGN AT THE BATTLE OF TRAFALGAR.

© JOHN LAMBERT   COMPLETED 17/12/1984   CH'D. 9/5/2002

L/S/441A

II. L/S/44/B HM 'Strath'-class Admiralty trawler, hull lines and detail, 1917

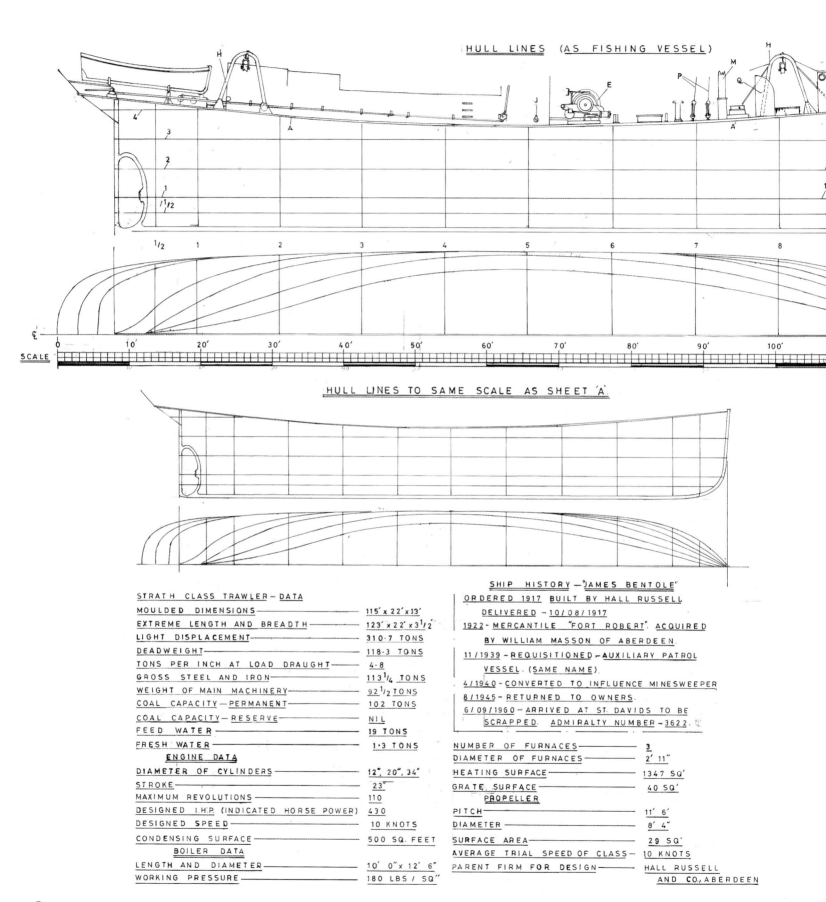

HULL LINES (AS FISHING VESSEL)

HULL LINES TO SAME SCALE AS SHEET 'A'

STRATH CLASS TRAWLER – DATA	
MOULDED DIMENSIONS	115' x 22' x 13'
EXTREME LENGTH AND BREADTH	123' x 22' x 3½'
LIGHT DISPLACEMENT	310·7 TONS
DEADWEIGHT	118·3 TONS
TONS PER INCH AT LOAD DRAUGHT	4·8
GROSS STEEL AND IRON	113¼ TONS
WEIGHT OF MAIN MACHINERY	92½ TONS
COAL CAPACITY – PERMANENT	102 TONS
COAL CAPACITY – RESERVE	NIL
FEED WATER	19 TONS
FRESH WATER	1·3 TONS
ENGINE DATA	
DIAMETER OF CYLINDERS	12", 20", 34"
STROKE	23"
MAXIMUM REVOLUTIONS	110
DESIGNED I.H.P. (INDICATED HORSE POWER)	430
DESIGNED SPEED	10 KNOTS
CONDENSING SURFACE	500 SQ. FEET
BOILER DATA	
LENGTH AND DIAMETER	10' 0" x 12' 6"
WORKING PRESSURE	180 LBS / SQ"

SHIP HISTORY – "JAMES BENTOLE"
ORDERED 1917 BUILT BY HALL RUSSELL
   DELIVERED – 10/08/1917
1922 – MERCANTILE "FORT ROBERT". ACQUIRED
   BY WILLIAM MASSON OF ABERDEEN.
11/1939 – REQUISITIONED – AUXILIARY PATROL
   VESSEL. (SAME NAME)
4/1940 – CONVERTED TO INFLUENCE MINESWEEPER
8/1945 – RETURNED TO OWNERS.
6/09/1960 – ARRIVED AT ST. DAVIDS TO BE
   SCRAPPED. ADMIRALTY NUMBER – 3622.

NUMBER OF FURNACES	3
DIAMETER OF FURNACES	2' 11"
HEATING SURFACE	1347 SQ'
GRATE SURFACE	40 SQ'
PROPELLER	
PITCH	11' 6"
DIAMETER	8' 4"
SURFACE AREA	29 SQ'
AVERAGE TRIAL SPEED OF CLASS	10 KNOTS
PARENT FIRM FOR DESIGN	HALL RUSSELL AND CO, ABERDEEN

© JOHN LAMBERT COMMENCED 16/10/2013   COMPLETED 5/11/2013   CH D 9/11/2013

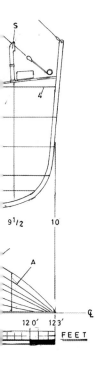

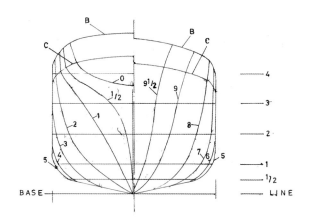

S

9 1/2   10

A

120'   123'   FEET

BASE

LINE

4

3

2

1

1/2

KEY TO DETAIL

A = EDGE OF DECK   L = SCUTTLE
B = LINE OF BULWARK   M = MAST
C = LINE OF DECK   N = GUARDRAIL
D = ℄ CENTRE LINE   P = MAST STAY
E = STEAM TRAWL WINCH   Q = COMPANION WAY
F = MAGNETIC COMPASS   R = CANVAS SCREEN
G = GALLEY FUNNEL   S = COWL VENTILATOR
H = GALLOWS   T = CLEARWATER (GUTTER)
J = LEECH LINE BLOCK   U = GALLEY DOOR
K = WHEELHOUSE   V = CHART ROOM
                              W = ANCHOR WINDLASS

SHIPS HISTORY
"JOSEPH ANNISON"
BUILDER- DUTHIE OF
ABERDEEN. LAUNCHED 19/09/1917 DELIVERED 2/11/1917
1922- SOLD TO MERCANTILE AND RETAINED THE SAME NAME, ACQUIRED BY
PERHELION A.F.C. OF GRIMSBY- PORT REG. GY 231
ACQUIRED BY STEPHEN FISHING CO OF ABERDEEN AND RENAMED WILLIAM STEPHEN
1939- NOVEMBER REQUISITIONED UNDER THE SAME NAME AND CONVERTED TO MINE-
SWEEPER 25/10/1943 SUNK BY E-BOAT,'S 74' OFF CROMER NORFOLK.

SHIP HISTORIES CONTINUED
"JAMES CURRY" ORDERED-1917 LAUNCHED-20/11/1917
DELIVERED- 28/12/1917 BUILDER-MURDOCH & MURRAY
AT PORT GLASGOW
1921- SOLD TO MERCANTILE AND RENAMED 'ADY'.
1939- REQUISITIONED AS A MINESWEEPER BELIEVED
AS FRENCH GENEVIVE
7/46 - PAID OFF LA VERON
1952 - SCRAPPED.

"JOHN BARRY" ORDERED 1917
LAUNCHED- 24/07/1917
DELIVERED- 29/08/1917 AND COMPLETED
AS MINESWEEPER.
BUILDER- HALL RUSSELL, ABERDEEN
1921- SOLD AND RENAMED
'CHRISTABELL' ACQUIRED BY
CONSOLIDATED FISHERIES
OF GRIMSBY PORT REG.
GY 1328 ACQUIRED BY
J. MACKIE OF ABERDEEN
PORT REG. A 360

SCALE 0   10'   20' FEET

ENLARGED DETAIL

MINESWEEPING KITE - WW I

FOR'D. SIDE OF BRIDGE

REAR OF GALLEY

III. L/S/43 HM *Castle*-class Admiralty standard trawler, general arrangement, 1917

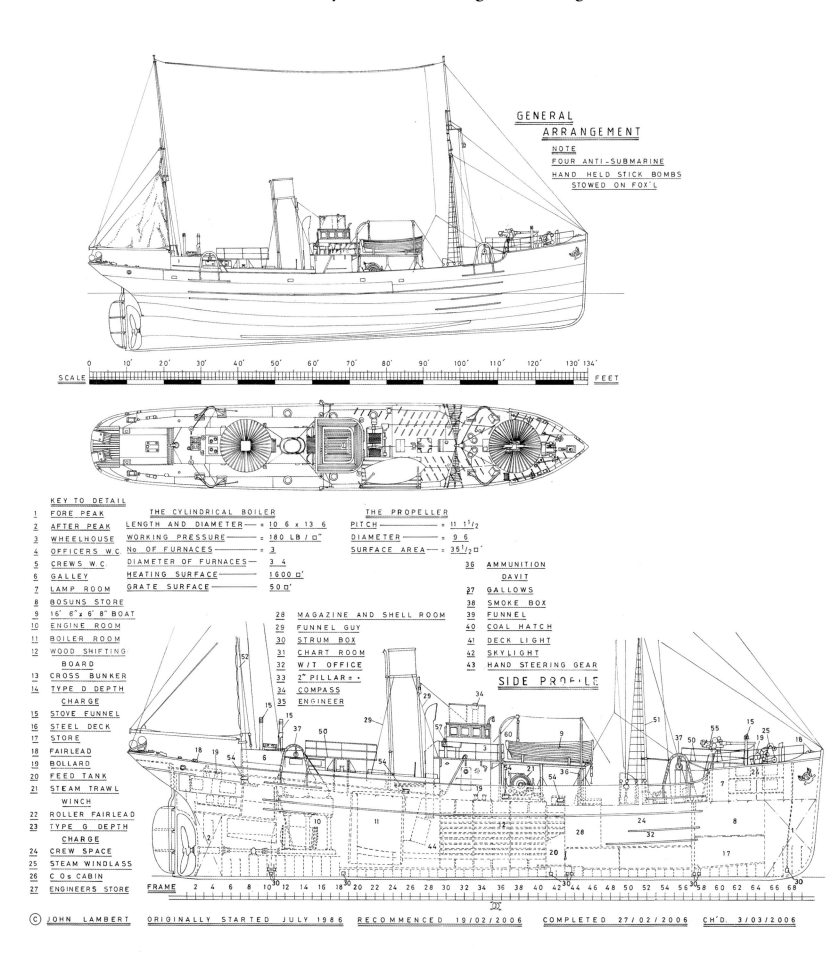

GENERAL
ARRANGEMENT
NOTE
FOUR ANTI-SUBMARINE
HAND HELD STICK BOMBS
STOWED ON FOX'L

SCALE — FEET

0 10' 20' 30' 40' 50' 60' 70' 80' 90' 100' 110' 120' 130' 134'

KEY TO DETAIL

1 FORE PEAK
2 AFTER PEAK
3 WHEELHOUSE
4 OFFICERS W.C.
5 CREWS W.C.
6 GALLEY
7 LAMP ROOM
8 BOSUNS STORE
9 16' 6" x 6' 8" BOAT
10 ENGINE ROOM
11 BOILER ROOM
12 WOOD SHIFTING
    BOARD
13 CROSS BUNKER
14 TYPE D DEPTH
    CHARGE
15 STOVE FUNNEL
16 STEEL DECK
17 STORE
18 FAIRLEAD
19 BOLLARD
20 FEED TANK
21 STEAM TRAWL
    WINCH
22 ROLLER FAIRLEAD
23 TYPE G DEPTH
    CHARGE
24 CREW SPACE
25 STEAM WINDLASS
26 C Os CABIN
27 ENGINEERS STORE

THE CYLINDRICAL BOILER

LENGTH AND DIAMETER — = 10 6 x 13 6
WORKING PRESSURE ——— = 180 LB / □"
No. OF FURNACES ——— = 3
DIAMETER OF FURNACES — 3 4
HEATING SURFACE ——— 1600 □'
GRATE SURFACE ——— 50 □'

28 MAGAZINE AND SHELL ROOM
29 FUNNEL GUY
30 STRUM BOX
31 CHART ROOM
32 W/T OFFICE
33 2" PILLAR = •
34 COMPASS
35 ENGINEER

THE PROPELLER

PITCH ——— = 11 1½
DIAMETER ——— = 9 6
SURFACE AREA — = 35½ □'

36 AMMUNITION
    DAVIT
37 GALLOWS
38 SMOKE BOX
39 FUNNEL
40 COAL HATCH
41 DECK LIGHT
42 SKYLIGHT
43 HAND STEERING GEAR

SIDE PROFILE

FRAME 2 4 6 8 10 12 14 16 18 20 22 24 26 28 30 32 34 36 38 40 42 44 46 48 50 52 54 56 58 60 62 64 66 68

© JOHN LAMBERT   ORIGINALLY STARTED JULY 1986   RECOMMENCED 19/02/2006   COMPLETED 27/02/2006   CH'D. 3/03/2006

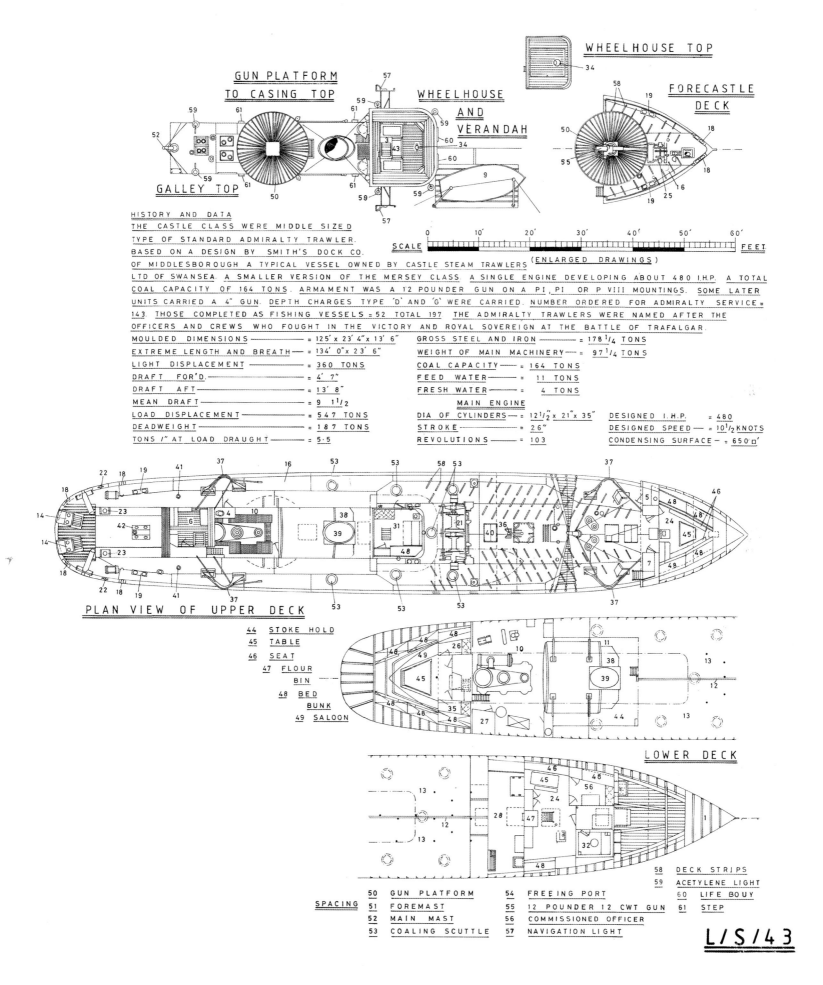

GUN PLATFORM
TO CASING TOP

GALLEY TOP

WHEELHOUSE
AND
VERANDAH

WHEELHOUSE TOP

FORECASTLE
DECK

HISTORY AND DATA
THE CASTLE CLASS WERE MIDDLE SIZED
TYPE OF STANDARD ADMIRALTY TRAWLER.
BASED ON A DESIGN BY SMITH'S DOCK CO.
OF MIDDLESBOROUGH A TYPICAL VESSEL OWNED BY CASTLE STEAM TRAWLERS (ENLARGED DRAWINGS)
LTD OF SWANSEA. A SMALLER VERSION OF THE MERSEY CLASS. A SINGLE ENGINE DEVELOPING ABOUT 480 I.H.P. A TOTAL
COAL CAPACITY OF 164 TONS. ARMAMENT WAS A 12 POUNDER GUN ON A PI, PI OR P VIII MOUNTINGS. SOME LATER
UNITS CARRIED A 4" GUN. DEPTH CHARGES TYPE 'D' AND 'G' WERE CARRIED. NUMBER ORDERED FOR ADMIRALTY SERVICE =
143. THOSE COMPLETED AS FISHING VESSELS = 52 TOTAL 197 THE ADMIRALTY TRAWLERS WERE NAMED AFTER THE
OFFICERS AND CREWS WHO FOUGHT IN THE VICTORY AND ROYAL SOVEREIGN AT THE BATTLE OF TRAFALGAR.

SCALE _____ FEET

MOULDED DIMENSIONS	= 125' x 23' 4" x 13' 6"	GROSS STEEL AND IRON	= $178\frac{1}{4}$ TONS
EXTREME LENGTH AND BREATH	= 134' 0" x 23' 6"	WEIGHT OF MAIN MACHINERY	= $97\frac{1}{4}$ TONS
LIGHT DISPLACEMENT	= 360 TONS	COAL CAPACITY	= 164 TONS
DRAFT FOR'D	= 4' 7"	FEED WATER	= 11 TONS
DRAFT AFT	= 13' 8"	FRESH WATER	= 4 TONS
MEAN DRAFT	= 9 $1\frac{1}{2}$	MAIN ENGINE	
LOAD DISPLACEMENT	= 547 TONS	DIA OF CYLINDERS = $12\frac{1}{2}$" x 21" x 35"	DESIGNED I.H.P. = 480
DEADWEIGHT	= 187 TONS	STROKE = 26"	DESIGNED SPEED = $10\frac{1}{2}$ KNOTS
TONS 1" AT LOAD DRAUGHT	= 5.5	REVOLUTIONS = 103	CONDENSING SURFACE = 650 □'

PLAN VIEW OF UPPER DECK

44 STOKE HOLD
45 TABLE
46 SEAT
47 FLOUR
   BIN
48 BED
   BUNK
49 SALOON

LOWER DECK

SPACING	50	GUN PLATFORM	54	FREEING PORT	58	DECK STRIPS
	51	FOREMAST	55	12 POUNDER 12 CWT GUN	59	ACETYLENE LIGHT
	52	MAIN MAST	56	COMMISSIONED OFFICER	60	LIFE BOUY
	53	COALING SCUTTLE	57	NAVIGATION LIGHT	61	STEP

L/S/43

IV. L/S/42 HM *Mersey*-class Admiralty trawler, general arrangement, 1917

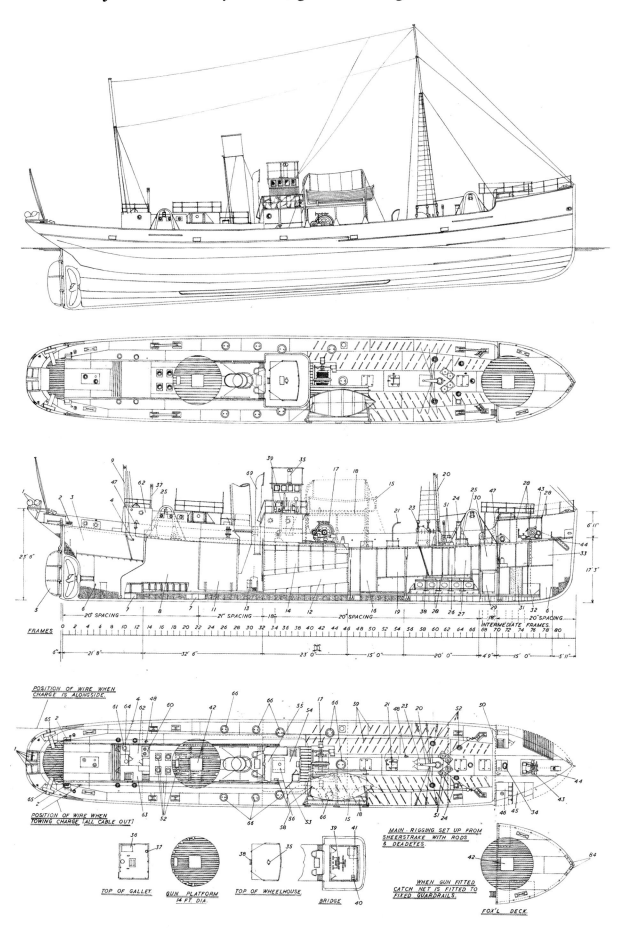

POSITION OF WIRE WHEN
CHARGE IS ALONGSIDE.

POSITION OF WIRE WHEN
TOWING CHARGE (ALL CABLE OUT)

TOP OF GALLEY

GUN PLATFORM
14 FT. DIA.

TOP OF WHEELHOUSE

BRIDGE

MAIN RIGGING SET UP FROM
SHEERSTRAKE WITH RODS
& DEADEYES.

WHEN GUN FITTED
CATCH NET IS FITTED TO
FIXED GUARDRAILS.

FOX'L DECK.

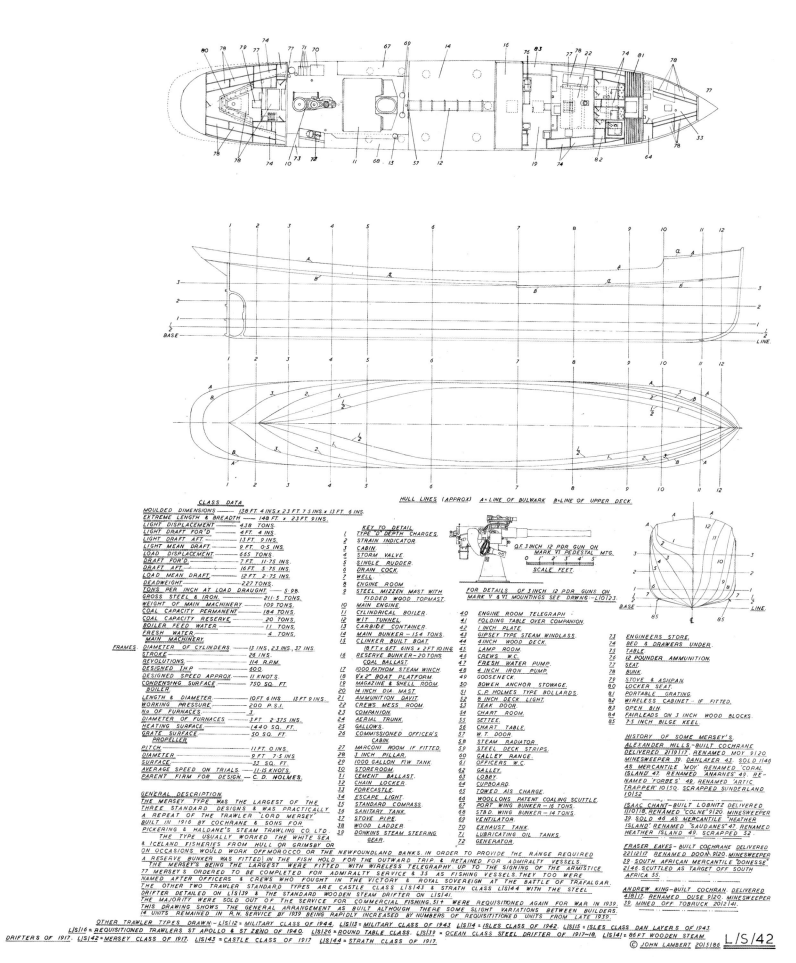

HULL LINES (APPROX) A = LINE OF BULWARK B = LINE OF UPPER DECK.

CLASS DATA

MOULDED DIMENSIONS	138 FT. 4 INS x 23 FT. 7.5 INS. x 13 FT. 6 INS.
EXTREME LENGTH & BREADTH	148 FT. x 23 FT. 9 INS.
LIGHT DISPLACEMENT	438 TONS.
LIGHT DRAFT FOR'D	4 FT. 4 INS.
LIGHT DRAFT AFT	13 FT. 9 INS.
LIGHT MEAN DRAFT	9 FT. 0.5 INS.
LOAD DISPLACEMENT	665 TONS.
DRAFT FOR'D	7 FT. 11.75 INS.
DRAFT AFT	16 FT. 5.75 INS.
LOAD MEAN DRAFT	12 FT. 2.75 INS.
DEADWEIGHT	227 TONS.
TONS PER INCH AT LOAD DRAUGHT	5.98.
GROSS STEEL & IRON	211.5 TONS.
WEIGHT OF MAIN MACHINERY	109 TONS.
COAL CAPACITY PERMANENT	184 TONS.
COAL CAPACITY RESERVE	20 TONS.
BOILER FEED WATER	11 TONS.
FRESH WATER	4 TONS.

FRAMES. MAIN MACHINERY.

DIAMETER OF CYLINDERS	13 INS, 23 INS, 37 INS.
STROKE	26 INS.
REVOLUTIONS	114 R.P.M.
DESIGNED I.H.P.	600.
DESIGNED SPEED APPROX.	11 KNOTS.
CONDENSING SURFACE	750 SQ. FT.

BOILER.

LENGTH & DIAMETER	10 FT. 6 INS. 13 FT. 9 INS.
WORKING PRESSURE	200 P.S.I.
No OF FURNACES	3.
DIAMETER OF FURNACES	3 FT. 2.375 INS.
HEATING SURFACE	1440 SQ. FT.
GRATE SURFACE	50 SQ. FT.

PROPELLER.

PITCH	11 FT. 0 INS.
DIAMETER	9 FT. 7.5 INS.
SURFACE	33 SQ. FT.
AVERAGE SPEED ON TRIALS	11.15 KNOTS.
PARENT FIRM FOR DESIGN	C. D. HOLMES.

GENERAL DESCRIPTION.

THE MERSEY TYPE WAS THE LARGEST OF THE THREE STANDARD DESIGNS & WAS PRACTICALLY A REPEAT OF THE TRAWLER 'LORD MERSEY' BUILT IN 1916 BY COCHRANE & SONS FOR PICKERING & HALDANE'S STEAM TRAWLING CO LTD. THE TYPE USUALLY WORKED THE WHITE SEA & ICELAND FISHERIES FROM HULL OR GRIMSBY OR ON OCCASIONS WOULD WORK OFF MOROCCO OR THE NEWFOUNDLAND BANKS. IN ORDER TO PROVIDE THE RANGE REQUIRED A RESERVE BUNKER WAS FITTED IN THE FISH HOLD FOR THE OUTWARD TRIP, & RETAINED FOR COMMERCIAL FISHING. 51+ WERE REQUISITIONED AGAIN FOR WAR IN 1939.
THE MERSEY'S BEING THE LARGEST WERE FITTED WITH WIRELESS TELEGRAPHY. UP TO THE SIGNING OF THE ARMISTICE 77 MERSEY'S ORDERED TO BE COMPLETED FOR ADMIRALTY SERVICE & 35 AS FISHING VESSELS. THEY TOO WERE NAMED AFTER OFFICERS & CREWS WHO FOUGHT IN THE VICTORY & ROYAL SOVEREIGN AT THE BATTLE OF TRAFALGAR. THE OTHER TWO TRAWLER STANDARD TYPES ARE CASTLE CLASS L/S/43 & STRATH CLASS L/S/44 WITH THE STEEL DRIFTER DETAILED ON L/S/39 & THE STANDARD WOODEN STEAM DRIFTER ON L/S/41. THE MAJORITY WERE SOLD OUT OF THE SERVICE FOR COMMERCIAL FISHING. 51+ WERE REQUISITIONED AGAIN FOR WAR IN 1939. THIS DRAWING SHOWS THE GENERAL ARRANGEMENT AS BUILT ALTHOUGH THERE SOME SLIGHT VARIATIONS BETWEEN BUILDERS. 14 UNITS REMAINED IN R.N. SERVICE BY 1939 BEING RAPIDLY INCREASED BY NUMBERS OF REQUISITIONED UNITS FROM LATE 1939.

KEY TO DETAIL

1. TYPE 'D' DEPTH CHARGES.
2. STRAIN INDICATOR.
3. CABIN.
4. STORM VALVE.
5. SINGLE RUDDER.
6. DRAIN COCK.
7. WELL.
8. ENGINE ROOM.
9. STEEL MIZZEN MAST WITH FIDDED WOOD TOPMAST.
10. MAIN ENGINE.
11. CYLINDRICAL BOILER.
12. W/T TUNNEL.
13. CARBIDE CONTAINER.
14. MAIN BUNKER - 154 TONS.
15. CLINKER BUILT BOAT 18 FT x 6 FT 6 INS x 2 FT 10 INS
16. RESERVE BUNKER - 20 TONS COAL BALLAST.
17. 1000 FATHOM STEAM WINCH.
18. 9' x 2" BOAT PLATFORM.
19. MAGAZINE & SHELL ROOM.
20. 14 INCH DIA. MAST.
21. AMMUNITION DAVIT.
22. CREWS MESS ROOM.
23. COMPANION.
24. AERIAL TRUNK.
25. GALLOWS.
26. COMMISSIONED OFFICER'S CABIN.
27. MARCONI ROOM IF FITTED.
28. 3 INCH PILLAR.
29. 1000 GALLON F/W TANK.
30. STOREROOM.
31. CEMENT BALLAST.
32. CHAIN LOCKER.
33. FORECASTLE.
34. ESCAPE LIGHT.
35. STANDARD COMPASS.
36. SANITARY TANK.
37. STOVE PIPE.
38. WOOD LADDER.
39. DONKINS STEAM STEERING GEAR.
40. ENGINE ROOM TELEGRAPH.
41. FOLDING TABLE OVER COMPANION.
42. 1 INCH PLATE.
43. GIPSEY TYPE STEAM WINDLASS.
44. 4 INCH WOOD DECK.
45. LAMP ROOM.
46. CREWS W.C.
47. FRESH WATER PUMP.
48. 4 INCH IRON PUMP.
49. GOOSENECK.
50. BOWER ANCHOR STOWAGE.
51. C.P. HOLMES TYPE BOLLARDS.
52. 8 INCH DECK LIGHT.
53. TEAK DOOR.
54. CHART ROOM.
55. SETTEE.
56. CHART TABLE.
57. W.T. DOOR.
58. STEAM RADIATOR.
59. STEEL DECK STRIPS.
60. GALLEY RANGE.
61. OFFICERS W.C.
62. GALLEY.
63. LOBBY.
64. CUPBOARD.
65. TOWED A/S CHARGE.
66. WOOLLONS PATENT COALING SCUTTLE.
67. PORT WING BUNKER - 16 TONS.
68. STB.D WING BUNKER - 14 TONS.
69. VENTILATOR.
70. EXHAUST TANK.
71. LUBRICATING OIL TANKS.
72. GENERATOR.
73. ENGINEERS STORE.
74. BED & DRAWERS UNDER.
75. TABLE.
76. 12 POUNDER AMMUNITION.
77. SEAT.
78. BUNK.
79. STOVE & ASHPAN.
80. LOCKER SEAT.
81. PORTABLE GRATING.
82. WIRELESS CABINET - IF FITTED.
83. OPEN BIN.
84. FAIRLEADS ON 3 INCH WOOD BLOCKS.
85. 7.5 INCH BILGE KEEL.

Q.F. 3 INCH 12 PDR GUN ON MARK VI PEDESTAL MTG.

SCALE FEET.

FOR DETAILS OF 3 INCH 12 PDR GUNS ON MARK V & VI MOUNTINGS SEE DRWNG:- L10123.

BASE LINE.

HISTORY OF SOME MERSEY'S.

ALEXANDER HILLS - BUILT COCHRANE. DELIVERED 21/9/17. RENAMED 'MOY' 9/20. MINESWEEPER 39. DANLAYER 43. SOLD 11/46 AS MERCANTILE 'MOY'. RENAMED 'CORAL ISLAND' 47. RENAMED 'ANARNES' 49. RENAMED 'FORBES' 49. RENAMED 'ARTIC TRAPPER' 10/50. SCRAPPED SUNDERLAND 10/52.

ISAAC CHANT - BUILT LOBNITZ DELIVERED 1/10/18. RENAMED 'COLNE' 9/20. MINESWEEPER 39. SOLD 46 AS MERCANTILE 'HEATHER ISLAND' RENAMED 'SAUDANES' 47. RENAMED HEATHER ISLAND 49. SCRAPPED 52.

FRASER EAVES - BUILT COCHRANE DELIVERED 22/12/17. RENAMED 'DOON' 9/20. MINESWEEPER 39. SOUTH AFRICAN MERCANTILE 'DONESSE' 2/46. SCUTTLED AS TARGET OFF SOUTH AFRICA 55.

ANDREW KING - BUILT COCHRANE. DELIVERED 4/8/17. RENAMED 'OUSE' 9/20. MINESWEEPER 39. MINED OFF TOBRUCK 20/2/41.

OTHER TRAWLER TYPES DRAWN:- L/S/12 = MILITARY CLASS OF 1944. L/S/13 = MILITARY CLASS OF 1943. L/S/14 = ISLES CLASS OF 1942. L/S/15 = ISLES CLASS DAN LAYERS OF 1943. L/S/16 = REQUISITIONED TRAWLERS St APOLLO & St ZENO OF 1940. L/S/26 = ROUND TABLE CLASS. L/S/39 = OCEAN CLASS STEEL DRIFTER OF 1917-18. L/S/41 = 86 FT WOODEN STEAM DRIFTERS OF 1917. L/S/42 = MERSEY CLASS OF 1917. L/S/43 = CASTLE CLASS OF 1917. L/S/44 = STRATH CLASS OF 1917.

© JOHN LAMBERT 20/5/86

L/S/42

V. L/S/39 *Ocean*-class Admiralty steel screw steam drifter, 1917–18

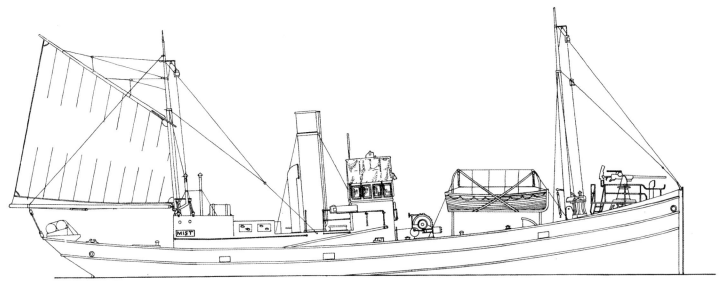

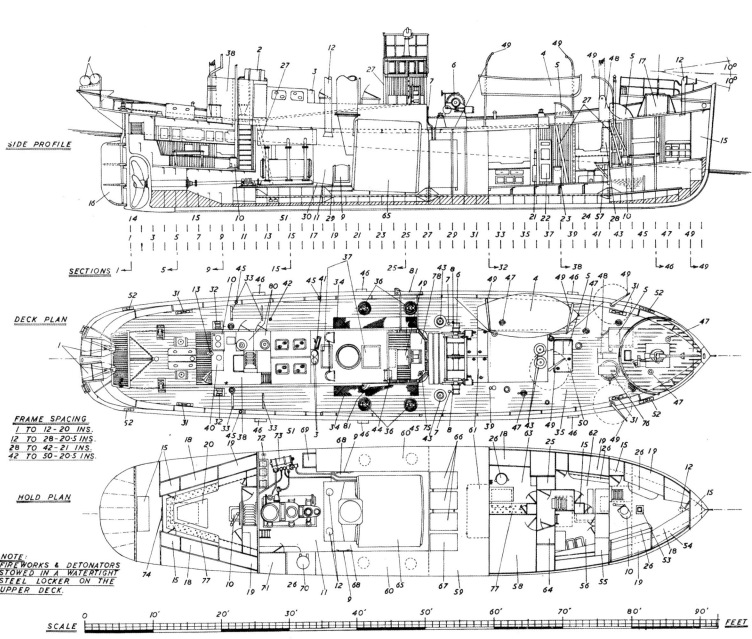

SIDE PROFILE

SECTIONS

DECK PLAN

FRAME SPACING
1 TO 12 - 20 INS.
12 TO 28 - 20.5 INS.
28 TO 42 - 21 INS.
42 TO 50 - 20.5 INS.

HOLD PLAN

NOTE:
FIREWORKS & DETONATORS
STOWED IN A WATERTIGHT
STEEL LOCKER ON THE
UPPER DECK.

SCALE 0 10' 20' 30' 40' 50' 60' 70' 80' 90' FEET

NOTE:—
MANY WAR BUILT STEEL DRIFTERS WERE SOLD TO COMMERCIAL FISHING FLEETS BETWEEN THE WARS. AT THE
OUTBREAK OF THE SECOND WORLD WAR SOME 20 STILL REMAINED IN ADMIRALTY SERVICE E.G. BRINE, CASCADE,
CLOUD FY3, COLDSNAP FY4, CRESCENT MOON FY5, EDDY FY12, HALO FY21, INDIAN SUMMER FY20, MIST FY40, ETC.
OVER 50 STEEL DRIFTERS THAT WERE SOLD OUT OF SERVICE AFTER WWI TO BE REQUISITIONED ON THE
OUTBREAK OF WWII. E.G. NORTHERN LIGHTS BUILT BY ROSE ST FOUNDRY & COMPLETED AS A FISHING VESSEL
16|4|19. SOLD & RENAMED SUNNYSIDE GIRL. REQUISITIONED DEC 39 SHE WAS
FITTED AS A ANTI-SUBMARINE VESSEL TO SURVIVE THE WAR & BE
RETURNED IN FEB. 46.

3 POUNDER HOTCHKISS
GUN ON MARK I
MOUNTING.
SEE DRAWING L10122

OTHER WWI TRAWLER & DRIFTER DRAWINGS.
L|S|41 86 FT. WOODEN STEAM DRIFTER.
L|S|42 MERSEY CLASS ADMIRALTY TRAWLER.
L|S|43 CASTLE CLASS ADMIRALTY TRAWLER.
L|S|44 STRATH CLASS ADMIRALTY TRAWLER.

CLASS DATA:-
MOULDED DIMENSIONS.— 86 FT x 18 FT 6 INS x 10 FT 6 INS.
LENGTH OVERALL.— 93 FT 3 INS.
EXTREME BEAM.— 18 FT 10 INS.
LIGHT DISPLACEMENT.— 148 TONS.
DRAFT FOR'D-LIGHT} MEAN 4 FT. 3 INS} 7 FT 4.5 INS.
DRAFT AFT - LIGHT} 10 FT 6 INS}
LOAD DISPLACEMENT.— 199.5 TONS.
DRAFT FOR'D LOAD} MEAN 6 FT 2.5 INS} 8 FT 10 INS
DRAFT AFT LOAD} 11 FT 5.5 INS}
DEADWEIGHT.— 51.5 TONS.
GROSS STEEL & IRON.— 69.5 TONS.
MAIN MACHINERY.— 42 TONS.
COAL CAPACITY.— 37 TONS.
FEED WATER.— 5.5 TONS.
FRESH WATER.— 2.75 TONS.
ENGINES:- DIA. OF CYLINDERS — 9.5 INS, 15.5 INS, 26 INS.
STROKE.— 18 INS.
REVOLUTIONS.— 140.
DESIGNED INDICATED HORSE POWER — 270
MAX. DESIGNED SPEED.— 9 KNOTS.
CLASS AVERAGE ON TRIALS.— 8.9 KNOTS.
CONDENSING SURFACE.— 275 SQUARE FEET.
BOILER LENGTH & DIA.— 9 FT 6 INS x 10 FT.
WORKING PRESSURE.— 180 LBS|SQ. INCH.
HEATING SURFACE.— 810 SQ. FT.
GRATE SURFACE.— 30.5 SQ. FT.

APPROX HULL SECTIONS

SECTIONS.

HISTORY— AT THE OUTBREAK OF WWI THE BRITISH ADMIRALTY POSSESSED NO DRIFTERS HOWEVER MANY
PRIVATELY OWNED VESSELS WERE REQUISITIONED FOR PATROL, CONVOY, WATER DUTY & FLEET ATTENDANCE
DUTIES THUS RELIEVING TRAWLERS FOR OTHER DUTIES. IN MARCH 1917 IT WAS DECIDED TO CONSTRUCT
115 DRIFTERS OF STEEL & WOOD AS SOON AS FIRMS COULD ACCEPT THEM. THE STEEL VESSELS WERE
BASED UPON THE DESIGN OF THOSE BUILT BY MESSRS A. HALL & CO. OF ABERDEEN, THE DRAWINGS BEING
MODIFIED TO ADMIRALTY REQUIREMENTS & SUPPLIED BY D.N.C. TO THE 21 SHIPYARDS EMPLOYED. BASED UPON
HALLS "OCEAN" TYPE. A COMBINED CHART ROOM & WHEELHOUSE WAS FITTED AT THE FOR'D END OF THE
BOILER CASING. A DECK HOUSE WAS FITTED AFT CONTAINED TWO W Cs GALLEY & COMPANION LEADING TO THE
CABIN BELOW WITH ACCOMMODATION FOR 5 MEN. FORE & MIZEN MASTS WERE FITTED WITH A FULL SUIT OF SAILS.
A 3 OR 6 POUNDER GUN WAS CARRIED. MANY WERE FITTED WITH W|T. COMPLEMENT— 10 OR 11 WITH W|T MOST
CARRIED FOUR D DEPTH CHARGES AS WELL AS MINESWEEPING GEAR. SOME NAMES & COMPLETION DATES:-
BILLOW-26|9|18. BLIZZARD-30|7|18 BRINE-17|7|18 CALM-18|6|18 CASCADE-2|6|18 CATSPAW-5|8|18 CLOUD-17|5|18 DAWN-11|6|18
DAYBREAK-15|8|18 DEW-6|9|18 DUSK-21|9|18 EDDY-27|8|18 FAIR WIND-31|8|18 FALLING STAR-21|9|18 FLASH-5|6|18
FLICKER-26|9|18 FORKLIGHTNING-22|11|18 FROTH-25|10|18 GLITTER-19|11|18 GLOW-21|11|19 GREY SEA-13|11|19

1 TWIN DEPTH CHARGE RACKS.
2 SANITARY TANK- 36 GALLONS.
3 ASH BUCKETS.
4 BOAT— 15 FT 0 INS x 6 FT 3 INS.
5 COMPANION.
6 STEAM WIRE WINCH.
7 AIR PIPE.
8 FILLING PIPE.
9 BUNKER DOOR.
10 COAL STOVE.
11 ENGINE ROOM.
12 COWL VENT.
13 7 INCH SCUTTLE.
14 SCREW- 6 FT 9 INS DIA.
15 LOCKER.
16 RUDDER.
17 GUN SUPPORT.
18 SINGLE BUNK.
19 2 BUNKS.
20 TABLE.
21 FOLDING LAVATORY.
22 DOOR TO STORE.
23 WASH BASIN.
24 STOOL.
25 STORE ROOM.
26 SEAT.
27 LADDER.
28 MESS KIT RACK.
29 BUNKER DOOR GUARD.
30 BUNKER END.
31 MOORING BOLLARD.
32 DECK FAIRLEAD.
33 MINE SWEEPING KITE RACKS.
34 STEEL CHEQUERED PLATE.
35 PINE DECK.
36 BUNKER SCUTTLE.
37 HATCH.
38 GALLEY.
39 HAND PUMP.
40 STEEL COAL BOX.
41 GRIND STONE.
42 4 INCH HAND PUMP.
43 SIDE BOLLARD.
44 HYDROPHONE SWITHBOARD.
45 SCUPPER PIPE.
46 WASH PORT.
47 DECK LIGHT.
48 MAST STEP.
49 DAVIT.
50 MAGAZINE HATCH.
51 RECIPROCATING STEAM ENGINE.
52 FAIRLEAD.
53 CHAIN BOX.
54 LAMPS UNDER.
55 RACK FOR DEPTH CHARGE PISTOLS.
56 MAGAZINE.
57 FOLDING TABLE.
58 SPACE FOR RADIO INSTALLATION.
59 CROSS BUNKER - 18 TONS
60 SIDE BUNKER- 21 TONS: TOTAL-39 TONS.
61 COALING HATCH.
62 SKIPPER & SECOND HAND CABIN.
63 COMMISSIONED OFFICERS CABIN.
64 PANTRY & STORE.
65 CYLINDRICAL BOILER.
66 BOILER FEED TANK- 416 GALLS.
67 FRESH WATER TANK- 416 GALLS.
68 STEP.
69 EXHAUST TANK.
70 GAS TANK.
71 ENGINEERS LOCKER.
72 W.C. DISCHARGE PIPE.
73 CONDENSER.
74 SLIDING DOOR.
75 ENGINE ROOM TELEGRAPH
76 CAPSTAN.
77 CUSHIONED SEAT.
78 CHART TABLE.
79 SHIPS WHEELHOUSE.
80 W.C.
81 NAVIGATION LIGHT.

© JOHN LAMBERT 29|9|81

L|S|39

VI. L/S/39/A *Ocean*-class Admiralty steel screw steam drifter, general arrangement, 1917

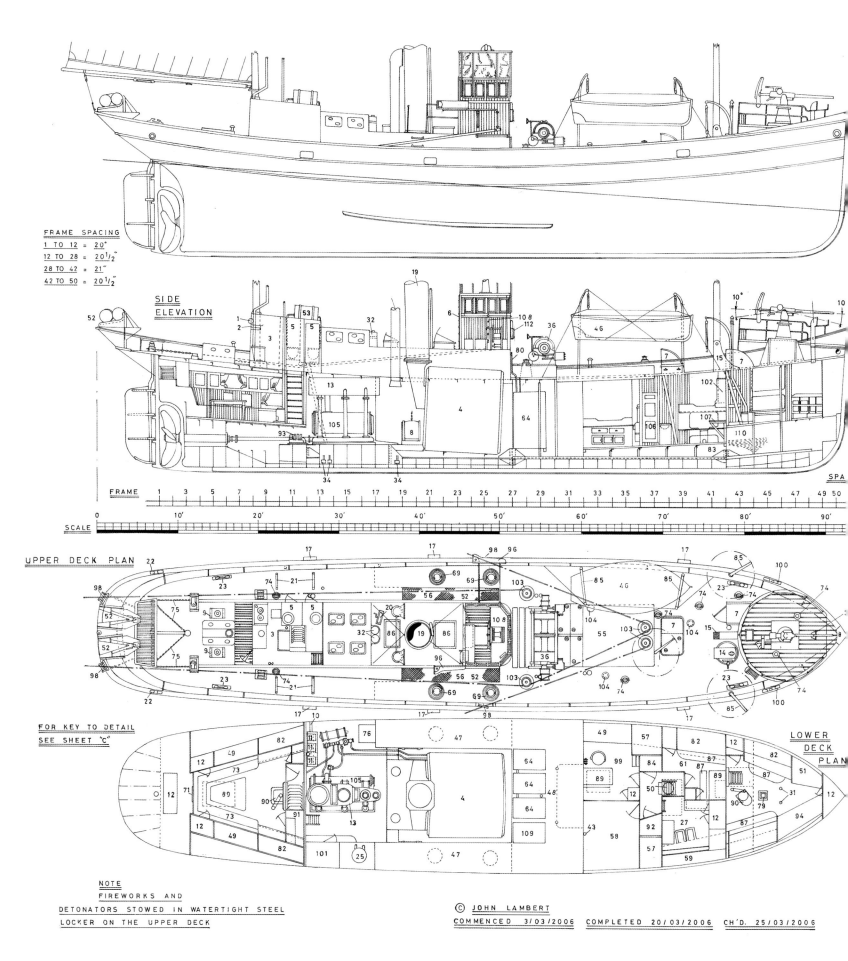

FRAME SPACING
1 TO 12 = 20"
12 TO 28 = 20 1/2"
28 TO 42 = 21"
42 TO 50 = 20 1/2"

SIDE ELEVATION

FRAME 1 3 5 7 9 11 13 15 17 19 21 23 25 27 29 31 33 35 37 39 41 43 45 47 49 50

SCALE 0 10' 20' 30' 40' 50' 60' 70' 80' 90'

UPPER DECK PLAN

FOR KEY TO DETAIL
SEE SHEET "C"

LOWER DECK PLAN

NOTE
FIREWORKS AND
DETONATORS STOWED IN WATERTIGHT STEEL
LOCKER ON THE UPPER DECK

© JOHN LAMBERT
COMMENCED 3/03/2006 COMPLETED 20/03/2006 CH'D. 25/03/2006

MOULDED DIMENSIONS	86' 0" x 18' 6" x 10' 6"
EXTREME LENGTH AND BREATH	93' 3" x 18' 10"
LIGHT DISPLACEMENT	148 TONS
LIGHT DRAFT FOR'D	4' 3"
LIGHT DRAFT AFT — MEAN — 7' 4½"	10' 6"
LOAD DISPLACEMENT	199·5 TONS
LOAD DRAFT FOR'D	6' 2½"
LOAD DRAFT AFT — MEAN — 8' 10"	11' 5½"
DEADWEIGHT	51·5 TONS
GROSS STEEL AND IRON	69·5 TONS
WEIGHT OF MAIN MACHINERY	42 TONS
COAL CAPACITY	37 TONS
FEED WATER	5·5 TONS
FRESH WATER	2·75 TONS
METACENTRIC HEIGHT—LIGHT	1·92 (GM)
METACENTRIC HEIGHT—LOADED	1·88 (GM)

MAIN ENGINES

DIAMETER OF CYLINDERS	9½", 15½", 26"
STROKE	18"
REVOLUTIONS (MAXIMUM)	140
DESIGNED i.h.p	270
N.H.P.	42
DESIGNED SPEED OF VESSEL	9 KNOTS
AVERAGE SPEED ON TRIALS	8·9 KNOTS
CONDENSING SURFACE	275 sq ft

BOILERS

LENGTH AND DIAMETER	9' 6" x 10'
WORKING PRESSURE	180 lbs
NUMBER OF FURNACES (PLAIN)	2
DIA. OF FURNACES (EXTERNAL)	3' 2"
HEATING SURFACE	810 sq ft
GRATE SURFACE	30·5 sq ft

PROPELLER

PITCH	8' 6"
DIAMETER	6' 9"
SURFACE	18 sq ft

HISTORY AND DATA

ON THE OUTBREAK OF WAR IN 1914 THE ADMIRALTY POSSESSED NO DRIFTERS, BUT IT WAS SOON FOUND NECESSARY TO REQUISITION PRIVATELY OWNED VESSELS FOR PATROL CONVOY WATER DUTY AND FLEET ATTENDANCE WORK THUS RELIEVING TRAWLERS FOR OTHER MORE IMPORTANT WORK. IN MARCH 1917 WITH THE OUTPUT OF TRAWLERS UNDER REVIEW IT WAS SUGGESTED THAT THE SITUATION COULD BE RELIEVED BY BUILDING DRIFTERS IN LIEU OF TRAWLERS. BY APRIL IT WAS APPROVED THAT DRIFTERS WOULD BE SUBSTITUTED FOR 50 TRAWLERS AND ORDERS WERE PUT IN HAND FOR 115 DRIFTERS TO BE BUILT AS SOON AS FIRMS COULD ACCEPT ORDERS. SMALLER CREW NUMBERS (15 TO 10) WERE REQUIRED AND DRIFTERS COULD UNDERTAKE MINESWEEPING DUTIES IN SUITABLE WEATHER.

THE ADMIRALTY STANDARD STEEL DRIFTER WAS BASED ON A DESIGN BY MESSRS A HALL OF ABERDEEN AND THAT COMPANY WAS ADOPTED AS THE 'PARENT' FIRM. THE DRAWING BEING MODIFIED BY DNC AS REQUIRED FOR ADMIRALTY SERVICE AND BASED UPON THE "OCEAN" TYPE OF FISHING DRIFTER.

A COMBINED CHART ROOM AND WHEELHOUSE WAS FITTED ON THE FOR'D. END OF THE BOILER CASING. A DECK HOUSE AFT CONTAINING TWO W.Cs, A GALLEY AND A COMPANION TO THE CABIN BELOW ACCOMMODATING FIVE MEN. CONTINUED ON SHEET "C".

REDRAWN FROM A COPY TRACED FROM A BLUEPRINT EX-A. HALL & COMPANY LIMITED OF ABERDEEN – DATED 23/11/1917 AND PASSED BY THE DIRECTOR OF AUXILIARY VESSELS (ADMIRALTY TRAWLERS & DRIFTERS) ON 27/09/1918

SHEET ONE OF THREE SHEETS   L/S/39/A

VII. L/S/39/B *Ocean*-class steel screw steam drifter, rigging plan and sheer drawing, 1917

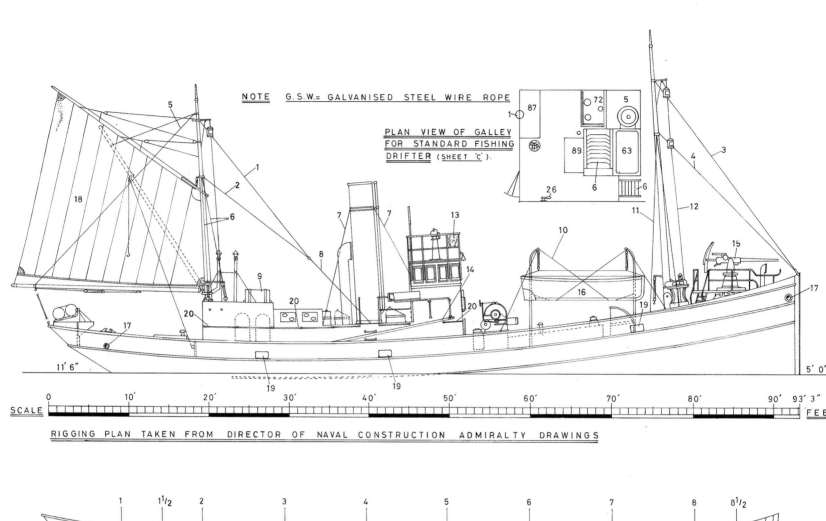

NOTE G.S.W.= GALVANISED STEEL WIRE ROPE

PLAN VIEW OF GALLEY FOR STANDARD FISHING DRIFTER (SHEET 'C').

SCALE |0 10′ 20′ 30′ 40′ 50′ 60′ 70′ 80′ 90′ 93′3″ FEET

RIGGING PLAN TAKEN FROM DIRECTOR OF NAVAL CONSTRUCTION ADMIRALTY DRAWINGS

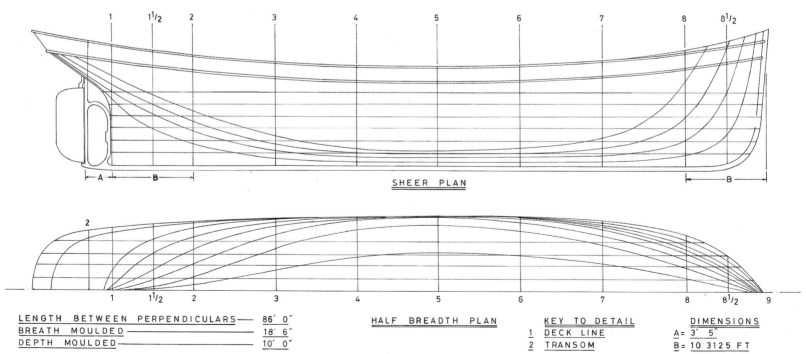

SHEER PLAN

HALF BREADTH PLAN

LENGTH BETWEEN PERPENDICULARS	86′ 0″
BREATH MOULDED	18′ 6″
DEPTH MOULDED	10′ 0″

KEY TO DETAIL	
1	DECK LINE
2	TRANSOM

DIMENSIONS	
A=	3′ 5″
B=	10 3125 FT

THE LINES ARE TAKEN FROM ORIGINAL DRAUGHT DRAWINGS OF FELLOWS AND CO LTD OF YARMOUTH

KEY TO DETAIL

1. $1\frac{1}{2}''$ G.S.W.R.
2. $2\frac{1}{4}''$ G.S.W.R.
3. $2''$ G.S.W.R.
4. $2\frac{1}{2}''$ G.S.W.R.
5. $1\frac{3}{4}''$ G.S.W.R.
6. $2''$ G.S.W.R. SET UP WITH DEAD EYES AND MANILLA LANYARDS
7. $1\frac{3}{4}''$ G.S.W.R. 4 OFF FUNNEL GUYS
8. $\frac{7}{8}''$ IRON ROD BRIDLED PALMED ON TO CASING
9. 36 GALLON SANITARY TANK
10. $1\frac{1}{4}''$ S.W.R. SERVED AND SPLICED TO NECK OF DAVIT
11. $2\frac{1}{4}''$ G.S.W.R. SET UP WITH $1''$ GALVANISED RIGGING SCREW
12. $2\frac{1}{4}''$ G.S.W.R. SET UP WITH BLOCKS AND FALLS
13. CANVAS ROUND SIDES OF COMPASS PLATFORM
14. STEERING GEAR CHAINS IN IRON PIPES
15. CANVAS COVER OVER 6 POUNDER Q F GUN
16. BOAT — 15' 0" x 6' 3"
17. TRACE OF BILGE KEEL

NOTE
WIRE, ROPE ETC IS
MEASURED BY ITS
CIRCUMFERENCE

17. MOORING PIPE
18. No 2 CANVAS
19. FREEING PORT
20. GRAB RAIL

SOME NAMES OF OCEAN CLASS STEEL DRIFTERS

NAME	BUILDER	COMPLETED
BACKWASH	COLBY	19 07 1918
BILLOW	WEBSTER & BICKERTON	26 09 1918
BLIZZARD	COLBY	30 07 1918
BRINE	OUSE	17 07 1918
CALM	DUTHIE TORRY	18 06 1918
CASCADE	OUSE	21 06 1918
CLOUD	DUTHIE TORRY	17 05 1918
DAWN	DUTHIE TORRY	11 06 1918
DEW	OUSE	6 09 1918
DUSK	DUTHIE TORRY	21 09 1918
EDDY	HALL	27 08 1918
FALLING STAR	HALL	21 09 1918
FLASH	COLBY	5 06 1918
FLICKER	HALL	26 09 1918
FORKLIGHTNING	BROOKE	22 11 1918
FROTH	HALL	25 10 1918
GLITTER	HALL	19 11 1918
GUST	HALL	6 12 1918
HALO	HALL	4 05 1918
HORIZON	HALL	30 03 1918
ICEBERG	HALL	1 07 1918
ICEPACK	HALL	11 07 1918
ICICLE	HALL	18 07 1918
INDIAN SUMMER	LEWIS	8 02 1918
LANDFALL	LEWIS	19 07 1918
LULL	LEWIS	9 04 1918
LUNAR BOW	LEWIS	19 07 1918
MIRAGE	LEWIS	16 12 1918
MIST	LEWIS	24 12 1918
MOONBEAM	LEWIS	30 09 1918
MOONSHINE	LEWIS	30 09 1918
MURK	LEWIS	13 11 1918

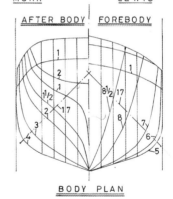

AFTER BODY | FOREBODY

BODY PLAN

NODE	COLBY	18 10 1918
NOONTIDE	COLBY	16 09 1918
NEBULA	ROSE St. FOUNDRY	19 11 1918
OVERFALL	COLBY	18 10 1918
QUICKSAND	COLBY	6 03 1919
SANDSTORM	HALL	31 05 1918
SPECTRUM	BROOKE	12 07 1918
SEABREEZE	HALL	9 01 1919
SHEEN	BROOKE	31 08 1918
SHOWER	BROOKE	30 09 1918
SEA FOG	WEBSTER & BICKERTON	18 12 1918
SLEET	BROOKE	6 11 1918
WHIRLPOOL	HALL	30 03 1920

SHEET TWO OF THREE SHEETS

L/S/39/B

© JOHN LAMBERT   COMMENCED 27/02/2006   COMPLETED 18/03/2006   CH'D. 21/03/2006

VIII. L/S/39/C *Ocean*-class steel screw steam drifter, modifications required for vessels to work as fishing drifters, 1918

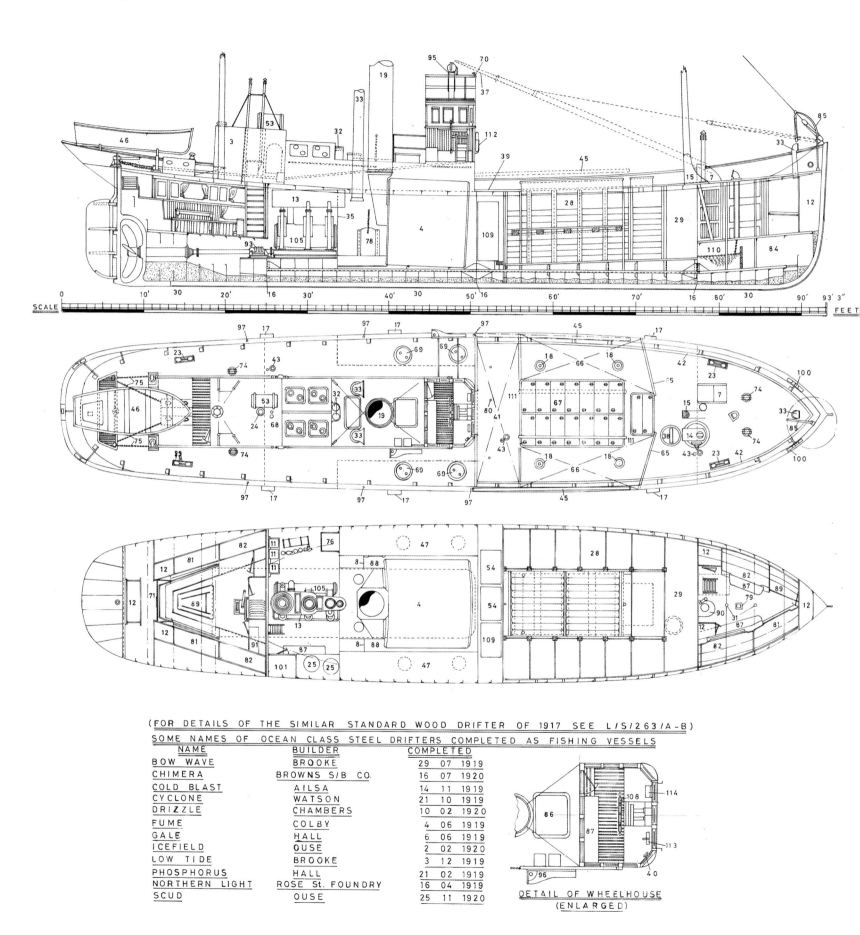

SCALE 0 10' 20' 30' 40' 50' 60' 70' 80' 90' 93' 3" FEET

(FOR DETAILS OF THE SIMILAR STANDARD WOOD DRIFTER OF 1917 SEE L/S/263/A-B)

SOME NAMES OF OCEAN CLASS STEEL DRIFTERS COMPLETED AS FISHING VESSELS

NAME	BUILDER	COMPLETED		
BOW WAVE	BROOKE	29	07	1919
CHIMERA	BROWNS S/B CO.	16	07	1920
COLD BLAST	AILSA	14	11	1919
CYCLONE	WATSON	21	10	1919
DRIZZLE	CHAMBERS	10	02	1920
FUME	COLBY	4	06	1919
GALE	HALL	6	06	1919
ICEFIELD	OUSE	2	02	1920
LOW TIDE	BROOKE	3	12	1919
PHOSPHORUS	HALL	21	02	1919
NORTHERN LIGHT	ROSE St. FOUNDRY	16	04	1919
SCUD	OUSE	25	11	1920

DETAIL OF WHEELHOUSE
(ENLARGED)

154

HISTORY (CONTINUED FROM SHEET "A")

THE FORE AND MIZEN MASTS WERE FITTED WITH A SUIT OF SAILS. FOR'D. A COMPANION LEAD TO THE FORECASTLE MESS ACCOMMODATING FIVE MEN. MACHINERY WAS COMMON FOR BOTH THE STEEL AND WOODEN DRIFTER. A TRIPLE EXPANSION ENGINE DEVELOPING ABOUT 270 ihp SUPPLIED BY STEAM FROM A SINGLE ENDED CYLINDRICAL BOILER FIRED FROM THE AFTER END. COAL BUNKERS WERE ARRANGED ON EACH SIDE OF THE BOILER, WITH ACCESS BY HINGED W/T DOORS WITH THE CROSS BUNKER IN THE FISH HOLD. THE HULL HAS THREE W/T BULKHEADS. HAND STEERING GEAR IS FITTED INSIDE THE WHEELHOUSE WITH STEERING CHAINS LEADING AFT TO THE RUDDER HEAD. A TRAWL STEAM WINCH WITH TWO DRUMS EACH CAPABLE OF TAKING 400 FATHOMS OF STEEL WIRE ROPE. THE MAGAZINE WAS LOCATED IN THE ORIGINAL FISH HOLD. ACCOMMODATION WAS REVISED TO PROVIDE FOR 14. BILGE KEELS SOME 26' LONG AND $7\frac{1}{2}$" DEEP WERE FITTED (ALTHOUGH NOT SHOWN ON THE G/A DRAWINGS). A 6 POUNDER GUN WAS THE USUAL DEFENSIVE ARMAMENT

62 STEEL DRIFTERS WERE BUILT FOR ADMIRALTY SERVICE WITH 63 MORE COMPLETED AS FISHING VESSELS. MANY RETURNED TO COMMERCIAL FISHING IN THE EARLY 1920's TO BE REQUISITIONED FOR DUTY IN WWII.

KEY TO DETAIL (SHEET 'A', 'B' AND 'C')

No.	Detail	No.	Detail	No.	Detail
1	7" OPENING LIGHT	42	WATERWAY ANGLE	71	SLIDING DOOR
2	POT RACK	43	4" HAND PUMP	72	COAL FIRED STOVE
3	GALLEY	44	CEMENTED FLOOR	73	CUSHIONED SEAT
4	CYLINDRICAL BOILER	45	WOOD ROLLER-19' 0"	74	DECK LIGHT
5	WC PORT SIDE	46	BOAT-15' 0"x 6' 3"	75	RUDDER CHAIN
6	LADDER	47	SIDE BUNKERS-21 TONS	76	EXHAUST TANK
7	COMPANION	48	CROSS BUNKER-18 TON	77	FILLING PIPE
8	BUNKER DOOR GUARD	49	1 BED-LOCKER UNDER	78	BUNKER DOOR
9	'G' DEPTH CHARGE RACK	50	WASH BASIN UNDER LADDER		
10	W.C. DISCHARE PIPE	51	TABLE WITH OIL TANKS UNDER		
11	OIL TANKS	52	DEPTH CHARGE RAIL		
12	LOCKER	53	36 GALLON SANITARY TANK		
13	MAIN ENGINE	54	BOILER FEED TANK-416 GALLONS		
14	CAPSTAN	55	HATCH TOP PLATED OVER		
15	MAST STEP	56	FLUSH WITH WOOD DECK		
16	WATER TIGHT B'HEAD	57	OPEN BINS -3' 0" HIGH 3 SHELVES OVER		
17	WASH PORT	58	SPACE FOR INSTALLATION OF W/T WHEN		
18	FISH SCUTTLE		REQUIRED		
19	FUNNEL	59	RACKS FOR ROCKET STICKS		
20	GRINDSTONE	60	FRESH WATER TANK CONNECTED		
21	KITE RACK		TO GALLEY PUMP	79	CHAIN BOX
22	FAIRLEAD	61	2 BEDS SKIPPER & 2 ND HAND		
23	MOORING BOLLARD	62	STEEL CHEQUERED PLATE	80	AIR PIPE
24	7" DEADLIGHT	63	150 GALLON FRESH WATER TANK	81	1 BED
25	GAS TANK (CARBIDE)	64	3 BOILER FEED TANKS CONNECTED	82	2 BEDS
26	GALLEY PUMP		WITH 2" PIPE.	83	STOOL
27	MAGAZINE	65	DECK POND BOARDS 2"DECKS	84	STORE
28	FISH HOLD		ON 9"x 2 1/2 THICK PINE	85	DAVIT
29	ROPE STORE	66	GRATINGS ON DECK WITH PORT-	86	HATCH
30	BALLAST		ABLE HATCHES	87	SEAT
31	2" PILLAR	67	2 1/2" PINE HATCH COVERS	88	STEP
32	ASH BUCKETS	68	AIR AND FILLING PIPE	89	TABLE
33	COWL VENTILATOR	69	COALING SCUTTLE	90	STOVE
34	STRUM BOX	70	VOICE PIPE TO WHEELHOUSE	91	PANTRY
35	BUNKER END				
36	STEAM M/S WINCH				
37	FOREMAST CRUTCH 15" OFF CENTRE TO PORT				
38	HATCH FITTED WITH HARDWOOD ROLLER AND STEEL PLATE COVER				
39	DECK SHEATHED 2 1/2" LARCH FROM FOR'D. END OF WHEELHOUSE				
40	VOICE PIPE TO ENGINE ROOM				
41	PORTABLE GRATINGS ON DECK				

No.	Detail	No.	Detail
92	PANTRY AND STORE	103	SIDE BOLLARD
93	THRUST BLOCK	104	6" MUSHROOM VENTILATOR
94	1 BED -LAMPS UNDER	105	CONDENSER
95	MAGNETIC COMPASS	106	DOOR TO STORE
96	NAVIGATION LIGHT	107	FOLDING TABLE
97	SCUPPER PIPE	108	SHIPS WHEEL
98	ROLLER FAIRLEAD	109	FRESH WATER TANK
99	COMMISSIONED OFFICER	110	CHAIN LOCKER
100	DOUBLE FAIRLEAD	111	WOOD ROLLER-12' 4"
101	ENGINEERS LOCKER	112	LIFE BUOY STOWAGE
102	MESS KIT RACK	113	ENGINE TELEGRAPH
		114	BINOCULAR BOX

SHEET THREE OF THREE SHEETS

L/S/39/C

IX. L/O/23 QF 3in 12pdr on Mark V pedestal mounting
QF 3in 12pdr on Mark VI pedestal mounting

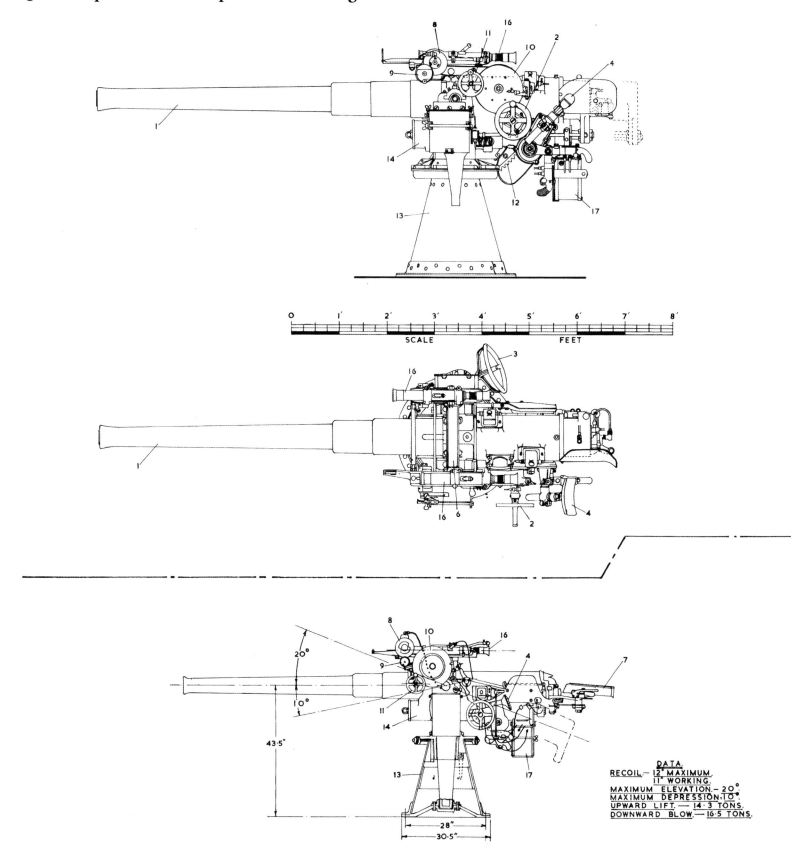

SCALE   FEET

DATA.
RECOIL.— 12" MAXIMUM.
         11" WORKING.
MAXIMUM ELEVATION.— 20°
MAXIMUM DEPRESSION.10°
UPWARD LIFT. — 14·3 TONS.
DOWNWARD BLOW.—16·5 TONS.

© JOHN LAMBERT   COMPLETED 24/5/1979   ENLARGED AND ENHANCED 5/5/2002

RECOIL.—— 12" MAXIMUM.
10·5" WORKING.
MAXIMUM ELEVATION.— 20°
MAXIMUM DEPRESSION —10°

DETAIL

1	GUN BARREL.
2	ELEVATING HANDWHEEL.
3	TRAINING HANDWHEEL.
4	BODY REST.
5	CRADLE.
6	SIGHT FRAME.
7	LOADING TRAY.
8	DEFLECTION DIAL.
9	DEFLECTION HANDWHEEL.
10	RANGE DIAL.
11	RANGE HANDWHEEL.
12	ELEVATING ARC.
13	PEDESTAL.
14	RECOIL CYLINDER.
15	GUN GUIDES.
16	TELESCOPIC SIGHTS.
17	BATTERY BOX.

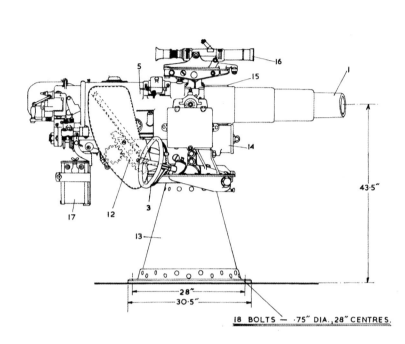

43·5"

28"

30·5"

18 BOLTS — ·75" DIA., 28" CENTRES.

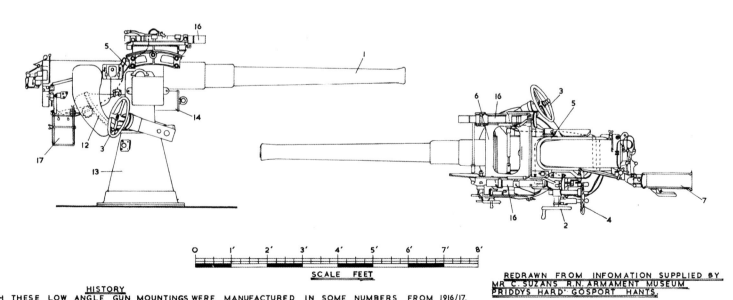

0   1'   2'   3'   4'   5'   6'   7'   8'

SCALE FEET

REDRAWN FROM INFOMATION SUPPLIED BY
MR C. SUZANS R.N. ARMAMENT MUSEUM
PRIDDYS HARD GOSPORT HANTS.

HISTORY

BOTH THESE LOW ANGLE GUN MOUNTINGS WERE MANUFACTURED IN SOME NUMBERS FROM 1916/17, BEING FITTED TO CONVOY & MINESWEEPING SLOOPS AS WELL AS SOME FLEET DESTROYERS & LIGHT CRUISERS. THE 12 PDR WAS GRADUALLY PHASED OUT OF SERVICE BEING REPLACED BY MORE POWERFUL & HARDER HITTING 4 INCH & 4·7 INCH GUN MOUNTINGS.

A SMALL NUMBER WERE RETAINED IN STORE & FITTED TO REQUISITIONED SMALL A/S TRAWLERS FROM 1939.

L/0/23

X. L/O/103 A First World War Hotchkiss 6pdr on a non recoil 1941 mounting

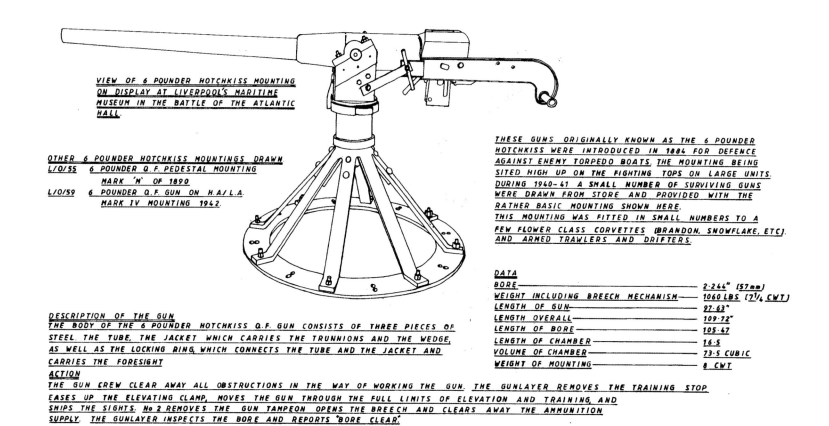

VIEW OF 6 POUNDER HOTCHKISS MOUNTING
ON DISPLAY AT LIVERPOOL'S MARITIME
MUSEUM IN THE BATTLE OF THE ATLANTIC
HALL.

OTHER 6 POUNDER HOTCHKISS MOUNTINGS DRAWN.
L/O/55   6 POUNDER Q.F. PEDESTAL MOUNTING
         MARK 'M' OF 1890
L/O/59   6 POUNDER Q.F. GUN ON H.A./L.A.
         MARK IV MOUNTING 1942.

THESE GUNS ORIGINALLY KNOWN AS THE 6 POUNDER
HOTCHKISS WERE INTRODUCED IN 1884 FOR DEFENCE
AGAINST ENEMY TORPEDO BOATS. THE MOUNTING BEING
SITED HIGH UP ON THE FIGHTING TOPS ON LARGE UNITS.
DURING 1940-41 A SMALL NUMBER OF SURVIVING GUNS
WERE DRAWN FROM STORE AND PROVIDED WITH THE
RATHER BASIC MOUNTING SHOWN HERE.
THIS MOUNTING WAS FITTED IN SMALL NUMBERS TO A
FEW FLOWER CLASS CORVETTES (BRANDON, SNOWFLAKE, ETC).
AND ARMED TRAWLERS AND DRIFTERS.

DATA

BORE	2·244" (57mm)
WEIGHT INCLUDING BREECH MECHANISM	1060 LBS (7¼ CWT)
LENGTH OF GUN	97·63"
LENGTH OVERALL	109·72"
LENGTH OF BORE	105·47
LENGTH OF CHAMBER	16·5
VOLUME OF CHAMBER	73·5 CUBIC
WEIGHT OF MOUNTING	8 CWT

DESCRIPTION OF THE GUN
THE BODY OF THE 6 POUNDER HOTCHKISS Q.F. GUN CONSISTS OF THREE PIECES OF
STEEL. THE TUBE, THE JACKET WHICH CARRIES THE TRUNNIONS AND THE WEDGE,
AS WELL AS THE LOCKING RING, WHICH CONNECTS THE TUBE AND THE JACKET AND
CARRIES THE FORESIGHT
ACTION
THE GUN CREW CLEAR AWAY ALL OBSTRUCTIONS IN THE WAY OF WORKING THE GUN. THE GUNLAYER REMOVES THE TRAINING STOP
EASES UP THE ELEVATING CLAMP, MOVES THE GUN THROUGH THE FULL LIMITS OF ELEVATION AND TRAINING, AND
SHIPS THE SIGHTS. No 2 REMOVES THE GUN TAMPEON OPENS THE BREECH AND CLEARS AWAY THE AMMUNITION
SUPPLY. THE GUNLAYER INSPECTS THE BORE AND REPORTS "BORE CLEAR".

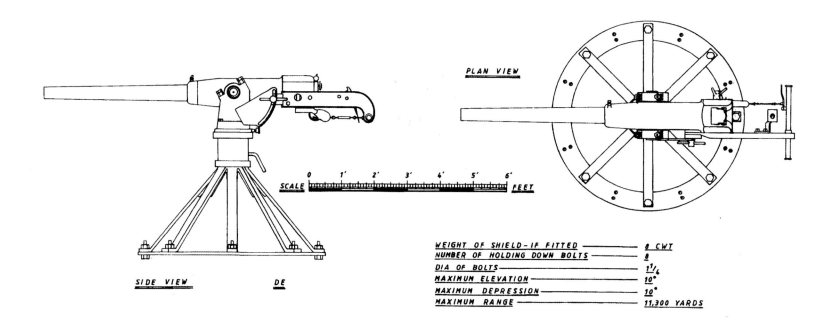

PLAN VIEW

SCALE [0 1' 2' 3' 4' 5' 6'] FEET

SIDE VIEW   DE

WEIGHT OF SHIELD-IF FITTED	8 CWT
NUMBER OF HOLDING DOWN BOLTS	8
DIA OF BOLTS	1¼
MAXIMUM ELEVATION	10°
MAXIMUM DEPRESSION	10°
MAXIMUM RANGE	11,300 YARDS

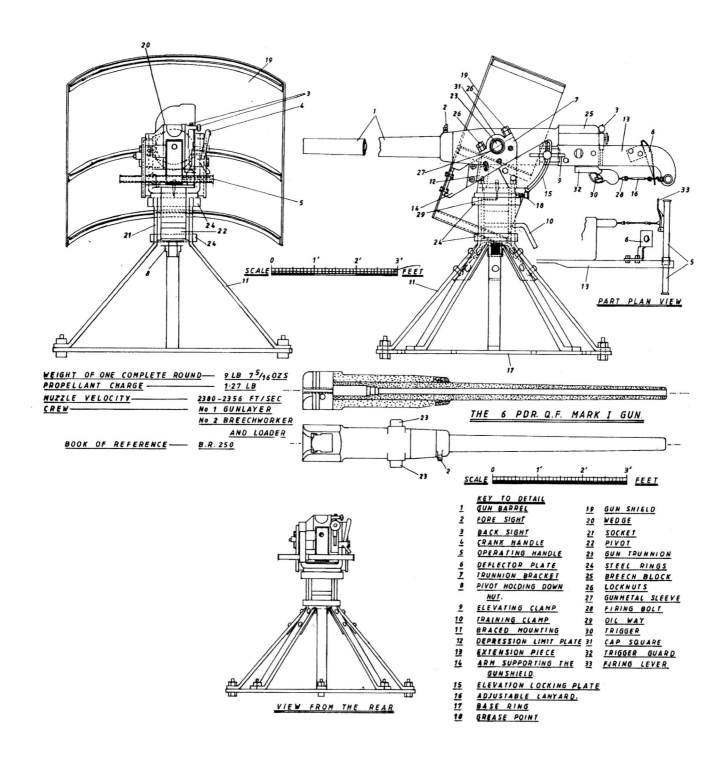

WEIGHT OF ONE COMPLETE ROUND —— 9 LB 7⁵/₁₆ OZS

PROPELLANT CHARGE —————— 1·27 LB

MUZZLE VELOCITY —————— 2380-2356 FT/SEC

CREW ———————————— No 1 GUNLAYER

No 2 BREECHWORKER

AND LOADER

BOOK OF REFERENCE —————— B.R. 250

THE 6 PDR. Q.F. MARK I GUN.

SCALE 0 1' 2' 3' FEET

VIEW FROM THE REAR

KEY TO DETAIL

1	GUN BARREL	19	GUN SHIELD
2	FORE SIGHT	20	WEDGE
3	BACK SIGHT	21	SOCKET
4	CRANK HANDLE	22	PIVOT
5	OPERATING HANDLE	23	GUN TRUNNION
6	DEFLECTOR PLATE	24	STEEL RINGS
7	TRUNNION BRACKET	25	BREECH BLOCK
8	PIVOT HOLDING DOWN NUT.	26	LOCKNUTS
9	ELEVATING CLAMP	27	GUNMETAL SLEEVE
10	TRAINING CLAMP	28	FIRING BOLT
11	BRACED MOUNTING	29	OIL WAY
12	DEPRESSION LIMIT PLATE	30	TRIGGER
13	EXTENSION PIECE	31	CAP SQUARE
14	ARM SUPPORTING THE GUNSHIELD.	32	TRIGGER GUARD
15	ELEVATION LOCKING PLATE	33	FIRING LEVER
16	ADJUSTABLE LANYARD.		
17	BASE RING		
18	GREASE POINT		

L/O/103

XI. L/S/190/A HM trawler *Quannet* (ex-*Dairycoats*), 'Tree'-class, general arrangement, converted to a boom defence vessel, May 1939

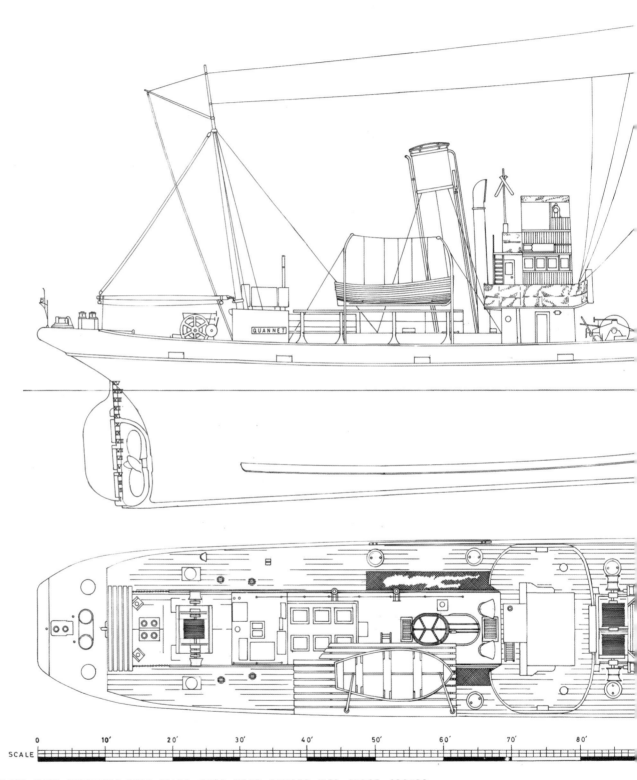

SCALE

| 0 | 10′ | 20′ | 30′ | 40′ | 50′ | 60′ | 70′ | 80′ |

NOTE EARLY IN 1939 20 TRAWLERS WERE PURCHASED FROM TRADE. THEY WERE DIVIDED INTO THREE GROUPS. 10 HAD ASDIC FITTED AS ANTI-SUBMARINE VESSELS. THESE WERE ADDED TO THE GEM GROUP. 6 CONVERTED TO MINE SWEEPING AND ADDED TO THE TREE GROUP AND THE REMAINING FOUR CONVERTED TO BOOM DEFENCE VESSELS AND RENAMED 'JENNET', 'PUNNET' 'QUANNET' AND 'RENNET.'

© JOHN LAMBERT COMMENCED 21/03/2006 COMPLETED 12/04/2006 CH'D. 18/04/2006

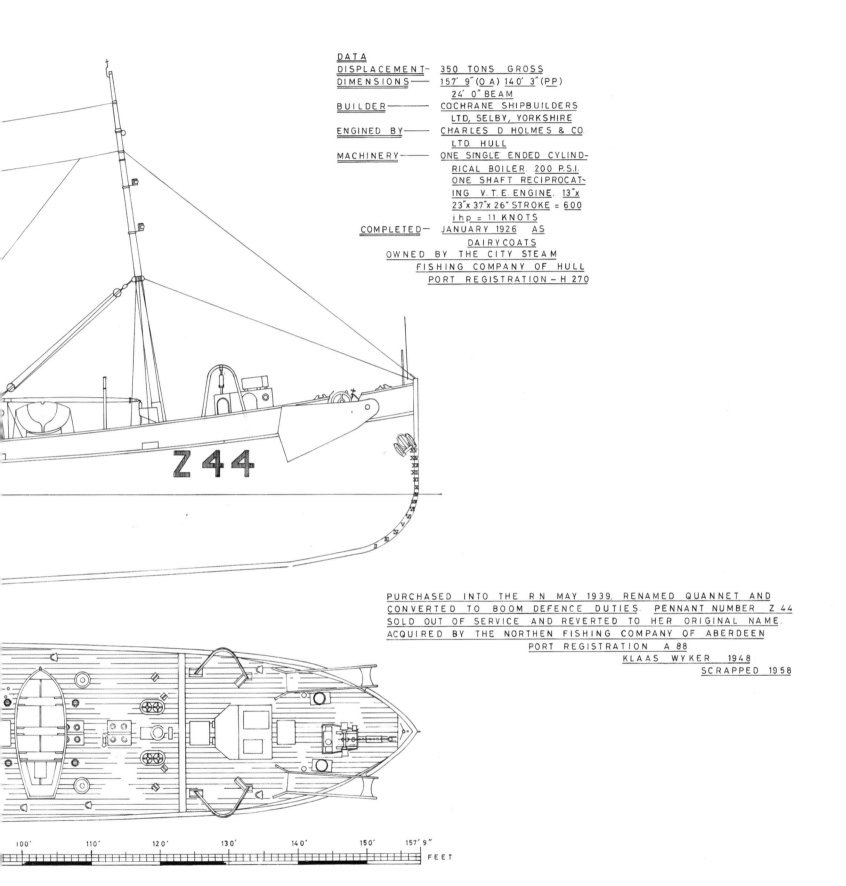

DATA
DISPLACEMENT- 350 TONS GROSS
DIMENSIONS —— 157' 9"(O A) 140' 3"(P.P)
            24' 0" BEAM
BUILDER ———— COCHRANE SHIPBUILDERS
            LTD, SELBY, YORKSHIRE
ENGINED BY—— CHARLES D HOLMES & CO.
            LTD. HULL
MACHINERY —— ONE SINGLE ENDED CYLIND-
            RICAL BOILER. 200 P.S.I.
            ONE SHAFT RECIPROCAT-
            ING V.T.E. ENGINE. 13"x
            23"x 37"x 26" STROKE = 600
            ihp = 11 KNOTS
COMPLETED— JANUARY 1926 AS
            DAIRYCOATS
   OWNED BY THE CITY STEAM
   FISHING COMPANY OF HULL
   PORT REGISTRATION – H 270

PURCHASED INTO THE R N MAY 1939. RENAMED QUANNET AND
CONVERTED TO BOOM DEFENCE DUTIES. PENNANT NUMBER Z 44
SOLD OUT OF SERVICE AND REVERTED TO HER ORIGINAL NAME.
ACQUIRED BY THE NORTHEN FISHING COMPANY OF ABERDEEN
            PORT REGISTRATION A 88
                KLAAS WYKER 1948
                    SCRAPPED 1958

100'   110'   120'   130'   140'   150'   157' 9"
                                                FEET

SHEET ONE OF TWO SHEETS
L/S/190/A

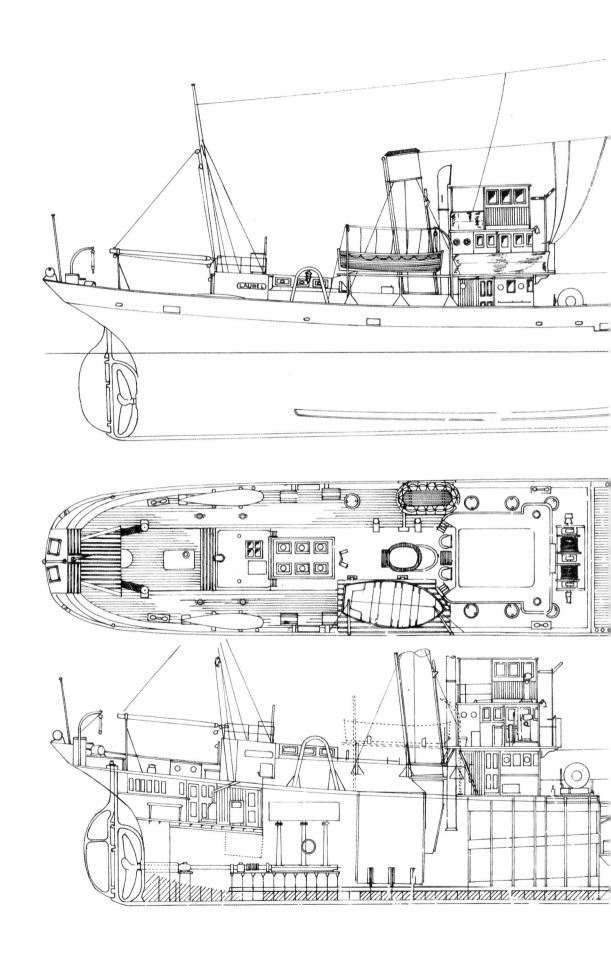

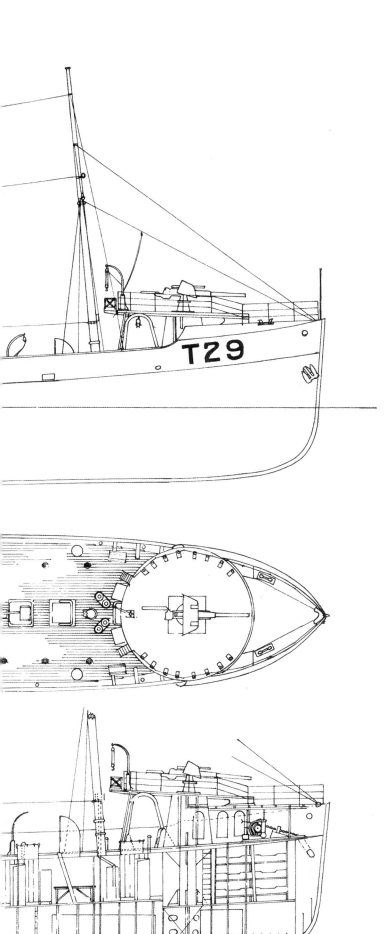

T29

L / S / 191 / A

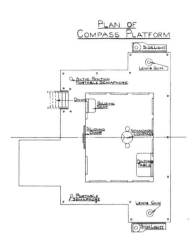

PLAN OF
COMPASS PLATFORM

¼" = ONE FOOT.

PROFILE.

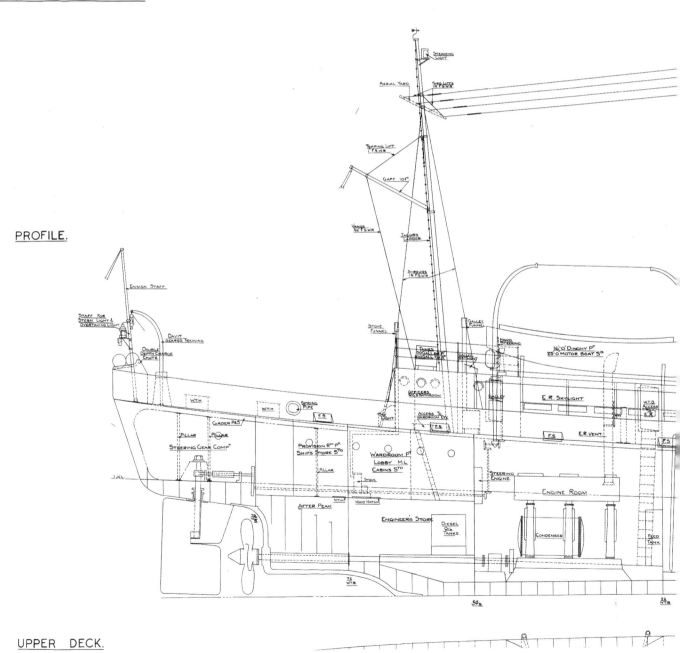

UPPER DECK.

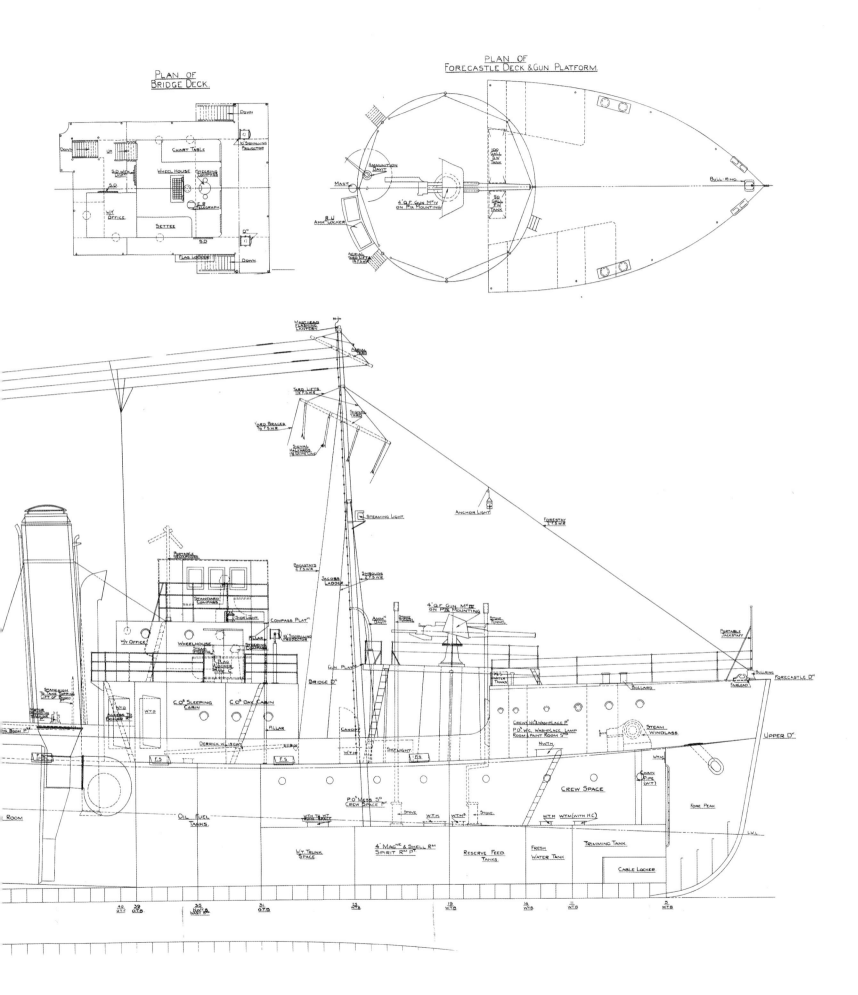

PLAN OF
BRIDGE DECK.

PLAN OF
FORECASTLE DECK & GUN PLATFORM.

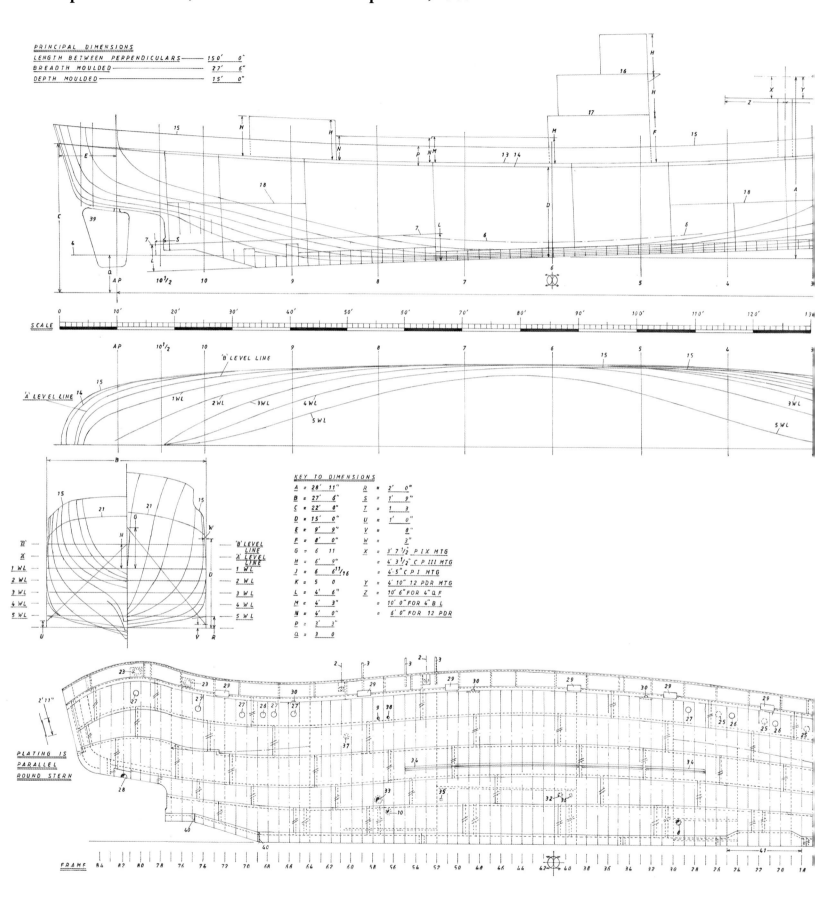

PRINCIPAL DIMENSIONS
LENGTH BETWEEN PERPENDICULARS —— 150' 0"
BREADTH MOULDED —— 27' 6"
DEPTH MOULDED —— 15' 0"

SCALE

'B' LEVEL LINE
'A' LEVEL LINE
1 WL
2 WL
3 WL
4 WL
5 WL

KEY TO DIMENSIONS

A	= 28' 11"		R	= 2' 0"	
B	= 27' 6"		S	= 1' 9"	
C	= 22' 0"		T	= 1 3	
D	= 15' 0"		U	= 1' 0"	
E	= 9' 9"		V	= 8"	
F	= 8' 0"		W	= 3"	
G	= 6 11		X	= 3' 7 1/2" P IX MTG	
H	= 6' 9"			= 4' 3 1/2" C P III MTG	
J	= 6 6"/16			= 4' 5" C P I MTG	
K	= 5 0		Y	= 4' 10" 12 PDR MTG	
L	= 4' 6"		Z	= 10' 6" FOR 4" Q F	
M	= 4' 3"			= 10' 0" FOR 4" B L	
N	= 4' 0"			= 6' 0" FOR 12 PDR	
P	= 3' 3"				
Q	= 3 0				

PLATING IS
PARALLEL
ROUND STERN

FRAME

© JOHN LAMBERT COMMENCED 15/5/2002 COMPLETED 18/8/2002 CHD 22/8/2002

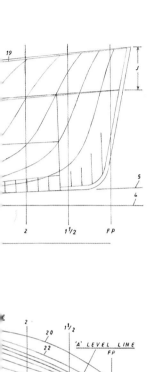

CLASS GUN DATA
MINESWEEPING TRAWLERS ONLY
12 POUNDER [3] 12 CWT GUN ON MARK IX MOUNTING
SEE L/O/13/A-B

ANTI SUBMARINE TRAWLERS   4" GUN MOUNTINGS
QUICK FIRING MOUNTINGS (QF)
P.IX MOUNTING (SEE L/O/07)
C.P.III MOUNTING (SEE L/O/86/A-E)
BREECH LOADING MOUNTING (BL)
CPI MOUNTING (SEE L/O/11)
NOTE PACKING RING ON ALL MOUNTINGS 1" THICK

KEY TO DETAIL

1 GUN PLATFORM TO BE PARALLEL WITH WL
2 ℄ OF BOAT DAVITS FIXED TO INSIDE OF BULWARKS
3 BOAT DECK SUPPORT FIXED TO INSIDE OF RAIL
4 BASE LINE TOP OF KEEL PLATE
5 TOP OF KEEL — PRODUCED
6 TRACE OF BILGE KEEL
7 ℄ OF PROPELLER SHAFT
8 4" SEA COCK (P) FOR FLOODING MAGAZINE AND SPIRIT ROOM
9 FIRE & BILGE PUMP DISCHARGE (P)
10 FIRE & BILGE PUMP INJECTION (P)
11 2½" SOLID ½" ROUND MOULDING ROUND SWEEP
12 RAIL BAR 6"x 3"x 34" BA HOOKED
13 DECK AT CENTRE
14 DECK AT SIDE
15 TOP OF BULWARK
16 COMPASS PLATFORM
17 BRIDGE DECK
18 LOWER DECK
19 FORECASTLE DECK
20 FORECASTLE DECK AT SIDE
21 UPPER DECK
22 UPPER DECK AT SIDE
23 MOORING PORT ~ 12"x 9"
24 ℄ OF GUN
25 SCUTTLE (P)
26 SCUTTLE (S)
27 SCUTTLE (P & S)
28 RUDDER BEARING
29 WASHPORT
30 SCUPPER
31 HAWSE PIPE (P & S)
32 AUXILIARY FEED PUMP INJECTION (S)
33 MAIN INJECTION VALVE (P)
34 BILGE KEEL FRAMES 27 - 55
35 BOILER BLOW DOWN (S)
36 ASH COOLING VALVE (P)
37 MAIN DISCHARGE (P)
38 BILGE DISCHARGE (P)
39 SINGLE RUDDER
40 WELDED BUTT
41 KEEL IN WAY OF ASDIC TRUNK
42 SPINDLE AND SOCKET
43 2½" SOLID COPE
44 JOGGLED DOOR
45 ·26" BULWARK
46 ⅛" DIA. OIL HOLE
47 2"x¼" FLAT STEEL
48 ½" DIA. RIVETS
49 STRINGER
50 1¼" DIA SPINDLE
51 ·40" BUTT STRAP
52 ·40" SHELL
53 BULWARK STAY

DETAIL OF WASHPORT DOORS

12" ½

2' 3" CLEAR

SECTION THROUGH DOOR

DETAIL OF SPINDLE AND SOCKET FOR WASHPORTS (2 OFF PER DOOR)

7 x ·35" BULB PLATE

FRAMES 83 82 81 80 79 78 77 FRAMES

12"

ARRANGEMENT OF SHELL PLATING IN WAY OF STERN CASTINGS

SPACING

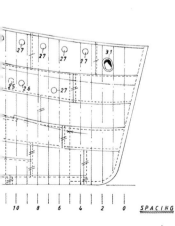

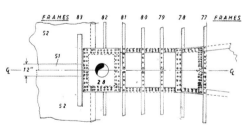

OR

DETAIL OF BILGE KEEL FRAMES 27 - 55

DETAIL OF BULWARK STAYS AROUND STERN TO BE ARRANGED AT SHIP

DETAIL OF DECK LUG TO STAYS

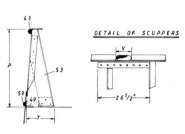

DETAIL OF SCUPPERS

2 6½"

L/S/192

XV. L/S/14 HM trawler *Lindisfarne*, Admiralty war construction 'Isles'-class

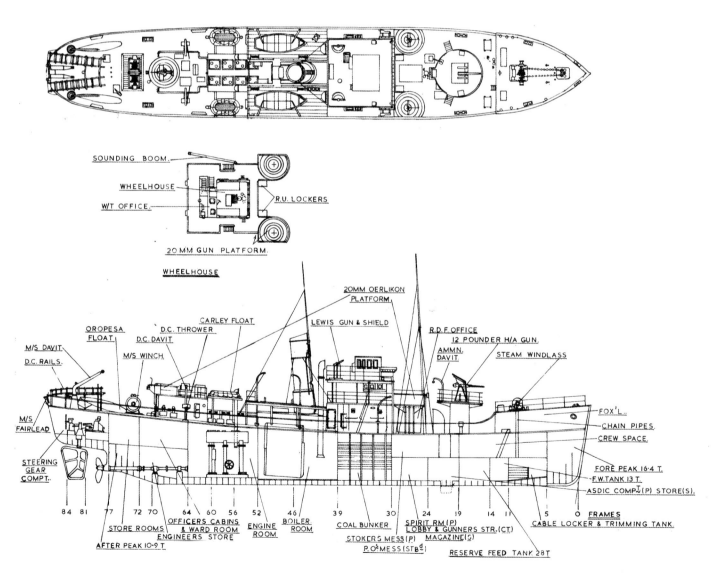

SOUNDING BOOM.
WHEELHOUSE
W/T OFFICE.
R.U. LOCKERS
20 MM GUN PLATFORM.

WHEELHOUSE

20MM OERLIKON PLATFORM
CARLEY FLOAT
LEWIS GUN & SHIELD
OROPESA FLOAT
D.C. THROWER
R.D.F. OFFICE
12 POUNDER H/A GUN.
D.C. DAVIT
AMMN. DAVIT
STEAM WINDLASS
M/S DAVIT.
M/S WINCH.
D.C. RAILS.
FOX'L.
CHAIN PIPES.
CREW SPACE
M/S FAIRLEAD
FORE PEAK 16·4 T.
F.W.TANK 13 T.
ASDIC COMP. (P) STORE(S).
STEERING GEAR COMPT.
84 81 77 72 70 64 60 56 52 46 39 30 24 19 14 11 5 0 FRAMES
STORE ROOMS
OFFICERS CABINS & WARD ROOM
ENGINEERS STORE
ENGINE ROOM
BOILER ROOM
COAL BUNKER
SPIRIT RM (P)
LOBBY & GUNNERS STR. (CT)
MAGAZINE(S)
CABLE LOCKER & TRIMMING TANK.
AFTER PEAK 10·9 T
STOKERS MESS (P)
P.O. MESS (STBd)
RESERVE FEED TANK 28T

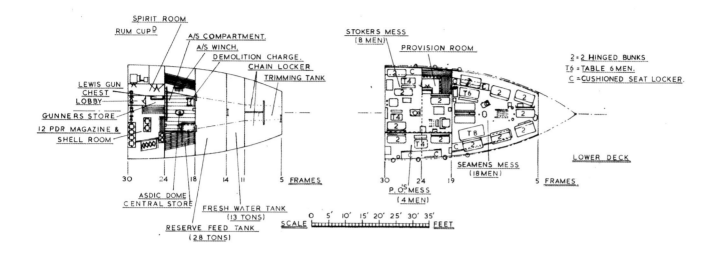

SPIRIT ROOM
RUM CUP^D
A/S COMPARTMENT.
A/S WINCH.
DEMOLITION CHARGE.
CHAIN LOCKER
TRIMMING TANK
LEWIS GUN
CHEST
LOBBY
GUNNERS STORE
12 PDR MAGAZINE &
SHELL ROOM
30   24   18   14   11   5   FRAMES
ASDIC DOME
CENTRAL STORE
FRESH WATER TANK
(13 TONS)
RESERVE FEED TANK
(28 TONS)

STOKERS MESS
(8 MEN)
PROVISION ROOM
2 = 2 HINGED BUNKS
T6 = TABLE 6 MEN.
C = CUSHIONED SEAT LOCKER.
LOWER DECK
30   25   24   19   5   FRAMES.
P.O. MESS
(4 MEN)
SEAMENS MESS
(18 MEN)

SCALE 0 5' 10' 15' 20' 25' 30' 35' FEET

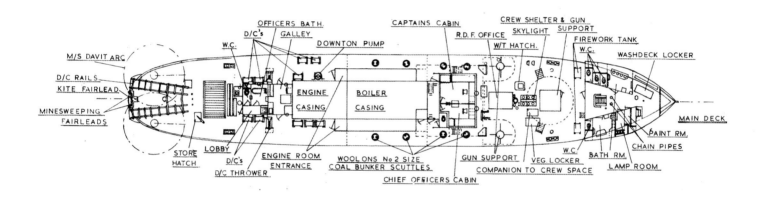

M/S DAVIT ARC
D/C RAILS
KITE FAIRLEAD
MINESWEEPING
FAIRLEADS
STORE
HATCH
LOBBY
D/C's
D/C THROWER
ENGINE ROOM
ENTRANCE
WOOLONS No 2 SIZE
COAL BUNKER SCUTTLES
CHIEF OFFICERS CABIN
GUN SUPPORT
COMPANION TO CREW SPACE
VEG LOCKER
W.C.
OFFICERS BATH.
D/C's
GALLEY
W.C.
DOWNTON PUMP
ENGINE
CASING
BOILER
CASING
CAPTAINS CABIN
R.D.F. OFFICE
W/T HATCH.
CREW SHELTER & GUN
SKYLIGHT   SUPPORT
FIREWORK TANK
W.C.
WASHDECK LOCKER
MAIN DECK
PAINT RM.
CHAIN PIPES
BATH RM.
LAMP ROOM

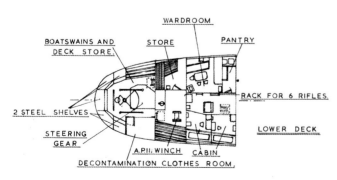

WARDROOM
BOATSWAINS AND
DECK STORE
STORE
PANTRY
2 STEEL SHELVES
STEERING
GEAR
A.P.II WINCH
CABIN
DECONTAMINATION CLOTHES ROOM.
RACK FOR 6 RIFLES.
LOWER DECK

DISPLACEMENT — 545 TONS
DIMENSIONS- 164 FT. OVERALL
150 FT. BETWEEN PERPENDICULARS.
27 FT 6 INS BEAM MOULDED.
10 FT 6 INS TO 15 FT DRAUGHT.
MACHINERY- 1 SHAFT RECIPROCATING ENGINE
(VERTICAL TRIPLE EXPANSION)
INDICATED HORSE POWER 850.
MAX. SPEED -12 KNOTS.
ARMAMENT- 1 H/A - 12 POUNDER (3 INCH).
3 SINGLE 20 MM OERLIKONS.
2 .303 INCH LEWIS L.M.G's.
6 .303 INCH RIFLES.
COMPLEMENT- 40

COAL CAPACITY
CROSS BUNKER - 126 TONS.
PORT WING — 29 TONS.
STARB^D WING — 29 TONS.
TOTAL - 184 TONS CAPACITY

BUILT BY COOK WELTON AND GEMMELL LTD.
OF BEVERLEY HULL.
LINDISFARN:-
LAID DOWN — 11/3/43.
LAUNCHED — 17/6/43.
COMPLETED — 17/9/43.
BUILDING TIME - 6 MTH 6 DAYS.
SCRAPPED — DOVER 26/4/58.

OF A TOTAL OF 129 BRITISH BUILT A/S-M/S TRAWLERS OF THE ISLES CLASS, 59 UNITS WERE
CONSTRUCTED BY COOK WELTON AND GEMMELL LTD. OF BEVERLEY.
REDRAWN AND REDUCED FROM THE ORIGINAL MAKERS DRAWINGS AS SUPPLIED BY S.J. BYATT ESQ.
OF CHARLES D. HOLMES AND COMPANY OF HULL.

FOR DETAILED ARMAMENT DRAWINGS SEE:-
L/O/13 - 12 POUNDER GUN ON MK IX H/A MOUNTING. [2 SHEETS]
L/O/2 - 20 MM OERLIKON.
L/O/3 - .303" LEWIS GUN.
L/O/16 - ANTI-SUBMARINE WEAPONS.

L/S/14

XVI. L/S/2/B Detail and general layout of the 'Round Table'-class minesweeping trawler

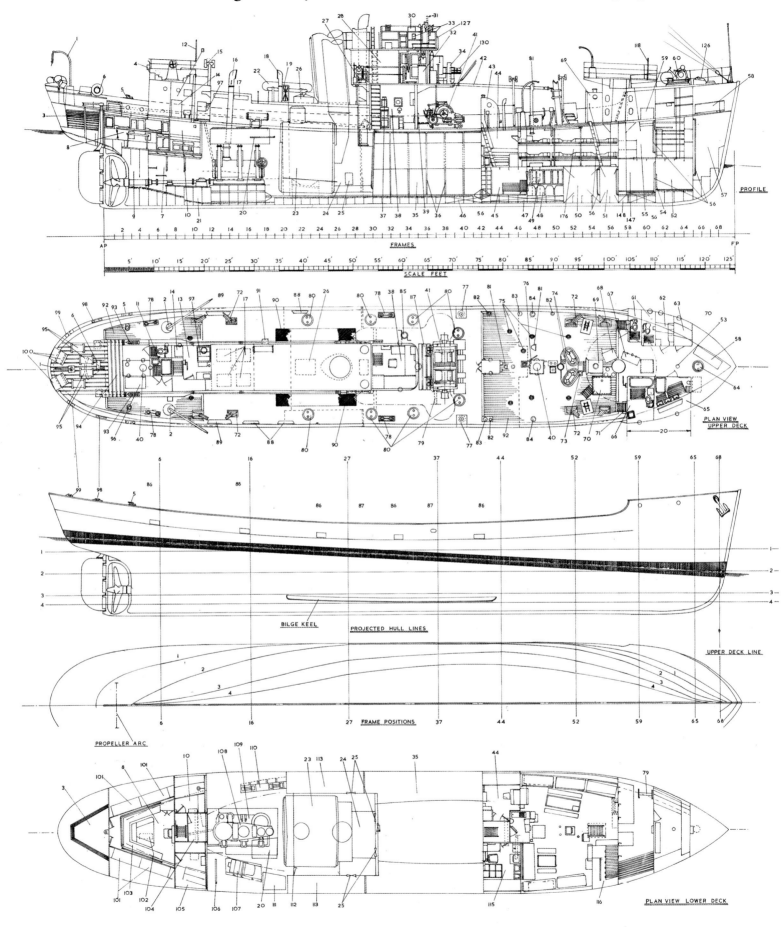

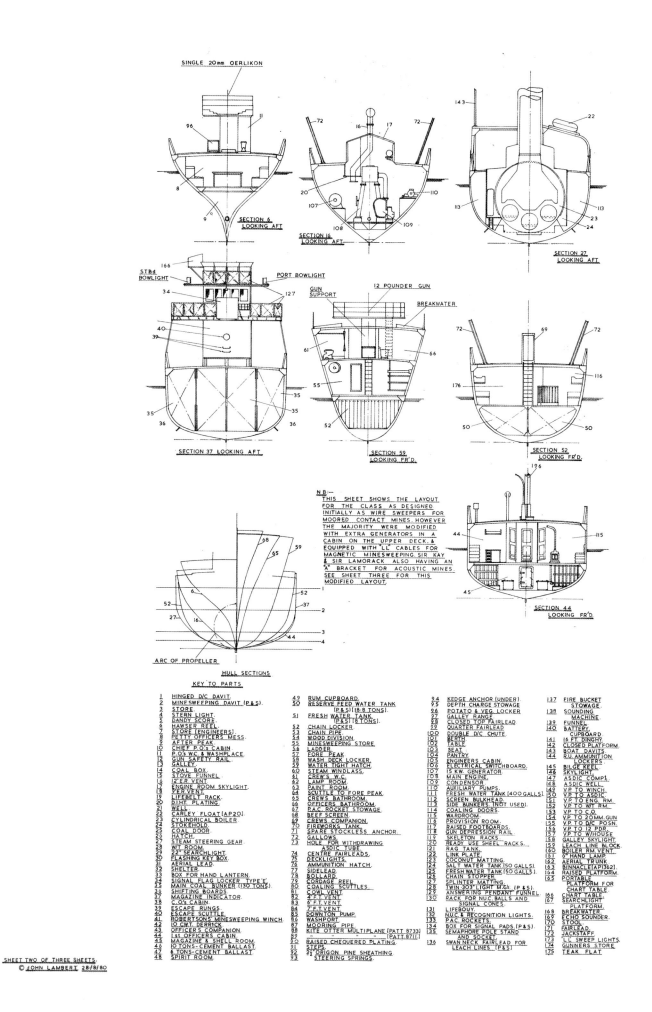

SINGLE 20mm OERLIKON

SECTION 6
LOOKING AFT

SECTION 16
LOOKING AFT

SECTION 27
LOOKING AFT

STBd
BOWLIGHT

PORT BOWLIGHT

GUN
SUPPORT

12 POUNDER GUN

BREAKWATER

SECTION 37 LOOKING AFT

SECTION 59
LOOKING FR'D.

SECTION 52
LOOKING FR'D.

N.B:—
THIS SHEET SHOWS THE LAYOUT
FOR THE CLASS AS DESIGNED
INITIALLY AS WIRE SWEEPERS FOR
MOORED CONTACT MINES. HOWEVER
THE MAJORITY WERE MODIFIED
WITH EXTRA GENERATORS IN A
CABIN ON THE UPPER DECK, &
EQUIPPED WITH "LL" CABLES FOR
MAGNETIC MINESWEEPING. SIR KAY
& SIR LAMORACK ALSO HAVING AN
"A" BRACKET FOR ACOUSTIC MINES.
SEE SHEET THREE FOR THIS
MODIFIED LAYOUT.

SECTION 44
LOOKING FR'D.

ARC OF PROPELLER

HULL SECTIONS

KEY TO PARTS

1 HINGED D/C DAVIT.
2 MINESWEEPING DAVIT (P&S).
3 STORE.
4 STERN LIGHT.
5 DANDY SCORE.
6 HAWSER REEL.
7 STORE (ENGINEERS).
8 PETTY OFFICERS MESS.
9 AFTER PEAK.
10 CHIEF P.O.S CABIN.
11 P.O'S WC. & WASHPLACE.
12 GUN SAFETY RAIL.
13 GALLEY.
14 COAL BOX.
15 STOVE FUNNEL.
16 12"E.R. VENT.
17 ENGINE ROOM SKYLIGHT.
18 9"E.R. VENT.
19 LIFEBELT RACK.
20 DINHT. PLATING.
21 WELL.
22 CARLEY FLOAT (AP20).
23 CYLINDRICAL BOILER.
24 STOKEHOLD.
25 COAL DOOR.
26 HATCH.
27 STEAM STEERING GEAR.
28 W/T ROOM.
29 22" SEARCHLIGHT.
30 FLASHING KEY BOX.
31 AERIAL LEAD.
32 SHELTER.
33 BOX FOR HAND LANTERN.
34 SIGNAL FLAG LOCKER TYPE 'E'.
35 MAIN COAL BUNKER (130 TONS).
36 SHIFTING BOARDS.
37 MAGAZINE INDICATOR.
38 C.O'S CABIN.
39 ESCAPE RUNGS.
40 ESCAPE SCUTTLE.
41 ROBERTSONS' MINESWEEPING WINCH.
42 10 CWT. DERRICK.
43 OFFICER'S COMPANION.
44 1st OFFICER'S CABIN.
45 MAGAZINE & SHELL ROOM.
46 10 TONS - CEMENT BALLAST.
47 6 TONS - CEMENT BALLAST.
48 SPIRIT ROOM.

49 RUM CUPBOARD.
50 RESERVE FEED WATER TANK
   (P&S) (18·8 TONS).
51 FRESH WATER TANK
   (P&S) (8 TONS).
52 CHAIN LOCKER.
53 CHAIN PIPE.
54 WOOD DIVISION.
55 MINESWEEPING STORE.
56 LADDER.
57 FORE PEAK.
58 WASH DECK LOCKER.
59 WATER TIGHT HATCH.
60 STEAM WINDLASS.
61 CREW'S W.C.
62 LAMP ROOM.
63 PAINT ROOM.
64 SCUTTLE TO FORE PEAK.
65 CREWS BATHROOM.
66 OFFICERS BATHROOM.
67 P.A.C. ROCKET STOWAGE.
68 BEEF SCREEN.
69 CREWS COMPANION.
70 FIREWORKS TANK.
71 SPARE STOCKLESS ANCHOR.
72 GALLOWS.
73 HOLE FOR WITHDRAWING
   ASDIC TUBE.
74 CENTRE FAIRLEADS.
75 DECKLIGHTS.
76 AMMUNITION HATCH.
77 SIDELEAD.
78 BOLLARD.
79 CORDAGE REEL.
80 COALING SCUTTLES.
81 COWL VENT.
82 4 F.T. VENT.
83 6" F.T. VENT.
84 7 F.T. VENT.
85 DOWNTON PUMP.
86 WASHPORT.
87 MOORING PIPE.
88 KITE OTTER MULTIPLANE (PATT 8733).
89   (PATT 8711).
90 RAISED CHEQUERED PLATING.
91 STEPS.
92 2" ORIGON PINE SHEATHING.
93 STEERING SPRINGS.

94 KEDGE ANCHOR (UNDER).
95 DEPTH CHARGE STOWAGE.
96 POTATO & VEG. LOCKER.
97 GALLEY RANGE.
98 CLOSED TOP FAIRLEAD.
99 QUARTER FAIRLEAD.
100 DOUBLE D/C CHUTE.
101 BERTH.
102 CABIN.
103 SEAT.
104 PANTRY.
105 ENGINEERS CABIN.
106 ELECTRICAL SWITCHBOARD.
107 15 KW. GENERATOR.
108 MAIN ENGINE.
109 CONDENSOR.
110 AUXILIARY PUMPS.
111 FRESH WATER TANK (400 GALLS).
112 SCREEN BULKHEAD.
113 SIDE BUNKERS (NOT USED).
114 COALING DOORS.
115 WARDROOM.
116 PROVISION ROOM.
117 RAISED FOOTBOARDS.
118 GUN DEPRESSION RAIL.
119 SKELETON RACKS.
120 READY USE SHELL RACKS.
121 RAG TANK.
122 LINK PLATE.
123 COCONUT MATTING.
124 SALT WATER TANK (50 GALLS).
125 FRESH WATER TANK (50 GALLS).
126 CHAIN STOPPER.
127 SPLINTER MATTING.
128 TWIN 303" LIGHT M.G's. (P&S).
129 ANSWERING PENDANT FUNNEL.
130 RACK FOR NUC. BALLS AND
    SIGNAL CONES.
131 LIFEBUOY.
132 NUC. & RECOGNITION LIGHTS.
133 P.A.C. ROCKETS.
134 BOX FOR SIGNAL PADS (P&S).
135 SEMAPHORE POLE STAND
    AND SOCKET.
136 SWAN NECK FAIRLEAD FOR
    LEACH LINES (P&S).

137 FIRE BUCKET
    STOWAGE.
138 SOUNDING
    MACHINE.
139 FUNNEL.
140 BATTERY
    CUPBOARD.
141 16 FT. DINGHY.
142 CLOSED PLATFORM.
143 BOAT DAVITS.
144 R.U. AMMUNITION
    LOCKERS.
145 BILGE KEEL.
146 SKYLIGHT.
147 ASDIC COMP'S.
148 ASDIC WELL.
149 V.P TO WINCH.
150 V.P TO ASDIC.
151 V.P TO ENG. RM.
152 V.P TO W/T RM.
153 V.P TO C.O.
154 V.P TO 20MM. GUN
155 V.P TO D/C POSN.
156 V.P TO 12 PDR.
157 V.P TO W/HOUSE
158 GALLEY SKYLIGHT.
159 LEACH LINE BLOCK.
160 BOILER RM. VENT.
161 6" HAND LAMP
162 AERIAL TRUNK.
163 BINNACLE (AP1362).
164 RAISED PLATFORM.
165 PORTABLE
    PLATFORM FOR
    CHART TABLE.
166 CHART TABLE
167 SEARCHLIGHT
    PLATFORM.
168 BREAKWATER.
169 ECHO SOUNDER.
170 STOOL.
171 FAIRLEAD.
172 JACKSTAFF.
173 LL SWEEP LIGHTS.
174 GUNNERS STORE.
175 TEAK FLAT.

L/S/26/B

XVII. L/S/26/A The 'Round Table'-class minesweeping trawler *Sir Galahad*

THESE GENERAL ARRANGEMENT VIEWS DEPICT THE ONLY TWO UNITS OF THE CLASS T226 SIR GALAHAD & T228 SIR LANCELOT TO BE COMPLETED TO THE ORIGINAL DESIGN THE REMAINING SIX UNITS WERE COMPLETED TO A MODIFIED DESIGN AS INFLUENCE MINESWEEPERS. SEE SHEET THREE FOR THOSE UNITS SO MODIFIED.

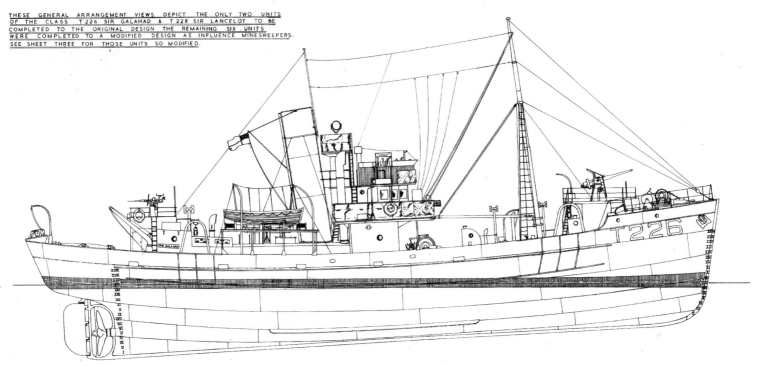

0   5'   10'   15'   20'   25'   30'   35'   40'   45'   50'   55'   60'   65'   70'   75'   80'   85'   90'   95'   100'   105'   110'   115'   120'   125'

SCALE FEET

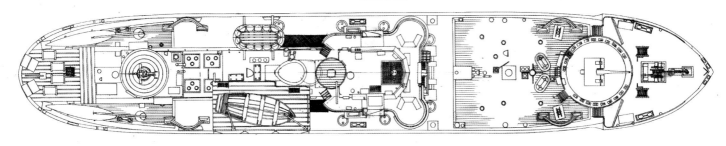

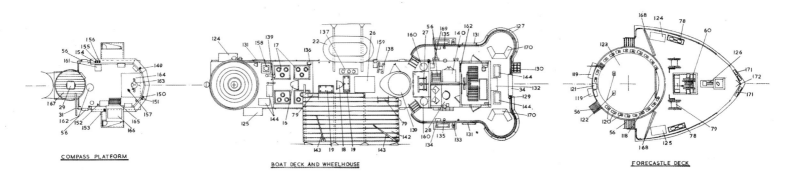

COMPASS PLATFORM

BOAT DECK AND WHEELHOUSE

FORECASTLE DECK

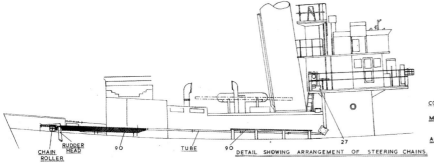

CHAIN ROLLER   RUDDER HEAD   90   TUBE   90   DETAIL SHOWING ARRANGEMENT OF STEERING CHAINS   27

CLASS DATA —
DISPLACEMENT —— 440 TONS. / 785 TONS
DIMENSIONS —— 126 FT (PP) 137 FT 9 INS (O.A.) 23 FT 9 INS - BEAM
11 FT 6 INS - DRAUGHT.
MACHINERY —— 1 SHAFT RECIPROCATING (V.T.E) ENGINE
I.H.P - 600 = 12 KNOTS.
1 - CYLINDRICAL BOILER. COAL BUNKER - 130 TONS.
SIDE BUNKERS NOT USED
ARMAMENT —— 1-12 PDR. A.A. 1-20mm OERLIKON. 2 OR 4 M.G's
COMPLEMENT —— 35
THE CLASS DESIGN WAS BASED ON HALL RUSSELLS COMMERCIAL
TRAWLER- STAR OF ORKNEY OF 1936.
MINESWEEPING EQUIPMENT FITTED TO CLASS. —— SEE SHEET L/S/26/C
CONTACT MINES —— MARK 3 SWEEP 1⅛" CIRC. SERRATED SWEEP WIRE.
SWEEP SPEED 7·5 K. KITE PATT. 8733 OTTER PATT. 8747 FLOAT PATT. 8742
MAGNETIC MINES —— MARK 2* LL SWEEP 2-50 KW. DIESEL GENERATORS.
NOMINAL POWER-70 KW DESIGNED CURRENT-2400 AMPS. LENGTH OF LONG
LEG-525 YDS. LENGTH OF SHORT LEG-200 YDS. MAX SWEEP SPEED-6 KNOTS
ACOUSTIC MINES —— S.A. TYPE A MARK 2 9" DIA DIAPHRAGM ⁷⁄₁₆" THICK ON
'A' BRACKET OPERATING APPROX. 12 FT BELOW SURFACE. THE DIAPHRAGM
DRIVEN BY A TYPE 'D' KANGO HAMMER.

THIS SET OF DRAWINGS IS BASED UPON THE "AS FITTED" GENERAL ARRANGEMENT DRG No 84/768
KINDLY SUPPLIED BY MR ROBERT McHATTIE NAVAL ARCHITECT OF HALL RUSSELL & CO SHIP-
BUILDERS & SHIPREPAIRERS OF ABERDEEN SCOTLAND & CLASS PHOTOGRAPHS AS SUPPLIED
BY M.O.D. (NAVY) AT BATH.
THESE DRAWINGS WERE ORIGINALLY COMMISSIONED FOR JOHN PIPER MODELS DURING JUNE 1978

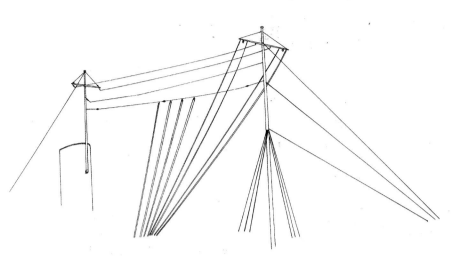

DIAGRAMATIC LAYOUT OF MASTS AERIALS & SIGNAL HALYARDS

CONTENTS OF MAGAZINE
12 PDR.- 80-S.A.P. SHELLS.
70-H.E.T.F. SHELLS.
10-SHRAPNEL SHELLS.
20-STAR SHELLS.
PLUS 20mm & S.A. AMMUNITION

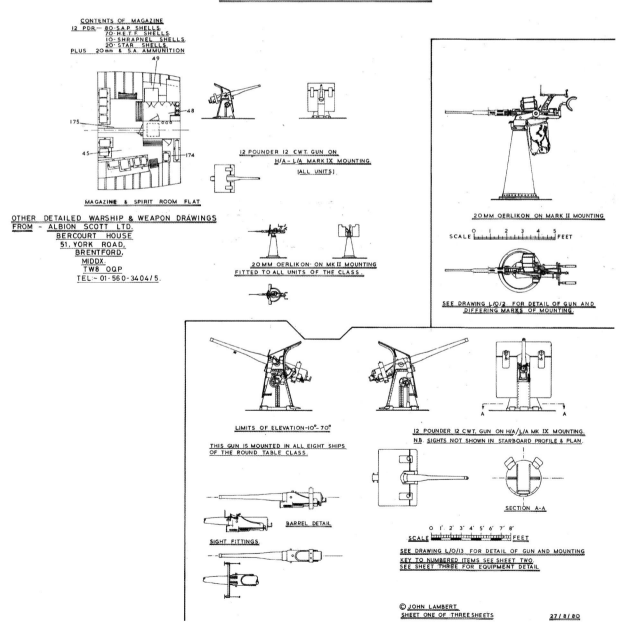

MAGAZINE & SPIRIT ROOM FLAT

OTHER DETAILED WARSHIP & WEAPON DRAWINGS
FROM - ALBION SCOTT LTD.
BERCOURT HOUSE
51, YORK ROAD,
BRENTFORD,
MIDDX.
TW8 OQP
TEL:- 01-560-3404/5.

12 POUNDER 12 CWT. GUN ON
H/A-L/A MARK IX MOUNTING.
[ALL UNITS]

20MM OERLIKON ON MK II MOUNTING
FITTED TO ALL UNITS OF THE CLASS.

20MM OERLIKON ON MARK II MOUNTING

SCALE 0 1 2 3 4 5 FEET

SEE DRAWING L/O/2 FOR DETAIL OF GUN AND
DIFFERING MARKS OF MOUNTING.

LIMITS OF ELEVATION-10°-70°

THIS GUN IS MOUNTED IN ALL EIGHT SHIPS
OF THE ROUND TABLE CLASS.

BARREL DETAIL

SIGHT FITTINGS

12 POUNDER 12 CWT. GUN ON H/A/L/A MK IX MOUNTING.
N.B. SIGHTS NOT SHOWN IN STARBOARD PROFILE & PLAN.

SECTION A-A

SCALE 0 1' 2' 3' 4' 5' 6' 7' 8' FEET

SEE DRAWING L/O/13 FOR DETAIL OF GUN AND MOUNTING
KEY TO NUMBERED ITEMS SEE SHEET TWO.
SEE SHEET THREE FOR EQUIPMENT DETAIL.

© JOHN LAMBERT
SHEET ONE OF THREE SHEETS   27/8/80

L/S/26/A

XVIII. L/S13 HMS *Coldstreamer*, 'Military'-class A/S trawler, 1942

T337

SCALE ⊢⊢⊢⊢⊢⊢⊢⊢⊢⊢⊢ FEET

0 10′ 20′ 30′ 40′ 50′ 60′ 70′ 80′

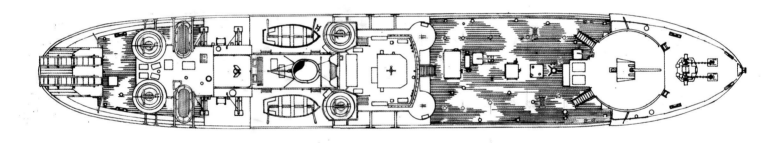

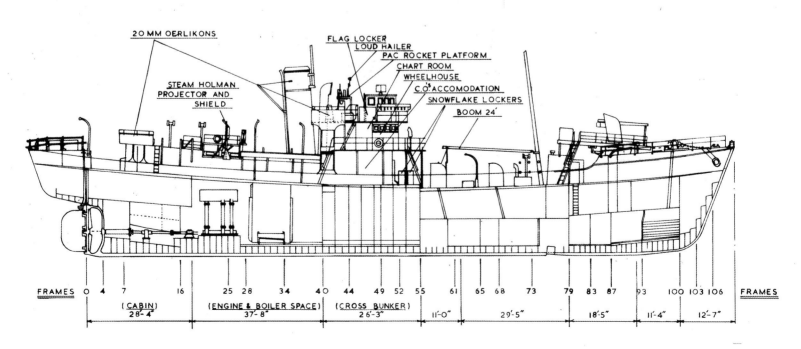

20 MM OERLIKONS

STEAM HOLMAN
PROJECTOR AND
SHIELD

FLAG LOCKER
LOUD HAILER
PAC ROCKET PLATFORM
CHART ROOM
WHEELHOUSE
C.O. ACCOMODATION
SNOWFLAKE LOCKERS
BOOM 24′

FRAMES 0 4 7 16 25 28 34 40 44 49 52 55 61 65 68 73 79 83 87 93 100 103 106 FRAMES

(CABIN)
28′-4″

(ENGINE & BOILER SPACE)
37′-8″

(CROSS BUNKER)
26′-3″

11′-0″

29′-5″

18′-5″

11′-4″

12′-7″

1941 PROGRAMME.

PENNANT No.	NAME.	LAUNCHED.	COMPLETED.
T 334	GRENADIER	26:9:42	10:2:43
T 335	LANCER	26:10:42	25:2:43
T 336	SAPPER	11:11:42	19:3:43

1942 PROGRAMME.

T 304	BOMBARDIER	23:1:43	19:5:43
T 337	COLDSTREAMER	10:12:42	10:4:43
T 305	FUSILIER	23:12:42	30:4:43

THE SIX EARLY MILITARY CLASS ANTI-SUBMARINE TRAWLERS (YARD Nos 703-708) WERE ALL
DESIGNED AND BUILT BY COOK WELTON AND GEMMELL LTD OF BEVERLEY. THE DESIGN WAS
BASED ON THEIR EARLIER PRE-WAR CIVILIAN TRAWLER DESIGNS.
THE THREE LATER UNITS (YARD Nos 732-734) UTILISED THE SAME HULL WITH AN
IMPROVED BRIDGE AND UPPER DECK LAYOUT (SEE DRAWING No L/S/12).

ARMAMENT 1-4 INCH MK XIX GUN ON A MK XXIII MOUNTING.
4-SINGLE 20 MM OERLIKONS.
2-TWIN .303" BROWNING LIGHT MACHINE GUNS.
1-STEAM HOLMAN PROJECTOR.
DEPTH CHARGES.

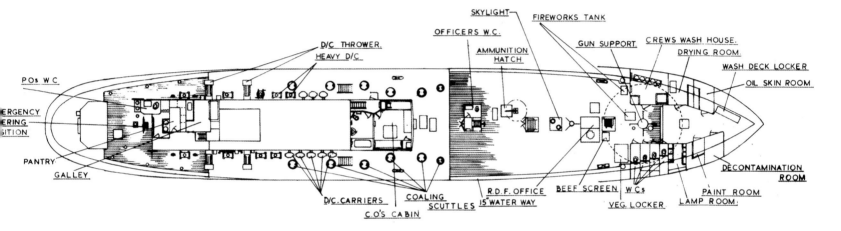

PLAN VIEW OF
WHEELHOUSE DECK

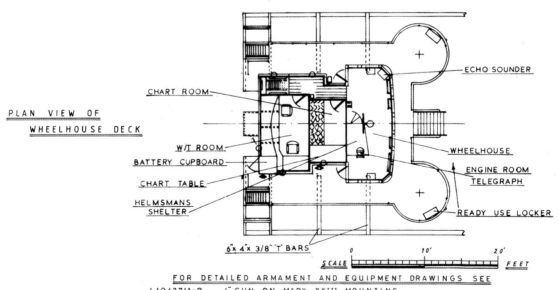

SCALE |_____| FEET
0   10'   20'

FOR DETAILED ARMAMENT AND EQUIPMENT DRAWINGS SEE

L/O/27/A-B	4" GUN ON MARK XXIII MOUNTING
L/O/02/A-B	THE SINGLE 20mm OERLIKON MOUNTING
L/O/16	ANTI-SUBMARINE WEAPONS
L/O/72/A-B	THE MARK II DEPTH CHARGE THROWER AND FITTINGS
L/O/63	THE STEAM POWERED HOLMAN PROJECTOR
L/O/120	THE MARK I DEPTH CHARGE RAIL
L/S/110	THE 16 FT TRAWLER BOAT

THIS SUBJECT, ALONG WITH L/S/12, WAS REDUCED AND REDRAWN FROM
ORIGINAL SHIPBUILDERS DRAWINGS PROVIDED BY S.J. BYATT ESQ. OF
CHARLES D HOLMES AND COMPANY OF HULL

L/S/13

XIX. Profile of HM anti-submarine trawler *Thuringia* as converted August–October 1939. Original drawing by W Gray & Co Ltd, ship builders and marine engineers, West Hartlepool

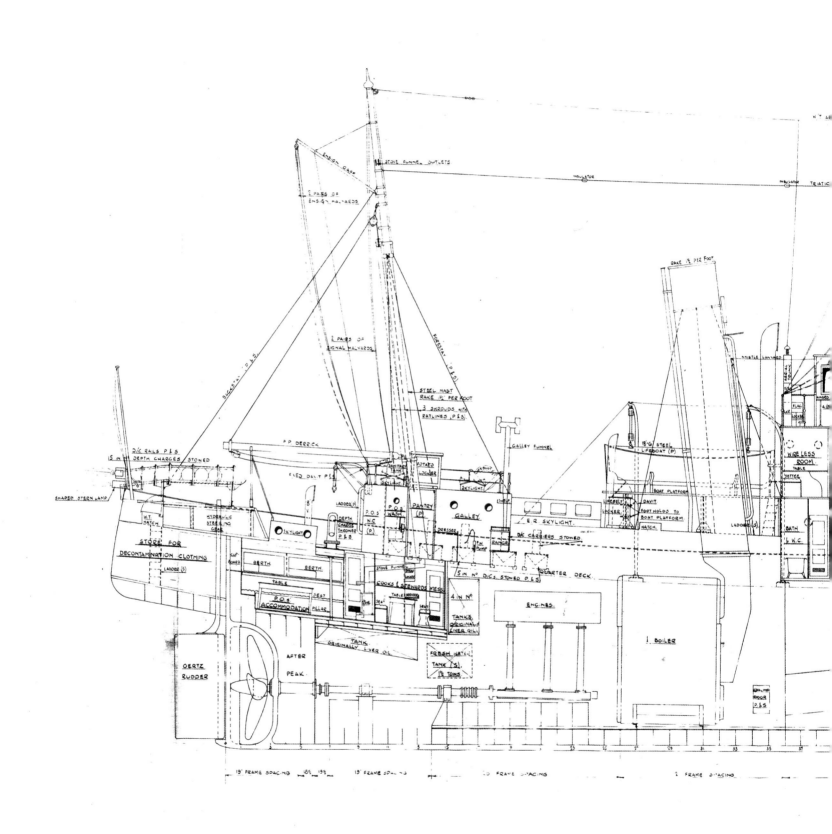

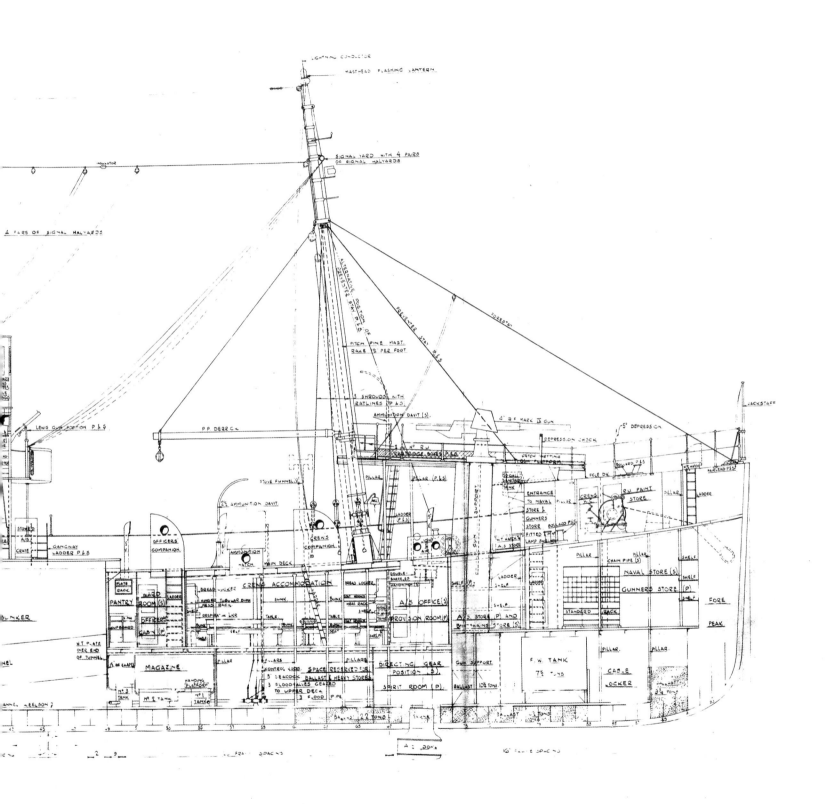

XX. HM anti-submarine trawler *Thuringia*, as converted August–October 1939.

Original drawing by W Gray & Co Ltd, ship builders and marine engineers, West Hartlepool.
Galley top, boat platform and wheelhouse, AS bridge and gun platform

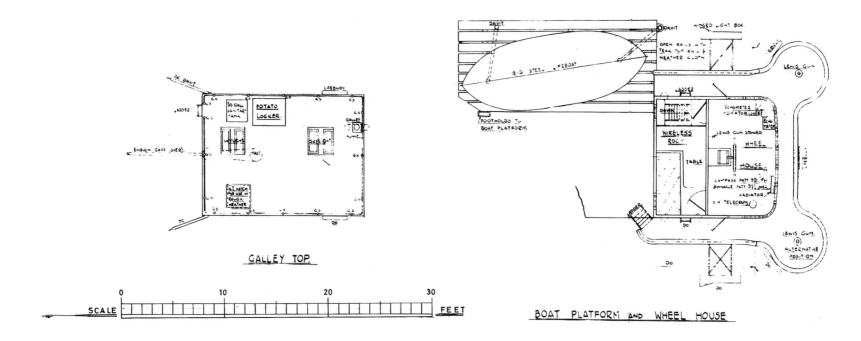

GALLEY TOP.

SCALE 0 10 20 30 FEET

BOAT PLATFORM AND WHEEL HOUSE

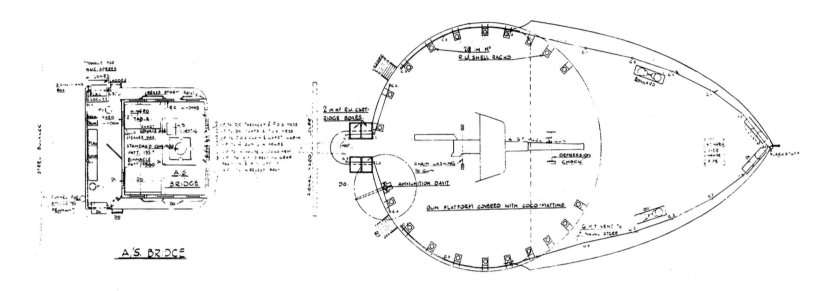

A.S. BRIDGE

GUN PLATFORM AND FORECASTLE DECK.

XXI. Decks of HM anti-submarine trawler *Thuringia* as converted August–October 1939. Original drawing by W Gray & Co Ltd, ship builders and marine engineers, West Hartlepool.

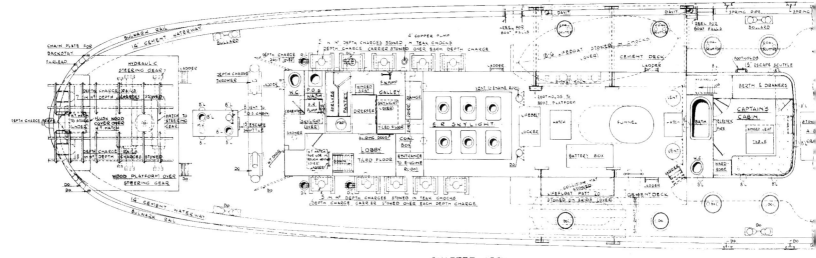

QUARTER DECK.

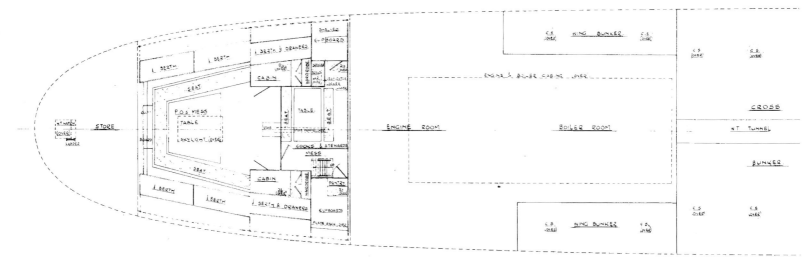

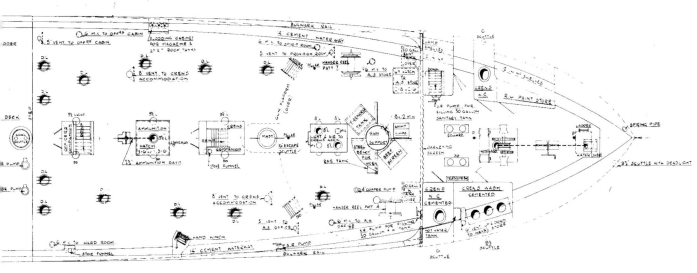

MAIN DECK.

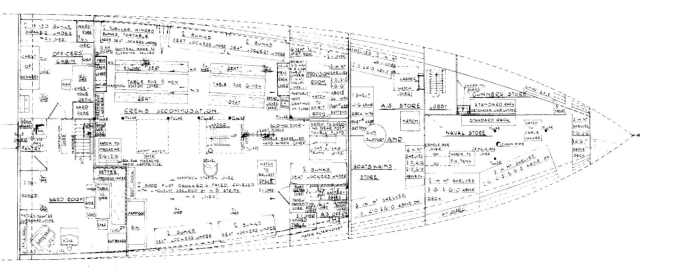

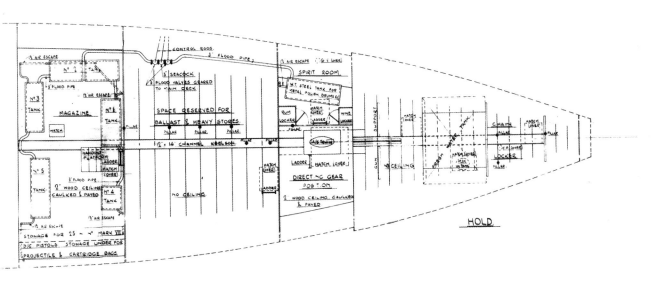

HOLD.

XXII L/S/26/C The 'Round Table'-class trawler *Sir Kay*, as modified for influence (acoustic & magnetic) minesweeping

CLASS HISTORY –
THIS CLASS OF 8 UNITS WAS THE SMALLEST TYPE OF NAVAL MINESWEEPING TRAWLER CLASS BUILT FOR THE ROYAL NAVY DURING THE SECOND WORLD WAR. OF SMALL SIZE & LIMITED RANGE THEY WERE LOCALLY EMPLOYED IN HOME WATERS. IN 1944 THE TWO WIRE SWEEP UNITS – SIR GALAHAD & SIR LANCELOT WERE EMPLOYED AS DAN LAYERS. ALL THE CLASS SURVIVED THE WAR & WERE SOLD OUT OF SERVICE IN THE EARLY POST WAR YEARS. SIR LANCELOT WAS DISARMED & USED BY THE FISHERY RESEARCH SERVICE FROM 1946 WHILST THE REMAINDER WERE SOLD INTO THE MERCANTILE SERVICE IN 1946/7.

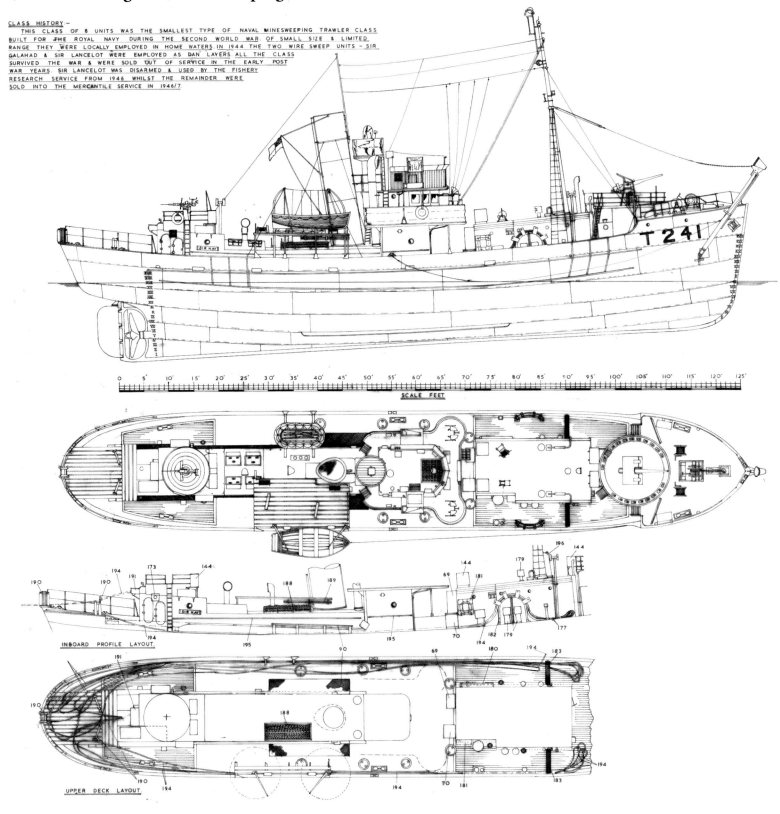

SCALE FEET

INBOARD PROFILE LAYOUT.

UPPER DECK LAYOUT.

APPEARANCE NOTES
WHILST THE CLASS WERE ALL OF THE SAME BASIC DESIGN & LAY OUT, MOST WERE COMPLETED AS INFLUENCE MINESWEEPERS, THUS THERE ARE A NUMBER OF OBVIOUS EQUIPMENT CHANGES. THE STEAM M/S WINCH & M/S DAVITS WERE DELETED & A DECKHOUSE BUILT FOR'D OF THE BRIDGE, TO HOUSE THE ADDITIONAL DIESEL GENERATORS TO PROVIDE THE 'PULSE' POWER & SWITCH GEAR FOR THE LL SWEEP. IT IS APPARENT THAT THIS EQUIPMENT INCREASED THE DISPLACEMENT TO SOME DEGREE 'LL' SWEEP LIGHTS SHOW THE PULSE PHASE (NOT ALL UNITS CARRIED THEM ON THE BRIDGE WINGS). THE DEPTH CHANGE GEAR WAS DELETED, FOR SPACE FOR STOWING THE 'LL' SWEEP CABLE WITH 'LL' ROLLERS AFT & ADDITIONAL GUARD RAILS. MANY WERE FITTED WITH MASTHEAD BALLOON KITE GEAR, SOME CARRIED SPLINTER MATTRESSES ON THE BRIDGE & SIGNAL DECK, SOME ONLY ON THE BRIDGE DECK & OTHERS LIKE SIR KAY, NONE. THE LIGHT MACHINE GUNS VARIED AS SHOWN. IFF INTERROGATORS WERE FITTED IN A FEW. THERE ARE ALSO SLIGHT DIFFERENCES IN THE LOCATION OF FIRE HOSE BASKETS, MUSHROOM VENTILATORS, LIFEBELT RACKS, FLOATNET STOWAGE POSITIONS ETC THROUGHOUT THE CLASS. A SINGLE ANCHOR WAS CARRIED ON THE STARBOARD SIDE. SIR KAY CARRIED AN EARLY THREE COLOUR WESTERN APPROACHES CAMOUFLAGE SCHEME. OTHER UNITS APPEAR OVERALL MEDIUM OR DARK GREY & WELL WEATHERED.

176 CREWS MESS
177 DIESEL GENERATOR EXHAUSTS [LED OVERBOARD]
178 EXPANSION TANK [SILENCER]
179 MUSHROOM VENTILATOR
180 VENTILATOR.
181 SPANNER RAFT.
182 'LL' CABLE GALLOWS.
183 CHEQUER PLATE OVER EXHAUSTS.
184 FLYING OFF BLOCK FOR KITE OR BALLOON.
185 KITE OR BALLOON WINCH. [4000FT WIRE]
186 LIGHTENING CONDUCTOR.
187 YANGI ARIEL IFF [IDENTIFICATION FRIEND OR FOE]
188 FLOAT NET STOWAGE.
189 LUMBER RACK.
190 M/S ROLLERS FOR "LL" CABLES.
191 TERMINAL BOX FOR "LL" CABLES.
192 KITE BALLOON WINCH.
193 GRINDSTONE.
194 'LL' CABLE STOWED LOOSELY ON UPPER DECK
195 HANDRAIL.
196 MAST.

'A' BRACKET DETAIL
[ACOUSTIC SWEEP GEAR]

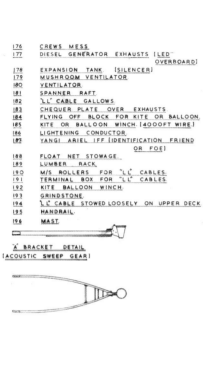

VIEW - AFTER END
STARBOARD SIDE
PORT SIDE
DETAIL - GENERATOR CABIN.
CABIN DETAIL PLAN
MAST DETAIL

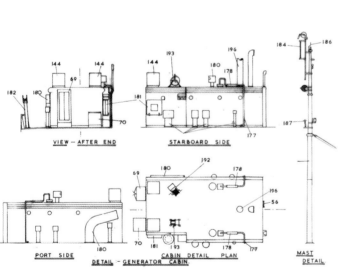

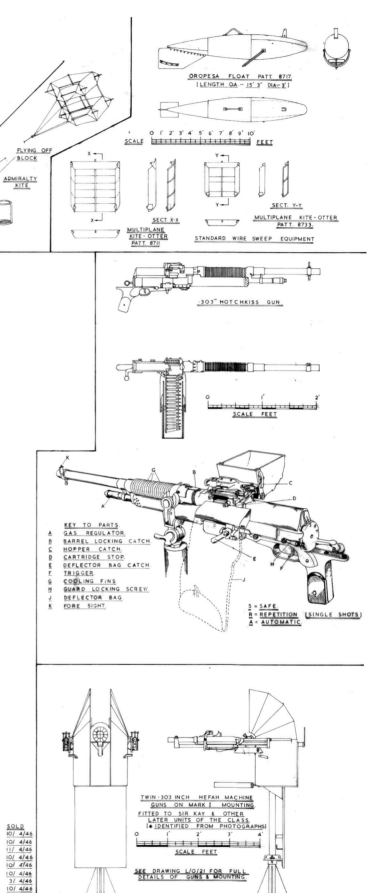

OROPESA FLOAT PATT. 8717.
[LENGTH OA.- 15' 3" DIA - 3']

SCALE 0 1' 2' 3' 4' 5' 6' 7' 8' 9' 10' FEET

SECT. X-X
MULTIPLANE KITE - OTTER PATT. 8711
SECT. Y-Y
MULTIPLANE KITE - OTTER PATT. 8733.
STANDARD WIRE SWEEP EQUIPMENT

FLYING OFF BLOCK
ADMIRALTY KITE.

·303" HOTCHKISS GUN

SCALE FEET 0 1' 2'

KEY TO PARTS.
A GAS REGULATOR.
B BARREL LOCKING CATCH.
C HOPPER CATCH.
D CARTRIDGE STOP.
E DEFLECTOR BAG CATCH.
F TRIGGER.
G COOLING FINS
H GUARD LOCKING SCREW.
J DEFLECTOR BAG
K FORE SIGHT.

S = SAFE.
R = REPETITION [SINGLE SHOTS]
A = AUTOMATIC.

TWIN ·303 INCH HEFAH MACHINE GUNS ON MARK I MOUNTING.
FITTED TO SIR KAY & OTHER LATER UNITS OF THE CLASS.
[* IDENTIFIED FROM PHOTOGRAPHS]

SCALE FEET 0 1' 2' 3' 4'

SEE DRAWING L/O/21 FOR FULL DETAILS OF GUNS & MOUNTING.

CLASS DETAILS

EQUIPMENT							NAME	P.No	BUILDER	ORDERED	LAID DOWN	LAUNCHED	COMPLETED	SOLD
/	L	S	H	B		- SIR	AGRAVAINE.	T 230	JOHN LEWIS & CO.	15/ 3/41	13/10 /41	18/ 3/ 42	12/ 6/42	10/ 4/46.
/	O	S	U	/		- SIR	GALAHAD.	T 226	HALL RUSSELL.	18/ 1 /41	13/ 6 /41	18/12/42	28/ 2/43	10/ 4/46
/	L	S	H	U		- SIR	GARETH.	T 227	HALL RUSSELL.	18/ 1 /41	13/ 6 /41	19/ 1 /42	29/ 4/42	11/ 4/46
/	L	S	*	B		- SIR	GERAINT.	T 240	JOHN LEWIS & CO.	13/ 6/41	20/11 /41	15/ 4/ 42	10/ 7/42	10/ 4/46
/	L	S				- SIR	KAY.	T 241	HALL RUSSELL.	24/ 7/41	27/ 2/ 42	26/10 /42	8/ 2/43	10/ 4/46
A	L	/	I	/		- SIR	LAMORACK.	T 242	HALL RUSSELL.	22/ 8/41	27/ 2 /42	23/11 /42	8/ 3/43	10/ 4/46
A	L	S	U	/		- SIR	LANCELOT.	T 228	JOHN LEWIS & CO.	21/ 1 /41	17/ 7 /41	4/12 /41	26/ 3/42	3/ 4/46
/	L	S	U	B		- SIR	TRISTRAM.	T 229	JOHN LEWIS & CO.	21/ 1 /41	2/ 9 /41	17/ 1 /41	15/ 5 /42	10/ 4/46

DETAIL OF CLASS FITTINGS OBTAINED BY EXAMINATION OF PHOTOGRAPHS.
THOSE UNITS FITTED FOR WIRE - OROPSA - SWEEPING =·O·. FITTED FOR MAGNETIC SWEEPING = 'L'.
FITTED FOR ACOUSTIC SWEEPING = 'A'. EQUIPPED WITH HEFAH MOUNTING=·*·. EQUIPPED WITH TWIN/SINGLE
HOTCHKISS GUNS='H'. FITTED WITH BALLOON KITE GEAR='B'. SPLINTER MATTRESS ON BRIDGE='S'.
UNABLE TO IDENTIFY I.E. GUNS COVERED ='U'. BOOM ON MAST='B'.

L/S/26/C

SHEET THREE OF THREE SHEETS. © JOHN LAMBERT 30/9/80

XXIII. L/S/15 HM trawlers *Bryher* and *Farne* (danlaying conversion), 'Isles'-class, 1943

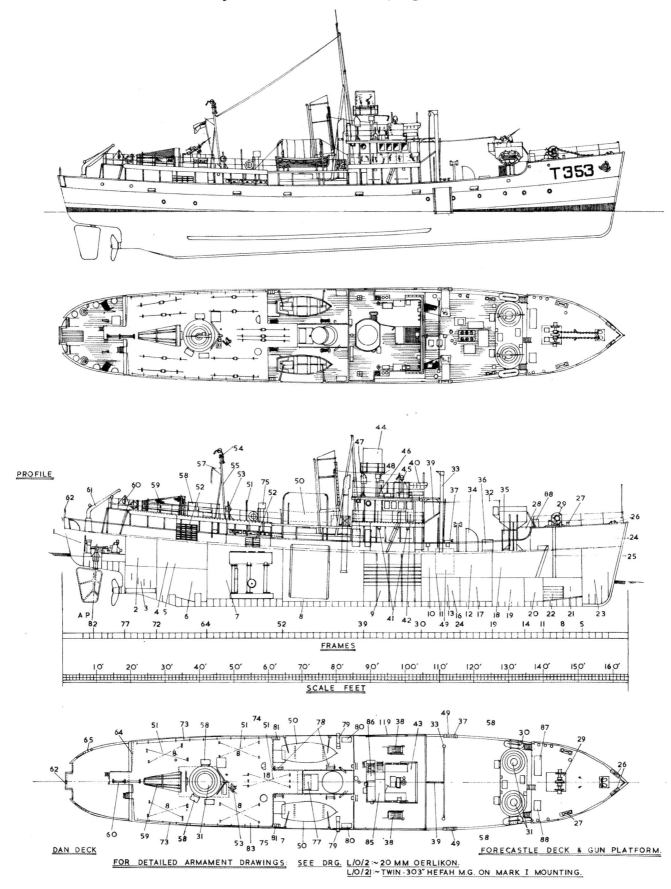

PROFILE

T353

FRAMES

SCALE FEET

DAN DECK

FORECASTLE DECK & GUN PLATFORM.

FOR DETAILED ARMAMENT DRAWINGS: SEE DRG. L/O/2 :~ 20 MM OERLIKON.
L/O/21 :~ TWIN ·303″ HEFAH M.G. ON MARK I MOUNTING.

L/S/189 OR L/S/110 :~ ADMIRALTY 16′ 0″ TRAWLER BOAT

© JOHN LAMBERT   COMPLETED 9/10/1997   ENLARGED AND ENHANCED 5/2002   CH'D 15/5/2002

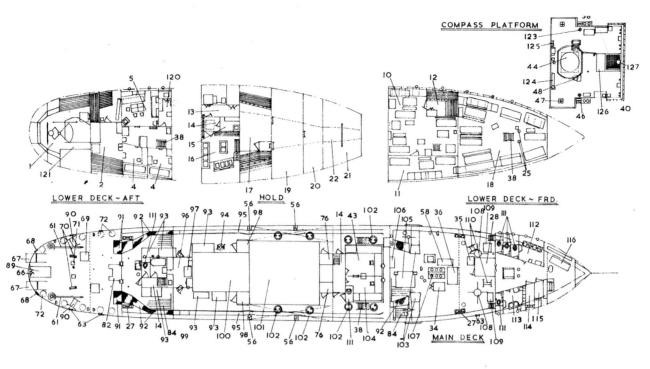

COMPASS PLATFORM

LOWER DECK ~ AFT   HOLD   LOWER DECK ~ FRD.

MAIN DECK

DETAIL — KEY

1	STEERING GEAR COMPARTMENT.
2	STORE ROOM.
3	AFTER PEAK [10·9 TONS]
4	OFFICERS CABIN.
5	WARDROOM.
6	ENGINEERS STORE.
7	ENGINE ROOM.
8	BOILER ROOM.
9	CROSS BUNKER. [126 TONS]
10	STOKERS MESS [8 MEN]
11	PETTY OFFICERS MESS [S]
12	PROVISION ROOM [P]
13	SPIRIT ROOM. [P]
14	LOBBY.
15	GUNNERS STORE.
16	MAGAZINE.
17	CENTRAL STORE.
18	CREWS MESS. [18 MEN]
19	RESERVE FEED TANK. [28 TONS]
20	FRESH WATER TANK. [13 TONS]
21	TRIMMING TANK.
22	CABLE LOCKER.
23	FORE PEAK [18·4 TONS]
24	FORECASTLE.
25	CHAIN PIPES
26	FAIRLEAD.
27	BOLLARD.
28	CREWS PROTECTIVE SHELTER.
29	STEAM WINDLASS.
30	CARLEY FLOAT. [6' 0"x 3' 4"]
31	SINGLE 20MM OERLIKON GUN.
32	VOICE PIPE TO FRD. GUNS.
33	STUMP MAST. [22' 4" ABOVE DECK]
34	COMPANION TO MESSDECKS.
35	BEEF SCREEN.
36	VEGATABLE LOCKER.
37	"SYLVANA" TYPE FAIRLEAD.
38	LADDER.
39	3" DIA. STAY.
40	WOOD WIND DEFLECTOR.
41	BUNKER VENT.
42	WHEELHOUSE.

43	C.O's CABIN.
44	TYPE 271 RADAR LANTERN.
45	10" SEARCHLIGHT.
46	P.A.C. PROJECTOR.
47	TWIN L.M.G. [TWIN ·303" HEFAH]
48	AERIAL TRUNK.
49	WOODCHOCKS COVERED WITH STEEL PLATE.
50	16' DINGHY.
51	DAN BOUY STOWAGE.
52	FLOAT STOWAGE
53	WINCH FOR KITE GEAR.
54	KITE BALLOON GEAR.
55	TUBULAR STEEL MAST. [5" DIA, 18' HIGH]
56	DAVIT SOCKET ON SEAT.
57	ENSIGN GAFF.
58	READY USE AMMUNITION LOCKER.
59	EXPANDED METAL CAGE.
60	TAUT WIRE MEASURING GEAR.
61	GEARED DAVIT.
62	ROLLER FAIRLEAD.
63	MOORING PIPE.
64	PORTABLE GUARD CHAINS
65	CLOSED TOP FAIRLEAD.
66	HINGED DOORS FOR SINKERS.
67	BULWARK HINGES DOWN TO FORM DAN PLATFORM. [P & S]
68	TOWING FAIRLEAD [P & S]
69	W.T HATCH TO STEERING GEAR.
70	EYE PLATE.
71	TELEPHONE BOX.
72	SINKER.
73	LASHING BAR.
74	12" COWL VENT TO ENGINE ROOM.
75	12" M.T. VENT TO FAN IN ENGINE ROOM
76	BOILER ROOM ENTRANCE.
77	AIR HATCH.
78	REEL FOR BOAT FALLS.
79	ASH SHOOT.
80	LIFEBOUY RACK.
81	PETROL CAN STOWAGE.
82	WINCH.
83	STEEL DECK.

84	WOOD DECK [5"x 2½".]
85	W/T OFFICE.
86	BATTERY CUPBOARD.
87	SALT WATER TANK. [100 GALLS.]
88	FRESH WATER TANK. [50 GALLS]
89	SINKER PLATFORM.
90	REEL FOR DAN BOUY MOORING ROPE.
91	PLATE FROM WOOD TO STEEL DECK.
92	CHEQUER PLATE.
93	STOWAGE FOR ELLIPTICAL FLOATS.
94	DOWNTON PUMP.
95	TROUGH FOR SINKERS [11" WIDE 10½"DEEP]
96	GALLEY.
97	RANGE.
98	ENGINE ROOM ENTRANCE.
99	COAL BOX.
100	ENGINE CASING.
101	BOILER CASING.
102	BUNKER SCUTTLES WOOLLONS No 2 SIZE.
103	MAT.
104	CHIEF OFFICERS CABIN.
105	T.S.D.S. WINCH.
106	DECK CONTROL BOX FOR MAGAZINE. FLOOD.
107	SKYLIGHT.
108	GUN PLATFORM SUPPORT TUBE.
109	FIREWORK TANK.
110	HAWSER REEL.
111	W.C.
112	CREWS BATHROOM.
113	P.O's BATHROOM.
114	LAMP ROOM.
115	PAINT ROOM.
116	WASHDECK LOCKER.
117	RUM CUPBOARD.
118	SPIRIT & METHYLATED CUPBOARD.
119	SOUNDING BOOM
120	PANTRY.
121	BOATSWAINS & DECK STORE.
122	DAN STORE.
123	PEDESTAL FOR ANTI-TANK RIFLE.
124	FLAG LOCKER.
125	RACK FOR 3 RIFLES.
126	CHART TABLE
127	STANDARD COMPASS.

52 DAN BOUYS CARRIED
RACKS ON DAN DECK STOW:~ 8 & 18 DANS

DATA:~
DISPLACEMENT:~ 545 TONS.
DIMENSIONS ~ 150 FT. [BP] 164 FT. [OA] 27 FT. 6 INS. [BEAM] 10 FT. 6 INS. [DRAUGHT]
MACHINERY:~ 1 RECIPROCATING ENGINE [VTE] [IHP] 850. SPEED~ 12 KNOTS [MAX]
1 CYLINDRICAL BOILER.
BUNKER CAPACITY:~ CROSS 126 TONS.~ PORT & STBD WING ~ 58 TONS :~ TOTAL 184 TONS.
ARMAMENT:~ 3~20 MM OERLIKONS ~ 2 TWIN ·303" LMG's ~ 2 A/T RIFLES

	H.M.S. BRYHER [JOB No 712]	H.M.S. FARNE [JOB No 713]
PENNANT No :~	T 350	T 353
ORDERED~	7/7/42	30/7/42
LAID DOWN:~	28/12/42	21/1/43
LAUNCHED:~	8/4/43	22/4/43
COMPLETED:~	24/8/43	7/9/43
FATE:~	SOLD 1947	SOLD 1946: LOST 12/48

BOTH BUILT BY :~ C.W. & G. HOLMES LTD

REDRAWN FROM THE "AS FITTED" DRAWINGS AS SUPPLIED BY THE BUILDERS.

L / S / 15

XXIV. L/S/16REV Anti-submarine trawlers *St Apollo* and *St Zeno*

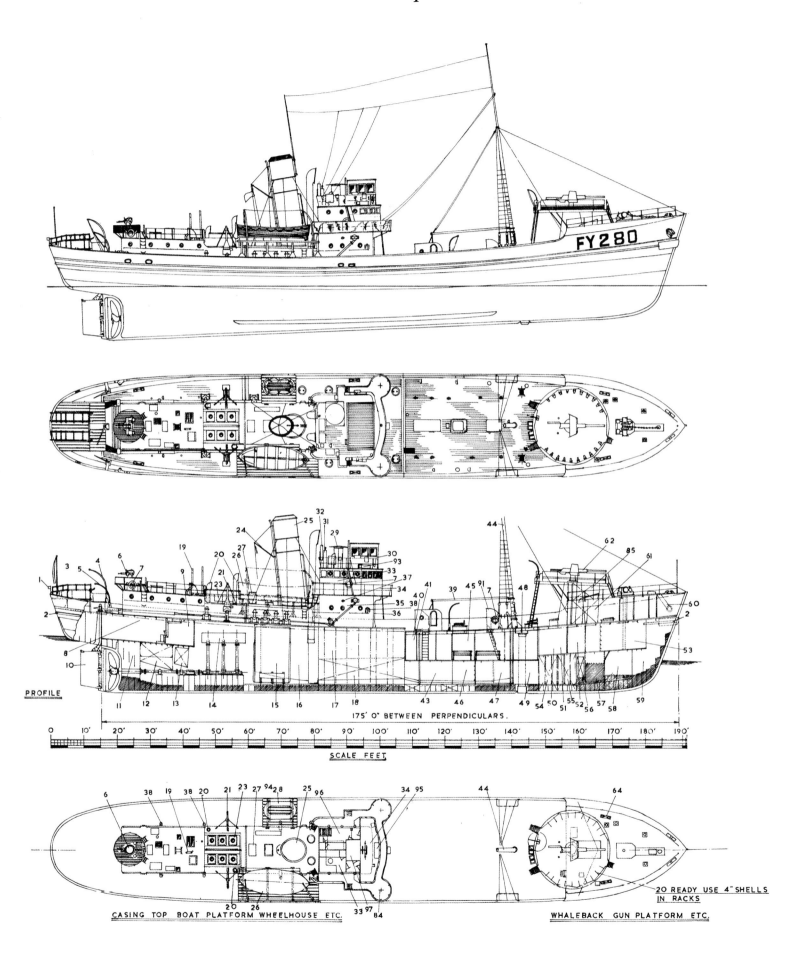

FY 280

PROFILE

175' 0" BETWEEN PERPENDICULARS.

0   10'   20'   30'   40'   50'   60'   70'   80'   90'   100'   110'   120'   130'   140'   150'   160'   170'   180'   190'

SCALE FEET

CASING TOP   BOAT PLATFORM WHEELHOUSE ETC.

WHALEBACK   GUN PLATFORM ETC.

20 READY USE 4" SHELLS
IN RACKS

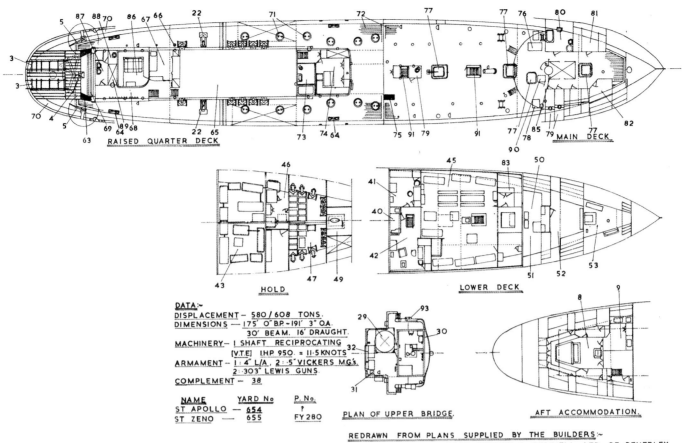

RAISED QUARTER DECK

MAIN DECK

HOLD

LOWER DECK

PLAN OF UPPER BRIDGE.

AFT ACCOMMODATION.

DATA:~
DISPLACEMENT ~ 580/608 TONS.
DIMENSIONS ~ 175' 0" B.P. ~ 191' 3" O.A.
30' BEAM. 16' DRAUGHT.
MACHINERY~ 1 SHAFT RECIPROCATING
[V.T.E] I.H.P. 950. = 11.5 KNOTS.
ARMAMENT ~ 1: 4" L/A, 2:·5" VICKERS M.G's.
2:·303" LEWIS GUNS.
COMPLEMENT ~ 38

NAME	YARD No	P. No.
ST APOLLO	654	?
ST ZENO	655	FY280

REDRAWN FROM PLANS SUPPLIED BY THE BUILDERS:~
COOK WELTON & GEMMELL LTD. OF BEVERLEY.

FOR DETAIL OF ARMAMENT SEE ~
L/0/07 = 4" MARK IV GUN ON P.IX MOUNTING
L/0/39 = 4" MARK IV GUN ON MARK 'J' MOUNTING
L/0/57/A-B = TWIN 0·5" VICKERS MACHINE GUNS ON MARK IV MOUNTING

KEY TO DETAIL.

1. STERN LIGHT.
2. D.G. COIL.
3. D.C. RAIL'S [15 D.C's]
4. D.C. DAVIT~ HINGED TYPE.
5. D.C. DAVIT. [P & S]
6. VICKERS ·5"GUN ON TWIN MARK IV MOUNTING.
7. LIFEBOUY.
8. P.O's MESS.
9. PANTRY. [P]
10. "HYDROGAP" PATENT RUDDER.
11. AFTER PEAK BALLAST TANK.
12. F.W. TANK~3500 GALLS.
13. F.W. TANK~ 575 GALLS.
14. MAIN ENGINE~STEAM RECIP.
15. CYLINDRICAL BOILER~225 P.S.I.
16. WING BUNKERS. [47 TONS]
17. MAIN BUNKER. [240 TONS]
18. W.T. TUNNEL.
19. CABIN STOVE FUNNEL.
20. 12" COWL VENT.
21. DEPTH CHARGE DAVIT [P & S]
22. D.C. THROWER [P & S]
23. E.R. SKYLIGHT.
24. GAFF ON WASTE STEAM PIPE.
25. FUNNEL.
26. CLASS I LIFEBOAT~22'x 7'3"x2'9".
27. LIFEBELT CHEST.
28. CARLY FLOAT. [P].
29. CRUCIFORM SHELTER.
30. UPPER BRIDGE.
31. AERIAL TRUNK.
32. FLAG LOCKER.
33. W/T ROOM.
34. WHEELHOUSE.
35. C.O's ACCOMMODATION.
36. CASING OVER VOICE PIPES.
37. 5" TORPEDO VENT.
38. FAIRLEAD. [P & S].
39. PITCH PINE DERRICK~ 23' 6" LONG x 7" DIA.
40. PANTRY.
41. CABIN. [P].
42. WARDROOM. [S].
43. MAGAZINE.
44. 16" DIA. PITCH PINE MAST.
45. CREWS MESS. [14 MEN]
46. SPIRIT ROOM.
47. DEPTH CHARGE MAGAZINE.
48. HAND WINCH FOR A/S GEAR.
49. ASDIC DIRECTING COMP!
50. A/S STORE. [P].
51. BO'SUN'S STORE [S]
52. NAVAL STORE.
53. GUNNERS STORE.
54. FEED WATER & BALLAST TANK [21 TONS].
55. DRINKING WATER. [18 TONS]
56. F.W. TANK ~ 650 GALLS.
57. 52 TONS PIG IRON BALLAST.
58. CHAIN LOCKER.
59. FORE PEAK.
60. HAWSE PIPE~STB'S SIDE ONLY.
61. CREWS SHELTER.
62. 4" Q.F. MK IV GUN ON MARK IX MOUNTING.
63. CHEQUER PLATE STOPS [P&S]
64. MOORING BOLLARD.
65. ENGINE & BOILER CASING.
66. 4" COPPER HAND PUMP.
67. GALLEY.
68. PASSAGE.
69. WOOD GRATING.
70. 18" CEMENT WATERWAY.
71. WOOLLNS BUNKER SCUTTLES.
72. 5"x 3" PITCH PINE DECKING.
73. C.O's BATH ROOM.
74. C.O's CABIN.
75. STEP.
76. VEGETABLE LOCKER.
77. HATCH.
78. FIREWORKS TANK.
79. CREW'S W.C.
80. CREWS WASH HOUSE.
81. R/USE PAINT STORE.
82. DECONTAMINATION ROOM.
83. PROVISION ROOM.
84. LEWIS GUN MOUNTING[P&S]
85. GUN CREW SHELTER.
86. MESS ROOM.
87. P.O's WASH HOUSE.
88. P.O's W.C.
89. LIGHT & AIR TRUNK.
90. BEEF SCREEN.
91. COMPANION.
92. CHART TABLE.
93. BOW LIGHTS [P&S]
94. COLLISION MAT.
95. HELMSMAN'S SHELTER.
96. CHART ROOM.
97. DONKINS VERTICAL STEAM STEERING GEAR

HISTORY:~ BOTH UNITS WERE UNDER CONSTRUCTION BEFORE THE OUTBREAK OF THE SECOND WORLD WAR. OWING TO THEIR LARGE DIMENSIONS THEY WERE REQUISITIONED AS ANTI~SUBMARINE ESCORT TRAWLERS & FITTED WITH ASDIC AND ARMAMENT WHILST BUILDING. THEY COMPLETED IN FEBRUARY & MARCH 1940 RESPECTIVELY. ST APOLLO JOINED THE 3RD ESCORT GROUP ON 11/5/41 SHE CARRIED OUT DEPTH CHARGE ATTACKS ON U201 CAUSING DAMAGE. ON 22 11 41 ST APOLLO WAS LOST BY COLLISION OFF THE HEBRIDES. ST ZENO WAS LOANED TO THE UNITED STATES NAVY IN THE SPRING OF 1942 TO HELP BALANCE THEIR LACK OF ESCORTS. SHE WAS RETURNED IN 1945 AND SOLD IN MAY 1946.

© JOHN LAMBERT   ORIGINALLY DRAWN 26/9/1979   ENLARGED 11/2000   RECHECKED 7/7/2001

L/S/16

XXV. Misc Details of trawler design; Oropesa sweep and davits

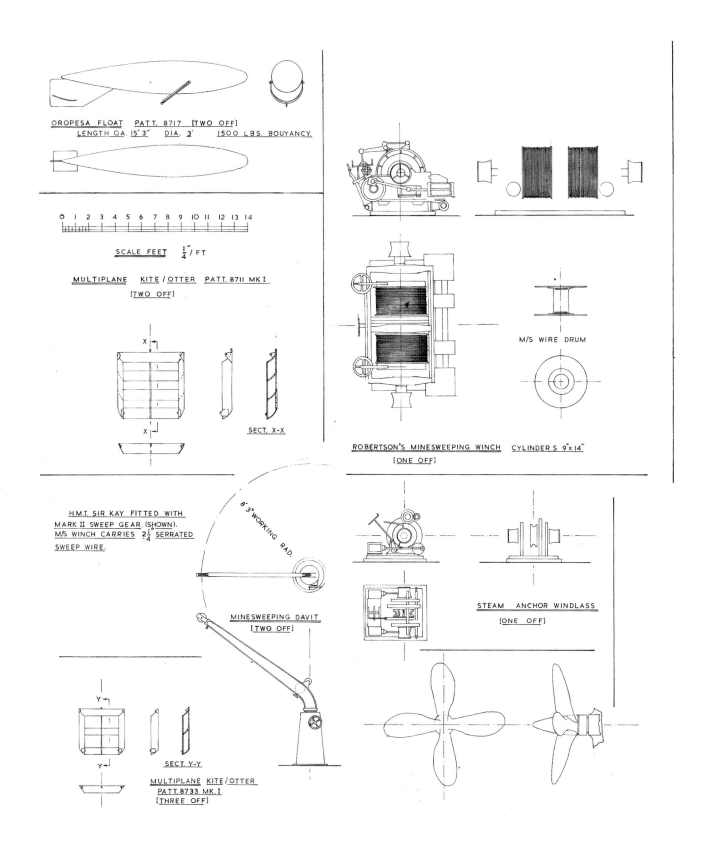

OROPESA FLOAT PATT. 8717 [TWO OFF]
LENGTH O.A. 15' 3"   DIA. 3'   1500 LBS. BOUYANCY.

0 1 2 3 4 5 6 7 8 9 10 11 12 13 14

SCALE FEET $\frac{1}{4}$"/FT

MULTIPLANE KITE/OTTER PATT. 8711 MK I
[TWO OFF]

X

SECT. X-X

M/S WIRE DRUM

ROBERTSON'S MINESWEEPING WINCH   CYLINDERS 9"x 14"
[ONE OFF]

H.M.T. SIR KAY FITTED WITH
MARK II SWEEP GEAR. (SHOWN).
M/S WINCH CARRIES 2$\frac{1}{4}$" SERRATED
SWEEP WIRE.

8' 3" WORKING RAD.

MINESWEEPING DAVIT
[TWO OFF]

STEAM ANCHOR WINDLASS
[ONE OFF]

Y

SECT. Y-Y

MULTIPLANE KITE/OTTER
PATT. 8733. MK. I
[THREE OFF]

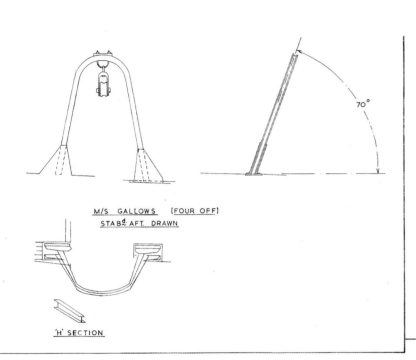

M/S GALLOWS [FOUR OFF]
STAB.S AFT. DRAWN

'H' SECTION

70°

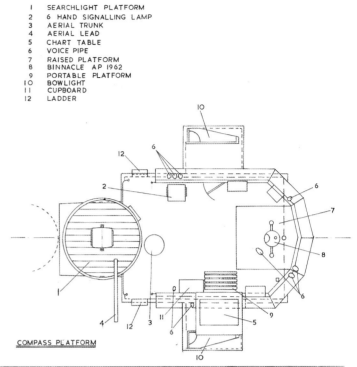

1 SEARCHLIGHT PLATFORM
2 6 HAND SIGNALLING LAMP
3 AERIAL TRUNK
4 AERIAL LEAD
5 CHART TABLE
6 VOICE PIPE
7 RAISED PLATFORM
8 BINNACLE AP 1962
9 PORTABLE PLATFORM
10 BOWLIGHT
11 CUPBOARD
12 LADDER

COMPASS PLATFORM

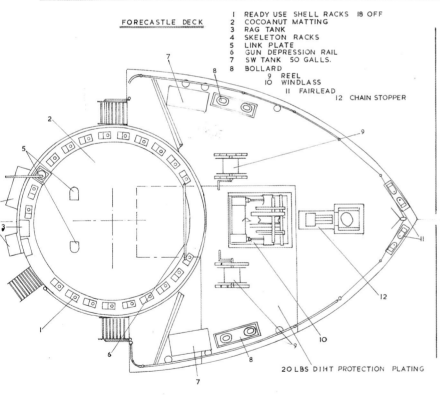

FORECASTLE DECK

1 READY USE SHELL RACKS 18 OFF
2 COCOANUT MATTING
3 RAG TANK
4 SKELETON RACKS
5 LINK PLATE
6 GUN DEPRESSION RAIL
7 SW TANK 50 GALLS.
8 BOLLARD
9 REEL
10 WINDLASS
11 FAIRLEAD
12 CHAIN STOPPER

20 LBS D1HT PROTECTION PLATING

DETAIL ~ SIR KAY

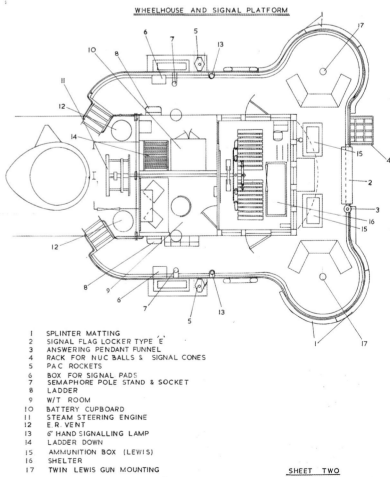

WHEELHOUSE AND SIGNAL PLATFORM

1 SPLINTER MATTING
2 SIGNAL FLAG LOCKER TYPE 'E'
3 ANSWERING PENDANT FUNNEL
4 RACK FOR NUC BALLS & SIGNAL CONES
5 PAC ROCKETS
6 BOX FOR SIGNAL PADS
7 SEMAPHORE POLE STAND & SOCKET
8 LADDER
9 W/T ROOM
10 BATTERY CUPBOARD
11 STEAM STEERING ENGINE
12 E.R. VENT
13 6" HAND SIGNALLING LAMP
14 LADDER DOWN
15 AMMUNITION BOX (LEWIS)
16 SHELTER
17 TWIN LEWIS GUN MOUNTING

SHEET TWO
JOHN LAMBERT 18/7/78.

XXVI. L/O/59 6pdr Hotchkiss QF gun HA/LA Mark VI on a Second World War mounting, 1942

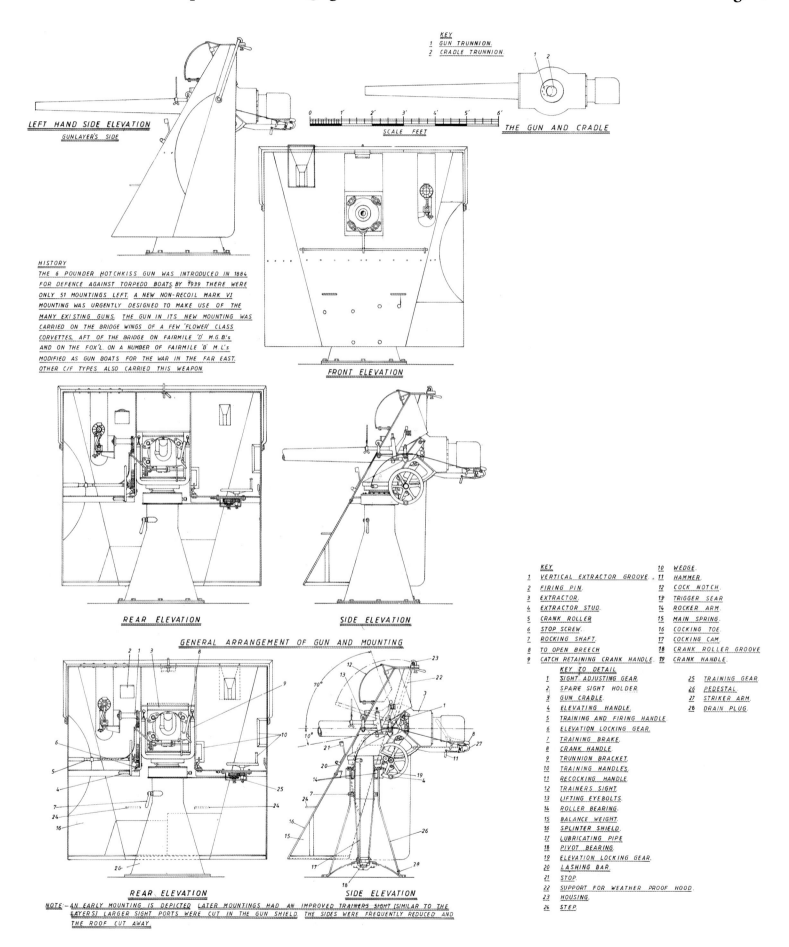

KEY
1 GUN TRUNNION.
2 CRADLE TRUNNION.

LEFT HAND SIDE ELEVATION
GUNLAYER'S SIDE

SCALE FEET

THE GUN AND CRADLE

HISTORY
THE 6 POUNDER HOTCHKISS GUN WAS INTRODUCED IN 1884
FOR DEFENCE AGAINST TORPEDO BOATS. BY 1939 THERE WERE
ONLY 51 MOUNTINGS LEFT. A NEW NON-RECOIL MARK VI
MOUNTING WAS URGENTLY DESIGNED TO MAKE USE OF THE
MANY EXISTING GUNS. THE GUN IN ITS NEW MOUNTING WAS
CARRIED ON THE BRIDGE WINGS OF A FEW 'FLOWER' CLASS
CORVETTES, AFT OF THE BRIDGE ON FAIRMILE 'D' M.G.B's
AND ON THE FOX'L ON A NUMBER OF FAIRMILE 'B' M.L's
MODIFIED AS GUN BOATS FOR THE WAR IN THE FAR EAST.
OTHER C/F TYPES ALSO CARRIED THIS WEAPON.

FRONT ELEVATION

REAR ELEVATION

SIDE ELEVATION

GENERAL ARRANGEMENT OF GUN AND MOUNTING

KEY
1 VERTICAL EXTRACTOR GROOVE.
2 FIRING PIN.
3 EXTRACTOR.
4 EXTRACTOR STUD.
5 CRANK ROLLER
6 STOP SCREW.
7 ROCKING SHAFT.
8 TO OPEN BREECH
9 CATCH RETAINING CRANK HANDLE.
10 WEDGE.
11 HAMMER.
12 COCK NOTCH.
13 TRIGGER SEAR
14 ROCKER ARM.
15 MAIN SPRING.
16 COCKING TOE.
17 COCKING CAM.
18 CRANK ROLLER GROOVE
19 CRANK HANDLE.

KEY TO DETAIL
1 SIGHT ADJUSTING GEAR.
2 SPARE SIGHT HOLDER.
3 GUN CRADLE.
4 ELEVATING HANDLE.
5 TRAINING AND FIRING HANDLE.
6 ELEVATION LOCKING GEAR.
7 TRAINING BRAKE.
8 CRANK HANDLE.
9 TRUNNION BRACKET.
10 TRAINING HANDLES.
11 RECOCKING HANDLE.
12 TRAINERS SIGHT.
13 LIFTING EYEBOLTS.
14 ROLLER BEARING.
15 BALANCE WEIGHT.
16 SPLINTER SHIELD.
17 LUBRICATING PIPE
18 PIVOT BEARING.
19 ELEVATION LOCKING GEAR.
20 LASHING BAR.
21 STOP.
22 SUPPORT FOR WEATHER PROOF HOOD.
23 HOUSING.
24 STEP.
25 TRAINING GEAR
26 PEDESTAL
27 STRIKER ARM.
28 DRAIN PLUG.

REAR ELEVATION

SIDE ELEVATION

NOTE:- AN EARLY MOUNTING IS DEPICTED. LATER MOUNTINGS HAD AN IMPROVED TRAINERS SIGHT [SIMILAR TO THE
LAYERS] LARGER SIGHT PORTS WERE CUT IN THE GUN SHIELD. THE SIDES WERE FREQUENTLY REDUCED AND
THE ROOF CUT AWAY.

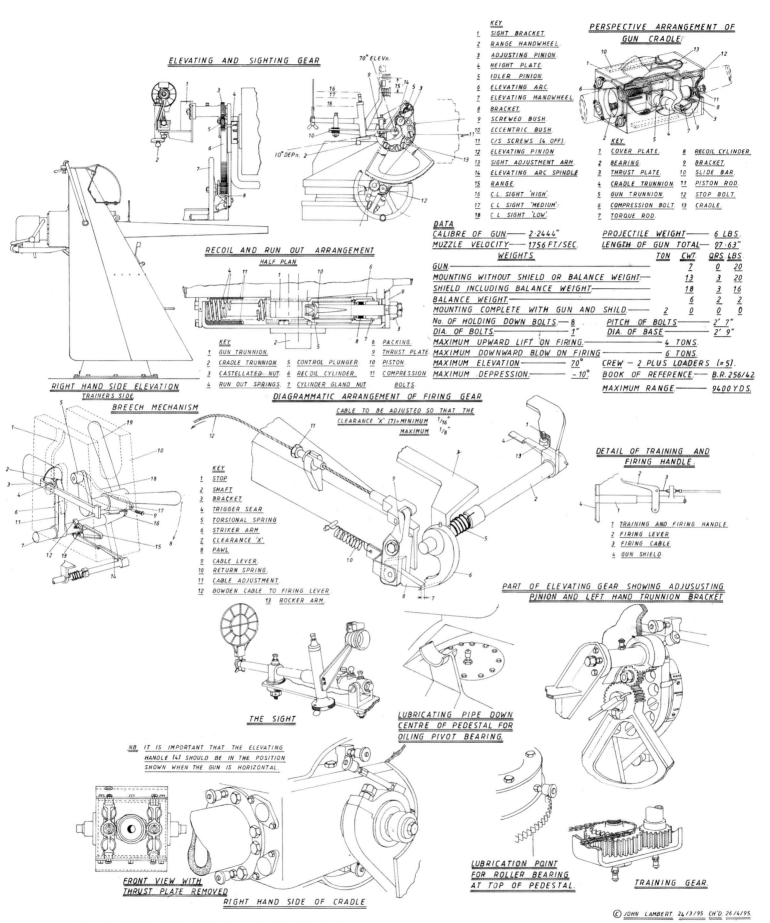

ELEVATING AND SIGHTING GEAR

70° ELEVn.

10° DEPn.

KEY

1 SIGHT BRACKET.
2 RANGE HANDWHEEL.
3 ADJUSTING PINION.
4 HEIGHT PLATE.
5 IDLER PINION.
6 ELEVATING ARC.
7 ELEVATING HANDWHEEL.
8 BRACKET.
9 SCREWED BUSH.
10 ECCENTRIC BUSH.
11 C/S SCREWS (4 OFF).
12 ELEVATING PINION
13 SIGHT ADJUSTMENT ARM.
14 ELEVATING ARC SPINDLE
15 RANGE.
16 C.L. SIGHT 'HIGH'.
17 C L SIGHT 'MEDIUM'.
18 C L SIGHT 'LOW'.

PERSPECTIVE ARRANGEMENT OF GUN CRADLE

KEY

1	COVER PLATE.	8	RECOIL CYLINDER.
2	BEARING.	9	BRACKET.
3	THRUST PLATE.	10	SLIDE BAR.
4	CRADLE TRUNNION	11	PISTON ROD.
5	GUN TRUNNION.	12	STOP BOLT.
6	COMPRESSION BOLT.	13	CRADLE.
7	TORQUE ROD.		

DATA

| CALIBRE OF GUN | 2·2444" | PROJECTILE WEIGHT | 6 LBS. |
| MUZZLE VELOCITY | 1756 FT./SEC. | LENGTH OF GUN TOTAL | 97·63" |

WEIGHTS

	TON	CWT.	QRS.	LBS.
GUN.		7	0	20
MOUNTING WITHOUT SHIELD OR BALANCE WEIGHT		13	3	20
SHIELD INCLUDING BALANCE WEIGHT		18	3	16
BALANCE WEIGHT.		6	2	2
MOUNTING COMPLETE WITH GUN AND SHIELD	2	0	0	0

No. OF HOLDING DOWN BOLTS	8	PITCH OF BOLTS	2' 7"
DIA. OF BOLTS.	1"	DIA. OF BASE	2' 9"
MAXIMUM UPWARD LIFT ON FIRING.			4 TONS.
MAXIMUM DOWNWARD BLOW ON FIRING			6 TONS.
MAXIMUM ELEVATION	70°	CREW - 2 PLUS LOADERS (=5).
MAXIMUM DEPRESSION.	-10°	BOOK OF REFERENCE.	B.R. 256/42
		MAXIMUM RANGE.	9400 YDS.

RECOIL AND RUN OUT ARRANGEMENT

HALF PLAN

KEY

1 GUN TRUNNION.
2 CRADLE TRUNNION.
3 CASTELLATED NUT.
4 RUN OUT SPRINGS.
5 CONTROL PLUNGER.
6 RECOIL CYLINDER.
7 CYLINDER GLAND NUT.
8 PACKING.
9 THRUST PLATE.
10 PISTON.
11 COMPRESSION BOLTS.

RIGHT HAND SIDE ELEVATION
TRAINERS SIDE

BREECH MECHANISM

KEY

1 STOP
2 SHAFT
3 BRACKET
4 TRIGGER SEAR
5 TORSIONAL SPRING
6 STRIKER ARM
7 CLEARANCE 'X'
8 PAWL
9 CABLE LEVER
10 RETURN SPRING.
11 CABLE ADJUSTMENT
12 BOWDEN CABLE TO FIRING LEVER.
13 ROCKER ARM.

DIAGRAMMATIC ARRANGEMENT OF FIRING GEAR

CABLE TO BE ADJUSTED SO THAT THE
CLEARANCE 'X' (7) = MINIMUM 1/16"
MAXIMUM 1/8"

DETAIL OF TRAINING AND
FIRING HANDLE.

1 TRAINING AND FIRING HANDLE.
2 FIRING LEVER
3 FIRING CABLE
4 GUN SHIELD.

PART OF ELEVATING GEAR SHOWING ADJUSTING
PINION AND LEFT HAND TRUNNION BRACKET

THE SIGHT

LUBRICATING PIPE DOWN
CENTRE OF PEDESTAL FOR
OILING PIVOT BEARING.

NB IT IS IMPORTANT THAT THE ELEVATING
HANDLE (4) SHOULD BE IN THE POSITION
SHOWN WHEN THE GUN IS HORIZONTAL.

FRONT VIEW WITH
THRUST PLATE REMOVED

RIGHT HAND SIDE OF CRADLE

LUBRICATION POINT
FOR ROLLER BEARING
AT TOP OF PEDESTAL.

TRAINING GEAR.

© JOHN LAMBERT 24/3/95 CH'D. 26/4/95.

L/0/59

THIS IS YET ANOTHER WEAPONS SYSTEM THAT I HAVE BEEN TRYING TO TRACE FOR A NUMBER OF YEARS. IN DECEMBER 1994 AFTER MY PLEA FOR HELP
IN WARSHIP WORLD (VOLUME 5-1) I WAS PUT IN TOUCH WITH THE MINISTRY OF DEFENCE PATTERN ROOM THE ENFIELD BUILDING C/O ROYAL ORDNANCE P.L.C.
KINGS MEADOW ROAD NOTTINGHAM NG2 1EQ. WHO HOLD A COPY OF B.R. 256/42 AND B.R.1086B. MY GRATEFUL THANKS TO MR H.J. WOODEND AND HIS STAFF

XXVII. L/O/02/A 20mm Oerlikon gun on Mark I, IIA, VIIA & VIIIA mountings, as extensively fitted to the armed trawlers.

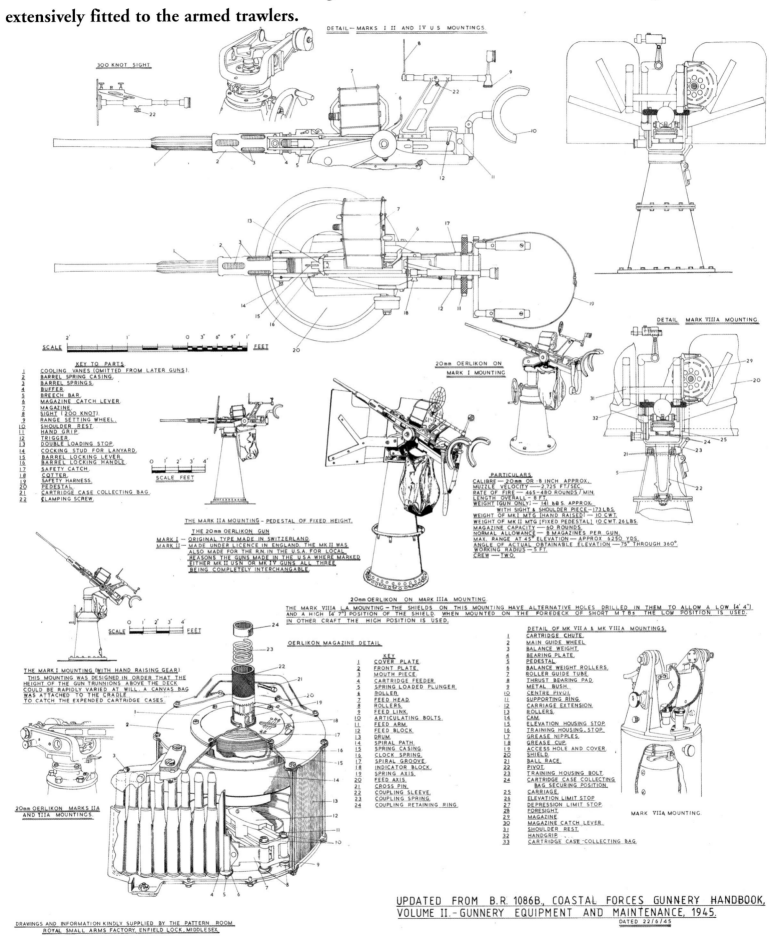

DETAIL—MARKS I II AND IV U S MOUNTINGS

300 KNOT SIGHT

SCALE 2' 1' 0 3" 6" 9" 1' FEET

KEY TO PARTS

1. COOLING VANES (OMITTED FROM LATER GUNS).
2. BARREL SPRING CASING.
3. BARREL SPRINGS.
4. BUFFER.
5. BREECH BAR.
6. MAGAZINE CATCH LEVER.
7. MAGAZINE.
8. SIGHT (200 KNOT).
9. RANGE SETTING WHEEL.
10. SHOULDER REST.
11. HAND GRIP.
12. TRIGGER.
13. DOUBLE LOADING STOP.
14. COCKING STUD FOR LANYARD.
15. BARREL LOCKING LEVER.
16. BARREL LOCKING HANDLE.
17. SAFETY CATCH.
18. COTTER.
19. SAFETY HARNESS.
20. PEDESTAL.
21. CARTRIDGE CASE COLLECTING BAG.
22. CLAMPING SCREW.

SCALE FEET 0 1' 2' 3' 4'

THE MARK IIA MOUNTING – PEDESTAL OF FIXED HEIGHT.

THE 20mm OERLIKON GUN

MARK I — ORIGINAL TYPE MADE IN SWITZERLAND.
MARK II — MADE UNDER LICENCE IN ENGLAND. THE MK II WAS ALSO MADE FOR THE R.N. IN THE U.S.A. FOR LOCAL REASONS THE GUNS MADE IN THE U.S.A. WERE MARKED EITHER MK II USN OR MK IV GUNS ALL THREE BEING COMPLETELY INTERCHANGABLE.

SCALE FEET 0 1' 2' 3' 4'

THE MARK I MOUNTING (WITH HAND RAISING GEAR)
THIS MOUNTING WAS DESIGNED IN ORDER THAT THE HEIGHT OF THE GUN TRUNNIONS ABOVE THE DECK COULD BE RAPIDLY VARIED AT WILL. A CANVAS BAG WAS ATTACHED TO THE CRADLE TO CATCH THE EXPENDED CARTRIDGE CASES.

20mm OERLIKON MARKS IIA AND IIIA MOUNTINGS.

20mm OERLIKON ON MARK I MOUNTING

20mm OERLIKON ON MARK IIIA MOUNTING.
THE MARK VIIIA L.A. MOUNTING – THE SHIELDS ON THIS MOUNTING HAVE ALTERNATIVE HOLES DRILLED IN THEM TO ALLOW A LOW (4' 4") AND A HIGH (4' 7") POSITION OF THE SHIELD. WHEN MOUNTED ON THE FOREDECK OF SHORT M.T.Bs THE LOW POSITION IS USED. IN OTHER CRAFT THE HIGH POSITION IS USED.

DETAIL MARK VIIIA MOUNTING

PARTICULARS
CALIBRE — 20mm OR .8 INCH APPROX.
MUZZLE VELOCITY — 2.725 FT./SEC.
RATE OF FIRE — 465-480 ROUNDS/MIN.
LENGTH OVERALL — 8FT.
WEIGHT (GUN ONLY) — 141 LBS. APPROX.
    WITH SIGHT & SHOULDER PIECE — 173 LBS.
WEIGHT OF MKI MTG (HAND RAISED) — 10 CWT.
WEIGHT OF MK II MTG (FIXED PEDESTAL) 10 CWT. 26 LBS.
MAGAZINE CAPACITY — 60 ROUNDS.
NORMAL ALLOWANCE — 8 MAGAZINES PER GUN.
MAX. RANGE AT 45° ELEVATION — APPROX 6250 YDS.
ANGLE OF ACTUAL OBTAINABLE ELEVATION — 75° THROUGH 360°.
WORKING RADIUS — 5 FT.
CREW — TWO.

OERLIKON MAGAZINE DETAIL

KEY

1. COVER PLATE
2. FRONT PLATE
3. MOUTH PIECE
4. CARTRIDGE FEEDER
5. SPRING LOADED PLUNGER
6. ROLLER
7. FEED HEAD
8. ROLLERS
9. FEED LINK
10. ARTICULATING BOLTS
11. FEED ARM
12. FEED BLOCK
13. DRUM
14. SPIRAL PATH
15. SPRING CASING
16. CLOCK SPRING
17. SPIRAL GROOVE
18. INDICATOR BLOCK
19. SPRING AXIS
20. FEED AXIS
21. CROSS PIN
22. COUPLING SLEEVE
23. COUPLING SPRING
24. COUPLING RETAINING RING

DETAIL OF MK VII A & MK VIIIA MOUNTINGS.

1. CARTRIDGE CHUTE
2. MAIN GUIDE WHEEL
3. BALANCE WEIGHT
4. BEARING PLATE
5. PEDESTAL
6. BALANCE WEIGHT ROLLERS
7. ROLLER GUIDE TUBE
8. THRUST BEARING PAD
9. METAL BUSH
10. CENTRE PIVOT
11. SUPPORTING RING
12. CARRIAGE EXTENSION
13. ROLLERS
14. CAM
15. ELEVATION HOUSING STOP
16. TRAINING HOUSING STOP
17. GREASE NIPPLES
18. GREASE CUP
19. ACCESS HOLE AND COVER
20. SHIELD
21. BALL RACE
22. PIVOT
23. TRAINING HOUSING BOLT
24. CARTRIDGE CASE COLLECTING BAG SECURING POSITION
25. CARRIAGE
26. ELEVATION LIMIT STOP
27. DEPRESSION LIMIT STOP
28. FORESIGHT
29. MAGAZINE
30. MAGAZINE CATCH LEVER
31. SHOULDER REST
32. HANDGRIP
33. CARTRIDGE CASE COLLECTING BAG

MARK VIIA MOUNTING.

UPDATED FROM B.R. 1086B, COASTAL FORCES GUNNERY HANDBOOK, VOLUME II.—GUNNERY EQUIPMENT AND MAINTENANCE, 1945.
DATED 22/6/45

DRAWINGS AND INFORMATION KINDLY SUPPLIED BY THE PATTERN ROOM ROYAL SMALL ARMS FACTORY, ENFIELD LOCK, MIDDLESEX.

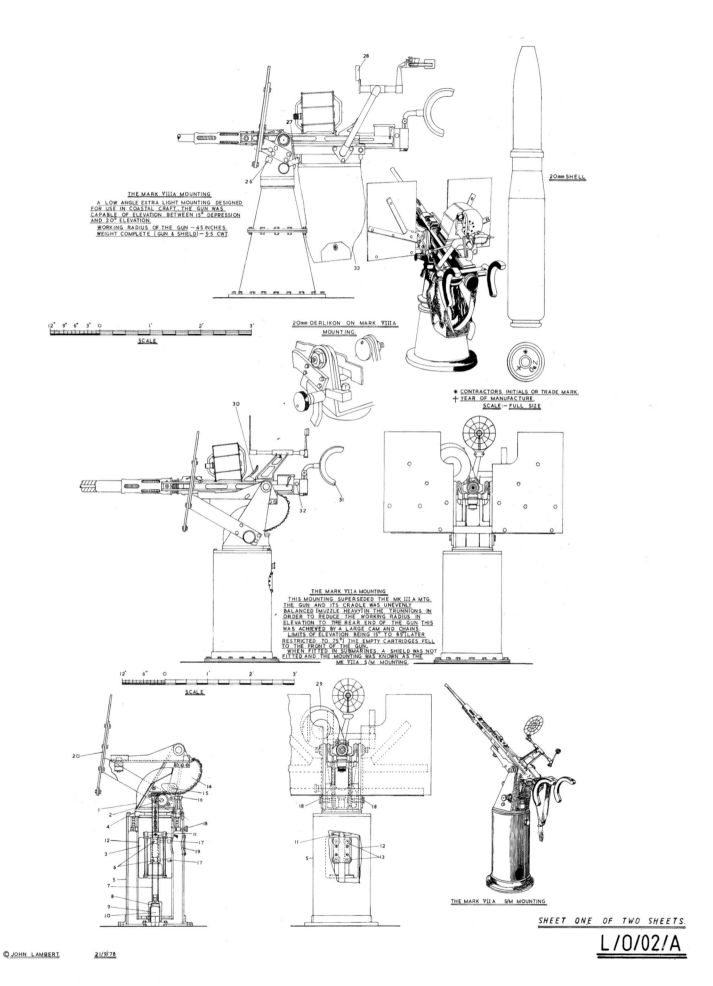

THE MARK VIIIA MOUNTING

A LOW ANGLE EXTRA LIGHT MOUNTING DESIGNED
FOR USE IN COASTAL CRAFT. THE GUN WAS
CAPABLE OF ELEVATION BETWEEN 15° DEPRESSION
AND 20° ELEVATION.
WORKING RADIUS OF THE GUN – 45 INCHES
WEIGHT COMPLETE (GUN & SHIELD) – 5·5 CWT.

20mm SHELL

20mm OERLIKON ON MARK VIIIA
MOUNTING.

12" 9" 6" 3" 0   1'   2'   3'
SCALE

* CONTRACTORS INITIALS OR TRADE MARK.
† YEAR OF MANUFACTURE.
        SCALE:– FULL SIZE

THE MARK VIIA MOUNTING

THIS MOUNTING SUPERSEDED THE MK IIIA MTG.
THE GUN AND ITS CRADLE WAS UNEVENLY
BALANCED (MUZZLE HEAVY) IN THE TRUNNIONS IN
ORDER TO REDUCE THE WORKING RADIUS IN
ELEVATION TO THE REAR END OF THE GUN. THIS
WAS ACHIEVED BY A LARGE CAM AND CHAINS.
LIMITS OF ELEVATION BEING 15° TO 85° (LATER
RESTRICTED TO 75°) THE EMPTY CARTRIDGES FELL
TO THE FRONT OF THE GUN.
WHEN FITTED IN SUBMARINES, A SHIELD WAS NOT
FITTED AND THE MOUNTING WAS KNOWN AS THE
MK VIIA S/M MOUNTING.

12" 6" 0   1'   2'   3'
SCALE

THE MARK VIIA S/M MOUNTING

SHEET ONE OF TWO SHEETS.

L/0/02/A

UPDATED 11/6/94.   © JOHN LAMBERT   21/9/78

XXVIII. L/O/22 3pdr Hotchkiss gun on the Mark I, I* 50° conversion, Mark V, VI, VI* mountings, 1942

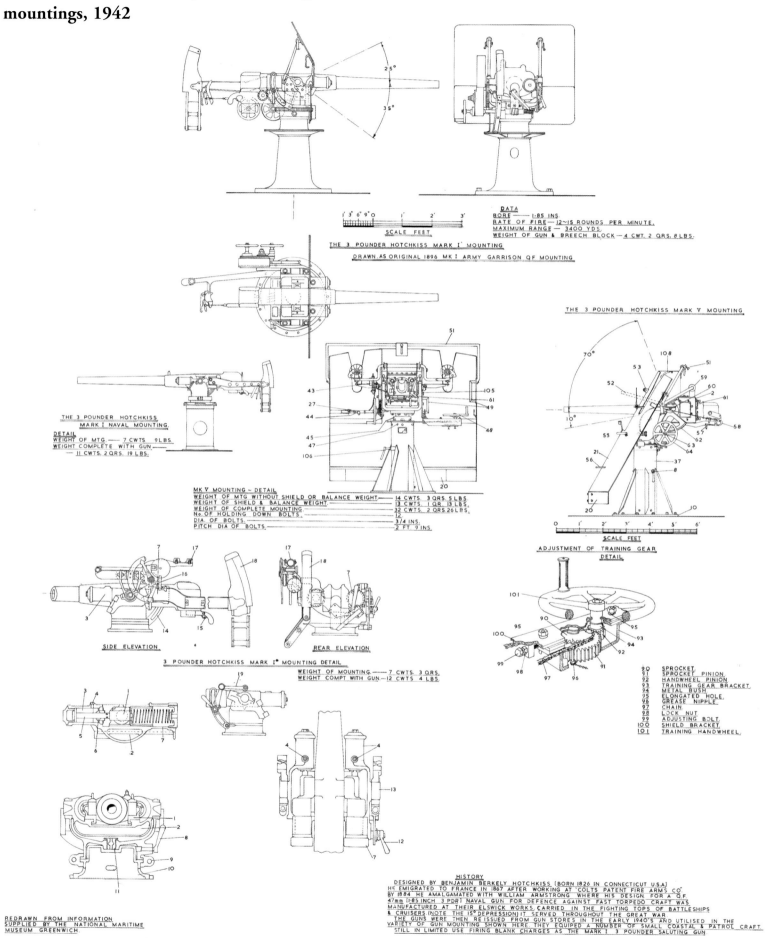

SCALE FEET

DATA
BORE —— 1·85 INS·
RATE OF FIRE — 12~15 ROUNDS PER MINUTE.
MAXIMUM RANGE — 3400 YDS.
WEIGHT OF GUN & BREECH BLOCK — 4 CWT. 2 QRS. 8 LBS.

THE 3 POUNDER HOTCHKISS MARK I MOUNTING
DRAWN, AS ORIGINAL 1896 MK I ARMY GARRISON QF MOUNTING

THE 3 POUNDER HOTCHKISS MARK V MOUNTING

THE 3 POUNDER HOTCHKISS
MARK I NAVAL MOUNTING.
DETAIL
WEIGHT OF MTG. —— 7 CWTS. 9 LBS.
WEIGHT COMPLETE WITH GUN ——
— 11 CWTS. 2 QRS. 19 LBS.

MK V MOUNTING ~ DETAIL
WEIGHT OF MTG WITHOUT SHIELD OR BALANCE WEIGHT —— 14 CWTS. 3 QRS. 5 LBS.
WEIGHT OF SHIELD & BALANCE WEIGHT. —— 13 CWTS. 1 QR. 13 LBS.
WEIGHT OF COMPLETE MOUNTING —— 32 CWTS. 2 QRS 26 LBS.
No. OF HOLDING DOWN BOLTS. —— 12
DIA. OF BOLTS. —— 3/4 INS.
PITCH DIA OF BOLTS —— 2 FT 9 INS

ADJUSTMENT OF TRAINING GEAR
DETAIL

SCALE FEET

SIDE ELEVATION

REAR ELEVATION

3 POUNDER HOTCHKISS MARK I* MOUNTING DETAIL
WEIGHT OF MOUNTING. —— 7 CWTS. 3 QRS.
WEIGHT COMPT WITH GUN.— 12 CWTS 4 LBS.

90	SPROCKET.
91	SPROCKET PINION.
92	HANDWHEEL PINION
93	TRAINING GEAR BRACKET.
94	METAL BUSH
95	ELONGATED HOLE.
96	GREASE NIPPLE.
97	CHAIN.
98	LOCK NUT
99	ADJUSTING BOLT.
100	SHIELD BRACKET.
101	TRAINING HANDWHEEL.

HISTORY
DESIGNED BY BENJAMIN BERKELY HOTCHKISS (BORN 1826 IN CONNECTICUT U.S.A.)
HE EMIGRATED TO FRANCE IN 1867 AFTER WORKING AT 'COLTS PATENT FIRE ARMS CO'.
BY 1884 HE AMALGAMATED WITH WILLIAM ARMSTRONG WHERE HIS DESIGN FOR A Q.F.
47mm (1·85 INCH 3 PDR) NAVAL GUN FOR DEFENCE AGAINST FAST TORPEDO CRAFT WAS
MANUFACTURED AT THEIR ELSWICK WORKS, CARRIED IN THE FIGHTING TOPS OF BATTLESHIPS
& CRUISERS (NOTE THE 15° DEPRESSION) IT SERVED THROUGHOUT THE GREAT WAR.
THE GUNS WERE THEN RE ISSUED FROM GUN STORES IN THE EARLY 1940'S AND UTILISED IN THE
VARIETY OF GUN MOUNTING SHOWN HERE THEY EQUIPED A NUMBER OF SMALL COASTAL & PATROL CRAFT
STILL IN LIMITED USE FIRING BLANK CHARGES AS THE MARK I 3 POUNDER SALUTING GUN

REDRAWN FROM INFORMATION
SUPPLIED BY THE NATIONAL MARITIME
MUSEUM GREENWICH.

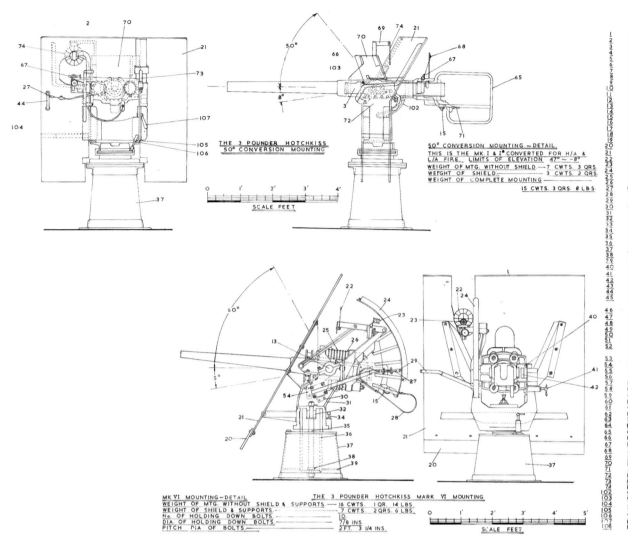

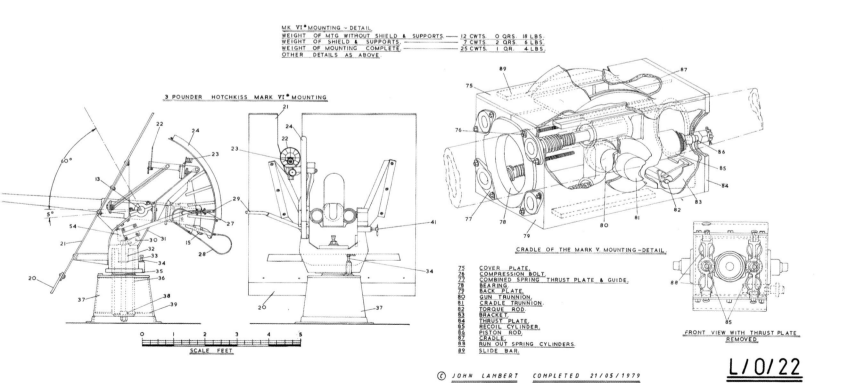

THE 3 POUNDER HOTCHKISS 50° CONVERSION MOUNTING

SCALE FEET

50° CONVERSION MOUNTING ~ DETAIL.
THIS IS THE MK. I & I* CONVERTED FOR H/A & L/A FIRE. LIMITS OF ELEVATION 47° ~ -8°
WEIGHT OF MTG. WITHOUT SHIELD ——— 7 CWTS. 3 QRS.
WEIGHT OF SHIELD ——————————— 3 CWTS. 2 QRS.
WEIGHT OF COMPLETE MOUNTING

15 CWTS. 3 QRS. 8 LBS.

MK VI MOUNTING ~ DETAIL
WEIGHT OF MTG. WITHOUT SHIELD & SUPPORTS.——— 16 CWTS. 1 QR. 14 LBS.
WEIGHT OF SHIELD & SUPPORTS.——————————— 7 CWTS. 2 QRS. 6 LBS.
No. OF HOLDING DOWN BOLTS ——————————————— 10.
DIA OF HOLDING DOWN BOLTS ——————————————— 7/8 INS
PITCH DIA OF BOLTS.——————————————————————— 2FT. 3 1/4 INS.

THE 3 POUNDER HOTCHKISS MARK VI MOUNTING

SCALE FEET

MK VI* MOUNTING ~ DETAIL
WEIGHT OF MTG WITHOUT SHIELD & SUPPORTS.——— 12 CWTS. 0 QRS. 18 LBS.
WEIGHT OF SHIELD & SUPPORTS.——————————————— 7 CWTS. 2 QRS. 6 LBS.
WEIGHT OF MOUNTING COMPLETE.——————————————— 25 CWTS. 1 QR. 4 LBS.
OTHER DETAILS AS ABOVE.

3 POUNDER HOTCHKISS MARK VI* MOUNTING

SCALE FEET

GUN MOUNTINGS DETAIL

1	TRUNNION BOX.
2	CRADLE.
3	RECOIL CYLINDER.
4	FILLING PLUG.
5	PISTON ROD.
6	STUFFING BOX.
7	SPRING CYLINDER.
8	TRAINING CLAMP.
9	CLIP RING.
10	BASE PLATE.
11	PIVOT BOLT.
12	ELEVATING CLAMP.
13	TRUNNION CAP.
14	ELEVATION CLAMP ARC.
15	TRIGGER.
16	RANGE HANDWHEEL.
17	TELESCOPE HOLDER.
18	SHOULDER PIECE.
19	AUTOMATIC BRAKE.
20	BALANCE WEIGHT.
21	SHIELD.
22	FORESIGHT.
23	BACKSIGHT.
24	ELEVATING ARM.
25	METAL WASHERS.
26	RUBBER BUSHES.
27	FIRING LEVER.
28	ARENS CONTROL.
29	TRAINING ARM.
30	ELEVATION STOP.
31	REVOLVING BRACKET.
32	RUBBER BUSH.
33	WASHER.
34	TRAINING LOCKING BOLT.
35	CENTRE PIVOT.
36	CENTRE TUBE.
37	PEDESTAL.
38	GUNMETAL THRUST WASHER.
39	SUPPORTING PLATE.
40	SLIDING CRADLE.
41	ELEVATION LOCKING BOLT.
42	RECOIL GUIDES.
43	RANGE SCALE.
44	TRAINING HANDLE.
45	BEARING PROTECTION & RETAINING PLATE.
46	CENTRE COLUMN.
47	LUBRICATOR TOP PEDESTAL BEARING.
48	TRAINING HANDWHEEL.
49	TRAINING HANDLES.
50	TRAINING GEAR.
51	SUPPORT FOR WEATHERPROOF HOOD.
52	SUPPORT IN POSITION FOR CARRYING WEATHERPROOF HOOD.
53	LIFTING EYE BOLTS.
54	DEPRESSION STOP.
55	LASHING BAR.
56	STEP.
57	RECOCKING HANDLE.
58	FIRING GEAR.
59	CROSS SHAFT FOR SIGHTING GEAR.
60	LUBRICATOR FOR FIRING CABLE.
61	CRANK HANDLE.
62	ELEVATING ARC.
63	ELEVATING IDLER PINION.
64	ELEVATING HANDWHEEL.
65	OPERATING ARM.
66	L/A FORESIGHT.
67	L/A BACKSIGHT.
68	APERTURE EYESHOOTING BACK SIGHT.
69	SIGHT BRACKET.
70	MANTLET PLATE.
71	CONNECTION FOR AREN DRIVE.
72	REVOLVING BRACKET.
73	REAR SHIELD STAY.
74	EYESHOOTING FORESIGHT.
102	CLAMPING ARC.
103	CLAMPING RING & STAY.
104	AREN DRIVE.
105	TRUNNION BRACKET.
106	TRAINING CLAMP.
107	ELEVATING CLAMPING HANDLE.
108	ELEVATION STOP.

CRADLE OF THE MARK V. MOUNTING ~ DETAIL.

75	COVER PLATE.
76	COMPRESSION BOLT.
77	COMBINED SPRING THRUST PLATE & GUIDE.
78	BEARING.
79	BACK PLATE.
80	GUN TRUNNION.
81	CRADLE TRUNNION.
82	TORQUE ROD.
83	BRACKET.
84	THRUST PLATE.
85	RECOIL CYLINDER.
86	PISTON ROD.
87	CRADLE.
88	RUN OUT SPRING CYLINDERS.
89	SLIDE BAR.

FRONT VIEW WITH THRUST PLATE REMOVED

© JOHN LAMBERT COMPLETED 21/05/1979

L/0/22

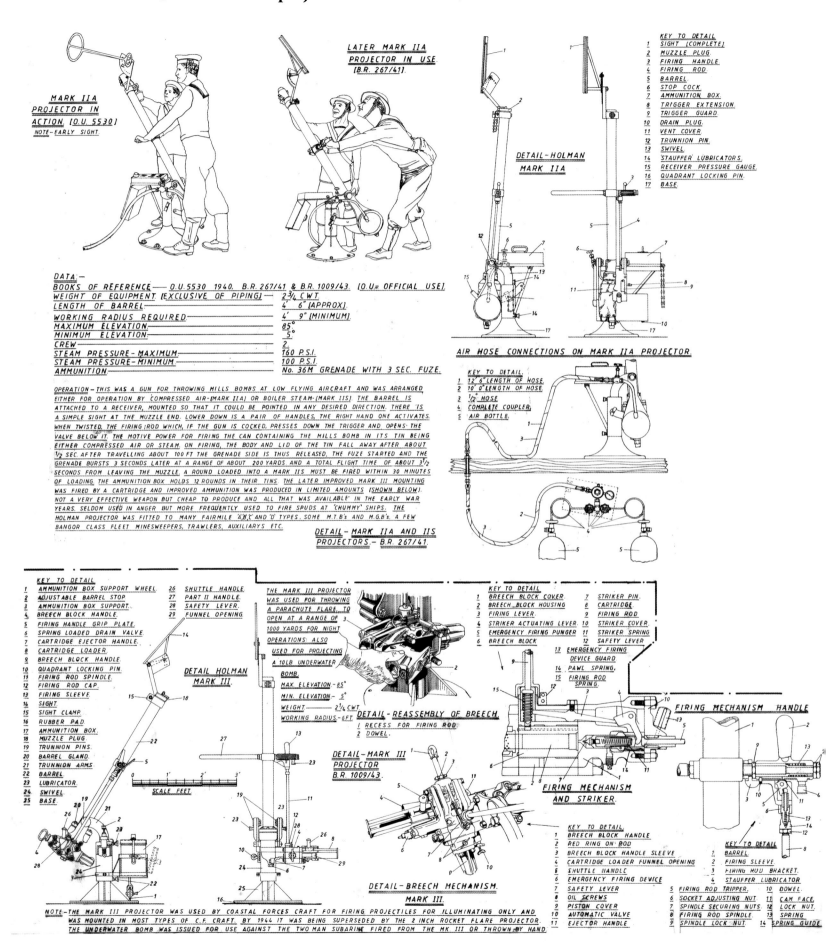

MARK IIA PROJECTOR IN ACTION. [O.U. 5530]
NOTE-EARLY SIGHT.

LATER MARK IIA PROJECTOR IN USE. [B.R. 267/41].

DETAIL-HOLMAN MARK IIA.

KEY TO DETAIL.
1 SIGHT [COMPLETE]
2 MUZZLE PLUG
3 FIRING HANDLE
4 FIRING ROD.
5 BARREL.
6 STOP COCK.
7 AMMUNITION BOX.
8 TRIGGER EXTENSION.
9 TRIGGER GUARD.
10 DRAIN PLUG.
11 VENT COVER.
12 TRUNNION PIN.
13 SWIVEL.
14 'STAUFFER' LUBRICATORS.
15 RECEIVER PRESSURE GAUGE
16 QUADRANT LOCKING PIN.
17 BASE.

DATA:-
BOOKS OF REFERENCE — O.U. 5530 1940, B.R. 267/41 & B.R. 1009/43. [O.U.= OFFICIAL USE].
WEIGHT OF EQUIPMENT. [EXCLUSIVE OF PIPING] — $2\frac{3}{4}$ CWT.
LENGTH OF BARREL — 4' 6" [APPROX].
WORKING RADIUS REQUIRED — 4' 9" [MINIMUM].
MAXIMUM ELEVATION. — 85°
MINIMUM ELEVATION. — 5°
CREW — 2
STEAM PRESSURE - MAXIMUM — 160 P.S.I.
STEAM PRESSURE - MINIMUM — 100 P.S.I.
AMMUNITION — No. 36M GRENADE WITH 3 SEC. FUZE.

OPERATION - THIS WAS A GUN FOR THROWING MILLS BOMBS AT LOW FLYING AIRCRAFT AND WAS ARRANGED EITHER FOR OPERATION BY COMPRESSED AIR-[MARK IIA] OR BOILER STEAM-[MARK IIS]. THE BARREL IS ATTACHED TO A RECEIVER, MOUNTED SO THAT IT COULD BE POINTED IN ANY DESIRED DIRECTION. THERE IS A SIMPLE SIGHT AT THE MUZZLE END. LOWER DOWN IS A PAIR OF HANDLES, THE RIGHT HAND ONE ACTIVATES. WHEN TWISTED, THE FIRING ROD WHICH, IF THE GUN IS COCKED, PRESSES DOWN THE TRIGGER AND OPENS THE VALVE BELOW IT. THE MOTIVE POWER FOR FIRING THE CAN CONTAINING THE MILLS BOMB IN ITS TIN BEING EITHER COMPRESSED AIR OR STEAM. ON FIRING, THE BODY AND LID OF THE TIN FALL AWAY AFTER ABOUT $\frac{1}{2}$ SEC. AFTER TRAVELLING ABOUT 100 FT THE GRENADE SIDE IS THUS RELEASED, THE FUZE STARTED AND THE GRENADE BURSTS 3 SECONDS LATER AT A RANGE OF ABOUT 200 YARDS AND A TOTAL FLIGHT TIME OF ABOUT $3\frac{1}{2}$ SECONDS FROM LEAVING THE MUZZLE. A ROUND LOADED INTO A MARK IIS MUST BE FIRED WITHIN 30 MINUTES OF LOADING. THE AMMUNITION BOX HOLDS 12 ROUNDS IN THEIR TINS. THE LATER IMPROVED MARK III MOUNTING WAS FIRED BY A CARTRIDGE AND IMPROVED AMMUNITION WAS PRODUCED IN LIMITED AMOUNTS [SHOWN BELOW]. NOT A VERY EFFECTIVE WEAPON BUT CHEAP TO PRODUCE AND ALL THAT WAS AVAILABLE IN THE EARLY WAR YEARS. SELDOM USED IN ANGER BUT MORE FREQUENTLY USED TO FIRE SPUDS AT 'CHUMMY' SHIPS. THE HOLMAN PROJECTOR WAS FITTED TO MANY FAIRMILE 'A','B','C' AND 'D' TYPES. SOME M.T.B's AND M.G.B's. A FEW BANGOR CLASS FLEET MINESWEEPERS, TRAWLERS, AUXILIARYS ETC.

DETAIL - MARK IIA AND IIS PROJECTORS.- B.R. 267/41.

AIR HOSE CONNECTIONS ON MARK IIA PROJECTOR.

KEY TO DETAIL.
1 12' 6" LENGTH OF HOSE
2 10' 0" LENGTH OF HOSE
3 $\frac{1}{2}$" HOSE
4 COMPLETE COUPLER.
5 AIR BOTTLE.

KEY TO DETAIL.
1 AMMUNITION BOX SUPPORT WHEEL.
2 ADJUSTABLE BARREL STOP
3 AMMUNITION BOX SUPPORT.
4 BREECH BLOCK HANDLE.
5 FIRING HANDLE GRIP PLATE.
6 SPRING LOADED DRAIN VALVE.
7 CARTRIDGE EJECTOR HANDLE.
8 CARTRIDGE LOADER
9 BREECH BLOCK HANDLE.
10 QUADRANT LOCKING PIN.
11 FIRING ROD SPINDLE.
12 FIRING ROD CAP.
13 FIRING SLEEVE.
14 SIGHT.
15 SIGHT CLAMP.
16 RUBBER PAD.
17 AMMUNITION BOX.
18 MUZZLE PLUG.
19 TRUNNION PINS.
20 BARREL GLAND.
21 TRUNNION ARMS.
22 BARREL.
23 LUBRICATOR.
24 SWIVEL.
25 BASE.
26 SHUTTLE HANDLE.
27 PART II HANDLE.
28 SAFETY LEVER.
29 FUNNEL OPENING.

DETAIL HOLMAN MARK III.

THE MARK III PROJECTOR WAS USED FOR THROWING A PARACHUTE FLARE, TO OPEN AT A RANGE OF 1000 YARDS FOR NIGHT OPERATIONS: ALSO USED FOR PROJECTING A 10LB UNDERWATER BOMB.
MAX. ELEVATION-85°
MIN. ELEVATION-5°
WEIGHT — $2\frac{1}{4}$ CWT
WORKING RADIUS-6FT.

SCALE FEET

DETAIL-MARK III PROJECTOR B.R. 1009/43.

KEY TO DETAIL.
1 BREECH BLOCK COVER.
2 BREECH BLOCK HOUSING.
3 FIRING LEVER.
4 STRIKER ACTUATING LEVER.
5 EMERGENCY FIRING PLUNGER.
6 BREECH BLOCK.
7 STRIKER PIN.
8 CARTRIDGE.
9 FIRING ROD.
10 STRIKER COVER.
11 STRIKER SPRING.
12 SAFETY LEVER.
13 EMERGENCY FIRING DEVICE GUARD.
14 PAWL SPRING.
15 FIRING ROD SPRING.

DETAIL - REASSEMBLY OF BREECH.
1 RECESS FOR FIRING ROD
2 DOWEL.

FIRING MECHANISM AND STRIKER.

FIRING MECHANISM HANDLE

DETAIL-BREECH MECHANISM.
MARK III.

KEY TO DETAIL.
1 BREECH BLOCK HANDLE
2 RED RING ON ROD
3 BREECH BLOCK HANDLE SLEEVE
4 CARTRIDGE LOADER FUNNEL OPENING
5 SHUTTLE HANDLE
6 EMERGENCY FIRING DEVICE
7 SAFETY LEVER
8 OIL SCREWS
9 PISTON COVER
10 AUTOMATIC VALVE
11 EJECTOR HANDLE

KEY TO DETAIL.
1 BARREL.
2 FIRING SLEEVE.
3 FIRING ROD BRACKET
4 STAUFFER LUBRICATOR
5 FIRING ROD TRIPPER.
6 SOCKET ADJUSTING NUT.
7 SPINDLE SECURING NUTS.
8 FIRING ROD SPINDLE.
9 SPINDLE LOCK NUT.
10 DOWEL.
11 CAM FACE.
12 LOCK NUT.
13 SPRING
14 SPRING GUIDE

NOTE-THE MARK III PROJECTOR WAS USED BY COASTAL FORCES CRAFT FOR FIRING PROJECTILES FOR ILLUMINATING ONLY AND WAS MOUNTED IN MOST TYPES OF C.F. CRAFT. BY 1944 IT WAS BEING SUPERSEDED BY THE 2 INCH ROCKET FLARE PROJECTOR. THE UNDERWATER BOMB WAS ISSUED FOR USE AGAINST THE TWO MAN SUBARINE FIRED FROM THE MK III OR THROWN BY HAND.

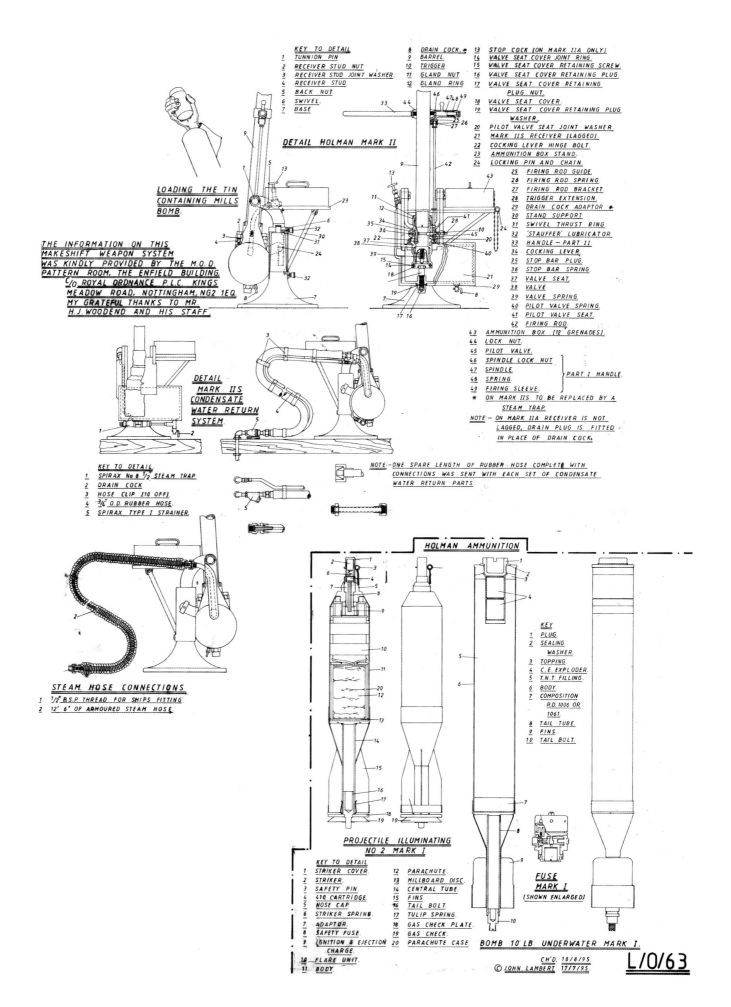

KEY TO DETAIL

1	TUNNION PIN
2	RECEIVER STUD NUT
3	RECEIVER STUD JOINT WASHER
4	RECEIVER STUD
5	BACK NUT
6	SWIVEL
7	BASE

8	DRAIN COCK.✦
9	BARREL.
10	TRIGGER
11	GLAND NUT
12	GLAND RING

DETAIL HOLMAN MARK II

LOADING THE TIN
CONTAINING MILLS
BOMB.

THE INFORMATION ON THIS
MAKESHIFT WEAPON SYSTEM
WAS KINDLY PROVIDED BY THE M.O.D.
PATTERN ROOM, THE ENFIELD BUILDING.
C/O ROYAL ORDNANCE P.L.C. KINGS
MEADOW ROAD, NOTTINGHAM, NG2 1EQ.
MY GRATEFUL THANKS TO MR.
H.J. WOODEND AND HIS STAFF.

13	STOP COCK (ON MARK IIA ONLY)
14	VALVE SEAT COVER JOINT RING
15	VALVE SEAT COVER RETAINING SCREW.
16	VALVE SEAT COVER RETAINING PLUG.
17	VALVE SEAT COVER RETAINING PLUG NUT.
18	VALVE SEAT COVER.
19	VALVE SEAT COVER RETAINING PLUG WASHER.
20	PILOT VALVE SEAT JOINT WASHER.
21	MARK IIS RECEIVER (LAGGED).
22	COCKING LEVER HINGE BOLT.
23	AMMUNITION BOX STAND.
24	LOCKING PIN AND CHAIN.
25	FIRING ROD GUIDE
26	FIRING ROD SPRING.
27	FIRING ROD BRACKET.
28	TRIGGER EXTENSION.
29	DRAIN COCK ADAPTOR ✱
30	STAND SUPPORT
31	SWIVEL THRUST RING
32	'STAUFFER' LUBRICATOR
33	HANDLE — PART II
34	COCKING LEVER.
35	STOP BAR PLUG.
36	STOP BAR SPRING.
37	VALVE SEAT.
38	VALVE.
39	VALVE SPRING.
40	PILOT VALVE SPRING.
41	PILOT VALVE SEAT.
42	FIRING ROD.
43	AMMUNITION BOX (12 GRENADES).
44	LOCK NUT.
45	PILOT VALVE.
46	SPINDLE LOCK NUT
47	SPINDLE
48	SPRING
49	FIRING SLEEVE

PART I HANDLE.

✱ ON MARK IIS TO BE REPLACED BY A
STEAM TRAP.

NOTE:- ON MARK IIA RECEIVER IS NOT
LAGGED, DRAIN PLUG IS FITTED
IN PLACE OF DRAIN COCK.

DETAIL
MARK IIS
CONDENSATE
WATER RETURN
SYSTEM.

NOTE:- ONE SPARE LENGTH OF RUBBER HOSE COMPLETE WITH
CONNECTIONS WAS SENT WITH EACH SET OF CONDENSATE
WATER RETURN PARTS.

KEY TO DETAIL

1	SPIRAX No 8 ½" STEAM TRAP
2	DRAIN COCK
3	HOSE CLIP (10 OFF)
4	³/₄" O.D. RUBBER HOSE.
5	SPIRAX TYPE I STRAINER.

STEAM HOSE CONNECTIONS

1	½" B.S.P. THREAD FOR SHIPS FITTING
2	12' 6" OF ARMOURED STEAM HOSE.

HOLMAN AMMUNITION

PROJECTILE ILLUMINATING
NO 2 MARK I

KEY TO DETAIL

1	STRIKER COVER.	12	PARACHUTE.
2	STRIKER	13	MILLBOARD DISC.
3	SAFETY PIN	14	CENTRAL TUBE.
4	410 CARTRIDGE	15	FINS.
5	NOSE CAP.	16	TAIL BOLT.
6	STRIKER SPRING.	17	TULIP SPRING.
7	ADAPTOR	18	GAS CHECK PLATE.
8	SAFETY FUSE.	19	GAS CHECK.
9	IGNITION & EJECTION CHARGE.	20	PARACHUTE CASE.
10	FLARE UNIT.		
11	BODY.		

KEY

1	PLUG
2	SEALING WASHER.
3	TOPPING.
4	C.E. EXPLODER.
5	T.N.T. FILLING.
6	BODY.
7	COMPOSITION R.D. 1006 OR 1061.
8	TAIL TUBE.
9	FINS.
10	TAIL BOLT.

FUSE
MARK I
(SHOWN ENLARGED)

BOMB 10 LB UNDERWATER MARK I.

CH'D. 18/8/95
© JOHN LAMBERT 17/7/95

L/0/63

XXX. The 14ft 6in Admiralty drifter type boat

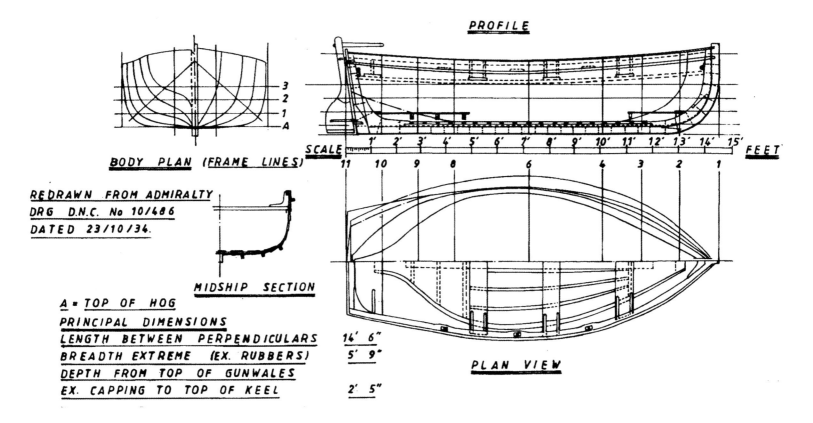

DETAIL— THE 14' 6" DRIFTER TYPE BOAT

PROFILE

BODY PLAN (FRAME LINES)

SCALE

1' 2' 3' 4' 5' 6' 7' 8' 9' 10' 11' 12' 13' 14' 15'   FEET

11   10   9   8   6   4   3   2   1

REDRAWN FROM ADMIRALTY
DRG D.N.C. No 10/486
DATED 23/10/34.

MIDSHIP SECTION

A = TOP OF HOG
PRINCIPAL DIMENSIONS
LENGTH BETWEEN PERPENDICULARS   14' 6"
BREADTH EXTREME (EX. RUBBERS)   5' 9"
DEPTH FROM TOP OF GUNWALES
EX. CAPPING TO TOP OF KEEL   2' 5"

PLAN VIEW

Appendices

Appendix 1:
Types of Mine in 1914

At the start of the First World War, there were effectively three types of mine, all detonated by electrical, chemical, direct or mechanical methods.

Moored harbour defence mines could be fired from a shore installation by triggering an electric current when an enemy vessel was deemed to be close enough to the mine or mines to be damaged. Many British ports had such devices installed, oddly under the management of the Royal Engineers.

Contact mines had one or more horns (the Hertz horn) which required contact by a vessel to cause an explosion. These horns (actually hollow lead protuberances) studded the upper half of the mine, each containing a glass vial filled with sulphuric acid. When a ship's hull crushed the metal horn, it cracked the vial inside it, allowing the acid to run down a tube and into a lead-acid battery which until then had contained no acid electrolyte. This caused an electrical current to flow from the battery, which detonated the explosive. This was the type of mine with which the Germans started the war.

Mechanical mines used an arm-operated firing mechanism which moved differentially to the body of the mine when the mine was disturbed by a vessel hitting it.

Appendix 2:
An Example of the Text of a 1914 T-124 Form

The several persons whose names are hereunto subscribed, being British subjects, and whose descriptions are set forth against their signatures, hereby agree with [name of RN officer] for and on behalf of the Lords Commissioners of the Admiralty to serve on board the said ship in the several capacities expressed against their respective names for any period not exceeding six months, but the Agreement to be terminable at a port in the United Kingdom after three months on either party giving seven days' notice.

(1.) The several persons whose names are hereunto subscribed agree that they shall be subject to the Naval Discipline Act:

(2.) Any offence committed by any such person shall be tried and punished as the like offence might be tried and punished if committed by any person in or belonging to His Majesty's Navy, and borne on the books of any of His Majesty's ships in commission:

(3.) Every such offender who is to be tried by Court-martial shall be placed under all necessary restraint until he can be tried by Court-martial:

(4.) On application made to the Lords of the Admiralty, or to the Commander-in-Chief, or senior officer of any of His Majesty's ships or vessels of war abroad authorised to assemble and hold Courts-martial, the Lords of the Admiralty, Commander-in-Chief, or senior officer (as the case may be) shall assemble and hold a Court-martial for the trial of the offender:

(5.) The officer commanding shall have the same power in respect of all other persons borne on the books or for the time being on board the same, as the officer commanding one of His Majesty's ships has for the being in respect of the officers and crew thereof or other persons on board the same:

(6.) The Naval Commander-in-Chief and senior Naval Officer in His Majesty's Service shall have the same powers over the officers and crew as if they have for the time being over the officers and crew of any of His Majesty's ships.

It is further agreed by the said [name of RN officer] provisions and clothing,* and allowances in connection therewith, will be issued according to the Regulations for H M Naval Service, and that in the event of death or injury caused by acts of the enemy pensions or gratuities in accordance with the Regulations printed on the last page hereof.

In witness whereof the same parties have subscribed their names on the other side hereof on the day specified against their respective signatures.

* Clothing is supplied to crews of Armed Merchant Cruisers only. In other ships, no uniform is required, and each person must provide his own clothes.

Appendix 3:
Admiralty Trawlers
1914–1918

Class	Number
Owned pre-war	16
Military	10
Ex-Portuguese	9
Strath	89
Castle	127
Mersey	69
Canadian *Castle*	60
Other Canadian	12
Indian	15
Prize	29
Axe	17
Total	453

Source: Dittmar and Colledge, *British Warships*, pp154–76

Appendix 4:
Admiralty Drifters
1914–1918

Type	Number
Wood	92
Canadian wood	100
Steel	126
Total	318

Source: Dittmar and Colledge, *British Warships*, pp220–31

Appendix 5:
Strath-, *Mersey-* and *Castle*-class Trawlers

	Strath	*Castle*	*Mersey*	**Total**	
Delivered by 11 Nov 1918	89	127	69	285	
Unarmed, completed after the Armistice	14	18	8	40	
Completed as fishing boats for onward sale	46	52	35	133	
Cancelled	18	20	44	82	
				540	

Source: Dittmar and Colledge, *British Warships*, pp220–31

Appendix 6:
Total Trawler and Drifter Losses by Cause, 1914–1918

	action	U-boat	mine	fire	collision	wrecked	various	unknown	total
Adm trawlers	1	3	4	0	5	2	1	2	18
Hired trawlers	5	14	140	1	35	34	9	8	246
Hired drifters	32	34	32	3	33	11	8	8	130

Source: *British Vessels Lost at Sea*, Section 1, p29

Appendix 7:
Admiralty-built Trawlers in the Second World War

Class	Year of launch	Tonnage	Number	Notes
WW1 vintage				
Axe	1916	390	4	
Strath	1916	311	1	
Castle	1917	360	3	
Mersey	1917/18	438	14	
Armentières	1917/18	440	3	
1935 onwards				
Gem/Tree	mixed	various	41	
Basset/Mastiff	1935/38	460/520	2	
Tree	1939/40	530	20	
Dance	1940/41	530	20	
Shakespearian	1940/41	545	12	
Isles	1940–3	545	145	16 Canadian built
Admiralty type (RNZN)	1941	600	3	all RNZN
Portuguese	1941/42	525	12	6 wooden hull, 6 metal, diesel engines
Brazilian	1942	680	6	immediately transferred to the Brazilian navy
Castle (RNZN)	1941–3	447	17	17 ordered, 3 cancelled, all RNZN
Hill	1941	750	8	
Fish	1941–43	670	10	
Round Table	1941–43	440	8	
Military	1942–44	750	9	

RNZN = Royal New Zealand Navy   Total number Admiralty-built trawlers Second World War: 338. Excludes forty-eight ordered for the Royal Indian Navy, of which twenty-five cancelled and four lost incomplete.

Appendix 8:
Trawlers and Drifters Sunk at Dunkirk

Name	Flag	Type
Argyllshire	RN	trawler
Blackburn Rovers	RN	trawler
Calvi	RN	trawler
Comfort	RN	drifter
Denis Papin	French	trawler
Emile Deschamps	French	trawler
Fairbreeze	RN	drifter
Girl Pamela	RN	drifter
Marguerite Rose	French	trawler
Ocean Lassie	RN	drifter
Ocean Reward	RN	drifter
Polly Johnson	RN	trawler
St Achilleus	RN	trawler
Stella Dorado	RN	trawler
Thomas Bartlett	RN	trawler
Thuringia	RN	trawler
Westella	RN	trawler

Appendix 9:
Trawlers Sent to Aid the US Navy in 1942

Trawler name	Registered	Notes
Le Tiger	Grimsby	
Coventry City	Do	
Hertfordshire	Do	
Norwich City,	Do	
Wellard	Do	
Bedfordshire	Do	sunk
Northern Chief	London but Grimsby based	German-built
Northern Dawn	Do	German-built
Northern Duke	Do	German-built
Northern Princess	Do	German-built, sunk
Northern Reward	Do	German-built
Arctic Explorer	Hull	
Cape Warwick	Do	
Kingston Ceylonite	Do	sunk
Lady Elsa	Do	
Pentland Firth	Do	sunk
St Cathan	Do	sunk
St Loman	Do	
St Zeno	Do	see plan XXIII
Stella Polaris	Do	
Senateur Duhamel	French	sunk
Whalers		
Wastwater		'Lake'-class
Buttermere		'Lake'-class

Source: Author's research

Sources

The following abbreviations will be used:

Institutions
IWM: Imperial War Museum, London
NA: National Archives, Kew
CAC: Churchill Archive, Churchill College, Cambridge
NMRN: National Museum of the Royal Navy, Portsmouth

Books
BW: Dittmar and Colledge, *British Warships 1914–1918*
CITNC: Kerslake, *Coxswain in the Northern Convoys*
FTDTSF:Marder, *From the Dreadnought to Scapa Flow*
WWW2:Lenton and Colledge, *Warships of World War II*

It is the convention that page numbers be given for citations. This is not always possible in the modern world. Some digitised documents lack page numbering, and some archives hold unnumbered single or multiple sheets in bundles under one reference or none at all. Thus, page numbers will be given where possible but the reader will understand that they are not always available or, indeed, necessary.

1
1. Fayle, *Seaborne Trade*, vol III, p 469
2. Daniel Defoe, *A tour thro' the whole island of Great Britain, divided into circuits or journies*, Letter 1, Pt 3
3. Murray, *Herring Tales* p 92
4. Robinson, *Fishermen*, pp11, 116
5. Ibid, p117
6. Book title, Margerison, see bibliography
7. Lambert, *Admirals*, p312
8. Crossley, *The Hidden Threat*, p111
9. Lambert, *Planning Armageddon*, p53
10. Goldrick, *Before Jutland*, p60
11. Bywater, *Strange Intelligence*, p41
12. Smith, *Into the Minefields*, p7
13. Kane report, ADM 231/10, NA
14. Bennett, *Charlie B*, p140
15. Marder, *FTDTSF*, vol I, p332
16. Ibid
17. GBR/0014/Hood, 6–6, CAC
18. DRAX1/11, CAC
19. Ibid

2
1. Scott, *Fifty Years in the Royal Navy*, p202
2. Dawson, *Gone for a Sailor*, pp131,133
3. ADM 186/604, NA
4. Ibid
5. Ibid
6. Ibid
7. DRAX 1/11,CAC
8. Ibid
9. D'Enno, *Fishermen Against the Kaiser*, p45
10. *Fraserburgh Times*, 4 August 1914
11. D'Enno, *Fishermen Against the Kaiser*, p60
12. Taffrail, *Swept Channels*, p69
13. ADM 186/604, NA
14. CHAR 13/42/48, CAC
15. Taffrail, *Swept Channels*, p242, and data from BW

3
1. Campbell, *With the Corners Off*, p198
2. ADM 1/8402/420, NA
3. Author's estimate from BW
4. Ibid
5. Taffrail, *Swept Channels*, p292
6. Jellicoe, *The Crisis of the Naval War*, p191
7. Docs 13075, IWM
8. E g 25 April 1915 ADM 137/1049, NA

4
1. ADM 186/604, NA
2. ADM 186/382, NA
3. Ibid
4. DRAX 1/11, CAC
5. Friedman, *Fighting the Great War at Sea*, p346
6. ADM 186/604 p15, NA
7. ADM 196/52/17, NA
8. ADM 186/382, NA
9. ADM 186/604, NA
10. *British Vessels Lost at Sea*, Section 1, p29
11. Taffrail, *Swept Channels*, p17
12. Quoted in the *Falmouth Packet*, 5 Nov 2018
13. CARD 4/2/4–5, CAC
14. Marder, FTDTSF, vol II, p242
15. CARD, 4/2/4–5, CAC
16. Taffrail, *Swept Channels*, p146
17. Ibid, p148
18. Winton, *Cunningham*, p24
19. Taffrail, *Swept Channels*, p154
20. D'Enno, *Fishermen against the Kaiser*, p122

20. Scott, *Fifty Years in the Royal Navy*, p286
21. Winton, *Cunningham*, p24
22. Taffrail, *Swept Channels*, p16
23. ADM 186/604, NA

5
1. Scott, *Fifty Years in the Royal Navy*, p286
2. Ibid p287
3. Winton, *Cunningham*, p30
4. 12 August 1915, MSS 255/6/4, NMRN
5. MSS 255/6/5, NMRN
6. DRAX 1/12, CAC
7. Ibid
8. *London Gazette*, no 30909, 17 September 1918
9. Taffrail, *Endless Story*, p222
10. Ibid
11. DRAX 1/12, CAC
12. Friedman, *Fighting the Great War at Sea*, p292
13. ADM 53/59342, NA
14. Ibid
15. Taffrail, *Swept Channels*, p55
16. Ibid
17. Docs 10977, IWM
18. Ibid
19. Ibid
20. *London Gazette*, no 30536, 19 February 1918
21. *British Vessels Lost at Sea*, section 1, p29

6
1. MT 23/517/5, NA
2. MT 23/662/6, NA
3. Docs 2867, IWM
4. Roskill, *Naval Air Service*, vol I, p630
5. Docs 12146, IWM
6. Ibid
7. Ibid
8. Fayle, *Seaborne Trade*, vol III, p465
9. Newbolt, *Naval Operations*, vol V, pp21–4
10. ADM 53/59125, NA
11. Hansard, vol 101 (29 January 1918)
12. Re-quoted in *Fishing News*, 8 October 2015
13. *New York World*, March 1917
14. *Fishing Trades Gazette*, 21 October 1916
15. *Sea Breezes*, May 2008
16. CHAR 13/63/72, CAC
17. *British Vessels Lost at Sea*, Section 1
18. *London Gazette*, no 29211, 29 June 1915
19. ADM 178/27, NA
20. Ibid
21. Quotes from Dorothy Ramser, *Shields Gazette*, 21 August 2018

SOURCES

22. Robinson, *Fishermen*, p136
23. *British Vessels Lost at Sea*, Section 2, p163

7
1. Taffrail, *Swept Channels*, p60
2. D'Enno, *Fishermen Against the Kaiser*, p60
3. Ibid p61
4. Ibid
5. Taffrail, *Swept Channels*, p174
6. *Far Horizons*, Uni of Hull
7. Hansard, vol 107 (24 June 1918)
8. Robinson, *Fishermen*, p145
9. Taffrail, *Swept Channels*, p67
10. Docs 12146, IWM
11. Ibid
12. LIDDLE/WW1/RNMN/REC/015
13. *Spectator*, 13 January 1917
14. Taffrail, *Swept Channels*, p71
15. Ibid
16. ADM 53/47265, NA
17. From Coxon, *Dover during the Dark Days*, p137
18. LIDDLE/WW1/RNMN/REC/015
19. Hansard, HC Deb vol 107, col 1026 (26 June 1918)
20. Docs 12146, IWM

8
1. Bacon, *The Dover Patrol*, vol I, p182
2. Winton, *Victoria Cross at Sea*, p146
3. Third Supplement to the *London Gazette*, Tuesday, 28 August 1917
4. Winton, *Victoria Cross at Sea*, p146
5. *London Gazette*, no 30363, 2 November 1917
6. Hansard, HL Deb vol 26, cols 801–34 (29 October 1917)
7. *London Gazette*, no 29076, 16 February 1915
8. Boothby, *Spunyarn*, p196
9. Little, *Through Cloud and Sunshine*, p41
10. Hansard, HC Deb vol 80, cols 1401–46 (7 March 1916)
11. Hansard, HL Deb vol 26, cols 801–34 (29 October 1917)
12. Bacon, *The Dover Patrol*, vol II, p389
13. *BW*, pp177–213
14. ADM 116/3367, NA
15. *BW*, p232–262
16. *Eastern Evening News*, 1 May 1920
17. Ibid
18. *British Vessels Lost at Sea*, Section 1, p28
19. Robinson, *Fishermen*, p179

9
1. *Statement of the First Lord of the Admiralty, Explanatory of the Navy Estimates, 1919–1920*
2. ADM 116/3600, NA
3. ADM 167/100, NA
4. Taffrail, *Swept Channels*, p215
5. ADM 116/3367, NA

6. Ibid
7. Ibid
8. Ibid
9. Roskill, *Naval Policy Between the Wars*, vol II, p228
10. Friedman, *British Naval Weapons of World War Two*, vol II, p10
11. Roskill, *Naval Policy between the Wars*, vol II, p228

10
1. Kerslake, *CITNC*, p1
2. Conversation with Leo Whisstock, secretary of the RNPSA
3. Featherbe, *Churchill's Pirates*, p12
4. DKNS III 1/2, CAC
5. Ibid
6. Ibid
7. Thwaites, *Atlantic Odyssey*, p5
8. *London Gazette*, 1 January 1917
9. Hansard, vol 355 (6 December 1939)
10. Author's estimate from *WWW2*
11. *WWW2*, p589
12. Featherbe, *Churchill's Pirates*, p12

11
1. Roskill, *The Navy at War*, p27
2. Warwick, *Really Not Required*, p110
3. *British Vessels Lost at Sea*, Section 2, p40

12
1. ADM 116/4446, NA
2. Kerslake, *CITNC*, p48
3. Supplement to the *London Gazette*, 2 September 1941
4. http://www.harry-tates.org.uk/tgtw.html ch11ff

13
1. ADM 116/4446, NA
2. Ibid
3. http://www.totleyhistorygroup.org.uk/documents/ww2-trawlers
4. Ibid
5. Elliott, *Allied Minesweeping in WW2*, p37
6. Ibid, p38
7. Ibid

14
1. Warwick, *Really Not Required*, p37
2. 9 July 1940, CAB 65/14/9, NA
3. CAB 69/1, NA
4. Thwaites, *Atlantic Odyssey*, p13
5. Ibid, p15
6. Warwick, *Really Not Required*, p255
7. Kerslake, *CITNC*, p56
8. Ibid, p59
9. Warwick, *Really Not Required*, p97
10. Kerslake, *CITNC*, p75
11. Ibid, p99

12. ADM 1/12300, NA
13. Kerslake, *CITNC*, pp113–14
14. Ibid, p114

15
1. Kerslake, *CITNC*, p45
2. Featherbe, *Churchill's Pirates*, p10
3. Kerslake, *CITNC*, p21
4. Ibid, p110
5. *Trawlers Go to War*, ch 7ff, http://www.harry-tates.org.uk/tgtw.html
6. Featherbe, *Churchill's Pirates*, p30
7. Warwick, *Really Not Required*, p124
8. Kerslake, *CITNC*, p46
9. Duke, *Report*, Introduction
10. Kerslake, *CINTNC*, p67
11. Warwick, *Really Not Required*, p4
12. Supplement to the *London Gazette*, 13 November 1940
13. Thwaites, *Atlantic Odyssey*, p93
14. Featherbe, *Churchill's Pirates*, p16
15. *London Gazette*, 7 June 1940
16. Sutherland and Canwell, *Churchill's Pirates*, p64
17. Supplement to the *London Gazette*, 1 January 1941
18. *Administrative History of US Naval Forces in Europe, 1940–1946*, vol. V, pp301ff
19. Elliott, *Allied Minesweeping in WW2*, p306
20. Maher, *A Passage to Sword Beach*, p120
21. *The Rotarian*, March 1941, p39
22. Hutson, *Grimsby's Fighting Fleet*, p77
23. Info from Scarborough Maritime Heritage Centre

16
1. Warwick, *Really Not Required*, p53
2. *London Gazette*, 16 August 1940
3. *British Vessels Lost at Sea*, Section 2, p38
4. Ibid
5. *British Vessels lost at Sea*, Section 2, pp56ff
6. Info from Scarborough Maritime Heritage Centre

Envoi
1. House of Commons Library, CDP 2017/0256, 6 December 2017
2. *Seafish Report SR 739*, Seafish Economics

Bibliography

The following books and other publications have been cited in the text. The place of publication is London unless otherwise indicated.

Primary sources

Various files in the ADM and MT series, individually cited, National Archives, Kew

Private Papers of Admiral Horace Hood, GBR/0014/Hood, Churchill Archive Centre, Churchill College, Cambridge

Private papers of the Admiral the Hon Sir Reginald Aylmer Ranfurly Plunkett-Ernle-Erle-Drax, DRAX, Churchill Archive Centre

Private papers of Admiral Sackville Carden, CARD, Churchill Archive Centre

Private papers of Admiral Sir David Scott, DKNS, Churchill Archive Centre

Papers of Sir Winston Churchill in the CHAR 13 series, Churchill Archive Centre

Private Papers of Admiral Henry Jackson, MSS 255, National Museum of the Royal Navy, Portsmouth

Oral History, Harry Chadwick-Smith, Liddle Collection, Brotherton Library, University of Leeds

Private papers of Commander K R Walker, Docs 13075, Imperial War Museum, London

Private papers of Captain W B Forbes, Docs 10977, Imperial War Museum

Private papers of F R Watt, Docs 2867, Imperial War Museum

Private papers of J Clarke, Docs 12146, Imperial War Museum

Secondary sources

Bacon R, *The Dover Patrol*, vols I and II, George H Doran (New York, 1919)

Bennett G, *Charlie B*, Peter Dawnay Ltd (1968)

Boothby H, *Spunyarn*, G T Foulis and Co (1929)

Bywater H and Ferraby H, *Strange Intelligence*, Constable (1931); republished Biteback (2015)

Campbell A, *With the Corners Off*, G G Harrap and Co (1937)

Corbett J and Newbolt H, *Naval Operations, The History of the Great War based on Official Documents, vol V*, republished Naval and Military Press and Imperial War Museum (2014)

Coxon S ('Dug Out'), *Dover during the Dark Days*, John Lane, The Bodley Head, (1919)

Crossley J, *The Hidden Threat*, Pen and Sword Maritime (Barnsley, 2011)

Dawson L, *Gone for a Sailor*, Rich and Cowan (1936)

Defoe D, *A tour thro' the whole island of Great Britain, divided into circuits or journies* (1724)

D'Enno D, *Fishermen Against the Kaiser*, Pen and Sword Maritime (Barnsley, 2010)

Dittmar F and Colledge J, *British Warships 1914–1918*, Ian Allen (1972)

Elliott P, *Allied Minesweeping in World War Two*, Patrick Stephens (Cambridge, 1979)

Fayle C, *Seaborne Trade*, vol III, John Murray (1924); republished Naval and Military Press (Sussex, undated)

Featherbe F, *Churchill's Pirates*, North Kent Books (Rochester, 1994)

Friedman N, *Fighting the Great War at Sea*, Seaforth Publishing (Barnsley, 2014)

Friedman N, *British Naval Weapons of World War 2*, vol II, Seaforth Publishing (Barnsley, 2019)

Goldrick J, *Before Jutland*, Naval Institute Press (Annapolis, 2015)

Hutson H, *Grimsby's Fighting Fleet*, Hutton Press (Beverley, 1990)

Jellicoe J, *The Crisis of the Naval War*, George H Doran Company (New York, 1920)

Kerslake S, *Coxswain in the Northern Convoys*, W Kimber and Co (1984)

Lambert A, *Admirals*, Faber and Faber Ltd (2009)

Lambert N, *Planning Armageddon,* Harvard University Press (Cambridge, Mass, 2012)

Lenton H and Colledge J, *Warships of World War II*, Ian Allen (1973)

Little S, *Through Cloud and Sunshine*, Brixham Heritage Museum (2008)

Lownie A, *The Mountbattens*, Blink Publishing (2019)

Maher B, *A Passage to Sword Beach*, Naval Institute Press (Annapolis, 1996)

Marder A, *From the Dreadnought to Scapa Flow*, vols I and II, OUP (1961, 1965); republished Seaforth Publishing (Barnsley, 2013)

Margerison J, *Our Wonderful Navy: The story of the sure shield in peace and war*, Cassell and Co (1919)

Murray D, *Herring Tales*, Bloomsbury (2016)

Robinson R, *Fishermen, the Fishing Industry and the Great War at Sea*, Liverpool University Press (Liverpool, 2019)

Roskill S, *The Navy at War, 1939–1945*, Collins (1960)

Roskill S, *Naval Policy Between the Wars*, vol II, Seaforth Publishing (Barnsley, 2016; originally published 1968)

Roskill S (ed), *The Naval Air Service, volume 1, 1908–1918*, Navy Records Society (1969)

Scott P, *Fifty Years in the Royal Navy*, John Murray (1919)

Smith P, *Into the Minefields,* Pen and Sword Maritime (Barnsley, 2005)

Spears J, *David G Farragut*, G W Jacobs (Philadelphia, 1905)

Sutherland J and Canwell D, *Churchill's Pirates*, Pen and Sword Maritime (Barnsley, 2010)

'Taffrail' [Captain Henry Taprell Dorling], *Swept Channels*, Hodder and Stroughton (1935)

'Taffrail', *Endless Story*, Hodder and Stroughton (1938)

Thwaites M, *Atlantic Odyssey*, New Cherwell Press (Oxford, 1999)

Warwick C, *Really Not Required*, The Pentland Press Ltd (Bishop Auckland, 1997)

Winton J, *Cunningham*, John Murray (1998)

Winton J, *The Victoria Cross at Sea*, Michael Joseph (1978)

Newspapers and magazines

Eastern Evening News
Falmouth Packet
Fishing News
Fishing Trades Gazette
Fraserburgh Times
London Gazette
New York World
Sea Breezes
Shields Gazette
The Rotarian
The Spectator
Whitaker's Red Book

Other

Administrative History of US Naval Forces in Europe, 1940–1946, vol V (1946)

British Vessels Lost at Sea, 1914–19 and 1939–45, Patrick Stephens Ltd (1988)

Hansard

Far Horizons, University of Hull, http://farhorizons.hull.ac.uk/distant-waters-william-oliver-and-the-worlds-greatest-fishing-port

House of Commons Library, Debate pack number CDP 2017/0256, 6 December 2017

Seafish Report SR 739, Seafish Economics, Edinburgh

Scarborough Heritage Maritime Centre

Statement of the First Lord of the Admiralty, Explanatory of the Navy Estimates, 1919–1920, HMSO (1 December 1919)

Summary Report by Commodore Duke, privately held by the RNPS association

Trawlers go to War, http://www.harry-tates.org.uk/tgtw.html

Totley History Group